LONDON

on £1,000 a day
(before tea)

"[*New York on $1,000 a Day*] offers readers everything they need to know . . . unusual spots both tourists and residents might otherwise overlook, as well as fascinating tidbits about famous places."

THE DALLAS SUNDAY NEWS

"The perfect guide to a lifestyle of champagne wishes and caviar dreams in the world's best city. A handy, almost biblical book . . . cram-packed with dazzling delights."

ROBIN LEACH

"A lavish, witty, informative—absolutely irresistible—guide to New York$$"

VICTORIA PRINCIPAL

"I loved it, but now the whole world knows my secrets for looking like a millionaire! *New York on a $1,000 a Day (Before Lunch)* really tells it all."

EILEEN FORD

"If you want to save yourself a grand a day and still have a great time in New York, try this book—before or after lunch. You'll love it."

REGIS PHILBIN

"After reading this book, I am reminded of the fact that I have been poor, and I have been rich—rich is better."

TONY RANDALL

"*New York on a $1,000 a Day (Before Lunch)* sings with the rhythm of my city. They are both glamorous, fun, and exciting."

BARBARA COOK

"Something for every taste, mood and moment filled with all the pleasures and treasures that New York has to offer."

ARLENE DAHL

"Forget your Filofax, *New York on a $1,000 a Day* has it ALL. Whether you've got a million or just 20 bucks to spend, this book will show you how to do it with real New York style. Now that's worth singing about!"

PATTI LA BELLE

LONDON

on £1,000 a day
(before tea)

FERNE KADISH
SHELLEY CLARK

PASSPORT BOOKS
a division of *NTC Publishing Group*
Lincolnwood, Illinois USA

cover photo: H. Armstrong Roberts

Published by Passport Books, a division of NTC Publishing Group,
4255 West Touhy Avenue,
Lincolnwood (Chicago), Illinois 60646-1975.
Manufactured in the United States of America.
Library of Congress Catalog Card Number: 90-63163

1 2 3 4 5 6 7 8 9 ML 9 8 7 6 5 4 3 2 1

Dedication

This book is dedicated to the world, and to all those who strive to protect us in it.

F.W.K.

For Theresa and John Behrendt, whose extraordinary kindness and generosity were invaluable in the completion of this book. And for my step-mother, Barbara Clark, who did so much to nurture my joie de vivre!

S.M.C.

Contents

CHAPTER FOUR

A Sudden Yen 206

*Nothing that a few pounds—sterling and otherwise—couldn't
satisfy*

CHAPTER SIX

Jewelry 360
Baubles, bangles, and beyond

Introduction

*"When a man is tired of London,
he is tired of life."*
—*Samuel Johnson*

Ditto for the distaff
—*Ferne Kadish*
Shelley Clark

*L*ondon. . . . It's Dickens and Shakespeare, Fortnum & Mason, Charles and Diana. The ghosts of Christmases past, present and future seem to rise from the mists of the Thames. Around that next corner, groping his way out of the mews, a villain from Sherlock Holmes' mysteries seems ready to spring at your taxi. London. . . a city of mystery and excitement, sophistication and style. It is, in so many ways, the gateway to Europe. London is indeed a foreign land to the British who live beyond its borders as well as to the visitors from across the ocean. It is a land where a road map is needed through its labyrinthine alleys, a guide to its special treasures, its most luscious luxuries, its most savoury settings.

London on £1,000 a Day (Before Tea) is the most direct route through the inscrutable wonders of this remarkable city. But it's more than a walking tour or a casual day-tripper's manual. Rather, it's an attempt to enter the heart and soul of the city, to enter the realm of tradition and ageless quality, to sample the *nouveau chic*, to save that most unreplenishable of commodities—time. And yes, money, too.

On these pages are the best ways to create that special mood, make that certain impression, find that wonderful corner of the universe to produce a magical memory that will never fade. In this sprawling metropolis that is 35 miles across, there are still pockets that date from Roman times, and there are plenty of treasures we didn't unearth. The opportunities for uncharted exploration are endless and should be taken. More than any other world capital, London is a patchwork of villages made up of neighbourhoods, each with its own distinctive character, community and customs. There is truly something for everyone.

At its core, there's The City, the once and present heart of the financial world as indispensable to global business and finance as Wall Street. Barren of fine hotels, shops and restaurants, it is nonetheless a tourist destination as the home of St Paul's Cathedral and the Tower of London. Still, its tiny one square mile is a world unto itself, managed by its own governing body from whom even the Queen, on ceremonial occasions, must ask permission to enter.

The City's ancestral rival is Westminster, with its centre, the West End. This is the real London to most visitors—where palaces and parks crowd elegant shops, restaurants and, of course, the theatre where *Les Misérables, Phantom of the Opera* and *Miss Saigon* made their debuts long before they hit the bright lights of Broadway.

Then there's Chelsea, that trendy little town which first engendered the style called "Mod." Up and down Fulham Road, green-haired punks rub shoulders with young nobles who seek to be more with-it than weird. Kensington, which Harrods calls home, has nothing style-wise on Chelsea but does edge it out on chic.

Farther along to the west, there's Richmond and to the east, Greenwich—two of England's most charming little towns, but like Westminster, Kensington and Chelsea, still a part of London. Beyond the city's limits stretches the rest of Britain, the verdant English countryside with its ancient inns and stately homes—an easy escape from the hustle and bustle of central London.

This, then, is a guide to a total London experience. Where to find an acceptable hangover cure may be as important as where to find the recognizably British ale or American cocktail that produced it. Then there are the tips on how to dress like a prince or princess, how to get that special table in that three-star restaurant (yes, haute cuisine has come to London), or how to find those front-row seats for that sold-out hit show.

In these pages you'll stumble upon members of "The Family" leaving their royal imprint all over town. You'll meet other royalty, too—culinary king Albert Roux and his heir apparent Nico Ladenis. You'll rub shoulders with Christopher, Bob, Nunzio and Michael, with their amazing network of contacts—as Jeeves may have told you, the hall porters hold the *real* power in London.

So whether you're rolling in the mighty pound sterling or in the dollar or in the super yen, whether you've just stepped off the Concorde or Virgin or arrived at Victoria Station, whether you're toting knapsack or Vuitton, whether your budget's a thousand quid a day (*before* tea, of course, my dear) or perhaps a thousand wishes, press on for a journey down the pathways and byways of olde London towne.

Ferne Kadish
Shelley Clark

CHAPTER ONE

Transportation

Getting there in style

*I*n Dickensian London of the 1800s, the Artful Dodger generally found it most opportune to lam around town on very fleet feet. There's still a Fleet Street in the heart of London today and, indeed, with congestion only deeper since the motorcar replaced the horse-drawn shay, your own two feet may still be the most efficient conveyance of all, even though they won't put a dent in the thousand pounds you have to spend by teatime.

But for those intent on plowing through the daily allowance, there are ample means to do so, starting with your arrival in the glamorous style of one of the world's great trains, the legendary *Orient Express*. No unwashed hordes to contend with, no marathon walk through endless corridors, no lost luggage—just a big dent in your £1,000 before tea!

Or how about disembarking in Southampton after a hedonistic four-day voyage aboard Cunard's luxurious *Queen Elizabeth II?* Consider the crossing a warm-up to your vacation or the calm before the storm if you're travelling on business. And it's a sure-fire way to avoid jet lag! The only problem—the *QE2's* schedule is heavily committed to cruising, interrupted only by the occasional transatlantic run, which is why we don't discuss the option in detail. But take it from us, it's the experience of a lifetime, *if* you've got the time and the money to do it up posh—first class, outside cabin. After all, the British coined the term "Port Out, Starboard Home"; the initials POSH, stamped on the ticket of the premier cabins on the steamers to India, were guaranteed to shield the wealthy bearers from the blistering sun of the equator, assuring them comfortable voyages to and from the colonies.

Today, of course, there are alternatives—and should time and itinerary dictate you must fly, don't fret. With London increasingly perceived as the English-speaking gateway to a vast, single European market, major carriers are in heated competition to improve facilities, service and schedules. Indeed, they're bent on coddling passengers on the lucrative London routes, doing their best to make your few hours in the air as pleasant as possible. They're even tackling and conquering the tasteless airline food issue. And once you deplane, if you've haven't hired a car, you've got one of life's great treats in store—the London cabdriver.

To a man, polite, respectful and possessed of an unfailingly colourful command of the English language, the London cabby skillfully negotiates London's often horrendous traffic in spotlessly clean, roomy, sturdy vehicles. The cabs are unique, unchanged since they were first designed so that gentlemen would not have to remove their top hats; the drivers are throwbacks to a gentler age as well. Given the slightest encouragement, they'll embark on an informative narrative en route. These boys know their stuff—not only *where* you're going, but also *what* you're going to see when you get there and its social or historical significance.

Still, with a turn around the block likely to run £8 or more these days, even on £1,000 a day, you probably shouldn't sniff at the thought of public transportation. In London it's the tube or the underground—unfailingly precise like everything British. After all, you *are* riding in a tube under the ground! Daily, weekly or monthly travel passes are on sale at most of the big tube stations, and they're good for unlimited mileage above and below the ground. In any other city, you'd pay a premium just for the views you get for free from the top of London's double-decker buses; and with a pass, you can leap on and off with cheerful abandon, whenever you just can't walk that extra few blocks.

But when you alight from the bus and take to your feet, remember one lifesaving eternal constant. Traffic arrives from the right. Look to the left and you'll wind up a shepherd's pie. Except where there are special bus lanes. The best rule is the one natives use: think twice and look both ways before crossing.

SCHEDULED SERVICE

British Airways

1-800-AIRWAYS (in the U.S.)
081-897-4000 (in the U.K.)

Ostensibly, the Concorde is British Airways' pride and joy, but we wonder. Those supersonic birds have been flying since 1976, and no one's talking about building any new planes to replace the aging fleet. Meanwhlie, British Airways has embarked on an ambitious programme to upgrade first-class travel on its conventional planes, and in fact has ordered 19 of the latest in Boeing's 747 series, the 747–400, for long-distance international flights. That suits us—fast is fine. And what's wrong with spending several hours nestled in the lap of luxury? You can relax, unwind, get some work done if you must, or just nap in British Airways' soothingly comfortable and very extendable sleeper seats.

The pampering, thanks to Michael Batt, head of marketing for British Airways, starts in the airport lounges dedicated to first-class passengers. Complimentary refreshments abound, and there's a healthy supply of fax machines and telephones to take care of last-minute details—with no charge for local calls.

Once on board, it's as if you'd become a member of an exclusive club. Served by its own cabin crew, it's a club which benefits from truly world-class catering, as well as thoughtful touches like fresh flowers and Floris fragrances and lotions in the toilets. There are also individual video screens and swivel tables that make getting in and out of your seat, even during meal service, a breeze.

Of course, given the quality of the cuisine, we recommend you simply sit back and relax. Then there's the abundance of the food, which helps guarantee that you'll be able to while away the in-flight hours in a restful sleep. This makes the evening flight especially pleasant—we like the 9:00 P.M. out of New York's JFK arriving at Heathrow at 8:45 A.M. the next day. By the time you get into the city, it's a reasonable hour. Too often we've arrived at our hotel too early, say 7:30 or 8:00 in the morning, only to be told our rooms weren't ready. Thank goodness for the showers in British Airways' lounges.

At any rate, for dinner or supper, expect a full meal that would do most multi-starred restaurants justice. On our last trip we waded our way through four courses that started with a selection of canapés and ended with an assortment of cheeses and fruits. In between, we were treated to three choices of appetizers and main courses, not to mention a delightful selection of wines, ranging from a vintage champagne to a grand cru Margaux.

With direct services from Montreal, Boston, Hartford, Philadelphia, Pittsburgh, Detroit, Toronto, Chicago, Seattle, San Francisco, Los Angeles, San Diego, Denver, Dallas, Houston, Miami, Tampa, Orlando, Washington *and* New York, you can fly British Airways to London from just about anywhere in North America. Indeed, as Britain's flagship airline, you can fly BA, as it's affectionately known, from almost any corner of the globe.

Wherever you're coming from, you might also investigate BA's flights into Gatwick. Once a sleepy, secondary airport for the charter trade, it has, in recent years, become a full-fledged international airport minus the chaos of Heathrow, the world's largest. And the easily accessible train service to London's centrally located Victoria Station is tough to beat, even with a car and driver.

Once firmly on the ground, you can still enjoy British Airways' special brand of service. Visit its smart new West End store at 156 Regent Street, a first in travel retailing. Much more than a reservation and ticketing facility, its staff dispenses travel advice, and you can follow it right on the premises with BA's immunization services and pharmacy.   ❦

Trans World Airlines

200 Piccadilly	071-439-0707
London W1V 0DH	(Toll-free in the U.S.) 800-892-4141

Back in the good old days, when Britannia ruled the waves and the U.S. reigned supreme in the sky, Pan American and Trans World were always duking it out for transatlantic preeminence. Pan Am was first to cross to Europe, but it was TWA that inaugurated all-sleeper luxury service from New York and eventually became the first airline to offer all-jet service. And, even though the indignities that both airlines have suffered as the unexpected fall-out of deregulation have taken their toll.

In the face of financial uncertainty, TWA maintains a proud stance. After all, doomsayers have predicted its demise a number of times over its 70-odd-year history. But it has proved as plucky as the man who was once its principal stockholder—Howard Hughes—and perhaps he imparted some of his inventive vision on the company. TWA adopted the

Doppler radar navigation system shortly after FAA approval, and its New York–London flights became the first transatlantic flights (commercial *or* military) ever operated without a professional navigator aboard. Furthermore, it was the only American carrier that put its money where its jet stream was with regard to supersonic transport (think Concorde) by placing an order for the first U.S.-built SSTs. By the time Congress pulled the plug on the program in 1971, TWA had upped the order to 12. Of course, the government reimbursed the company for the funds it had invested in SST research and development, but the prospect of another aviation first was lost.

Fortunately, TWA had been just as supportive of the development of wide-bodied jets as it was of the narrow fast-flying birds. Consequently, it scored another first with the introduction of the 747 in the U.S. Even more monumental was the company's precedent-setting decision to offer nonsmoking sections on every aircraft in its fleet.

No doubt, there are those—especially smokers who are now forced to go without on all domestic flights—who will never forgive TWA. Even they, however, would be hard-pressed to hold a grudge after they've been coddled by its first-class service to London. These days, the comfy sleeper seats are a given. But what really sets TWA apart is the food service. Each plate for each course is attractively arranged by your flight attendant from a presentation rolling cart; no pre-set platters of plastic-looking food are plopped down before you. So, you can make your opinions known about portion size and also make a decision about whether or not to have sauce.

The other decision you have to make is where to fly from—Baltimore, Los Angeles, Philadelphia, San Francisco, or St. Louis.

TWA's U.S. based flights to London now land at Gatwick, which is the good news because it's grown up to be a more civilized version of Heathrow. ❧

Venice Simplon Orient Express

Victoria Station	071-928-6000
Suite 200	(FAX) 071-630-7663
Hudsons Place	
London SW1V 1JL	

No other mode of transportation rivals the *Orient Express*—"The Train of Kings, and the King of Trains"—for its images of romance, glamour, intrigue and luxury. While the glamour and intrigue quotient may be down since the original train's heyday prior to World War I, when it ran through a Europe still largely composed of kingdoms and carried the most important and glittering travellers of the day, the romance and luxury of the new train, inaugurated in 1982, is unparalleled. Indeed, there is no question that the Edwardian train was never so grand nor so luxurious as the refurbished cars which form the Venice Simplon Orient Express of today. (If you've ever wondered—we had—about the "Simplon" part of an otherwise obvious route-descriptive name, it refers to the Simplon Tunnel through the Alps which shortened the route when it opened in 1906.)

To our way of thinking, if you have the time to savour the complete VSOE experience—32 hours from Venice, 34 from Vienna—there is no other way to get to London from the Continent. Of course, it doesn't come cheap, £280 to £850 per person for double occupancy, depending upon the season and site of departure, but money shouldn't even be a consideration as the journey is an unqualified delight, guaranteed to spawn cherished memories. In fact, we would go so far to say it's a once-in-a-lifetime adventure, except for those like Liza Minelli, Gregory Peck, Neil Sedaka, Cher, James Coburn and Sidney Poitier, for whom it's not. And we understand that two gentlemen are head-to-head in a heated competition to rack up a record number of trips. They're still at it.

Naturally, both gentlemen are English, but in this instance they can't really be accused of eccentricity. Rather, they are obviously dedicated connoisseurs of the good life. They appreciate the lavish appointments of the painstakingly restored cars with their art-deco lamps, turn-of-the-century prints, and marquetry panels, and the masterful cuisine of chef Christian Bodiguel which has made the Orient Express an honorary member of the esteemed Relais et Châteaux. Table d'hôte lunch, afternoon tea, dinner and brunch are served en route and are included in the price. An extensive à la carte menu is available to those willing to pay the supplementary charges, but why bother when the "standard" fare features such seasonal specialities as quail stuffed with foie gras and ballotine of chicken with carmelized tangerines and brandy snaps? The restaurant is composed of three dining cars, each different—one boasts glorious Lalique glass panels, another is famous for its Chinese lacquer, and the third is decorated with superb marquetry. We always try to take a meal in each one—ask the maître d' to make the necessary arrangements.

It's a good idea to make friends with your cabin steward early on, as you'll be seeing a lot of him. He'll deliver your overnight luggage—the bulk is checked through—to your private compartment and unveil the secrets of the handsomely panelled and richly upholstered cabin. He'll show you how the curved, beautifully inlaid door conceals a washbasin equipped with fluffy towels and extravagant Donelle soap made especially for the train, and he'll point out the miniature writing desk. Of course, he won't desert you without showing off the spacious lavatories at the end of the car, where the mosaic floors can only be described as works of art. He'll retrieve you for lunch, serve tea in your cabin, and later he'll announce dinner. When you return to your cabin, he's also the fellow you can thank for transforming it into a snugly elegant bedroom.

Another member of the staff who's likely to become your new best friend is Giorgio, whose domain is the most popular car on the train—the splendid art-deco bar-salon. From late afternoon on, it fairly sparkles with animated conversation between the fashionably dressed passengers, the festive air enhanced by the talents of a pianist on the baby grand. As the evening wears on, the atmosphere has been known to become that of a gala party to which every one of the 176 passengers is invited. We have it on good authority that during one memorable trip some £15,000 worth of champagne was consumed between 4:00 P.M. and 6:00 A.M. And we're sorry we missed the evening the quick-witted piano player broke the tension prompted by a very abrupt stop in the midst of a nasty spell of hail by breaking into a rousing rendition of "Stormy Weather."

The bottom line is, don't bother burdening yourself with lots of reading materials for the trip. Despite your intentions to catch up, the spectacular scenery and the delights of the salon will sabotage your best efforts.

Upon arrival in Paris, fresh croissants along with the *International Herald Tribune* are brought on board and delivered to your cabin by your ever-faithful steward. Then it's on to brunch before disembarking at Boulogne to board a Sealink ferry for the trip across the English Channel. You're escorted to a special lounge for the exclusive use of Orient Express passengers where you're ensconced for the 90-minute voyage. At Folkstone, you're met by the sumptuous cream and brown Pullman carriages of the British section of the train, each outfitted with groupings of plush, commodious, tapestry-covered armchairs, surrounding damask cloth-adorned dining tables. Proper English afternoon tea is served as the train winds its way through the green countryside of Kent, the "Garden of England," on the way to your final destination, London's Victoria Station.

If you're short on time, you can pick up the train in Paris for a day's excursion to London. You'll be allotted a reserved seat in one of the dining cars, or you can book a cabin. The fare ranges from £280 for a seat alone to £480 for the privacy of a compartment.

Whether you indulge in the overnight trek or the day's jaunt, for the most popular months—June, July and September—you should reserve three months in advance. Remember, the train runs only twice a week and is extremely popular despite being—or, perhaps, because it is—the only overland vehicle we know of with a dress code. Men are expected to wear jackets and ties in the evening, preferably tuxedo for dinner and smart casual wear for day, while ladies will be most comfortable in dressy cocktail attire—it's not unusual to see Japanese women in formal national dress. Leave your jeans in your luggage. Regardless of the time of day, they're a no-no in the dining cars, and we have the distinct impression they're not welcome on any part of the train. Let's hear it for standards!

Virgin Atlantic

Virgin Megatsore	(in U.S.) 800-862-8621
527–531 Oxford Street	(in U.K.) 0293-562-000
London W1	

Deregulation was supposed to have been a boon to the U.S. airline industry. Instead it's been a big *bust*—witness flash-in-the-pan Peoples Express and New York Air, and look what it did to old standby Eastern, not to mention the flagship of the U.S. fleet, Pan Am. Of course, the laissez-faire policy opened up opportunities for non-U.S. carriers to make inroads and encouraged some entrepreneurs to test the skies. Freddie Laker's Airbus went the way of most of the start-up ventures in the United States, but his fellow countryman Richard Branson's Virgin Atlantic has become a hit, against all odds.

But that's the way the brash Branson likes it. The billionaire, who made his first million with a discount record mail-order business at the very tender age of 17 (hence the name *Virgin*, referring to his youth and lack of experience), thrives on challenge...on pushing "myself to new horizons." His own daring aviational exploits, including two record-setting hot-air balloon trips across the Atlantic, are legend. However, many would argue that his entry into the airline industry as an economy-oriented carrier was his biggest risk-taking adventure. After all, Branson charged onto the field just as his buddy Sir Freddie and others were retreating in defeat. But he knew what apparently they did not—it isn't enough simply to be cheaper than the competition, you've got to be different.

Richard drew on his roots in the music business to capitalize on minimizing the boredom of flying. Richard entertains his passengers with singers on some flights, book signings or wine tastings on others. Apparently his was an idea whose time had come in 1984 when Virgin Atlantic Airways was launched. In just over three years, with service offered from New York (JFK *and* Newark), Miami, Boston, Los Angeles, Tokyo and Moscow, the upstart airline is operating at a tidy profit—feat enough in an industry bleeding red.

Besides being fun, flying Virgin Atlantic is a bona fide good deal, especially where its "upper-class" service is concerned. It is equal and, indeed, superior to many a competitor's first class; its prices are comparable to their business service. Moreover, you get valuable freebies such as limo service from your home to the terminal and vice versa. Alternatively, upon arrival in London, you can opt for a free first-class Britrail pass to any destination on the mainland United Kingdom, or you may elect to take an Avis car for two days, gratis, including umlimited mileage, cellular phone and free pick-up and drop-off at any of Avis' 200 offices in the U.K.

If you need more convincing about the Virgin Atlantic difference, consider the roomy lounges and bars that give you an on-board destination, and the Sony Video Walkmans serviced by a cassette library of some 30 top-rated films (just in case the nonstop "skyshows" of the latest movies, music videos, news, sports, cartoons, and even BBC classics on the "big" screen or the live entertainment don't suit).

As for the food, it's beautifully presented on Wedgwood and good enough for Virgin Atlantic to be named overall Airline of the Year in 1990 by Britain's *Executive Travel* with a runner-up status in the Best In-Flight Food category. A selection of three main courses follows canapés and an appetizer and is complemented by very respectable wines.

So what does all this fun and excitement cost? From New York, you're looking at about £2,198 round-trip—or half that if you take into consideration that you can make the next trip "free" in economy where you still get to take the high-quality headphones with you as a memento of your flight!   ❧

Car/Limo Services

Camelot Barthropp Ltd

071-235-0234
(FAX) 071-823-1278

The first name evokes romantically chivalrous images of King Arthur's Round Table. (Barthropp is the name of the company's founding family.) The fact that this prince among limousine companies is a subsidiary of the Savoy Group ensures those images correspond to reality. Camelot Barthropp's fleet of Rolls-Royces, Daimler limousines, Mercedes, Jaguars and Ford or Volvo sedans are elegantly appointed coaches. Their chauffeurs—who need not apply unless they've had five years experience elsewhere—are unfailingly courteous and very natty in their uniforms, caps and company ties.

Managing director Barrie Salter, and general manager, Terry Smith, make sure the cars live up to their drivers—they're always immaculate, they have telephones for clients' use, and, since they're radio equipped, can usually be counted on at only an hour's notice. But, given London's iffy weather that can further snarl one of the world's most horrific traffic scenes, it's only fair to try to book ahead. They have six people manning the phones from 7:00 A.M. to midnight. After midnight your call is directed to a duty controller who will locate a chauffeur. Even the Frank Sinatras and the Gregory Pecks, along with executives from Walt Disney and Warner Brothers, call or fax their itineraries well in advance. They can't imagine London without Camelot Barthropp. Who else shows up at the airport or train station with a van for your luggage if they know you don't travel light? During the years of the Taylor–Burton road show, they regularly dispatched a van to deal with the couple's 60 to 70 bags.

Sans van, the ride from Heathrow costs from £36 in a Ford or Volvo to £100 in a Rolls or Bentley, exclusive of gratuity and the troublesome VAT—or value added tax. Once in London, the hourly rate for cruising around town, including four free miles, ranges from £15 to £40. Add tax and tip. As separated from the hoi polloi as riding in a Rolls equipped with a telephone makes one feel, we believe ourselves sufficiently distinguished touring for nine hours in a Daimler limo for £300. If a series of meetings or some serious shopping or sightseeing is on the agenda, consider the half-day rates which entitle you to four hours and 65 miles (London is a *very* big city) for £100 to £190. There are also published fees for popular day-trip destinations from London. And, of course, Barrie and Terry will be happy to quote rates for a little jaunt to the Continent.

For evening forays, defined as 7:00 P.M. to 7:00 A.M., on the London scene, a 15 per cent service charge is automatically added to the bill. Presumably there's some concern that a night's revels could cause one to forget to tip. Hard to believe. Camelot Barthropp's chauffeurs deliver such excellent service, we can't imagine anyone being so boorish. But if it happened, we suspect these fellows would manage to point out the oversight—in a very mannerly, obsequious way, of course! 🦃

CCS—Charlotte Chauffeur Services

071-381-4548
(Mobile phone) 860-638-738
(FAX) 0932-253-916

Proprietor Ralph Rose's card says it all: "personal chauffeur." Personal service is what Ralph and Charlotte Chauffeur Services (CCS) are all about. Even the choice of name is personal. Charlotte is Ralph's daughter, born of a marriage personally arranged by his former employer, the Baron Enrique de Portanova. Don't misunderstand. Ralph chose his ladylove himself, but the Baron flew her from London to Monte Carlo in his private jet, so Ralph could propose over a champagne dinner. You see, the Baron, and therefore Ralph, was in residence in the principality at the time and knew his prized chauffeur was smitten. He even went so far as to give Ralph a wedding at London's elegant Inn on the Park.

Now, you too can benefit from Ralph's services. Fit for a baron, not to mention London's Diplomatic Corps and assorted pop stars, CCS owns ten cars and has access to many more. The company specializes in English luxury vehicles—Rolls-Royce, Bentley, Jaguar and Daimler. The drivers are equally high class, outfitted in attractive blue uniforms. Like Ralph, they've all had military training and experience as diplomatic drivers. They know a thing or two about evasive tactics, so you can feel personally secure in their capable hands. But the best news is that none of CCS's charges include gratuities. Any reward for service is completely up to you. Consequently, CCS drivers routinely perform above and beyond the call of duty in order to get their 15 percent, or whatever *you* deem appropriate.

As for Ralph's fees, they're reasonable, considering the calibre of car and service. To or from Heathrow runs about £34.50. An evening on the town—a four-hour, 30-free-mile package—in a saloon car costs £60. Otherwise, it's £15 an hour. For a Jaguar, plan on a two-hour minimum at £25 per.

Any car you choose comes complete with a portable telephone, which you can take with you to meetings or lunches if you're inclined to do that sort of thing. The telephones are metered, so the bills are presented when you settle for the car—no nasty surprises later. Actually, no surprises at all. Ralph doesn't believe in using the telephones as a profit center. (Would that the hotels of this world adhere to that credo!) There's no surcharge tacked onto your legitimate talking time.

Should you wish to chat while trekking through the countryside, that's okay, too. You can get a CCS car for eight hours and 100 miles for £130. After the initial eight, it's £15 per hour, and £1 is charged for each mile over the allotted 100. And, of course, you'll spend every hour, travel every mile with Ralph's ever so attentive drivers. After all, they learned the ropes of being (very) personal chauffeurs from the master himself.

❧

CHAPTER TWO

Hotels

A hotel is not a home, but it's liable to be a house... or how the English countryside annexed the West End

I t is a tradition that goes back a thousand years. Chaucer's storytellers stopped at inns and hostels on their travels and told their tales. But even Britain's most famous storyteller would scarcely recognize most of what London calls hostelries today. What he would, no doubt, recognize is the warm welcome, the British charm, that certain sensibility of the unfailingly courteous and impeccable host that makes British hotels unique in the world.

If you joined us on our romp through *New York on $1,000 a Day (Before Lunch)*, you know we're hotel buffs. We're fascinated with their individual characters, the stages they provide for living out fantasies, the romance they promise, the excitement they deliver. That's why, in London, we're in paradise—hotel heaven. From the grandiose to the quaint, each carries a distinctive personality.

In this ancient city, there's a continuity of tradition and staff, ensuring that what you expect is what you get. Often, the gentleman's gentleman who brings you your tea has been "in service" at the establishment for decades. And in some cases, generations of a family have devoted themselves to a particular hostelry. It's such a pleasure to turn up and be welcomed, time and time again, by the same familiar face.

Of course, too much familiarity can breed contempt or, at least, an awkward moment, depending upon the nature of the last visit or the

13

company kept. So hotel-hopping is a popular sport of frequent visitors. They stay at one place when they're on business, another when they're on holiday, another for Ascot or Wimbledon, and another for a weekend rendezvous. The varied destinations make for a change of pace and players.

Hotel-hopping also makes for a change of viable dining venues. Hotel restaurants in London should not be considered last-ditch alternatives. Quite the contrary. In fact, at least four—namely, Ninety Park Lane at the Grosvenor House, the Four Seasons at the Inn on the Park, the Capital's dining room, and the Connaught's restaurant—are counted among the city's best. And the Savoy Grill, while not necessarily a bastion of culinary ingenuity, all but invented the power lunch and remains preeminent in the field.

Indeed, that's one of the elements that makes London hotels so special. Beyond serving the obvious function of providing special-event space for the natives, they are the warp and woof of the city's daily social fabric—not just tourist territory. Locals take tea at hotels and carouse in their affable bars—establishments devoted to the art of the cocktail, just as pubs remain committed to the pouring of ale. The Savoy is even credited with introducing the cocktail bar to Europe.

But as delightful as they are, the city's hotels have begun to face stiff competition from their country cousins, especially on weekends when the verdant landscape and relaxed pace of England's rustic countryside beckons. Within a couple hours' radius by car or train, a number of desirable destinations beckon for a weekend in the country—a former palace, a couple of spas, the occasional coaching inn and, of course, several authentic representations of the quintessential English country house. And you don't have to spend the night to enjoy their many charms—brunch or an early dinner will usually do it without blowing your £1,000 before . . . or after tea.

The Berkeley

Wilton Place	071-235-6000
Knightsbridge	(FAX) 071-235-4330
London SW1X 7RL	

Overlooking Hyde Park is a stylish hotel that caters to a select few, a very refined group of mostly English and American individuals who know exactly what they want. Although there are no flags, no blazing lights and no large signs, the elite find their way again and again to the very private Berkeley, where their needs are anticipated and instantly met.

Entering the spacious lobby, you're likely to see captains of industry, as well as celebrities like Peter Ustinov, Dustin Hoffman and Kirk Douglas.

Privacy and discretion are the key words here, and general manager Stefano Sebastiani dedicates himself to providing guests with just that. Stefano, a slim, elegant gentleman from Rome, is something of a celebrity himself, being a race car driver for more than 22 years on the leading circuits.

His challenge, he told us with a twinkle in his eyes, is to "provide guests with all that's best in the way of comfort, luxury and fine food." As you will discover, Stefano and his fine staff accomplish this with great élan!

The Berkeley was designed by the distinguished English architect Brian O'Rorke, and it opened in 1972 to replace the old Berkeley which had been a landmark hotel in Piccadilly since the turn of the century. The hotel's fine reputation was created under the talented management of Sir George Reeves-Smith, who was there for 41 years. That kind of continuity can only benefit the guests and, of course, it did.

After World War II, the Piccadilly area began to change, and it was felt the hotel should relocate to a new neighbourhood. Sir Hugh Wontner, the new managing director, chose Wilton Place in Belgravia. Acquiring the land and building the new hotel took 10 years. And when it opened in 1972, everyone in London took note: the Berkeley was referred to as the last truly deluxe European hotel.

Today, located near the fashionable Knightsbridge shops, the Berkeley more than lives up to the tradition of its predecessor, with a warmth and hospitality that you feel the moment you step inside.

The foyer bar, for example, exudes warmth with its rose and green decor and an exquisite 18th-century English crystal chandelier. The atmosphere here is elegant, and although ladies may wear trouser suits, gentlemen are requested to wear jackets and ties, especially at weekends.

If you're looking for a moment of quiet contemplation, be sure to stop in the Reading Room, which is from the original hotel and was designed by the famous architect Lutyens. It's a peaceful oasis amid the city's din.

One of the Berkeley's special features that we just love is the rooftop swimming pool. In summertime, the roof is drawn back so you can swim in the sunshine and gaze over Hyde Park. Or, if you're not in the mood for swimming, you can nibble a tasty snack from the poolside bar. It is certainly one of the most delightful ways to enjoy a warm London afternoon.

Living well is the best revenge, isn't it? But after all that great dining in London, our figures are grateful for the Berkeley's gym. There's Nautilus equipment, a trainer to help you work out, saunas, expert masseuses and hair stylists for men and women. What a great way to unwind from a day of meetings or touring, before going on to yet another superb dinner.

The hotel also has its own private cinema, where you can have a private screening of the latest movie without going out. We promise, the Berkeley will keep you in shape, physically and culturally!

Of course their food is not to be missed, either. The Restaurant is a subtle, relaxing room, decorated in colourful chintz fabrics, wall mirrors and limed-oak wood panelling. The outstanding classic French cuisine, prepared under the supervision of maître chef Clemens Schmidl, is well known in London.

We loved the creamed pumpkin soup garnished with nutmeg-scented gnocchi, risotto of langoustines and wild mushrooms, and, for dessert, leaves of crisp biscuit with a passion fruit mousse, and lemon and kumquat confit. Entrées average around £19 and, yes, the calories are worth it. You can always go to the gym again the next morning.

The Buttery, under manager Roberto Sorani, has fabulous prix fixe light buffet luncheons and suppers. This is a popular spot before and after the theatre.

Some of our Buttery favourites: smoked Scottish salmon and potted shrimps, Dover sole in apple brandy sauce and a lovely assortment of cheeses for dessert. If you just want the buffet, the price is £12.50; otherwise, you can order à la carte.

We hope you'll stop in at the Perroquet Bar, which serves drinks and snacks on three levels. It's really quite a happening spot, with delightful live piano music that starts from 7:00 P.M. and goes into the wee hours. Everyone wears the latest fashions, and men are preferred in jackets, although this is the one spot in the Berkeley where you can skip the tie, if you'd like.

The suites at the Berkeley are fabulous, many with marble fireplaces and fine furniture from the original hotel.

Suite 310 is a favourite of ours, with its peach and green fabrics and a huge sitting room that faces St Paul's Church. This is what's called a studio room, and it really is wonderful. There's a comfortable sofa and two cosy chairs, and the bedroom and bathroom are very large. We could be quite happy here for a month or two. This suite goes for £310.

Now, Suite 515—the Pavilion suite—is really at the top of our list. The conservatory is incredibly dramatic, all glassed in with a splendid 180° city view, taking in Hyde Park as well. The terrace will accommodate 100 of your dearest friends for cocktails. Or, if you're by yourself working, you can sit at the desk and make telephone calls while you look out over the rooftops of Knightsbridge.

The doors leading from the living room into the study are made of inlaid wood, showing the houses of Belgravia designed by Viscount David Linley, Princess Margaret's son.

The large living room has 18th-century paintings. The study is small, but it has an exquisite French Empire daybed, which works as a comfortable sofa, and two telephones.

The bedroom is very peaceful in soft grey and light blue, with French windows that open onto the patio terrace. And the huge marble bathroom has double sinks that face each other, which makes conversing with your spouse very easy in the morning or evening as you're dressing for dinner. This posh suite goes for £800 per night, and is worth it.

Perhaps the best way to convince you of the Berkeley's dedication to serving your every need is to tell you about head hall porter, Ray Balducci.

We hear that one of the hotel's guests had invited friends to the Longchamps races and to the theatre on the same day. With one event in one country and one in another, how could he possibly entertain his very important guests at both?

Well, of course, Mr Balducci figured it all out. He chartered the group a private plane for the ride to the races, got permission to land at Orly (usually this is strictly against the rules), and ordered a limo to pick them up and take them directly to the racetrack. Then he had the entire enclave waiting to whisk the group back to London just in time for the opening curtain.

A perfect day was had by all, and Mr Balducci received his proper thanks. And, we hope, a very big tip!

So you see, there's nothing they can't do for you at the Berkeley.

We're sure there are other "miracles" performed by the devoted and professional staff, but we know you will want to experience them yourself. Please do, and let us know about your discoveries. 🐾

Brown's Hotel

Albemarle Street and Dover Street   071-493-6020
London W1A 4SW   (FAX) 071-493-9381

If it's character you seek in the way of hotels, character of facility and staff, Brown's should be your address in London. Opened in 1837 (the year Queen Victoria ascended the throne) by James Brown, a retired gentleman's gentleman, Brown's in all the aristocratic glory of its slightly tattered finery and negligibly faded elegance is not everyone's cup of tea.

Actually, that's only true figuratively. From a literal standpoint, Brown's is absolutely everyone's "cuppa"—the hotel's daily £10.50 tea, served in the rich wood-panelled lounge is hugely popular. There aren't very many of the brightly cheerful, floral-covered sofas and armchairs—and no reservations are taken—so there's always a queue. As a nonresident, arrive early or late to get a seat. If you're a guest at Brown's, you're accommodated as a priority.

General manager Bruce Bannister, the dapper energetic Scot who has been in charge here for the last 15 years or so, is careful to point out that his is "afternoon" not "high" tea, as it is so often called. In actual fact, high tea is served in the North of England and is a cooked meal, not the selection of tiny sandwiches, pastries, cakes and scones with clotted cream that one expects and finds at Brown's. They're all scrumptious and the waiters, clad in morning coats, present them on elegant cake stands (a Scottish tradition Bruce introduced to London, now standard issue everywhere) in enough quantity to replace either lunch or dinner. Lingering in these serene surroundings over any one of the eight varieties of tea is one of life's great pleasures. And it's a luxury you'll be allowed, no matter how many people are queuing in the hall or scattering about the lobby. No one is ever rushed at Brown's; it's far too genteel an establishment for such crassly modern practices.

Indeed, to enter its portals from either Albemarle Street or Dover Street, entrances of equal stature on opposite sides of the hotel which converge in a lobby in the middle, is to step into a time warp of considerable historical significance. Brown's was one of the very few commercial establishments frequented by Queen Victoria; Napoleon III stayed here following the Franco-Prussian War; King George II of the Helenes held court here; Teddy Roosevelt was married in one of the suites; and nephew Franklin honeymooned with Eleanor at Brown's. Despite its growth from two 17th-century townhouses to fourteen, all would recognize it today. There's a continuity about Brown's, from the antique-laden decor to the very proper staff, that some find old-fashioned, even stodgy, but which we find comfortably like a home.

You see, Brown's was a "country house hotel" in Mayfair long before the term was coined, one whose uneven hallways and countless stairways invited guests to explore all its nooks and crannies. Rest assured, now there are elevators (as well as all the other modern conveniences of televisions and mini-bars), but the stairwells yield pleasant surprises, like Rudyard Kipling's elaborate brass inlaid desk, a pair of regal purple velvet armchairs distinguished by the gilt owls on the arms and by the fact that they belonged to Queen Victoria, and enchanting stained-glass windows. Even Bruce is occasionally startled by a discovery—during a round of refurbishments, he recently unearthed from behind "lots of wood" an especially glorious window. He had the colourful masterpiece restored and installed as a backlit focal point of the lounge.

But there are no surprises where the service is concerned. The staff is unfailingly attentive and courteous, clearly taking great pride in their positions at Brown's. Indeed, some view their jobs as a sort of patrimony. Ron Morton, the head valet, followed his father into service here, and Ron's son has signed on as a porter. Most have devoted their professional lives to Brown's and wouldn't have it any other way, even if they could advance their careers faster by accepting the offers from larger hotels that often come their way. Christopher Gransbury had to wait ten years to succeed to the position of head porter. Of course, he had the best of all possible training under the watchful eye of the legendary Gordon May who was at Brown's for 32 years. Christopher inherited Gordon's enthusiasm for performing tasks above and beyond the call of duty, as well as his appreciation of the ability of Brown's staff to give truly personal service—service which has been duly noted by a parade of illustrious personages. Witness the autograph book kept by Gordon, filled with laudatory comments from the likes of Douglas Fairbanks, Jr., Julie Andrews, Van Johnson, Orson Welles, Paul Robeson, Farley Granger, and Dolores Gray. Before he retired, Gordon admitted to having let it lapse; otherwise, there would have been some more au courant signatures as well. Perhaps Christopher will resurrect the practice.

What is certain is that Christopher will continue to keep to his post on the Albemarle side of the hotel, while Graham Wood mans the Dover Street entrance. Graham's been around for 34 years and can recount in detail every single one of them. He's a sweetheart, but beware of engaging him in conversation, as he'll talk your ear off. Still, we were ever so grateful for his unsolicited explanation one morning of the sudden ringing of bells accompanied by the rather frightening sound of slamming doors from all directions. He told us the fire bells are tested every Thursday at 11:00 A.M., and their alarm automatically shuts all the fire doors. Be forewarned.

We have another reason for valuing Graham's talkative nature. He once let it slip that room 20 was his favourite. We figured he ought to know. So on our last visit we opted for it, sight unseen, over the more impressive sounding Queen Wilhelmina Suite. Now it's our favourite, too—gargantuan and bright, its location, fireplace, ornate ceiling mouldings and the height of the ceiling suggest it was once a parlour. Any other hotel would define it as a junior suite instead of a room, given its spacious sitting area and palatial bathroom. With lovely green-print wallpaper, desk *and* vanity, it's about the nicest "room" we've ever stayed in, including those that fetch more than its £245-a-night pricetag. Other double rooms range from £190 to £225 and singles can be had from £155. All are equipped with devices actually recognizable as hair dryers tucked away in the wardrobes.

Of course, the Queen Wilhelmina Suite isn't easily dismissed. Named after the Dutch queen who stayed there, it's loaded with the cosy unassuming comfort which, like the charming story associated with it, is a Brown's specialty. Wilhelmina's daughter, later Queen Juliana, first asserted her independence when, as a small child, she left the confines of the suite and took a walk around the block. Having never before ventured beyond the boundaries of her family's several palaces, Juliana felt very grown-up and independent, unaware she was always within sight of the staff's watchful though carefully discreet eyes. You, too, can feel like a once-and-future queen in this one-and-a-half bedroom suite for £360.

But for only £30 more, we prefer Suite 161 (all three-digit rooms are on the Albemarle side; two-digit, on the Dover) named after another queen. Pictures of Victoria during every phase of her long life are testimony to the fact she actually spent time there. Tudor rose moulding in the dining room further underscores the suite's royal connections, and the exquisite kidney-shaped antique desk in the living room is probably worth a king's ransom.

Speaking of which, that's about what Trusthouse Forte has recently spent on renovating some of the suites and rooms. Others have been left alone, not so much for budgetary reasons as for the fact the regulars at

Brown's like things just the way they are and take a dim view of any changes, even or *especially* those viewed as improvements.

Consequently, the refurbishments are of a gentle nature like those of the Burlington Suite, number 191. A symphony in blue and green offset by a stunning red-lacquer Chinese deco coffee table, it boasts a beautifully restored wood mantelpiece and elegant window treatments. In addition to a living room, formal dining area and master bedroom, there's a usable dressing room with a small chamber beyond, perfect for a child. And the bathroom, all redone in what we have come to call Trusthouse Forte sand marble, is a knock-out in a hostelry where the facilities however functional are a bit primitive. At £375, the only problem with the suite is that it's so slick, it is likely to draw undesirables to Brown's—the sort of people incapable of understanding the hotel's unique character.

One aspect of Brown's everyone can and should appreciate, though, is the food. There are three ways to enjoy it—in your room, courtesy of the fastest room service known to man; in the lounge; or in the elegant wood pillared dining room. The latter is the domain of chef Martin Davis and is known as L'Aperitif Restaurant. It is not for the faint of appetite (for light meals, head for the lounge). Martin's is a creative English kitchen utilizing the best of fresh ingredients, many from his "secret sources in the Kent countryside," to produce rich, traditional dishes with innovative twists.

The clubby, decidedly masculine atmosphere and hearty three-course £25.75 menu, featuring favourites like steak, kidney and woodland mushroom pudding and pot-roasted Scottish fillet of beef with stuffed vegetables, make L'Aperitif heavily trafficked by businessmen at lunch. Too overpowering for us at midday, we like a leisurely evening meal in the restaurant when the glow of silk-shaded sconces and chandeliers softens the ambience. At dinner, choose between the £29.95 menu or a host of seasonal à la carte creations. Both menus are changed every few months. Either way, you can't go wrong as you're cosseted by the attentive but not obtrusive service.

Last time out we split the decision. From the fixed-price selections, it was a picture perfect terrine of lobster topped by a crosshatch of asparagus, followed by succulent lamb roasted in a feather-light pastry. From the à la carte, there was the unusual £12.75 combination of foie gras and fresh pineapple made sublimely palatable by an olive oil dressing, succeeded by steamed fillet of seabass resting on a bed of potato-and-onion salad knapped with a light lobster glaze for £15.50. Naturally, we both finished the meal with a selection of English cheeses from the trolley— included in the table d'hôte or £4.85 on its own.

We save our sweet tooth for the real Scottish shortbread, Walkers by name, so revered by Edinburgh-born Bruce. He makes a habit of noting special guests' arrivals with a personal presentation of a box. Who needs chocolates on a pillow, when you can nibble on Walkers' buttery sinfulness? Shortbread instead of chocolate, just one of the quirks that make up the atypical character of the hotel so treasured by Brown's habitués.

🍎

The Capital

22 Basil Street	071-589-5171
London SW3 1AT	(FAX) 071-225-0011

These days, with boutique hotels springing up on both sides of the Atlantic, it's easy to forget that 20 years ago the notion of a luxury, restaurant-driven townhouse hotel was novel, even radical. However, David Levin thought it was an idea whose time had come. He was so sure that in 1969 he successfully negotiated for a site in Knightsbridge, just behind Harrods, and built a 60-bedroom hotel. The rave reviews that heralded the Capital's 1971 debut ensured its status as the granddaddy of the world's small, exclusive hotels.

When it opened, the Capital was a high-tech, ultra-modern hostelry with metal doors, abstract paintings, superb service and a top-rated restaurant. It still boasts excellent service and a world-class eatery, but as the result of a £3.5 million refurbishment, the Capital's character has been softened considerably: Nina Campbell's rendition of *fin de siècle* decor has replaced the slick, contemporary decor in the intimate public areas, while richly coloured fabrics and graceful antiques impart a sense of comfortable extravagance in the sleeping rooms.

General manager Jonathan Orr-Ewing, formerly of the Pelham, one of the more successful incarnations of the concept pioneered by the Capital, is justifiably proud of the house that David built. Tall and elegant with an easy charm, Jonathan is a perfect counterpoint to his more animated boss, who's known as one of London's great storytellers. David Levin is also considered one of the best hoteliers in Europe with his penchant for perfection here and at his other property next door, L'Hotel. No detail is too small to escape his attention nor that of his wife Margaret who was responsible for the sumptuous but homey quality of the bedrooms. Who else would think of draping a warm-'n'-fuzzy blanket over the back of a sofa so that you can curl up like a couch potato in front of the tube. . . or of placing reading lamps where they are really useful?

When it came to decorating the hotel's 48 rooms and suites—the Capital lost 12 rooms during the renovation to make the accommodations more spacious—Margaret turned to her favourite designer, Ralph Lauren, for inspiration. So for once Ralph, who has been so clever at making his shops look like very desirable private homes, put his debonair stamp on an establishment you can really move into. Lush, Lauren-designed fabrics cover the walls of the rooms; Margaret also purchased most of the rugs, small pieces of furniture, and all of the accessories from Ralph.

One of our favourite rooms is 428, a standard (if there is such a thing at the Capital) double which goes for £175. You feel as though you were sitting pretty in an English garden, as the walls are blanketed with an opulent, rose-print material. Lustrous mahogany furniture, including a massive wardrobe and a wonderful antique desk with real workspace, add to your sense of well-being. The marble bathroom may be a bit on the tiny side, but when the wicker tray arrives for a cosy breakfast in bed, all is forgiven.

Now, don't misunderstand, as a guest here you are not consigned to your room for the morning meal. You can dine, as many local business people do, in the restaurant. Either way, even at breakfast, the food will be noteworthy, so much so that we deal in depth with the Capital's restaurant in the section of this book devoted to dining establishments. At any rate, we like our breakfast trays much better than the bulky room-service carts that do duty elsewhere. It's much more personal, like so many services at the hotel. The housekeeping staff routinely unpacks for guests and whisks away any wrinkled garments for a quick press. One regular always sends his bags a day ahead, so that when he does arrive, briefcase in hand, he can head straight for "his" room (*always* the same one) where he will find all his belongings neatly put in their places, his suits pressed, ties hung and shoes polished.

That's the kind of attention habitués expect and get at the Capital—a fussy lot, including Douglas Fairbanks, Jr., Charles Aznavour, Elizabeth Taylor and Diahann Carroll. Regardless of your celebrity status, records are meticulously kept, detailing your preferences in rooms, food, drink, flowers and laundry. Even birthdays, anniversaries and other special dates are noted so that if one falls during your stay, it will be properly celebrated.

Actually, we can think of few better places to observe a romantic anniversary. Cuddle up for a couple of days in one of the eight expansive £265-a-night suites, such as 231 with its sumptuous jewel tones and *two bathrooms* for the one bedroom. All that plumbing certainly helps romance, as does the 24-hour room service from the award-winning kitchen. If you care to dine *à deux* downstairs, plan ahead. Being a guest in the hotel does not necessarily mean you'll be guaranteed a reservation in the restaurant. Indeed, Jonathan suggests you book a table at the same time you make arrangements for your room. And he recommends you call at least a month in advance; though he assures us that once you're a regular you'll always get a room. Given the supply-and-demand equation here, we haven't the foggiest idea how he does it, but he's a proven miracle worker, which is why David had the good sense to hire him in the first place.

Still, Jonathan isn't the only mental marvel on the premises. Bob Gould, the hall porter, has made a habit of accomplishing the impossible since the Capital first opened its doors for business. Indeed, we suspect that Bob, with his winning ways and smile, has been a major factor in the hotel's success. Bob's been known to pick up regular patrons' transiting children at the airport or train station, dole out pocket money to them and safely dispatch them to their final destinations. He's a whiz at keeping recalcitrant teens entertained with educational itineraries disguised as fun. And he's a lifesaver when it comes to last-minute shopping—give Bob a list and you can count on everything being delivered to your room without delay.

In fact, the only task we can imagine that might prove too daunting for Bob is asking him to secure an impromptu reservation in the Capital's restaurant. Never mind, there's always room service, which offers an identical menu. And as far as we're concerned, any of the hotel's rooms is more attractive than the restaurant. Actually, if you're on your own, we can't think of anything more self-indulgently decadent than consuming chef Philip Britten's inspired cuisine in the lavish privacy of one of the £175 singles. There, all wrapped up in the fluffy terry bathrobe which you'll find hanging in the bathroom, you can toast your good taste at staying at the Capital. Better yet, salute your good fortune at being able to afford that Astin Martin you've got tucked away in the hotel's garage, yet another of the Capital's special amenities—the garage, not the car—

that make it one of only two London members of the prestigious Relais et Châteaux group. The other is the venerable Claridge's. Pretty good company, wouldn't you say?   🌱

Claridge's

Brook Street	071-629-8860
London W1A 2JQ	(FAX) 071-499-2210

The expression "fit for a king" has been with us for a long time—so has Claridge's, since 1814 in fact. And indeed, it's not impossible that the phrase was coined to describe the hotel James Mivart fashioned from two houses perched at the corner of Brook and Davies streets. The Prince Regent put the royal stamp of approval on the hotel when he took a permanent suite. The royal connection, once established, has never been broken. During Ronald Jones' first week as general manager, the hotel hosted three queens and two kings. "All reigning," he's quick to add as testimony to the fact that Claridge's, known as "the Resort of Kings and Princes," remains fit for them.

It's also plenty fit for anyone else who hankers for Claridge's dignified environment, coupled with its legendary level of personal care and service. When you have a manager like Michael Bentley overseeing every personal detail of your stay, the combined effect makes you feel like royalty from the moment you enter the imposing foyer with its black-and-white marble floors and sparkling chandeliers. You *know* you've arrived the first time you spot a liveried footman. It won't take you long—the staff-to-guest ratio is a remarkable 2 to 1. And to the man or woman, they stand ready to assist you in ways unheard of in most hostelries. Evening maids think nothing of being asked to brush a lady's hair or to run her bath. Their daytime counterparts routinely unpack and pack, interleaving the clothes with tissue paper to keep them from wrinkling. We have one gentleman friend whose heart was irretrievably won by Claridge's when he discovered the valets tie a flawless bow tie; no more frantic last-minute fumblings for him!

We could go on and on waxing poetic about the staff in general, but we would be doing you a disservice if we didn't introduce you to one member in particular, head hall porter par excellence John Spahr. He's been with the hotel for 35 years and has earned a well-deserved reputation as the master of the improbable, as well as the impossible. One client requested that he locate a fully trained female hound, one that also "spoke"

Italian. "Certainly, sir," was John's reply. We understand client and dog are doing well.

Another regular guest complained to John that when he got home to New York he lost his taste for tea. He and John speculated that it was a matter of the difference in water. So John regularly bottles some tap water for him and sends it to New York. Now, that guest has his authentic London tea every afternoon at home. This is the sort of thing that Claridge's defines as its "high standards of service," standards to which every staff member adheres, even relatively young ones, such as John's assistant Thomas Keatley. Thomas is only 29, but he's been at Claridge's for 14 years and is a consummate professional.

But service is only half the unique Claridge's equation. The other half is the spectacular nature of the accommodations. Take, for example, Suite 312, a presidential or royal suite, depending upon your leanings toward democracy versus monarchy. The Chinese-red entry hall highlighted by a gold-lacquered Japanese cabinet leads to a majestic high-ceilinged living room with wood-burning fireplace. The room overflows with late Victorian objets d' art and is so large that a baby grand piano is almost dwarfed.

The rose-toned bedroom successfully mixes traditional and art deco furnishings with a red damask canopied bed. The lighting fixtures date from the '20s, as does the Italian marble bathroom, which features double sinks and a tub for two. And, of course, it sports one of the famous Claridge's oversized showerheads, so popular that many guests order them for their bathrooms back home.

What does all this magnificence cost? Our guess is that if you have to ask the price, you can't afford it. The suite's rate is only quoted on request and certainly not published.

Another beauty, also with a mystery pricetag for security reasons, has a location which we cannot identify. It's another of the three royal (or presidential) suites and it, too, has a large foyer, and the dining room can seat twelve for dinner. But its most distinguishing feature resides in the pale yellow living room with its exquisite Aubusson-style carpet—a piano that belonged to Sir Arthur Sullivan of Gilbert and Sullivan fame. If it doesn't inspire you to sit down and write a ditty or two, perhaps the huge pink marble bathroom will.

When it comes to suites with prices we *can* reveal, we like number 412 at £400 per night. Its pine-panelled living room is an ideal place to lounge or entertain, with its working fireplace (there are 40 throughout the hotel), massive desk, comfy sofa and large coffee table. The bedroom is pale blue and made particularly memorable by its enormous closets, two dressing tables, acres of mirrors and luxurious eiderdown quilts. Again, the bathroom is noteworthy—this one is black-and-white marble and boasts a truly grand soaking tub and a waterfall shower.

All the hotel's 136 rooms and 55 suites are spaciously proportioned, as are the hallways that join them—wide enough for ladies in full crinolines to pass comfortably and have benefitted from a recent £2.2 million improvement program. Consequently, while the buttons in every room, meant for calling maids, butlers or waiters, may look quaint, be advised that the hotel is wired into the latest technology. It is completely air-conditioned, and dual-line, computer- and fax-ready telephones grace every room.

Moreover, £4.4 million was spent to reconfigure maître chef de cuisine Marjan Lesnick's kitchen into one of the most modern in Europe—only a 100-year-old gas oven large enough to cook a whole lamb remains from its former life. Sleek, clean and colourful, the new kitchen has allowed Marjan and his team of 60 cooks to improve upon the quality of the cuisine, which was already deemed fit for a queen and a king—Her Majesty Queen Elizabeth frequently entertains here. King Hussan II hosted a Moroccan feast in her honor in the Oswald Milne-designed ballroom.

For less protocol-laden occasions, the Causerie is a delight with its lunchtime smorgasbord of 33 different entrées, from £13.50 to £16.25, depending upon the number of courses that entice you. Or dine in the Restaurant under Christopher Ironside's fantastic mirrored mural. And, of course, taking tea in the foyer where you are served by those liveried footmen and serenaded by the fabled Hungarian Quartet is one of the things you should really do at least once, just for the sheer fun of it.

Likewise, you should stay at Claridge's at least once, just for the pure self-indulgent pleasure of it. Of course, it's likely to become a habit. Some 70 per cent of the clientele are repeaters. And Ronald Jones, supported by the elegance and amazing memory of manager Michael Bentley, constantly strives to increase that percentage. A picture-perfect rendition of *the* English gentleman with the requisite wit and charm, it's no wonder he was named Hotelier of the Year in 1988. That same year, his grateful client, Queen Elizabeth, honored him for his services to the British hotel industry by inducting him into the prestigious Order of the British Empire.

Our opinion? We think it would be fitting if Ronald was annointed King of Hoteliers. ❦

The Connaught

Carlos Place   071-499-7070
London W1Y 6AL   (FAX) 071-495-3262

Enter London's elegant and dignified Connaught Hotel, and you leave the city behind for another world. Here you'll discover privacy and serene comfort at its best, within an atmosphere of days gone by.

The Connaught's loyal clientele return again and again to luxuriate in their favourite comfortable suites and to be coddled by the gracious staff with smiles and service par excellence. The Connaught is run today exactly as it has always been run: like a good private house. And we know you, too, will feel at home the minute you step inside its hallowed halls.

The Connaught's legacy dates back to 1803, when Alexander Grillon, chef to Lord Crewe, opened a hotel on London's Albemarle Street. A few years later an offshoot to his hotel was opened in a pair of elegant Georgian houses at 14–16 Charles Street, Grosvenor Square, on property belonging to the Duke of Westminster.

As the Duke was an entrepreneur, he decided to redevelop the area at the end of the 1880s into what is known today as Carlos Place. In 1894, a new hotel was built by owner August Scorrier, who named it the Coburg, after Prince Albert of Sax-Coburg, consort of Queen Victoria.

The Coburg established a sterling reputation for itself that carries on to its successor, the Connaught, as the hotel was renamed at the beginning of World War I.

An historic Coburg brochure, which the Connaught staff treasures, proudly boasted that "the cuisine, and the cellar alike will be sans reproche, and the Coburg Hotel will be found in every possible detail to justify its association with a part of London which has been for generations, and is likely always to be, instinctively identified with all that is aristocratic, refined and luxurious in metropolitan society."

Heady stuff, indeed, but the Connaught does live up to this creed. However, managing director Paolo Zago has relaxed things a bit and says that his ongoing objective is for the hotel to be "a down-to-earth home, where guests feel comfortable and at ease."

It's impossible not to feel at ease, especially when Paolo is there to greet you himself. And it is certain if you have been a guest at the Connaught before, that Paolo will remember everything important about you. He keeps all your likes and dislikes on a 3 x 5 card in his private rolodex. He knows your favourite room, cocktail, flower, even your birthday. No computers for Paolo, they are much too impersonal! We'd like to have a look at his notes, but they are for his eyes only.

Of course, the entire staff of 300 want nothing more than to take care of your needs and see that all is well in your life while you are under their roof. And we promise that all will be well.

Surely you'll get to know head hall porter Alan Bromley. He's really an exceptional man. After all, he's been with the Connaught for nearly 20 years. He started out as a page boy and worked his way through the ranks. Today he will keep everything in your life running smoothly, no matter what it is that you need. The word *no* just is not present in his vocabulary, and we hear that he performs miracles of all kinds. Name your needed miracle, and it will be performed.

Besides the wonderful staff, the ambience here is going to make you feel right at home. Just off the entrance hall, you'll see a very inviting lounge, resplendent in dusty rose velvet and solid wing tapestry chairs. The fresh flowers and elegant tea tables invite you into an oasis of calm, security and warmth. Even if you're not a guest, you'll be welcome here for tea.

For lunch or dinner you will need reservations for the Restaurant and the Grill because they are considered to be among London's finest spots for dining. People come to do business and to see and be seen here.

The kitchen, under maître chef des cuisines, Michel Bourdin, is the same for both restaurants, but each room has its own atmosphere and clientele. The Grill with maître d' Pastore, who has been here 20 years, is much less formal than the Restaurant, though jacket and tie are required, but both have chef Bourdin's magic touch. Just select the room that suits your mood that day, and the staff will make sure a place is reserved for you and your friends.

The Grill has only 11 tables, spaced within the intimate spring-green walls, and overlooks the loveliest tiny garden. You can order all sorts of delicious à la carte items from the menu at lunch or dinner, Monday to Friday.

If you're feeling more like dressing up for an elegant evening, you'll feel right at home in the Restaurant, with its gleaming mahogany wall panelling, extraordinary chandelier, hand-blown crystal glasses and exquisite bone china.

This is where London's smart set meets to socialise. Usually, you start off in the lounge with cocktails and give your dinner order to the bell captain. When the first course is served, you're called into the dining room to sit down to a delicious classic French or traditional English dinner. It's just like going to a friend's home. Somehow you totally forget you're in a hotel dining room.

The Restaurant has one seating at lunch and one at dinner, and it seats only 80. It is open seven days a week, with Jean Pierre Chevallier as maître d'. He knows everyone and everything. He should, he's been here nearly 20 years.

Now, if you want to have a party that everyone will always remember, talk with Mr J. Perez, the private parties manager. He will help you create the perfect menu for the Carlos Room, where 14 to 22 guests can dine among 19th-century paintings and furniture. This is a perfect place to entertain those new city friends.

The Connaught has so many wonderful rooms to choose from, you'll probably want to try them all. The rooms on the lower floors are bigger, so keep that in mind when you write for reservations. And written reservations really are a must, especially for first-time guests. Walk-ins are simply not considered good taste at the Connaught, though telephone calls from repeat clients are more than welcome.

We like Suite 217–218 on the Mount Street side, with its high ceilings and comfortable sofas and chairs. A living room fireplace creates a very romantic mood. In the bedroom is a good-sized dressing table, leading to a shiny marble bathroom. The bathroom is perhaps a speck small, but it has nice high ceilings and all the amenities you ever could want. This suite will make you feel instantly at home and goes for £400.

Suite 225–226 is airbrushed in heavenly soft tones of cream, yellow and gold. It's quite large, and you can have a real fire in this suite. The beautiful chinoiserie cabinet bar stands at your service, with an ever-filled ice bucket, fresh lemons and just the proper glass for water, wine or brandy. You might not make it to dinner if you stay in this suite.

Gracing your bedside table are silver thermos jugs filled with soothing ice water. And towel warmers are in the sublime very large bathroom, with its enormous deep tub and nice bright mirrors. The vanity has three-way mirrors, just perfect for checking that hem on your gown.

And, of course, all the rooms have buttons that you push to summon a maid, valet or waiter instantly. The staff members are waiting for your call, so don't hesitate if they can be of service.

Even the Connaught's room keys were designed with imagination: instead of the usual plastic or wood, they are made from English gunmetal. You might be tempted to take a key home as a souvenir, but do ask Mr Zago first, if you're ever planning on returning to the hotel. He'll probably give you one, and then note it on your personal index card!

Anyone who is a regular guest at the Connaught doesn't even consider other hotels in London. With only 90 rooms and 24 suites, Connaught guests love the intimacy, friendliness and the feeling of being at home. To these discerning individuals, the Connaught is not a hotel at all, it's a way of life. And it's their London home away from home.   ❦

The Dorchester

Park Lane	071-629-8888
London W1A 2HJ	(FAX) 071-409-0114
	(from U.S.A. only) 800-727-9820

If you liked the old Dorchester, you'll love the new and improved version. Its recent renewal was not your garden-variety refurbishment. Instead, the Sultan of Brunei determined that his latest prize should become, as it once was, the ultimate in elegance and luxury enhanced by state-of-the-art facilities and technology. Hence, the hotel was shut down completely for almost two years to allow for a bottom-to-top restoration that meant gutting much of the property in order to install contemporary plumbing, air-conditioning with individual climate control in each room, an additional passenger lift along with new service lifts, and kitchens boasting the latest equipment. In the process, the 280 rooms were reduced to 252, including 55 suites, to increase the average size of the accommodations. But the essential character of this architectural gem on Park Lane that first opened its doors in 1931 remains unchanged.

To begin with, many of the rooms and features of the hotel are architecturally listed as being of special significance, which means they could not be changed. The distinctive look of the windows, for instance, could not be altered even though, in the spirit of upgrading the physical plant, they were all double-glazed—in fact, triple-glazed along Park Lane to shut out all the traffic noise. Special frames, identical to the original design, had to be made to incorporate the glazing in a manner that would not be apparent. Even more sensitive treatment was applied to the legendary Oliver Messel decorated chambers on the seventh and eighth floors, painstakingly restored to the fanciful splendour which made them the city's most sought-after rooms in the fifties and sixties.

Under the direction of one of Messel's assistants, the last examples of the flamboyant theatrical designer's work in London have been meticulously renovated according to the master's inspired concepts. The legendary Oliver Messel Suite (Liz Taylor's favourite) on the seventh floor and The Penthouse/Pavilion Suite on the eighth have further benefitted from the enthusiastic interest of Lord Snowden, Messel's nephew. What a relief to la Taylor and the suite's many other fans that Messel's flights of fantasy have come home to roost—latticework as picture frames, a television encased in a miniature theatre, bird cages as wall sconces, water spouting from a golden fish into a porcelain canopied bathtub, and a fireplace as pagan altar with the figure of Bacchus under a leafy trellis.

We share Liz's passion for the one-bedroom Oliver Messel Suite, which at £850 a night—not including VAT—is pure unadulterated Hollywood glamour. It looks like the sort of palace a movie queen (or king, or both) should inhabit. Indeed, it looks like the set for one of Noel Coward's sophisticated comedies, an observation apparently shared by Mr Coward himself, as it was always his suite of choice. Surely the garden terrace off the living room with its magnificent views over London's skyline is just the sort of place where the principals of *Private Lives* rediscovered each other. And you can just imagine a blithe spirit feeling very much at home hovering over the bed alcove, which is draped in chintz and framed by mirrored doors decorated with painted trees from which hang silk pictures of frolicking monkeys.

A little too whimsical for your taste? Try Suite 711 which overlooks Hyde Park. Reminiscent of the drawing room of an 18th-century English country house, the pine-panelled walls are hung with oil paintings and French tapestries, and graceful columns separate the living and dining areas. Typical of the hotel, the expected modern conveniences, such as a television and mini-bar, are disguised to fit in with the decor. In this instance, they are hidden in beautiful Chinese lacquer cabinets. It's all yours for a nightly rate of £650 plus tax.

Rooms, all decorated in keeping with the look of (what else?) the ever popular country house—here in the style of the between-the-wars years—can be had for £180 to £240. Each is unique in terms of finishes, fabrics, colours and layout and is equipped with safes and lavishly marbled bathrooms, most with a window and all benefitting from superb lighting, courtesy of well-placed Lalique fixtures. In keeping with the

pretense, everything that is brand-spanking new has the respectable patina of age; the tubs are oversized footed gems specially commissioned in
Germany, and those good old-fashioned brass room keys are in actual
fact part of an advanced electronic security system. Corresponding
codes are programmed into the keys and locks for the duration of a
guest's stay, and then reprogrammed for the next occupant.

Another Dorchester tradition that has been carefully preserved and,
indeed, improved upon is the cuisine. Willi Elsner, former deputy to the
legendary Anton Mosimann who put the Dorchester on the culinary
map, is the executive chef overseeing a staff which has been increased to
115 from a "mere" 85. He needs each and every one of them to properly
operate the hotel's kitchens. Each of the three restaurants has its own
kitchen, in addition to one dedicated to banquet service. The famous
Grill Room remains a temple to the best of British fare—cock-a-leekie
soup, smoked finnan haddie, and Dover sole—while the rococo Terrace
continues to set a sumptuous stage for the finest of French cuisine.

But there's some new action on the dining scene—the descriptively
named Oriental Restaurant. Situated on two levels on the Park Lane
side, it is loaded with fascinating Far Eastern objets d'art, making it one
of the few truly smart Oriental eateries in town. Primarily committed to
Cantonese dishes, the restaurant occasionally features other Oriental
cuisines that reflect its eclectic decor.

And speaking of action, there's plenty of it in the new nightclub downstairs. Taking a cue from The Ritz in Paris, this chic little enclave is the
preserve of authentic members—being a guest allows you to apply for
temporary membership, as long as you do it 24 hours in advance and
plan on spending £50 for yourself and a guest. Still, if the club is fully
booked by regular members, your application will be denied. If you plan
to spend any time here, enquire about permanent membership in the
Dorchester Club in order to mingle with the elite who regularly enjoy
the three Ds of its charming Georgian townhouse style—drinking, dining
and dancing.

The membership rule also applies to the Health Club for local residents. It's yet another innovation, but one which has roots in the Dorchester's past. It is located on the site of the Turkish Baths which were
part of the original design of the hotel. However, over the years they fell
into disuse, and during the war they served as an air-raid shelter. In their
latest incarnation, they've been transformed into a luxurious spa specializing in "relaxation" and "stress reduction"—the approved terminology

for fitness in the nineties. There is no charge to hotel guests for the use of the facilities, just for treatments such as massages and facials.

Still as au courant as the Dorchester can now claim to be (the instalation of a high-tech business center is another improvement), there is much about it that hearkens to another era. The emphasis on service continues to be unprecedented. As director and general manager Ricci Obertelli says, "Personal care and attention are key." Waiters, maids and valets are beckoned by the press of a button. They appear almost instantly to cheerfully and efficiently do your bidding, obviously taking great pride in the professionalism of their work. And indeed, many of them have been performing up to the Dorchester's exacting standards for quite some time. Despite the two-year hiatus, fully 30 per cent of the hotel's staff who were in service when it closed have returned to their duties. That means the familiar moustached countenance of John West still greets you at the door and the unflappable John Curry will seat you in the Grill Room. A 23-year fixture, John is worth cultivating not only for a prime seat, but also for the telling of one of his many tales. Ask him about the time he enforced his domain's former dress code by ever so politely barring the entrance of a lady in a pantsuit. Without any fuss she decamped to change, only to return wearing very little other than the jacket to her suit! Gracious to a fault, John conceded defeat and seated her, to the delighted amusement of his other guests.

Such memories and such people give the hotel a soul, something that no amount of paint and plaster can produce. Fortunately for the Dorchester, its soul remains intact while its body got a mid-life facelift which has restored the hotel to its youthful splendour.

The Draycott

| 24–26 Cadogan Gardens | 071-730-6466 |
| London SW3 2RP | (FAX) 071-730-0236 |

We succumb to a chronic illness whenever we spend any length of time in London—it's an urban version of island fever that possesses us with the notion of purchasing a flat to call our very own. We may have developed an immunity to this bothersome disease though, now that we've discovered the Draycott. It's just what the doctor ordered—a small hotel run like a private home with an ongoing house-party atmosphere. Indeed, it was a vintage 19th-century residence, or rather two of them, that fate dictated should be reincarnated into one of the best of the city's ever-increasing crop of intimate inns. You see, by coincidence the two residences became available on the same day, and Peter Morris just happened to be walking by as "For Sale" signs were going up. Driven by apparently divine intervention, Peter negotiated the deal in a matter of hours.

The story is even more amazing when you consider the fact that Peter had no experience as a hotelier. Nonetheless, he fearlessly spent £1.5 million on renovations, and then proved his good business sense by selling his creation to Ashford Hotels, at a profit. He knew he was putting it in good hands. The Ashford folks own and operate Ireland's two leading properties, Ashford and Dromoland castles.

The ebullient Sue Gregory has real power as the hotel's general manager. A hands-on manager, Sue is the Draycott's personality, a peculiar though very satisfying blend of grande luxe and home-like atmosphere. Amenities like refrigerators, fresh flowers, remote control televisions, hair dryers, and 24-hour room service suggest the bustling convenience of a large luxury hotel, while the lack of a uniformed staff, a concierge desk and a formal restaurant speak to a more relaxed hostel. It's a place where you can depend on an amiable chat with fellow guests over tea or cocktails in the English country house elegance of the drawing room. You can even count on it being an interesting conversation, because Sue is as particular about her guests as she is about her hospitality. She shares 18th-century author John Fothergill's opinion, expressed in *The Innkeeper's Diary*, that boring guests should be subjected to a surcharge. In reality, Sue doesn't go quite that far—she simply doesn't accept any future reservations from proven dullards.

The policy hasn't hurt the Draycott's occupancy rate and has probably helped maintain its popularity with folks like Angela Lansbury, John Malkovich, Jeremy Irons, Michelle Pfeiffer, Richard Dreyfuss, Sean Connery, Victoria Principal, Glenda Jackson, Michael Feinstein and Joan Collins. Joan Collins in a hotel without a concierge or a restaurant? Hard to believe, but true. Put it down to the hotel's unusual character and the fact that anything a properly "keyed" concierge can do, Sue or night manager Ali Gursoy can do, and in some instances, do it better. Witness the case of the out-of-print book we'd been searching for in vain. On a hunch, we gave them the title, and they were able to track down a copy.

As for the restaurant issue, who needs one when the chef in the basement kitchen is fully prepared to cater to your every whim any hour of the day or night? Breakfast at two in the afternoon or at two in the morning? No problem. Should you wish to share the wealth of the excellent fare with a few friends, that, too, is easily arranged. The Club Room is available for private parties and can seat up to 16. At night with the fireplace blazing, candles lit and a glorious flower arrangement (a Draycott trademark) in the centre of the beautifully appointed table, we can imagine few better settings for an elegant dinner party. Neither could John O'Sullivan, who hosted a little soirée for four cabinet ministers and their wives here.

For more casual entertaining, there's the drawing room we mentioned, with its stunning mantel over the wood-burning fireplace and its windows overlooking the enchanting gardens, or the smoking room near the entrance. Don't be put off by the name—it's more tradition than reality. This is an inviting persimmon-coloured library/bar, where the familial warmth is enhanced by a number of handsome portraits. The identities of these "ancestors" is a bit uncertain because the story changes, depending upon which member of the staff is telling it or how much champagne has been consumed by a regular guest who's taken a proprietary interest in the paintings.

Most of the sophisticated charm of the "public" rooms has been re-created in the 24 guest accommodations. Antiques lend authenticity to the engaging decor—pictures of English country scenes and gilt mirrors cover the walls, while decorative accessories on mantels and tables dismiss even the remote possibility of an institutional look. All bedrooms sport conversational furniture groupings—settee and armchair, table and chairs—and many have gas fireplaces. Even the bathrooms have more than state-of-the-art fixtures to recommend them. Many of them have a mosaic of handpainted tiles, each different, the work of a Cornwall artist who blows paint through a straw to colour the tiles one by one. High ceilings and garden views complete the rosy picture, unless you've made the mistake of booking one of the six singles for £65 to £95 a night. They're small, very small. . . too small.

Even if you're travelling alone, spring for one of the commodious doubles at £165. And if you hanker for something downright palatial, ask for a "superior double" at £185.

Whatever your space requirements or budget, be sure to book at least a month in advance. The Draycott has been a big hit since it opened in 1988. In addition to its unique character, the hotel is favoured by a convenient location on an exclusive residential street just steps from Sloane

Street and Knightsbridge. Of course, if you haven't stayed here before and your reservation request is declined, you can take comfort in the fact that it truly is a matter of availability (or rather lack thereof), not a comment on your personality. But if you *have* had the pleasure of being a guest at the Draycott and Sue turns you down, you may never know!

🍷

Dukes Hotel

| St James's Place | 071-491-4840 |
| London SWLA 1NY | (FAX) 071-493-1264 |

When asked about why they've developed a partiality for one hostelry over another, most people will mutter something about the size of the rooms, the lavishness of the bathrooms or the competency of the staff ...unless Dukes is the subject of their preference. In that case, while Dukes scores points on all of the above, habitués will start waxing poetic about the bar, aptly if unimaginatively named, The Bar.

Don't dismiss them as lushes. Their appreciation of Dukes's bar is a sign of their refined good taste and of their cognizance of the better things in life. What sets The Bar apart from the hordes of intimately elegant, gentlemen's clubby drinking establishments is a world-class collection of armagnacs and cognacs dating from as far back as 1789. Salvatore Calabrese acts as curator of these precious wines, claiming he "sells history by the glass." And history doesn't come cheap—a glass of that 1789 will set you back £425. For less than half that you can sip a tumbler of 1811, while the 1878 goes for "only" £75.

Salvatore is relentless in the pursuit of his bottles of history, and when he finds them, he keeps them locked up in the cellar. You have to know to ask about them, and even then he may test your knowledge of their relative merits before pouring. "I never sell the last measure in a bottle. It would be like losing a child"—a child he went to great lengths to find in the first place, never missing a sale or auction with pal Lucien Celentino of Ma Cuisine often in tow. Since Lucien's passion is for ports, Salvatore lets him get away with the pick of those lots, though The Bar benefits from an impressive selection of Portugal's answer to cognac, as well. We spotted one bottle of port dating from 1915 that sells for £10 a glass, but we settled for a 1970 at £7.50 a pop. And we learned the hard way not to even consider chasing this or any other alcoholic libation with a cup of coffee in Salvatore's domain. To his way of thinking, The Bar is a bar, period. For coffee or tea, the lovely lounge next door does very nicely, thank you very much.

You see, The Bar is sacred, somehow the heart and soul of the hotel. Its very name is derived from the portraits of three dukes—Wellington, Beaufort and Marlborough—that have hung in the hunter-green snuggery since the Edwardian building first opened as a hotel in 1908. Recently purchased by Cunard, the 26 suites and 36 rooms have been sympathetically refurbished to retain the tranquility and charm for which the hotel has been known for decades. Indeed, many of Dukes's valued traditions remain intact, most notably and importantly, the service. Under the brilliant orchestration of general manager Hugh Williamson-Noble, it is clearly paramount and carried out to the nth degree. No mini-bar in the room? No problem. Hugh is more than happy to install a full bar stocked with your personal favourites. And Thom Broadbent, the head hall porter who is also the president of the UK's branch of Clef d'Or (the professional organisation for concierges), is just the man to see about tickets to the latest Cameron MacKintosh production. If he can't get them, no one can!

Other more tangible legacies from Dukes's rich history include the ritual hand lighting of the gas lamps in the flower-filled courtyard which marks the entrance. And while the rooms have been enlarged, each has been decorated individually and with great care to resemble accommodations in a well-bred private residence, except when it comes to the bathrooms. Redone in sumptuous Italian marble, they could only be ascribed to a palace.

One of our favourites among the suites is 26. Bright and cheerful with its yellow walls, it has all the comforts of home, including an overstuffed sofa, thriving plants, ornamental knicknacks on the mantel, the odd ancestral portrait, real removable dress and suit hangers and a well-equipped kitchen. Actually, all the suites have kitchens; electric fireplaces in the sitting rooms; two telephones, each equipped with two lines; and a pricetag of £450 a night. Suite 12 is differentiated by pretty pink patterned fabrics and a sweeping bay window with a bench—an ideal spot for a good long afternoon's read.

Other suites have a more tailored, masculine look, like number 15. The sitting room is elegant yet vibrant with its dark red-striped fabric wall-coverings, while the dominance of a soft green makes the bedroom a restful refuge. But the real excitement here is in the bathroom where

the pressurized fixtures can be regulated to suit your individual shower-
ing preferences.

Now, about all those kitchens—useful and practical, yes. But given the
quality of the food service here, hardly necessary. Room service operates
24 hours a day, and the 40-seat restaurant overlooking the garden is a
delight—its chipper gentility is reminiscent of the dining room of an Old
Guard country club. Renowned for fine English cooking, the menu has
long depended on the delights of grilled Dover sole and traditional roast
goose. Now in the capable hands of Anthony Marshall, who is considered one of London's top chefs, having paid his dues at the Dorchester,
the Palace Hotel in St. Moritz, and the Savoy, the restaurant also boasts
dishes like ragout of turbot, sole, lobster and halibut served with a chervil and caviar sauce.

But the printed offerings serve only as a guide. Regular guests know
restaurant manager George Batz will persuade the kitchen to prepare
most anything they have in mind for consumption either in the dining
room or in their own cosy chambers. Should you opt for the latter, the
meal is served course by course, rather than rely on insulated units to
keep the food hot or cold.

And even the more modestly priced rooms at Dukes, which start at
£175 for singles and £205 for doubles, are spacious enough to encourage
taking advantage of such service. Furthermore, they tend to have lots of
closet and shelf space. Their bathrooms are just as grand as those of the
suites and are outfitted with the same amenities—plush towels, bathrobes and full-size bottles of Floris toiletries.

The one drawback at Dukes, if you are sensitive about the possibility
of staff and fellow guests assessing your financial standing, is the fact that
all the suites are on one side of the building and all the rooms are on the
other, each served by its own mahogany-lined elevator. The direction in
which you head after that nightcap with Salvatore, or his alternate
Gilberto, defines your suite-versus-room status. But Dukes's modest size
dictates that even regulars may not be able to secure the accommodations they desire or can afford. Reception manager Julie Murphy O'Connor suggests reserving in February for May and June, and at the
beginning of July for the Fall. From late November through Christmas
the situation eases when the CEOs who favour Dukes are sticking close
to home.

One final note about our unequivocal favourite feature of Dukes—you
guessed it, The Bar. Both Salvatore and Gilberto are dispensers of what

have been cited by a number of verifiable experts as some of the city's finest cocktails. They make a mean martini of ice-cold perfection, and their Manhattans—that most difficult of mixtures—are absolutely sublime. Moreover, they are both engaging hosts who make you feel very much at home, even if you're a lady on her own. Indeed, it's ironic—or perhaps very fitting—that this edifice which began life as a block of gentlemen's flats convenient to their St James's clubs (Boodle's, White's and the like) should now sport what may be the best bar in town.   🦃

Fortyseven Park Street

Mayfair   071-491-7282
London W1Y 4EB   (FAX) 071-491-7281

We've known a hotel or two that has spawned a truly world-class restaurant, but the reverse is seldom the case—a restaurant giving birth to a hotel of international repute. But Fortyseven Park Street is the exception that proves the rule. Having been crowned king of the cadre of Britain-based chefs by virtue of the extraordinary Le Gavroche (see entry in the restaurant section), Albert Roux determined to rise to the top of the ranks of hoteliers as well. He explains that courtesy of his culinary fame he had been "fortunate to visit all the best places. I wanted to create [a hotel] as good as all those top places in the world, but one thing is missing in them—privacy." It was Albert's dream to institute a tranquil, very private and supremely comfortable hostelry which would approximate his vision of a perfect lodging environment.

As luck would have it, he was already occupying part of the perfect property ("perfect" figures prominently in Albert's vocabulary, indicative of his drive to strive for perfection in every aspect of his hotel and restaurant). Le Gavroche, since opening in 1967, had inhabited the basement of a grand Edwardian townhouse. Built by the first Baron Milford, the imposing red brick structure encased a series of flats meant to be pieds-à-terre for gentlemen of quality. What better place to fashion Albert's "perfect world"—an all-suite establishment in a superb location serviced by one of Britain's two Michelin three-star restaurants?

In 1981, backed by Swedish tycoon Bengt Nygren, Albert purchased the building and embarked on an extensive renovation of the 52 suites. With the help of his wife Monique, who devised unique decors for each suite while employing a warmly soothing colour scheme of soft pinks,

Wedgwood blues and greens throughout, he was ready to open for business in 1982. And the rest, as they say, is hospitality history.

Fortyseven Park Street has flourished under the guidance of the Rouxs who run it as a large and luxurious family home, where the guests' wishes are the order of the day. "If you want to talk, we talk to you," says Albert. "If you want to be unknown, you are unknown. If you want to cook an omelette, ask the concierge to get the eggs, and use the kitchen in your suite to cook the omelette. And if it sticks to the pan, call me and I'll come up and tell you why it is sticking." Many would argue that this perquisite alone—the opportunity to get the occasional cooking tip from Albert—is reason enough to stay here. We're more persuaded by the fact that being a guest here is about the only way to assure a table at Le Gavroche. Hotel residents are given first priority for reservations. Actually, when you call to book your suite, you're asked about your dining requirements vis-à-vis the restaurant.

We say "your" suite because Fortyseven Park habitués tend to adopt their favourite and make their travel plans according to its availability. Suites range from £225 to £535 per night.

As a first-timer your tastes in decor and preferences in layout are gently solicited so that you will be assigned accommodations which most closely approximate them. Regular or newcomer, you're made to feel very welcome by the festive greeting of a bottle of vintage bubbly nestled in a gleaming silver ice bucket. What bliss to kick off your shoes after a hard day's travelling, sink into the sofa of your very own drawing room, and relish the restorative power of the champagne! You don't even have to deal with the rigours of unpacking and getting settled. Head housekeeper Janet Sparkes and your own personal chambermaid will see to that, just as they see to your rooms being supplied with fresh flowers every day.

Janet, a veteran of one of those top but impersonal places Albert had visited, is typical of the staff here. She is a consummate professional and regards the hotel as a very special place. She feels privileged to work here because, "we have the facility to always be able to say 'yes' to anything anybody wants." In fact, she's said 'yes' so often to us, we were stunned when she uttered an unequivocal "No!" to our entreaty that she become a part of our household. In actual fact, she's had better offers than ours, but she wouldn't dream of budging for love nor money.

Neither would Keith Bradford, who as director and general manager has met Albert's brief to "create a jewel, just like Le Gavroche." Behind his brooding dark good looks and dignified demeanor lies a passion for his job, a passion which places him neck-'n'-neck with Albert in the pursuit of perfection. He's the one who makes sure you're kept up-to-date with world events by having English, French and Italian newspapers delivered to each suite daily. And it is at Keith's direction that the suites boast generously stocked bars of wine and spirits. Indeed, the full complement of glasses, coupled with the china, flatware and cooking equipment in the kitchen, makes the notion of Fortyseven Park Street being your "home away from home" more than lip service.

Certainly, given the fully equipped kitchen and the 24-hour room service from Albert's world-renowned kitchen, entertaining en suite is a breeze. But if you want to throw a cocktail soirée or a large dinner party, there's a majestic private dining room at your disposal. Lest you think the hotel is the private preserve of the leisure classes, you should know the latest in international communications technology and superb secretarial support are also available. And you can indulge in the delights of the kitchen with impunity, as Fortyseven Park has an arrangement with a health club just two minutes' walk away. There you can work off the calories in the pool and gym or relax in the jacuzzi.

It seems that the Rouxs and Keith have thought of most everything. Rest assured, however, that if by chance they—or you—have forgotten anything, head concierge Peter Barwick will get it for you. In our considerable experience, he has never been daunted by any request. Peter simply does not understand the concept of "cannot" or "unable"—he epitomizes what Keith describes as the "passionate professionalism" of the staff, which in the final analysis is what truly sets Fortyseven Park apart from its many worthy competitors.   ❦

Grosvenor House

Park Lane	071-499-6363
London W1A 3AA	(FAX) 071-493-3341

There she sits looming over Hyde Park, an ocean liner docked at Park Lane—the stately Grosvenor House. Opened in 1929 on the former site of the Duke of Westminster's London house, this matriarch of London's grand hotels occupies more than two acres of land and offers a range of facilities unrivalled by any other: 70 suites, 390 rooms, 160 apartments, a health club, a business center, three restaurants, a conference center, a hairdressing salon, a florist *and* Europe's largest ballroom.

Despite its address and the fact that it was the first hotel built on Park Lane, the main entrance isn't on that noble boulevard at all, but on the quieter, quainter Park Street. That is, the parallel street is quieter and quainter until you turn into the Grosvenor House's driveway where invariably a phalanx of roaring high-tech vehicles lurks—Rolls-Royces, Jaguars, Porsches, Bentleys and Mercedes, most with London plates, testimony to the hotel's status as social function central. The doormen do an admirable job of directing the congested scene, but they could use the skill of a professional traffic manager. We can't tell you how many times we've abandoned cabs at the entrance of the driveway rather than have the driver battle his way to the door.

Once inside, unless you're attending a dinner for 1,500 or so in the gargantuan Great Room, the Grosvenor House is, given its size, a surprisingly tranquil place. Or perhaps it's *because* of the expansive proportions that it seems devoid of the hustle and bustle of a property accommodating some 700 guests and residents attended by an equal number of staff. The size of the rooms simply engulfs the hordes and deadens the accompanying babble. Remember, it was built when space was not at a premium. Witness the former Olympic size of the lobby, a calm blue-green ocean punctuated by whitecaps of Oriental art. But the ocean is being broken up into a series of seas—having spent £25 million refurbishing the guest rooms, Trusthouse Forte is embarking on a £6 million renovation of its flagship's lobby. Smaller, more intimate spaces are being created, using English stone rather than marble to avoid the sleek coldness of so many modern lobbies. A library/bar for the exclusive use of guests is being carved out, a place where they can cosy up to two fireplaces. And the giant sophisticated coffee shop/restaurant that is the Pavillion, with its sweeping view of Hyde Park, is being transformed into a wood-panelled grill room.

However, when the work is completed, one lobby fixture will emerge unchanged—the Grosvenor House's ambassador Jimmy Welch who has been welcoming guests here for 45 years. With more than a hint of Charles Boyer in his countenance and a large dose in his charming persona, Jimmy claims he used to greet people at Southampton disembarking from Cunard's Queens and now he's receiving their grandchildren fresh off the Concorde.

But Jimmy's just the tip of the hospitality iceberg. There are eight concierges and four guest relations managers to attend to your every whim. And that's not even counting the manager of the Crown Club, the hotel within the hotel on the fifth floor. It takes a special key to persuade the lift to stop on the club level, which is complete with a board room and lounge. Here, too, service is the keynote—the staff are equipped with beepers to assure prompt response to guest requests, like those of the Sultan of Brunei who called the Crown Club his London home while awaiting the renovation of the Dorchester.

Since we figure anything that's good enough for a sultan is good enough for us, we usually request accommodations in the club—the two-line telephones also have something to do with our preference for the fifth floor. Of course, you pay a bit more—£225 for a single as opposed to £195 elsewhere, £250 versus £225 for a double—but you get to attend a private cocktail reception every evening in the lounge. It's a terrific way to meet your fellow club members and do a little international networking. The extra we spend on our quarters, we make up for in dinner invitations, even when we opt for one of the appropriately described small suites.

We're partial to 571 at £360 a night with its pleasant proportions—a good-sized foyer separates the sleeping and living areas. The handsome bedroom boasts an enormous closet, one with enough height to actually accommodate gowns and fur coats without letting them drag on the floor. The sitting room is a more feminine counterpoint with dainty, vaguely Victorian rose-velvet-covered furniture and the suite's second remote-control television. Should nature call, you can even follow an engrossing program in the bathroom where the sound is piped in at the turn of a knob. The bathroom is further distinguished by the size of the tub which could pass as a lap pool, but is otherwise a clone (right down to the nasty built-in hair dryers) of those of the recently redone suites at Brown's. Trusthouse Forte must, somewhere, own an immense quarry yielding a bounty of sand-coloured marble.

For more space with a view, ask for Suite 545 which delivers broad vistas of the park from its corner location while embracing you in its rosy warmth. Twin sofas nestle in front of the fireplace, and ornamental moulding softens the edges. A built-in vanity in the bedroom is a nice touch, as are the pale blue floral upholstered headboard and the ample closets, which seem to be a Grosvenor House trademark. The long foyer-cum-corridor and the size of the rooms make you feel as if you're in a one-bedroom apartment rather than a hotel suite—even one that goes for £745.

And speaking of apartments, one whole section of the building that sports a separate entrance is devoted to them. Fully serviced one- to five-bedroom residences, they're available for long-term tenants like the Duchess of Argyle and for transients from £225 per night. They're tastefully decorated in country-house chic, right down to the collection of antique tomes arranged on the bookshelves that flank the fireplace in 49. You might well wonder if Nina Campbell was involved in the decor, but it turns out to be the work of Olga Polizi who does most of the decorating for Trusthouse Forte's London properties. Not coincidentally, she is Lord Forte's daughter.

Yes, there is a Lord Forte very much in charge of the world's most profitable hotel company, which used to be headquartered at Grosvenor House. However, Lord Forte and his executive staff have moved elsewhere, leaving room for the creation of 86 Park Lane, London's newest, most sophisticated conference center. Many of the rooms are equipped with cleverly concealed state-of-the-art communications technology, and none of them bears any resemblance to your typical hotel function room. Take the Bourbon, a richly wainscoted chamber with a fireplace and a magnificent table seating 22. Then there's the gem revealed behind the panelling in Lord Forte's former oval (literally and figuratively) office—a baroque mirrored jewelbox of a room supported by ornate gilt columns, perfect for an elegant dinner party.

Downstairs, you'll find more state-of-the-art equipment in the gym of the Grosvenor House Health Club, the largest, most complete of any in a London hotel. In addition to the extensive range of exercise apparatus, there are a 60-foot pool—suitable for swimming, rather than the splashing availed by most postage-stamp hotel pools—jacuzzi, sauna, steambath, and health bar which serves a variety of juices and nutritious snacks.

If the very idea of a health bar strikes you as a contradiction in terms, never fear, there are plenty of places to imbibe. Besides the Pavillion, there's Ninety Park Lane, the hotel's signature restaurant that rates its own entry in this book, as well as Pasta Vino e Fanastasia offering Northern Italian cuisine in a gently festive atmosphere and the Red Bar— pretty much what its name suggests. It is most definitely red, splendid lacquered red from stem to stern, from floor to ceiling, and it's dedicated to the convivial consumption of alcoholic beverages.

So, other than the sultan and the duchess, who are you likely to find at Grosvenor House? Just about anybody who appreciates (or needs) every modern convenience packaged with all the luxurious trappings of a truly grand hotel. And if you're into royal watching, this is a better place than most—one of the family shows up at least once a month to attend one function or another.   🍇

Halcyon Hotel

| 81 Holland Park | 071-727-7288 |
| London W11 3RZ | (FAX) 071-229-8516 |

Resplendent in its belle époque lavishness, the Halcyon is a bit off the beaten track of Bond Street, Knightsbridge and Park Lane. But that's the whole point. As its name suggests, this small hotel is a haven for those seeking tranquil privacy. It is also ideal for those intent on attending Henley, Ascot or Wimbledon—all are easily accessible from its Holland Park site on a stately, tree-lined residential street. But for these events, it's necessary to reserve at least five months in advance.

For non-sporting weeks, it's still advisable to think ahead where the Halcyon is concerned. The competition is stiff for getting in here— you're up against some pretty heavy hitters. Michelle Pfeiffer, Mick Jagger, Bruce Willis, Demi Moore, Yoko Ono, Carly Simon, Lauren Bacall and Liza Minelli all consider it their home away from home. For good reason. It once was a private residence, two magnificent early Victorian mansions, to be more precise, that were meticulously restored to the tune of £9 million in preparation for the May 1987 opening. Furthermore, the young, attractive, respectfully friendly *and* plentiful staff—65 for the 44 rooms—make it clear it's their great pleasure to serve you and to have you take advantage of the extra-special niceties they offer, like one-hour pressing, secretarial service, babysitting and 24-hour room service.

The illusion of being a guest in a very wealthy friend's townhouse begins when you cross the threshold into the reception area-cum-drawing room, with its tapestry-covered Empire chairs and settee, majestic grandfather's clock and rococo moulding. It's a breathtakingly formal room, softened by a profusion of beautifully arranged flowers. A parlour in the old-fashioned sense is more show that anything else; the real lounging goes on in the snug little bar down a flight of stairs. A truly discreet hideaway, its purposely dim lighting lends a touch of mystery to the wood-panelled chamber. Who is occupying the barely 20 seats, the comfy striped sofas and chairs meant for lingering? It's almost impossible to identify anyone by sight, and the staff will never tell, as the bar serves as a watering hole for a very exclusive neighbourhood that includes Kensington Palace.

We do know that Prince and Princess Michael of Kent have been for dinner at the adjacent Kingfisher Restaurant. We can only speculate as to whether or not any of their relatives like Charles and Di, Margaret, and the Duke and Duchess of Gloucester have entered the haven. With such prestigious potential patronage, it's too bad the room is a bit on the dreary side—this, despite the fact that large French doors open onto a rather delightful garden. There's something very pedestrian about the decor which relies heavily on latticework. Fortunately, there's nothing mundane about the food, thanks to the talents of Robert Ridley. He offers an imaginative menu, and the prices are, by hotel standards, diner-friendly—£3.50 to £9 for starters and £8.50 to £15.50 for main courses.

At these prices you could forgive some culinary transgressions, but a meal of wild mushroom risotto, followed by steamed turbot with leeks and grain mustard vinaigrette had nary a one. And the noisettes of venison with prunes and celeriac purée was downright sensational.

No matter how much you cotton to Robert's cooking, however, you won't spend nearly as much time in his restaurant as you will in your room—which is the good news since all the rooms are brilliantly decorated. Each is unique, striking in its individuality. The air-conditioned spaciousness and the marble bathrooms are the only common denominator, courtesy of the creativity of Barbara Thornhill, who hails from Washington, D.C. Interesting that a colonial was entrusted with replicating the atmosphere of an English country house. But she proved up to the task, producing a genial, slightly eccentric ambience which is absolutely authentic to the traditions of that great British institution. Take the Egyptian Suite—its bedroom resembles a blue-and-white striped tent camped at a palm-shaded desert oasis, as depicted by a wraparound wall mural. It's exactly the sort of thing a Victorian adventurer might have commissioned for his manse to commemorate his travels. Charming and witty, you can make like Richard Burton (the explorer, not the actor) or a pharaoh in it for £275 a night.

Enchanting, often humorous details like the Egyptian Suite's mural and the inventive use of trompe l'oeil throughout are a hallmark of the hotel. The glass ceiling of the Halcyon Suite's sun-drenched conservatory is shaded by a colourful collection of parasols hanging upside down from the rafters at a dizzying array of angles. Pale bamboo and gaily painted wooden furniture complete the winsome room, which is complemented by a bedroom draped floor-to-ceiling in pretty pastel striped fabric. Yours for £550 a night.

For more traditional accommodations, check suite 41. In this junior suite you'll find more soft ice-cream cone colours adorning the overstuffed sofa and chairs. The twin beds are made one by the crowning glory of a ceiling-high canopy, its yards of material seemingly gathered by a cheerfully romantic bow. One of our favourites, it goes for £325 a night. Doubles can be had from £185; singles from £165.

Whichever room you choose, you'll be entitled to the use of one of London's smartest health clubs which is nearby. Its facilities include an indoor pool, a high-tech gym and a sauna. There is no fee for any of them, but you will be charged reasonable rates for the club's beauty treatments. Just contact the hall porter, Oscar Jacobs, who will make all the necessary arrangements. He's also the fellow to see about horseback riding which is also available in close proximity to the hotel. And should you prefer getting around on two legs—yours—Oscar will map out a jogging route through the park for you. Tennis anyone? That, too, can be arranged.

With its hospitable aura, exceptional decoration and easy access to such varied activities, it's no wonder the hotel is a destination in itself. People go to the Halcyon to stay there, to enjoy its amenities. To habitués, the Halcyon is more than just a place to hang their hats, it's a place to call home.   🍒

Hotel Conrad Chelsea Harbour

Chelsea Harbour	071-823-3000
London SW10 0XG	(FAX) 071-351-6525

Self-serving superlatives run rampant in the hotel industry, and one of London's newest hotels is no exception. Europe's first built-from-the-ground-up luxury all-suite establishment, the Hotel Conrad Chelsea Harbour aims to be London's finest business hostelry and maintains that in order to accomplish that feat it has to make certain it's the city's finest hotel—period.

Our suggestion to the dashing John Serbrock, who as general manager so diligently pursues the 160-room hotel's stated goal, is to keep plugging away at the business angle. There he may have it locked, but it's unlikely that the Conrad will ever be rated best of show. It's too new, too far west and too comfortably predictable to join the ranks of Claridge's and the Connaught.

Which is not to say the Conrad isn't a worthy contender. It is, with a lot to recommend it to business and leisure travellers alike. For one, there's the location, a 20-minute cab ride from Hyde Park, in the smart new Chelsea Harbour complex right on the Thames where, looking like a multidecked cruise ship, the hotel dominates a marina. Anathema to some, we found the quiet, contained atmosphere of the development a pleasant change from the hustle and bustle of the heart of the West End. And what could be more enjoyable than getting to more populated areas of the city by riverbus? Furthermore, if you're an antiques aficionado, the scores of shops strung along Kings Road are just a ten-minute stroll away.

But once at the Conrad, you don't actually have to go anywhere if you don't want to. You're right on top of the sophisticated dining and shopping of Chelsea Harbour that is making it a destination for locals as well as for tourists. Here, you'll find Ken Lo's Memories of China and Lord Linley's Deals (see restaurant section) in addition to a wine bar, a deli and respectable French and Italian eateries. Then there are the specialty shops and services geared to catering to the newly built neighbourhood in which £300,000 flats are not uncommon.

As for the hotel, it's a marbled beauty with a grand hotel magnificence about its public spaces, although their splendour is slightly muted by modern translations of classic symbols such as columns and staircases. A properly impressive lobby of lofty proportions greets guests—properly impressive because, like all the interiors, it was designed by internationally heralded decorator David Hicks. It's his first hotel, and the old boy's verifiably proud of it, spending lots of time entertaining his chums here to show off his work. As pretty as we find the Georgian columns soaring to the cloud-mural ceiling, what we like best about the lobby is that you don't have to spend much time in it. The rigours of registration are taken care of in your suite—a nice touch, as is the fact there's no charge for early arrival or late departure, if the hotel is not fully booked.

So you walk in and are whisked away, literally, in the bank of very fast elevators to your own little domicile, minimally a bedroom/living area serviced by an entrance hall, plenty of closets and a large bathroom complete with standard-sized, rather than sample, toiletries. Spacious and comfortably, if somewhat unimaginatively, decorated—all the colours are a little too soothing, while the prints generate too much of an ensemble effect—such accommodations go for £175, plus VAT, on the lower floors and £195, plus tax, on the upper.

Like all the Conrad's suites, they glory in two exceptional features: a bleached wood conference-table-like desk and a corresponding secretary which serves as the hospitality and entertainment center. The desk can handle a personal computer *and* a fax machine (both of which the Conrad is equipped to provide) and it still leaves space for an open briefcase, along with room to pen a handwritten note or two, not to mention the telephone. You should know there are three telephones in every suite, the other two phones located at bedside and in the bathroom.

As for the deceptively rustic-looking secretary, it conceals what may be the best stocked mini-bar in the universe—caviar, cheese and other edible delicacies are stacked alongside the usual assortment of liquid refreshments. Actually, not so usual. Here you have a mini wine cellar, with the reds correctly stored in a separate unrefrigerated unit. Even more awe-inspiring is the complete collection of glasses, ranging from champagne flutes to red *and* white wine glasses, to tumblers. The wonders of this piece of furniture continue to astound when you open the upper double doors to discover a remote-control television and VCR. The staff will happily tape any show you are unable to catch, compliments of the house.

It all adds up to a good deal, but another £50 buys you considerably more space in a superior suite. We like 202 with its sweet little balcony overlooking the marina. Light and airy in soft cheery blues, it has a formal living room, the door of which, like that of the bedroom and *one* of the bathroom's, opens onto a foyer. We're talking about lots of doors— another door directly connects the bedroom with the bath, and the commode area is separated by yet another one. In fact, there are so many doors (all fire-doors are outfitted with spring-loaded hinges that automatically close them) that two people roaming around one of these suites can feel as if they're rehearsing a French farce—doors slamming everywhere. Admittedly from an architectural standpoint, all this is well laid out, ensuring privacy for the simultaneous conducting of a business meeting in the living room and a snooze in the bedroom.

And there are the safety considerations, which are rightfully of paramount importance in such new construction. One member of the young, enthusiastic and attractive staff pointed out all the sprinklers (which seem to rate at least a one-to-one ratio with the doors) with the good-natured observation that one is more likely to drown here than to burn.

Certainly you can come close to drowning in luxury in any of the six penthouse suites which take up the entire top floor. In addition to the super-secure electronic locks throughout the hotel, you need a special key to take the lift up to the penthouse level. When the doors open, it's like entering a completely different world. Gone are the cheerful limed-oak wood wainscoting and chrome fittings that give other hallways the look of a contemporary Bavarian lodge. They are replaced by rich dark mahogany and polished brass. The room proportions are nothing short of palatial, and all, except the bathrooms, open onto wide terraces with breathtaking views downriver toward the centre of London.

Again, the layout is ingenious, enabling the entire floor to act as one giant enclave with six bedrooms, six living rooms and three dining/conference rooms, all benefitting from exclusive round-the-clock butler service for a special rate of £3,000 a night. That's the way one "mega-star" took it during a concert series in the Docklands, downstream. The unnamed singing sensation even took advantage of the White Eagle, the hotel's 51-foot cabin cruiser (which is available to all guests), using it as transportation to and from the gig.

Since we don't travel with an entourage, the £1,000 a night two-bedroom Presidential Suite suits us just fine. Occupying the southeastern corner of the floor, a large porthole affords an amazing view from the master bedroom; another one distinguishes the breakfast nook; and the dining room has a floor-to-ceiling bay window that offers a different but equally spectacular vista. Speaking of which, how about the sauna and the huge jacuzzi in the master bath?

Obviously your basic executive isn't going to occupy such extravagant quarters, so why are we so confident that the Conrad will become a mecca for business people? Well, there are the desks, the well-thought-through layout of the suites, and a business center open daily from 8 A.M. to 8 P.M. Its efficient staff can arrange for couriers, provide cellular phones, do translations and take dictation. Moreover, photocopying, fax and telex services are available 24 hours a day, seven days a week. Indeed, their radical policy of not charging for incoming faxes is in and of itself reason enough to make us regulars.

Add to that a clubby bar, an elegant lounge, a friendly restaurant and an in-house health club with a 25-metre indoor pool, and you've got a pretty compelling argument for the Conrad's future preeminence. ❧

Hyde Park Hotel

| 66 Knightsbridge | 071-235-2000 |
| London, SW1Y 7LA | (FAX) 071-235-4552 |

The crown in the logo of the Hyde Park Hotel is more significant than one might imagine. It's not simply indicative of the hotel's status as the most palace-like of any of London's hostelries; the crown points to the Hyde Park's long-standing association with Buckingham Palace, a relationship closer than that between any other hotel and the royals. Indeed, since the Hyde Park opened, an entrance on the park side of the hotel has been reserved for the exclusive use of the royal family.

It is a tradition born of necessity rather than an intent to tie the hotel's destiny to the House of Windsor. It seems the turreted red-brick building began life in 1892 as the Hyde Park Court, London's tallest building and an exclusive block of "residential chambers for gentlemen." The uproar about the "vast pile" and the "Tower of Babel" did nothing to deter the smart set from readily embracing it as one of the most fashionable addresses in the city. But a decade after its debut, which had led Parliament to enact a law limiting the height of new construction, the lease was obtained by the Bennett family of hoteliers. They reopened it as London's grandest hotel in 1908, with a new address.

The Queen would not allow any commercial advertising in Hyde Park, and therefore insisted the main entrance with the hotel's name above it be moved to the Knightsbridge side. The original portal was preserved as the Royal Entrance and has been opening regularly for the family ever since. Indeed, during the early years, Queen Mary was so constant a visitor that she was given her personal retiring room equipped with an old-fashioned commode—the ladies' powder room was some distance from the Royal Entrance and a queen is, after all, entitled to her privacy.

So are future queens. When Victor Edelstein shows his collections here, Princess Diana is treated to a private viewing in the ballroom. Afterwards she's been known to drop into The Park Room for a spot of tea, a ritual frequently enjoyed by her husband and sister-in-law when they were children accompanying papa Prince Philip. The Duke of Edinburgh engaged in more adult pursuits here as well—the Hyde Park was the setting for all his polo cocktail parties.

While the association with royalty, British and otherwise, put the hotel on the map, it also ushered in an unfortunate chapter in the Hyde Park's history when, during the 1960s, the staff coped uneasily with a clientele of newly minted millionaires. Uncomfortable with the trappings of royalty, the jet setters deserted the hotel for other, less formal environments; and the Hyde Park suffered a period of decline which saw a number of ill-considered transformations of its regal decor.

But over the last few years, a concerted effort has been made to restore the hotel to its former glory. General manager and Gorbachev double, Paolo Biscioni, has been charged with the brief of making the Hyde Park one of the top three five-star hotels in London and the jewel in the crown of the Trusthouse Forte chain. The charming Paolo, who is equally adept at greeting King Constantine of Greece at a wedding in the rococo ballroom as he is at welcoming a jittery young honeymoon couple awed by the grandiose surroundings, has a lot to work with in the unrivalled extravagance of the physical plant. Eight different marbles from an equal number of countries gleam in the ornate two-tiered lobby. And the multi-million-pound refurbishment, which has seen every square foot lavishly restored, has revealed long forgotten mosaics and fireplaces in other public rooms, as well as the lovely murals on the Edwardian wardrobes. In the process, one-and-a-half acres of elaborate frieze work has been regilded, hundreds of pieces of antique furniture repolished, and acres of specially commissioned carpet have been installed.

The result is spectacular. The Hyde Park is once again attracting a clientele capable of keeping the £1,250-a-day Royal Suite consistently occupied. No wonder. It is nothing short of magnificent. Georgian chandeliers glitter in rooms awash in priceless antiques like the exquisite Louis XV writing table in the drawing room and the grand Regency table seating eight in the dining room. The walls of the master bedroom are covered in gold silk brocade, and rich Carrara marble lines the bathrooms. French doors lead from each of the rooms to a wide Palladian balustraded terrace overlooking Hyde Park. No detail is left to chance from the delicate handpainted cornicing to a cellarette for the storing of the occupant's vintage wines to a design offering complete security.

All the other 19 less exhorbitantly priced suites, like the one-bedroom Presidential at £750 and the £800 King Gustav Adolf, the dignified 6th-floor favourite of the Swedish monarch, are also located on the park side of the hotel. And all enjoy butler and valet service. Tea is served upon your arrival while your luggage is unpacked. Every evening your personal Jeeves signals the end of the day with complimentary champagne and canapés. Ah, the joys of gracious living.

But you don't have to check into a suite to experience the hotel's accommodating service. It embraces you from the moment landmark doorman Harry Payne helps you out of your car or cab. Harry's been practising the hospitable arts here for years, acting as the hotel's welcoming vanguard to the world's richest and most famous—people like Ava Gardner, with whom he was reputedly in love, and more recently Richard Gere, Joanne Woodward, Harry Belafonte, Princess Ira Von Furstenberg, Nicola Trussardi and Frank Zappa. He turns them and you over to the very elegant, tailcoat-clad Donald Sloan, who spends much of his time greeting guests and ushering them on their way—up the majestic staircase to the polished mahogany registration desk where yet another warm welcome awaits. . . or beyond to The Park Room.

One of the city's loveliest, most tranquil restaurants with an unparalleled panoramic view across the verdant acres of Hyde Park, the room is pioneering the power breakfast in London. Captains of industry and finance fill The Park Room daily, plotting their deals over the £13 full English breakfast or the £18 Knightsbridge which features a split of champagne along with fresh-squeezed orange juice, scrambled eggs wrapped in smoked salmon, half a melon with lemon sorbet, and fresh croissants. There's also a simple Continental offering, but the powerbrokers tend to ignore it, and so do we, in order to enjoy The Park Room to the fullest.

So should you. A substantial meal to linger over is essential for watching the daily ritual of the Queen's Horse Guards marching by around 10:30 A.M. on their way to Buckingham Palace. Otherwise, book a table for lunch just before noon, so you can settle down to witness the Guards returning to their barracks. If for some reason you miss them, chef Adriano Paganini's food will make up for any disappointment. This talented 24-year-old has introduced a new style of north Mediterranean cooking to London. It's a fresh, health-conscious cuisine that eschews butter and cream in favor of olive oil and light, herb-scented sauces. At lunch he offers a table d'hôte menu of two courses for £18, three for £20.50, and four for £24.50, inclusive of service and tax, featuring dishes as varied as tortellini with aubergines, salmon steak braised with thyme, or boned breast of chicken stuffed with vegetables.

Later on, The Park Room becomes one of the most romantic settings for dinner in town. The 22.3-carat gold leaf trim which sparkles against the pale blue-grey of the walls during the day, takes on a lustrous glow from the crystal chandeliers and the tall tapers on the tables. And the subtle character of the beautiful blue-and-peach floor covering, so unusual in a country full of tens of thousands of miles of truly garish carpet, becomes even more appreciated. It's an environment meant for long leisurely dining, for working your way through Adriano's "menu gastronomico." At £35 it's a four-course feast, including treats like artichoke hearts with scampi topped by a chervil sauce, followed by a wild mushroom risotto for starters. The main course might be escallope of salmon served with fresh asparagus, and the dessert will definitely be your selection from the tempting trolley.

For heartier traditional fare, try the oak-panelled grill room downstairs. It has its own separate street-level entrance, or you can reach it from the rear of the lobby by following your nose—the seductive aroma of just-roasted meats sitting on carving tables tends to waft its way up the back staircase. Even here, in this former temple of traditional English cooking, a lighter touch is in evidence. A gold crown identifies those dishes on the menu prepared with a minimum of oil and dairy products. As the result, what was once a male preserve is now being frequented by the ladies who lunch. No doubt they, like us, are kicking themselves for missing the solicitous attentions of manager Ernesto Cacace all these years. He couldn't be sweeter or more entertaining. Ask him to tell you about the time he got an urgent phone call for His Majesty and had to ask, "Which Majesty?"

But no one at the Hyde Park tops Nunzio Nestola in the story-telling department. As head concierge for more than 20 years, he's been asked to do just about everything and has, "as long as it's legal." Mr Tact himself, he would never reveal the whos, but he's a terrific teller of the whats, which include the recent purchase of a private jet for a guest.

Unfortunately, we've never had the opportunity to test Nunzio's procuring skills to such an extent. But when we stay here, we feel as if we could afford to do so. A day or two at the Hyde Park and we feel like royalty, no matter whether we're in a suite or a room. Indeed, one of the joys of the hotel is the spaciousness and inherent comfort of the single and double rooms, ranging from £199 to £265. They tend to be uncommonly large with an uncontrived serenity of decor that allows for instant relaxation. Thank goodness for the abundant closet space because once settled at the Hyde Park, we're usually persuaded to stay a while. ❦

Inn on the Park

Hamilton Place, Park Lane   071-499-0888
London W1A 1AZ   (FAX) 071-493-6629/01

Despite being a relatively new hotel and decidedly not a subscriber to the country-house trend, the Inn on the Park possesses quantifiable charm unexpected in a 228-room property built as the British beachhead of a North American chain. The first Four Seasons hotel in Europe, the Inn on the Park is a refined hybrid of the sleekly modern and the snugly traditional, a combination which makes it particularly popular with American visitors, as well as show-biz people from all points, and keeps its occupancy rate the highest of any hotel in London. The management aims for 90 per cent occupancy and gets it, even though it's the only hotel of any size we know that does not officially offer a discounted corporate rate. Nonetheless, it has been voted the best hotel in Britain for three consecutive years by international business travellers in the Executive Travel/Expotel Awards.

There's something so very civilized about the Inn on the Park, a quality first exhibited at check-in even at the busiest times. Instead of lining up at a commercial-looking counter, you're invited to sit in one of the amiable groupings of antique and gently contemporary furniture that soften the lustrous marble and redwood lines of the lobby. A receptionist retrieves you from your comfortable perch and ushers you to one of the elegant Regency desks that cleverly conceal all the necessary accoutrements of registration—computers and credit card imprinters.

From there, one of the receptionists, captivating conversationalists one and all, escorts you to your room. All the singles and doubles, starting at £190 (plus tax) are commodious, done in soft tones enlivened by accent colours in the crown moulding, one of the many unanticipated decorative touches in a circa 1970 building. The comely, Empire-style furniture is specially made for the Inn and is complemented by elaborate drapes and valances, framing windows that actually open. Large closets contain individual electronically operated safes. And, in addition to the ubiquitous robe and toiletries (Floris, in this instance) the bathrooms boast telephones, yet another example of the hotel's civilized nature.

As pleasant as the "standard" rooms are, we prefer the Four Seasons variety, like room 401 which has a sweet little balcony overlooking the Inn's private park. At £385 it features a sitting room, separated from the bedroom by folding French doors, and a queen-size bed set back in a sheltering alcove. Decorated in a soothing celadon and rose scheme, it is very homey in a plush sort of way, made all the more so by the clever artifice of fresh flowers arranged in interesting containers, such as silver teapots.

Glitzier and completely unique in London are the second floor's Conservatory rooms and suites. Inaugurated just three years ago, they have proved so popular that the design is being incorporated in the Four Seasons' new Paris property. Number 225 for £305 is typical in that you enter directly into the bedroom, only to be dazzled by the light streaming through the glass-enclosed sitting room beyond. To say the effect—enhanced by a glossy marble floor, artfully arranged plants and the hotel's hallmark mixture of antique and traditional furnishings—is dramatic is to understate the case.

Even more spectacular is Suite 216, which would seem to be more at home overlooking Lake Worth in Palm Beach than poised in the middle of Mayfair. Here a large marbled foyer leads into what must be the brightest, most jovial room in London, bathed in streams of dancing light. The outer glass wall and ceiling blur the distinction between outdoors and in. Is the planted terrace, resplendent with statuary, inside or out? Hard to tell, but it's just where the pool and deck would be on Florida's Gold Coast. Likewise, the room has the well-bred international look of one expertly and expensively decorated with an eye to creating a casual grandeur befitting the Palm Beach lifestyle. The two oversized, overstuffed sofas glory in their bold floral prints and provide a lush counterpoint to the stark marble dining table. Its harsh lines are muted by the graceful decanters displayed on an antique console, which in turn is topped by a stunning Empire mirror. Interesting ceiling detail, a richly veined green marble floor and the dominance of the happy combination of yellow and purple pull it all together.

If a room right out of *HG* isn't enough to justify your expenditure of £900 a night, consider the two complementary bedrooms and the three bathrooms as part of your rationalization.

For masculine tastes, there's the aptly named Wellington Suite, its massive living area flanked by two conservatory equipped bedrooms, making it the largest suite in the hotel...maybe in the whole city. Tycoons can mount campaigns from the living area, spreading documents over the ancient sea chest that serves as a coffee table. They can marvel at their own clever countenances in the outstanding floor-to-ceiling gilt mirror. And they can savour their victories enthroned in the marvelous leather chair balanced on great gilt feet. This is a suite for people with strong personalities and healthy bank balances at £950 per night.

Like all the rooms at the Inn, the Wellington Suite is absolutely immaculate—not a hint of the tiredness that affects most other heavily trafficked hotels, no matter how fine and/or pricey. The trick here is that the Inn is in a constant state of renewal, as opposed to the periodic refurbishment of most other properties. General manager Ramon Pajares, the elegant Spaniard who has shaped the Inn's character for much of its 21 years, strives to redecorate about 60 rooms a year, while sustaining an aggressive ongoing approach to maintenance and touch-ups. He also endeavours to enhance the individuality of the hotel by regularly adding to its impressive collection of antiques, the pride of which is the unique double-face grandfather's clock standing guard in the lobby at the bottom of the sweeping redwood staircase. Everyone asks, but no one seems to know its provenance. The exquisite marble table at the entrance of the Four Seasons restaurant fares better—Italian circa 1860—as does the handsome china gracing the shelves of Lanes Bar—manufactured by Rockingham about 1825. And if you have wondered, in light of our earlier assertion, about the slightly worn quality of the upholstery on the lobby's carved walnut armchairs, consider the fact that it is antique Persian carpet proudly proclaiming its age.

Should you be inspired to do a little antique hunting of your own, ask head concierge Michael Milojkovic for guidance. He'll direct you to the most intriguing shops, calling ahead to make any necessary introductions. He's also the man to see about dinner reservations—he can almost always get them for even the hottest tables in town and is a whiz at recommending establishments to suit your mood and pocketbook. And don't be put off should one of his first suggestions be either of the Inn's restaurants. His declaration of their attractions is not self-serving; they are genuinely two of the best and most popular dining spots around. Indeed, the sophisticated Four Seasons stands alone as one of London's most renowned eateries, having earned a Michelin star—a feat almost unheard of among hotel-based restaurants. (Its attractions are addressed in detail in the restaurant section of this book.)

The more informal Lanes is always packed for lunch due to its three set menus which include a sensational hors d'oeuvres buffet and unlimited wine. While the £27 Masters Choice (including tax and service)— hors d'oeuvres selection or soup, followed by a main dish such as Dover sole or medallions of veal, and dessert—is tempting, accompanied by that endless supply of wine, it knocks us out for the afternoon. So we opt for the Mayfair Choice at £23.25, a lighter alternative for which the buffet serves as the main course after soup as a starter. For dinner, the price of the entrées such as £25.50 roast prime of Scottish beef and £22.50 lasagna with morels includes the cold buffet but not dessert. And the celebrated After Theatre Supper, served after 11:00 P.M. for £21, mirrors our favourite lunch here, minus the generous supply of wine.

While Lanes is a frequent haunt of locals who consider it "their" neighbourhood spot, the Inn is careful always to have tables available either in the restaurant or in the bar for residents of the hotel—a fact that is much appreciated on damp wintery evenings when the very thought of going out is abhorrent and the prospect of being confined to one's room (however lovely) is equally distasteful. The cheerful ambience, splendid food and praiseworthy service of Lanes make it a very desirable destination in its own right—one of the many charms which keep the name of its parent property from being a misnomer. Despite its size, this truly is an inn on a park.   ❦

The Pelham Hotel

15 Cromwell Place	071-589-8288
London SW7	(FAX) 071-584-8444

It was entirely fitting that we first heard about the Pelham over dinner at the Capital with then general manager, Keith Williams. He was about to decamp to take charge of a huge new resort complex. But he was leaving, happy in the knowledge that his not-easy-to-fill shoes would be filled by his annointed successor, Jonathan Orr-Ewing, who happened to be dining across the room with the Capital's owner. At the time, Jonathan was running the Pelham, the latest and plushest incarnation of the rage for townhouse hotels started by the Capital. Talk about things coming full circle!

In any event Jonathan is now happily ensconced at his new post and Sally Bulloch, formerly of the Draycott (designated a country house rather than townhouse establishment) has taken over where he left off, putting the Pelham on the map. It's a less than arduous task, as this 37-room gem, owned by Tim and Kit Kemp, burst upon the scene in August 1989 in full-blown splendour. Word has it that no one has ever built a hotel to such extravagant specifications as the Kemps did, and certainly not in ten-and-a-half months, a record time. Of course, it helps to have your own construction company when you take on gutting a former student hostel with the intent of transforming it into a world-class hotel.

And we do mean gut. Only three walls were left standing. Their "take-no-prisoners" approach enabled the Kemps to install a unique heating and air-conditioning system that filters and humidifies the air, then heats or cools it once it reaches the rooms—no dry heat, the bane of so many other hotels. The treated air is good not only for the guests but also for the priceless panelling and exquisite fabrics that make the Pelham so very glamorous. While it has all the accoutrements of a major property—concierge, 24-hour room service, mini-bars, private board/dining room and restaurant—it has the look of a home that has benefitted from loads and loads of money. And it did. No one will say exactly how much, but we did weasel out of Sally the sum of £35,000 for the 18th-century pine panelling from a house in Suffolk—*before* it was restored and installed in the drawing room.

One can only imagine the cost of executing Kit Kemp's inspired decorating schemes that look so dazzling, yet so "undone." There's not a commercial-looking fabric in sight. Rather, expensive silks and damasks abound, materials not meant for the unavoidable wear and tear of a hotel. Moreover, Kit carried through themes in a manner seldom seen in a purpose-built public space. For instance, the drawing room's 200-plus-year-old panelling dictated an 18th-century fireplace, period paintings and certain other circa 1700s museum-quality furnishings. The effect is incredibly elegant, yet surprisingly relaxed. You don't feel as if there were invisible "do not touch" signs everywhere. Quite the contrary, the room begs you to sink into the pillow-plump sofa in front of the fireplace and order some tea.

No wonder guests, once settled in, seem loathe to leave the premises. After all, many come here intent on *not* being seen and treasure the sumptuous cocoon quality of the hotel. And if they do feel like being sociable, they can count on Sally Bulloch to introduce them to copacetic souls. Still, she exercises her natural cruise ship activity director skills with less abandon than she did at the Draycott, in keeping with the Pelham's quieter, more formal nature.

Since there are only two or three rooms on each floor, you could conceivably stay here for quite some time without ever seeing another guest. But since that's not our style, we like to hang out in the lush library-like Smoking Room where some guests gather every afternoon for a cocktail.

Waiters are on hand to take your order as you stake out territory in the uncommonly handsome room lined with rich 18th-century mahogany. Kit's decorating details are especially absorbing here—the haunting portrait of a woman clutching a flower is framed in silk blossoms, for instance. And we gasped the first time we saw a waiter set a silver tray laden with drinks, olives and biscuits on the large tufted ottoman in front of the fireplace, until we realized it was meant to double as a coffee table.

The components of the sleeping quarters are no less compelling. Each distinctively different, they all profit from fearless combinations of prints and colours like those of room 101, which is all done up in florals and stripes in blues, purples and reds. The thronelike king-size bed sits up high so you can recline under the gorgeous canopy and look out through the windows, beyond the red-tiled terrace to the activity in the bustling intersection below. There's an enticing little love seat and the fashionably draped "table" conceals the mini-bar. The room's stunning polished granite and mahogany bathroom is standard issue throughout the hotel, as are the unattached hair dryers, and the bedside free-standing Roberts radios—no built-in hotel models for the Pelham.

The room sells for £155 and might be considered smallish by some, but it's so pretty and gracefully laid out that only a clumsy lout would find it cramped. Ditto, room 8 at £110, which reminds us of the master's cabin in a very yar sailing yacht. You can't help feeling just as snug as a bug in a rug in the welcoming comfort of its seductive brown, mustard, blue and rose colour scheme.

But no one could possibly quibble over the spaciousness of either of the Pelham's two suites. Number 102 looks as if it were right out of the pages of *Interiors* magazine, where in fact it was featured. Magnificent, opulently draped gold silk curtains cap the glorious sweep of the bedroom and parlour, which are separated by sliding double doors. Bright and cheery, with rococo ceilings and crystal chandeliers, everything about it luxuriously spells home right down to the candles in the crystal candlesticks on the marble mantle. Make it your London residence for £250 a night.

Like any sophisticated dwelling, the Pelham maintains a notable kitchen, servicing the 38-seat basement-level restaurant, also named the Pelham, which is a controlled riot of mix-and-match fabrics, pulled together by a collection of equestrian-themed prints saluting Tim and Kit's steeplechase champion, Pelham Suite. His racing colours, blue and gold, feature prominently in the room, as does the staff of life—the corners are decorated with peculiarly pretty columns of dried wheat and breads. It's a lovely hideaway to enjoy one, or every, meal while you're at the hotel.

If you prefer to do your own cooking but would like the option of world-class room service in a setting as posh as the Pelham's, check out the hotel's sister property, Durley House. Located a few blocks away on Sloane Street, across from Cadagon Park which guests are entitled to use—tennis courts and all—the former block of serviced flats has been transformed by the talented Kit into a series of sumptuously furnished, kitchen-equipped suites. We're talking about operational, fully stocked kitchens, not service galleys. You can exercise your culinary skills or take advantage of those of Durley House's chef whose kitchen is directly connected with each suite via dumbwaiter. Rates for the one- and two-bedroom suites, complete with VCRs, current reading materials and board games like Monopoly and Scrabble, range from £230 to £250. Call 071-235-5537 for reservations.

Like the Pelham, Durley House is for those who want to relish their creature comforts in peace and quiet and who want to get away from it all without giving up one ounce of luxury or convenience—in other words, refugees from chain hotels. 🐛

The Ritz Hotel

Piccadilly   071-493-8181
London W1V 9DG   (FAX) 071-493-2687

In the heart of Mayfair on Piccadilly, just across Green Park from Buckingham Palace, stands one of London's most famous landmark hotels, the Ritz.

What other hotel has been immortalized by the musical genius of Irving Berlin, whose 1937 melody "Putting On the Ritz" told the world what fun they were missing? What other hotel has been blessed with surprise performances by Pavlova, last-minute appearances by Charlie Chaplin and historical meetings of Churchill, de Gaulle and Eisenhower?

Today, the magnificent 130-room Ritz is still frequented by the famous and the fashionable who luxuriate in the grand Louis XVI decor, the superb service and, of course, the timeless British tradition of afternoon tea. On any given afternoon in the elegant Palm Court, you could be sharing crustless cucumber sandwiches with author Jackie Collins or jazz great Cab Calloway.

The Ritz opened May 15 in 1906, to owner Cesar Ritz who called it, "a small house to which I am proud to see my name attached." The Ritz was an immediate success and, according to Lady Diana Cooper, became London's first hotel to which young, unmarried women were allowed to enter unchaperoned! How lucky for us.

This trust has been earned from the tender loving care the staff takes with each and every guest, a reputation that began in 1906 and continues today.

The general manager of the Ritz, David Hopkins, who is as good looking as he is softspoken, has stated his goal: to "fulfil my guest's once-in-a-lifetime dreams." And he shares this goal with every member of his highly trained and experienced staff. So, of course, we headed right over and checked in.

We heard that head hall porter, Michael De Cozar, took this mission to heart by helping a frequent Ritz guest achieve *her* dream. It seems that the woman was in New York, awaiting a saddle she had ordered from Bristol for a special horse race in the States. When she learned that the saddle's delivery to New York would be too late for the race, she telephoned Michael for help. He immediately sent a messenger by train to pick up the saddle in Bristol, and he sent it to New York via Concorde, hand-carried by another Ritz guest, who was only too happy to cooperate in the last-minute plan. We don't know if our lady's horse won the race, but we do know she was thrilled to have her saddle in time. For Michael, it was just another way to demonstrate that nothing is too much to ask when it comes to caring for guests at the Ritz, whether they are there at the time or not!

This attention to service and detail extends to the hotel's restaurants as well. Maître d' Michael Twomey has presided over the lovely Palm Court for over 40 years, where some 55,000 teas a year are served to royals and mere mortals, who relax by the extravagantly sculptured fountain each afternoon at 3:15 and 4:30, with treats like scones and strawbery jam, almond slices with marzipan, and glazed kiwi and grape pastries. We promise, the calories are worth it! Maître d' Twomey requests reservations, men in jackets and ties, and would be pleased "if ladies would wear their best hats."

In the dining room, beneath a magnificently painted ceiling done in 1906 and ornate chandeliers, you will feast on head chef Keith Standley's haute cuisine. Although Keith is only 33, he entered the culinary world at the tender age of 19 and has been creating magic ever since. The menu is so diverse, you really must take the time to study it carefully, lest you miss a memorable morsel.

Our unforgettable meal consisted of lamb's tongue and toulouse sausages on a bed of lentils and mangetout (£8.75), terrine of seafish on a cider sauce (£8.50), and roulade of salmon and langoustine with saffron sauce (£16.75). Fortunately, we saved room for the dessert trolley, which overflowed with fresh pastries and cream cakes.

If you're not in the mood to choose, Chef Standley will select a special daily menu for you, including entrée, coffee and dessert for £39.50. For the vegetable lover, he also does fabulous three-course vegetarian dinners.

When you want to have a private party, you may choose from the opulent Marie Antoinette Suite (where Churchill, Eisenhower and de Gaulle met during World War II); the elegant Trafalgar Suite which offers dinner service on priceless Nanking china; or the Berkeley Suite, with a seventh-floor view of Green Park.

Of course, you need never leave your room, because the Ritz thoughtfully offers 24-hour room service. And you may never want to leave because they are some of the most beautifully appointed rooms we've seen.

Decorated in delicate, pastel colours and gold leaf, Louis XVI furnishings and elegant marble fireplaces, many rooms and suites have the original brass beds. Every room features a fully stocked mini-bar, international direct-dial telephone, and satellite television channels, and most rooms and suites are air-conditioned.

Through a gracious entry hall, you enter room 516 to find lovely high ceilings, a queen-size bed and closets that will embrace a full complement of designer gowns and custom tailored suits. The fabrics and carpet are cheerful pastel prints, and the bath is all terra-cotta marble, with separate shower stall and bath tub. A perfect home away from home for £225 per night.

Suite 218–219 features an elegant living room in soft rose hues, a fireplace with two large comfy sofas, and chairs that overlook Green Park and Piccadilly. All the light fixtures, mouldings and the fireplace are 1906 originals. Notice the exquisite, discreetly placed wall clocks to keep you prompt for that busy calendar of yours. The spacious bedroom has a wonderful dressing table with mirrors, and loads of closets. This suite goes for £560 per night.

Besides the exquisite rooms and restaurants, one of the joys of staying at the Ritz is the proximity to London's most interesting sights and shopping. The Ritz has created an excellent walking guide for you that features a number of one- to two-hour walks beginning just outside their front door.

Nearby, for example, is London's oldest royal park, St James, created by Henry VIII in 1532, and the favourite jousting park of Queen Elizabeth I. Another walk takes you to Shepherd Market and No. 10 Hertford Street, home to dramatist R.B. Sheridan, author of *School for Scandal.* Yet another stroll will take you to Burlington Arcade, where you can shop for cashmere, silver, pewter, paintings or anything else your heart desires.

At different times of the year, the Ritz plans special events like lessons in grouse shooting on a private estate, limousine picnics to the 150-year-old Holland & Holland gun factory and, at Christmas, carolling and roasted chestnuts.

If the goal of the Ritz is to fulfil the dreams of each and every guest; and to be, in the words of Cesar Ritz, "the most fashionable hotel in the most fashionable city in the world," then we must say our dreams have become reality here.

Savoy Hotel

| The Strand | 071-836-4343 |
| London WC2R OEU | (FAX) 071-240-6040 |

It has been said that a great hotel depends on the quality of its guests, its staff and its property. Well, if you blend all these important attributes into one hotel, then the Savoy is one of the world's greats.

And as the Savoy is over 100 years old, history supports us in this compliment.

Opening in 1889, the Savoy was the brainchild of Gilbert and Sullivan impresario Richard D'Oyly Carte. After constructing the Savoy Theatre for Gilbert and Sullivan's operas, D'Oyly Carte decided to build a hotel to feed and house the theatre's patrons.

Who could have known he would build one of the most innovative hotels in the world?

Right from its birth, the Savoy perfected the art of avoiding obscurity. Construction began in 1884 with a concrete and steel structure designed to be fireproof, with glazed terra-cotta tiles to resist pollution. Lifts, then a novelty, were installed and referred to as "ascending rooms."

"Speaking tubes" allowed communication between floors, and under the basement was an artesian well and two electricity generators prepared to operate within 20 seconds of a power break. And a grand total of 67 private baths were added, an unheard-of luxury for the time.

To attract the kind of clientele the Savoy deserved, D'Oyly secured Cesar Ritz, known as the world's premier hotelier, as his manager. Ritz then imported Auguste Escoffier as the hotel's chef, who was hailed as "Emperor of Cooks." With this noble team in place, the Savoy opened its doors to the wealthy and the aristocratic. And they came in record numbers.

By 1914, the Savoy was the glittering spotlight for international stars, both on and off the stage. Maharajahs were in residence, the Archbishop of Canterbury applauded the cabaret, and even soprano Luisa Tetrazzini's pet crocodile was welcomed! We do hope she kept him on a leash.

In the Ballroom, guests were treated to George Gershwin's first London performance of "Rhapsody in Blue." Sir Winston Churchill bowed as Mrs Eleanor Roosevelt received the Pilgrim Society's guest of honour award. Pavlova danced, and Jascha Heifetz took bagpipe lessons on the roof from Harry Lauder. The parties were legendary, and so was the Savoy.

Today, the Savoy continues to be a magnet for stars, politicians, journalists and business tycoons from the world's capitals. You'll most certainly run into barons of industry, like Sir James Goldsmith or Lord Young, making mega-deals over lunch in the famous Grill.

The Grill has its own stardust sprinkled over it, with the regulars—like Jeffrey Archer or editor of the *Sunday Times*, Andrew Neill—striding in each day to claim their usual spots at the white linen-covered tables.

Where you sit, whether alongside the curtained window overlooking the courtyard or at the comfy banquettes in the corner, says as much who you are as does the title on your business card.

Angelo Maresca, the maître d'hotel, has the very sensitive job of assigning the daily seating, which may be similar to presiding over a United Nations council meeting.

Angelo says that a non-regular customer has about as much chance of booking a regular's table as being allowed in without a jacket and tie. "We would never promise a table to someone we didn't know," he smiles. "We have businessmen in here doing deals worth millions of pounds, and they want their regular waiter who knows what they want, so they won't be disturbed."

Tony Carmona, the head sommelier, started at the Grill in 1947 and remembers serving his "regulars," then Sir Winston Churchill, Princesses Elizabeth and Margaret and Noel Coward.

Don't fret, however, we promise there will be a table there for you, too, probably in the centre, where the regulars don't sit.

You might even try the vegetarian lunch. They do have sausages and mash though, if you want a more English-style meal.

At dinner, the Grill becomes much less business oriented and much more social, as smartly dressed couples dine before rushing off to make a theatre show nearby. It is definitely a spot where you'll see and be seen.

And after theatre, it's just perfect to return to the hotel's Thames Foyer for coffee and dessert. Or stop into the American Bar for a cocktail, and enjoy Terence O'Neill's stunning photographs of Liza Minelli, Faye Dunaway and Paul Newman. Of course, they may be in the bar, too, sipping one of head barman Peter Dorelli's famous martinis!

Everywhere you gaze at the Savoy, there is something beautiful to behold. The art deco mouldings around the doors are quite stunning, the charming elevator is painted in red Chinese lacquer and has a leather bench inside, and the Reading Room in the back of the lobby is a serene oasis of Savoy memorabilia.

The flair and impeccable British style that D'Oyly Carte created over 100 years ago is flourishing today, as is the independence the hotel maintains in its daily operation.

The Savoy, proud holder of a Royal Warrant, roasts and grinds its own coffee. And the hotel still maintains its own power supply, so if London goes dark, the Savoy will still blaze with light.

The attention to detail at the Savoy will impress you. Take the handmade mattresses: a single has 836 springs wrapped in cotton, padded with white curled horsehair, cushioned with lambswool, encased in cotton felt and enveloped in ticking of linen and cotton. Surely you will have a heavenly night's rest on one of these!

And the attention to the decor of the rooms is just as impressive, as no two of the 152 rooms and 48 suites are alike.

One of our favourites, Suite 311, has a wonderful desk right by the window and overlooks the River Thames. We know you'll be inspired there gazing out over the city. Perhaps you'll start that novel you've been planning.

The sitting room has incredible mouldings along the high ceilings, as well as restful blue carpets. What a perfect place to curl up with the newspaper.

Of course, you could stretch out in front of the fireplace in the bedroom, or lounge in your club chair or chaise. Or perhaps organize your ensembles inside the grand mirrored wardrobes. You'll be very happy here just enjoying the luxury of the room.

The suite can be expanded to two bedrooms if you'd like, and is a delightful combination of traditional, contemporary and art deco styles, which work together to create a perfectly marvellous haven. This suite goes for £600 or £820 per night, depending on the number of bedrooms you want.

We love number 614 also, because of the spectacular view at night of Big Ben, the bridges and the Royal Festival Hall. It's so romantic just to sit and have a drink while you watch the lights blink on. At the end of the hall, you can see the Thames, St Paul's Cathedral and Waterloo Bridge. Quite a sight!

We love padding about on the thick carpet in this suite and enjoying the pastel plaid sofas and chairs. The walls are a soft rose pink with white mouldings, which is the perfect shade for a woman's complexion, you know. And, of course, there's the fireplace to keep you cosy. There are mirrors everywhere, even a three-way makeup mirror on the vanity. It all works to create a memorable ambience.

You've probably heard about the Savoy's famous showerheads. They are $9^3/4$ inches around, and water cascades straight down from 290 holes; and may we tell you the effect is quite astonishing. No matter what kind of day you've had, just stand underneath one of these showerheads, and all your cares are pummelled away, and you emerge a totally refreshed human being. Many guests end up so relaxed, they order them for their own showers back home costing £60 plus shipping. We recommend that you do, too.

Yet, for all the attention to material conveniences, managing director Giles Shepard feels that the Savoy's secret of success is in having "managers with flair, virtuoso chefs and waiters, receptionists with understanding of their guests . . . professionals at every level who know how to attend to the smallest detail without being obtrusive."

We found all this to be absolutely true during our unforgettable visit to the Savoy, and we are sure the hotel will continue welcoming important clients, while refusing to compromise in the grand tradition created over a century ago. 🍏

The Stafford

St James's Place	071-493-0111
London SW1A 1NJ	(FAX) 071-493-7121

The legacy of the great gentlemen's dining and drinking (mostly drinking) clubs lingers still in St James—the area sports two of the city's best bars. They're so good that their fame transcends that of their parent establishments, two of London's better hotels. Like Dukes, any discussion of the Stafford must begin with its bar and with Charles Guano, the man who has held sway there for over 30 years.

Neither quaint nor particularly charming, the Stafford bar is most definitely unusual. Virtually every inch of wall and ceiling space is covered with Charles' staggering collection of ties, baseball caps, football helmets, yacht club burgees, and other sporting memorabilia. Named Barman of the Year in 1988 by the *Hideaway Report,* Charles is a little vague about how it all got started. He claims not to remember exactly, but he thinks, "probably some American came in here wearing a baseball cap—you know some older Americans wear them around in the summer—and I probably said, joker that I was, 'that's nice, I think I'll have that,' and he gave it to me. Same thing with somebody's tie. Then it got to be a regular thing." So regular that today Charles is armed with a stack of Stafford ties he trades with customers for additional decorations for his bar . . . though God only knows how he finds space to display his new trophies.

But there's more here than meets the eye. The palate is well served, too. Charles mixes a superior martini and challenges anyone in London to approach his deft touch with a martini dry. Perhaps Dukes and the Stafford should mount a martini-off? At any rate, in addition to his talents as a world-class mixologist, Charles is a verbose charmer and lives up to his self-characterization as a joker. He can be counted on to be excellent company. As if all that weren't enough to recommend what has become known as the American Bar, excellent light fare is served here, too. It's a convivial place in which to have lunch or a late-night snack. And during the summer months the bar's private courtyard, located in the mews behind the hotel, is a pleasant retreat from the madding crowds.

But the Stafford's justified reputation for libatious hospitality doesn't end here. The 300-year-old wine cellar, once used to keep the wines from St James's Palace, is also the scene of a fair amount of activity. Not only is it home to countless bottles representing over 400 vintages, but its private dining room is the site of many a lovely candle-lit dinner party. The cellar also serves as shrine to the years when the Stafford's status as a hotel was interrupted, when during World War II the hotel became a club for American and Canadian officers. Today, the Better Hole Club, a small room off the main cellar, is filled with wartime mementoes and a guestbook with the names of the North Americans who sought refuge here when the bombs fell.

In more recent times, the Stafford has provided refuge from another sort of hell, that of the fast-paced modern world. Managing director Denis Beaulieu views his domain as a very special place where he's trying to make time stand still, to continue the gracious traditions of a bygone era. To a great extent he's been extraordinarily successful—many of his staff, like the legendary Charles, have been here for decades and steadfastly refuse to be lured to any other hostelry. Consequently, the service, from that of hall porter Colin Short to that of head housekeeper Bernadette Leahy, is superb in a quiet and very protective way. The staff's respect of guests' privacy is unparalleled.

Witness the story of the American executive who left instructions not to be disturbed. Despite the persistence of one caller from Washington, D.C., the staff politely but firmly adhered to his wishes. It wasn't until a pair of black limos arrived at the Stafford's predictably discreet entrance with persuasive emissaries from the U.S. Embassy in tow that George Schultz received the telephone call from President Reagan, inviting him to serve as Secretary of State!

Okay, so it's got a great bar, a terrific wine cellar, and a stellar staff of 140 for the 74 rooms. Did we mention the location on a quiet cul de sac, just a stone's throw from bustling Piccadilly? But what about the actual accommodations? Well...they're nice—warm and somewhat old-fashioned, despite all the modern necessities of direct-dial telephones, colour television, well-appointed bathrooms and ample wardrobes. A description in a January 1849 issue of *The Times* of No. 17 St James's Place, the 18th-century centrepiece of the structure which was once three separate houses, somehow says it all: "An extensive and fashionable mansion, in perfect substantial and ornamental repair, having all the agreements required by a family moving in the higher circles of society, and all the accommodation and convenience of a large establishment." The Stafford is a place for old, low-key money. If your ship just came in, dock elsewhere. It's unlikely the Stafford will be glitzy enough for you. Check out its sister hotel, the Ritz, just around a couple of corners and also owned by Cunard (whose vice president and managing director Terry Holmes cut his hotel-keeping teeth at the Stafford under the not-always-supportive guidance of Charles).

But for those who don't require—or expect—tons of gold leaf or studied, country-house elegance, the Stafford's rooms are comfortingly familiar and cheerful. We're especially fond of Suite 202. Its sitting room reminds us of living rooms we have known in Chevy Chase or Gross Point—boxy armchairs covered in a pretty peachy pink, accented by green piping and textured yellow wallpaper. The exotic peach, green and yellow floral print of the drapes is reflected in a handsome gilt mirror over the mantle, which is white—like all the other woodwork. The bedroom, sporting twin beds with upholstered headboards, is a variation on the theme. Nice, very nice for £350 a night.

Room 212, with two double beds, is a bright alternative, all done up in brilliant oranges, colourful paisley prints and lacquered bamboo furniture. It looks a lot better than it sounds and, like all the Stafford's rooms, benefits from crisp Irish linens and lovely flower arrangements. The rack rate for it and most other doubles is £215; £190 for singles.

But back to the more public aspects of the Stafford which we find most endearing. The restaurant is worthy of a visit whether or not you're staying here. Under the 42-year stewardship of manager K. Chris Paschalides—Mr Chris to the cognoscenti—it has earned a well-deserved reputation as one of the city's finer hotel dining rooms. There's a quiet grandeur about it, courtesy of elaborate white mouldings set off by salmon walls and the glow of crystal chandeliers. This sets an appropriate stage for head chef Armando Rodriguez's masterful creations. A comparative newcomer with only 26 years in service here, Armando is assisted by 13 other chefs in his presentation of traditional dishes and imaginative specialities that make creative use of fresh native ingredients—seagull eggs, available off the coast of Dover just two weeks a year, and wild oysters from Scotland.

This is the place for a special occasion, when you want your meat sauced and desserts flambéed. There's not a better £19 steak Diane or £10.50 cherries jubilee in town. We also like the breast of chicken cooked in white wine sauce with mushrooms and finished with cream for

£15.25. And the sublime bisque de homard, loaded with lobster stock, brandy, butter and cream is a meal in itself at £8.25. Whatever you order, master sommelier Gino Nardella, an 18-year veteran, stands ready to offer assistance in the selection of a wine from the lengthy and most impressive list.

Between the bar, the cellar, the staff and the restaurant we've been known to check in at the Stafford and hardly venture forth for days. But then we're old London hands. Newcomers should take advantage of yet another of the hotel's noteworthy amenities—Patrick, the driver, who's on call 24 hours a day to conduct guided tours. A beguiling storyteller, his encyclopaedic knowledge of the city ensures an outing that will produce lasting, even useful, memories.   ❦

The Westbury

| Bond Street at Conduit | 071-629-7755 |
| London W1A 4UH | (FAX) 071-495-1163 |

Don't be put off by the beige marbled slickness of the Westbury's lobby. Behind the building's bland 1950s facade and the characterless (except for the green marble manteled and brass-railed fireplace) late 1980s lobby, lies a genuine charmer that combines the best of British traditions with American comforts at an unbeatable location. Indeed, when it opened in 1955 as the first luxury hotel to be built in the West End in a quarter century, the Westbury was operated by Knott Hotels Corporation, the oldest hotel chain in the U.S. As the first hostelry in Britain to be run by an American company, the Westbury claimed its ice water to be "the coldest in London and the Martinis the dryest"—two very important considerations for visiting Yanks, one which again brings up the battle of the city's hotel bars and barmen.

Omar Sharif once announced on Johnny Carson's *Tonight Show* that George Lopez, who has overseen the Polo Bar at the Westbury for 24 years, "has the best bar in London." So where does that leave Dukes and the Stafford? In St James, that's where. We'll take a neighbourhood approach to this very partisan issue and declare a tie for first place in St James, giving best honours to the Westbury in Mayfair.

Polo memorabilia and murals depicting the history of the sport of kings decorate the room's green walls. Polo ponies gallop across the specially commissioned carpet. Even the bar's shape can be construed as an instrument of the game, the mallet. Okay, so we've employed a little poetic licence—the long, narrow "handle" actually ends in a round, rather than oblong, shape, but you get the idea. Still, you don't have to have a passion for polo (the association comes from the game's hallowed grounds in Westbury, Long Island) to enjoy the ambience or the charming attentions of George. Portuguese by birth, he's pure English when it comes to standards of service, but not with regard to reserve. He'll be the first to tell you about Omar's claim and will readily volunteer that he's penning a book about champagne. He professes to know so much about the bubbly because the British consume more of it than any other people in the world. Did you know that? We didn't, but now we do, thanks to the ever sociable George.

There's more knowledge to be gained by trivia buffs at the Westbury. What honeymooning couple caused an international sensation here that virtually ruined the newlywed husband's career? Jerry Lee Lewis and his early-adolescent bride, who also happened to be his cousin, caused quite a stir back in 1958. The scandal was back in the news 31 years later, when Hollywood descended to tell their story. The hotel's penthouse suite, which retains much of its '50s glamour according to Sir Norman Hartnel's original design, figured prominently in the movie *Great Balls of Fire*, starring Dennis Quaid.

Even if Suite 733 weren't an authentic site, it would have been the perfect interior set. Its size alone spells star power. The first time we stayed there, we "lost" a bedroom for two days. Or more accurately, it took us that long to discover its existence, what with the huge master bedroom, two full baths, safe and mini-bar hidden behind the bookshelves flanking the mantel in the massive living/dining room, and the terrace fit for entertaining 75 or so of our nearest and dearest. It took so long for us to wind our way from the velvet couches grouped in front of the fireplace to the front door that one guest gave up ringing the bell and was halfway back to the lift before we got there. That same guest was relegated to sleeping on one of the living room's sofas until a casual remark by a hotel executive tipped us off to the additional bedroom. We still wonder what the maids must have thought of her makeshift nest, while a perfectly good twin-bedded room was left in a pristine state!

This palatial retreat goes for £550 a night and is located on the seventh floor known as that of the musicians in honour of the broad range of talents who have stayed on it, from Gene Pitney to André Previn. Their pictures line the corridor. This top floor of the hotel is further distinguished by a lounge for the exclusive use of members of the Polo Club.

It caters to guests of this London hotel as well as to those of its like-named sister property on Madison Avenue in New York City. Membership means myriad networking opportunities over complimentary coffee or cocktails in the lounge.

Although Polo Club members are entitled to other special privileges as well, all guests at the Westbury have the use of the health and leisure facilities of the Metropolitan Club. Just three minutes away on foot, the club's amenities include steam room and sauna, swimming pool, Nautilus-equipped gym, exercise studio and jacuzzi spa pools.

Indeed, the Westbury is unique in its concern for the health of its guests. In addition to providing for the exercise of their bodies, it offers meals low in fat and cholesterol for their systems. Certain dishes on the menu of the hotel's restaurant, named Polo (what else?) are designated as "lifestyle," having been created for "those who prefer a lighter diet, who, through necessity or choice, eat with their health in mind." Healthy or not, as prepared by chef Sergio Marenghi, the 30-year-old wunder-kind who began his career in the Westbury's kitchens as a porter at the age of 16, they are devastatingly delicious. The marinated fresh salmon with a caviar sauce is an inspired hors d'oeuvre, and the breasts of poussin stuffed with Dublin Bay prawns, topped by a lobster sauce are a delightful entrée at £15.50.

Between Sergio's cooking and the restaurant's attractive gold-toned formality, softened with graceful curving banquettes, it's no wonder the Polo is a popular luncheon spot for the tony set that the hotel's proximity to Sotheby's and much of London's best shopping attract.

For more relaxed lunching, a buffet is set up in the pine-panelled lounge with its comfy chintz furnishings. At £13.50 (£11.50 without dessert), it's high on the lists of locals who appreciate the genteel surroundings and the fact that the lounge shares a separate outside entrance with the bar. We suspect that the fact that the room is open 24 hours a day for refreshments is another attraction.

In the evening, the lounge is made all the more appealing by the presence of a piano player, who dispenses delightful background music until he moves over to the restaurant. Except for his efforts there during dinner, things are considerably quieter than they are at lunch—which is just fine with us. We like to savour our evening meal in peace, especially when we're not watching our diets and decide to work our way through the three-course £20.50 menu, rather than pick at the à la carte or lifestyle selections. Last time out, we both opted for a delicate salad of avo-

and marinated scallops served in a raspberry dressing. Then we split our votes between the sinfully rich fillet of beef topped with a foie gras pâté and knapped by a Madeira sauce and the roast of the day carved at the table—succulent lamb, in this instance, which is a speciality of the house. As for dessert, you can't miss with either the selection from the pastry-laden trolley or the collection of English and French cheeses.

It's also impossible to be disappointed by any of the hotel's accommodations, which have recently benefitted from a facelift. You already know about the penthouse suite, but if either its dimensions or its price is daunting, there's plenty more to choose from, on both counts—singles from £155 to suites starting at £255. Among the former, we highly recommend room 230 with its prettily draped table, fringed slipper chairs and bold print bedspread. Some might call it small, but we think its cosy and decidedly comfortable for £180. If space is what you seek, try one of the junior suites. Their layout has the feel of an apartment, rather than a hotel suite due to the good-sized foyer and a little dressing area with a built-in, well-lit vanity. We are especially fond of 236. A Chinese deco lacquered coffee table is the perfect counterpoint to the traditional overstuffed chair and sofa, and the pale hue of the faux silk moiré wallpaper pulls the whole look together, a look which will cost you £350 per night.

Perhaps our pal who counts his Polo Club membership as one of his most prized possessions sums it up best when he says (as he frequently does), "The Westbury is a *very* nice hotel—not grand, but nice." Nice as in agreeable, congenial, friendly and pleasant. We couldn't agree more.

🍇

IN THE COUNTRY

Bath Spa Hotel

| Sydney Road | 0225-444424 |
| Bath, Avon BA2 6JF | (FAX) 0225-444006 |

In the mood for a sumptuous country mansion, where you'll be pampered in total privacy and luxury, yet still be within a stone's throw of the pleasures a thriving city? Then hop the train from Paddington Station for the one hour and fifteen minute trip west to discover the Bath Spa Hotel and its namesake city.

Renowned for its ancient Roman baths and graceful Georgian architecture, Bath offers countless fascinating places to explore: museums, galleries, shops and arcades, antique collections and, in late spring, the Festival of Music and Art. And there the joys of strolling in Sydney Gardens, Henrietta Park, and along the picturesque River Avon should not be overlooked. But there's a new reason to visit Bath—the Bath Spa Hotel, opened in early 1990 as Trusthouse Forte's second five-star hotel outside London.

The mansion that is the nucleus of the hotel began life in 1835 as Vellore House, the home of General Augustus Andrews, who served in India before returning to Bath to build his dream home. In 1870, a wing was added and it became a boys' school known as Bath College. Vellore House had its first taste of the future during the early part of the century when it was transformed into a hotel. Having served admirable duty as a Royal Navy hostel during World War II, it was briefly reopened to the public before becoming a residence for nurses. Then, in 1986, a £20 million restoration was undertaken by Alan Bouvier Associates of London to convert the property into Trusthouse Forte's vision of a world-class spa. The results of the work guided by that vision are nothing short of spectacular. As internationally acclaimed architect Mies van der Rohe declared about the renovation, it "had God in the details." We quite agree, and so apparently do Richard Harris and Joan Collins, who enjoyed the hotel as their home base while performing at Bath's Theatre Royal.

Those divinely inspired details start with lushly landscaped grounds. Overlooking the city, the hotel sits at the end of a long, elegantly curved tree-lined drive, its handsome Bath stone façade adorned with an abundance of exotic greenery. And speaking of exotic, this is the only hotel we know where you can meander across the lawn to survey a Grecian temple and Victorian grotto. A final graceful note is added by a lyrical line of stone columns called the Colonnade which is enveloped by formal flower beds.

Inside, the classical reception area is tastefully ornate, with rococo ceiling mouldings, brightly patterned carpets over marble tile floors, and inviting dark green striped couches. Bouquets of fresh flowers from the gardens grace the stately antique furniture. Beyond, the cinnamon-hued Drawing Room is resplendent in oak panelling, wood-burning fireplaces, more elaborate mouldings and Greek columns. Built-in bookcases bulge with all the great literature you should have read at school. We think it the perfect place to curl up with a classic and a steaming cup of tea.

For sustenance of the tummy, as opposed to that of the mind, the Vellore Restaurant is equally gratifying. In fact, it has become a favourite haunt of Bath residents who find chef Berndt Meister's resourceful approach to English and French classics a breath of fresh air. And the room's soaring columns, welcomed to the ceiling by unusual porcelain chandeliers, in combination with the enormous red-draped picture windows overlooking the grounds, make it one of the most attractive restaurants in town. Of course, as a resident of the hotel, you get first crack at reservations, which are necessary particularly at lunch when the table d'hôte menus—£15.50 for two courses, including service and tax; £18.50 for three—make it a food bargain hunter's dream.

Cost considerations aside, we usually skip lunch here in favour of dinner. Why dash back from our exploration of Bath or interrupt our rigorous regime at The Laurels, the hotel's health and leisure spa? The £28 inclusive fixed-price menu might feature first courses like a terrine of game bound in liver mousse and enlivened by wild mushrooms and pistachios and main dishes such as pan-fried supreme of salmon with sorrel, but we think it's more fun to wander through the à la carte selections. A £4.75 haddock and red pepper soup described as "wholesome" certainly was and proved a delightful surprise, while a crab soufflé nestled in a fillet of sole knapped with a ginger and coriander-scented sauce for £12.75 could be addictive. Ditto the roasted John Dory fillet with scallops in an orange tomato sauce for £18.75. And although we know we should stay away from this sort of thing, *especially* at a spa, we couldn't resist the £26 fillet of Scottish beef topped by a horseradish and green peppercorn cream served with a red wine sauce.

If all this sounds as if it's specifically designed to negate the good work you've done under the careful tutelage of Laurel's manager Tracey Oberheim, be assured the kitchen willingly prepares plain grilled items. In fact, the menu notes that the chef will "be pleased to prepare your own favourite dish."

As for Tracey and her health club, neither should be missed. Outside membership is limited to 100 lucky souls, so the facilities are always available to hotel guests. The pool is great for laps or the aqua aerobics led by Tracey's staff. There's also a gym outfitted with all the latest in exercise equipment, not to mention the sauna, jacuzzi, solarium and outdoor tennis and croquet courts. The former coach house encompasses a steam room, thermal pool and beauty treatment rooms where you can indulge in facials, manicures and massages. Highly trained specialists design exercise and beauty programs geared to your individual needs and dispense good advice about nutrition.

Of the hotel's 102 rooms, all equipped with comfortable armchairs and white marble bathrooms made doubly dramatic by dark mahogany accents, we're particularly fond of 417. Done in one of twelve colour combinations used throughout, its peach-striped wallpaper is nicely juxtaposed by the green and cream curtains, quilt and chairs. As in all the rooms, fresh flowers, fruit and a selection of reading materials are much appreciated touches. Like all the rooms, it's yours for £115 as a single, £150 as a double. Suites start at £200.

Among the seven suites, the Imperial stands out in its magnificence as the original sitting room of Vellore House, where General Augustus Andrews and, later, Emperor Haile Selassie entertained. Now a one-bedroom suite, the original coving has been beautifully restored, and the tall windows afford panoramic views of Bath. Antiques abound—an engraved wardrobe and dressing table in the wine-and-cream-coloured bedroom, French chandeliers in the cheerful yellow living room. Of course, we think the cunning four-poster bed alone is worth the £375 price of admission.

Should meetings be on your mind, the Admiralty Room where Winston Churchill made it a habit of consulting with his naval officers should inspire your strategizing. Or try the adjoining Kennet and Avon rooms. The latter's three truly splendid Venetian glass chandeliers will shed light on your plans. And your audiovisual needs have been carefully planned for in the smaller Syndicate rooms. Indeed, given the one-to-one staff-to-guest ratio, modern conference facilities, superb health spa, elegant restaurant, and proximity to Bath, the hotel is an ideal site for a management retreat...or a personal one.

The Bell Inn

Aston Clinton	0296-630252
Buckinghamshire HP22 5HP	(FAX) 0296-631250

Long before it was fashionable to drop out of the fast lane in favour of a simpler, back-to-basics lifestyle, Gerard Harris walked away from his career as a successful solicitor to fulfil his dream of owning a small congenial country pub. He broadened the scope of his ambitions when he came across the Bell, originally an 18th-century coaching inn on the well-travelled route from London to Buckingham. With its quaint red-brick structure, pretty garden and outbuildings affording room for expansion, he realized its potential of becoming a first-class hostelry serving the best in food and wine. Gerard bought the Bell in 1939 and set about making it the popular afternoon-or-weekend-in-the-country destination it is today.

By the early 1950s, the Bell Inn had earned a far-flung reputation for exceptional food and hospitality, a reputation acknowledged as fact by the inn's designation as the first Relais et Châteaux in Britain. The quality of the cuisine, the warmth of the service and its status among the prestigious international association of hotels and restaurants remain intact under the stewardship of Gerard's son Michael and his wife Patsy. They've continued to develop the inn's possibilities, discreetly transforming the old brewery and stables into sleeping accommodations and adding a terraced pavilion for large parties. But the growth—there are now 21 sleeping rooms and the pavilion can seat 300—has in no way detracted from the Bell's essential character, that of a small family-run establishment where attention to detail is evident everywhere. The rooms benefit from the soft scent of frequently replenished potpourri and are thoughtfully supplied with a range of reading materials—from books to current periodicals. And a welcoming tray of olives, pickles, peanuts and popcorn whets your appetite as you review the menu in the picturesque drawing room.

But we're getting ahead of ourselves. To do the Bell justice, we should start at the beginning, at your inclination to duck as you cross the threshold—the diminutive doorway, serving as a reminder that when the Bell was built (about 1797), people were smaller. Once inside you're enveloped by a sense of the past. The vestibule with its large wooden tavern clock and rough-hewn floor has changed little since the adjoining bar dispensed fortifying libations to travellers over 200 years ago. Indeed, the bar itself remains in a time warp. The snug candle-lit flagstone-floored, ancient beamed chamber complete with large copper-edged fireplace and not entirely comfortable bare wood furniture looks like a Smithsonian re-creation of an 18th-century tavern. Only the drawing room, its knotty pine panelling graced by intricate crown moulding, seems to have been gently nudged into the 20th century. Comfy sofas and parlour chairs are arranged in conversational groupings around the room, which is decorated with a number of handsome prints and oil paintings—a particularly attractive one by Anne Wright was given in memory of Gerard by his friends.

Besides the blast from the past as you enter, you're wrapped in the infectious warmth of the greeting of Patsy Harris, general manager Paul White or Paul's deputy, Stephen Quigley. If you're here for the typical three- to four-day stay, they'll get you settled. If it's sustenance you seek, they'll usher you into the drawing room and present you with chef Kevin Cape's intriguing menu, a studied combination of traditional and contemporary dishes.

The restaurant is open daily with a limited menu on Sunday and Monday evenings and a £16.75 fixed-price luncheon available Tuesday to Saturday. Just over an hour by car or rail from London, we think Saturday or Sunday brunch at the Bell is a delightful country outing, a popularly held opinion that makes it necessary to reserve at least a week in advance for either. We've even been known to be ambitious enough to visit one of the nearby historic homes like Blenheim, Waddesdon, Claydon and Woburn before or after brunch; but more often than not, we make the meal our principal day's activity.

In the winter it's such a treat to cosy up to the roaring fire in the drawing room, sip a glass of warming sherry and grapple with deciding what to order. It's a tough call, and we often find ourselves soliciting opinions from other equally perplexed guests. The room encourages a seductive camaraderie that tempts you to sip and chat all day long. But, eventually the spell is broken and you're summoned to your table, a pleasant journey along the curved corridor known, because of its shape, as "Regent Street." Jocelyn Richards' whimsical murals of a fanciful garden full of arbours, trellises, birds and fruits are a delightful prelude to the dining room which relies on the Bell's real gardens for decor. Lined with French doors, it seems to invite nature indoors to share the high-backed tufted leather banquettes, which alternate as seating with English Chippendale tables and chairs.

We always ask for a banquette since we plan our brunches at the Bell to be our only significant meal of the day. We loiter well into the afternoon, working our way through the à la carte choices and possibly trying the patience of the French staff. However, since service isn't included in the tariff, we've never seen any evidence of their being annoyed. Typically we'll order three or more hors d'oeuvres like warm salad of rabbit with a compote of aubergine tossed in a chive and lemon dressing, a light compote of mushrooms with fricassee of wild woodland mushrooms for £8, and £15 fresh sautéed goose liver served on a nest of Belgian endive and raviolis of truffle.

Reason prevails when it comes to the entrées, only one each: fillet of steamed turbot enveloped in Parma ham and served in a fricassee of ceps and salsify for £19.50 and a combination of venison of the season with braised cabbage and a mosaic of vegetables at £23.50, perhaps. Or we might opt for the traditionally roasted, locally bred Aylesbury duckling for two at £31.50. And we never fail to find a suitable wine from the extensive list, Chilean to fine French, trivial to serious.

Kevin's desserts, such as homemade pistachio ice cream crowned with chestnut leaves and served with pralines for £4.50, are monumental works of art. But our fondness for port stimulated by the excellent, in some cases amazing, choices dictates cheese.

After such a magnificent meal, there's no greater pleasure than a nap—reason enough to book a room here. But the accommodations have an inherent charm that stands on its own. We're especially fond of 53 upstairs with its little raised sitting room and pretty tiled bathroom. It goes for £110 a night, including tax, service, and a Continental breakfast. And the massive four-poster nestled under the garret-like sloping ceiling in 52 is very inviting at £125.

Across the lane, the former brewery and stable house newer but still quaint quarters surrounded by manicured grounds. There's a miniature Swiss-chalet quality about 6 which sells for £125. Perched at the top of an outside flight of stairs and overlooking a trellised garden, it boasts a peaked beamed ceiling in the sitting room and a sweet cabin-like bedroom. Like all the other rooms in this part of the complex, its state-of-the-art bathroom is anything but country-inn scale.

Should fine food and drink not be entertainment enough during your stay, croquet is available, and tennis can be played in nearby Aylesbury. Fishing is also a popular pastime here, and there's a golf course at Woburn which guests may use. But most people are content to relax, catch up on their reading and do some undisturbed walking in between eagerly anticipated meals. That's the school we enthusiastically attend during our sojourns at the Bell.

Chewton Glen

New Milton	0425-275341
Hampshire BH25 6QS	(FAX) 0425-272310
	(Toll-free from U.S.) 800-223-5581

We've addressed the ersatz country house hotels that proliferate in the urban environment of London's West End, but here we turn our attention to the forerunner of the *real* English country house hotel—an aristocratic residence actually located in an area with abundant flora and fauna which has been transformed into a commercial lodging establishment. For more than 200 years, Chewton Glen did admirable duty as a comfortable country seat for a succession of would-be squires, most notably Captain Frederick Marryat. The good captain was an author who wrote his successful novel here, *The Children of the New Forest* (1847), which explains why the guestrooms have monikers like The Little Savage and Mr. Midshipman Easy—all of the 13 suites and 45 bedrooms are named after the characters from Marryat's books or the ships he commanded.

In any event, as was the case with so many edifices of its ilk, the house became an anachronism in the new Britain that emerged after World War II. Its potential as a hotel was first recognized in 1963 when it was purchased by the Duval family for that purpose. They put a stop to the steady deterioration that had plagued the house for decades, but it wasn't until Martin Skan and his wife Brigitte purchased the property in 1966 that Chewton Glen got a new lease on life. The glamorous Skans embarked on a massive modernization plan, based upon instinct rather than proven formula—hard to believe, but in those days there were few other country house hotels, even *in* the country. Consequently, they wrote the book and set the standards for those who would follow by producing what many devotees feel is the perfect country retreat. We happen to share that opinion, but you don't have to take our word for it—Chewton Glen has a list of awards that make its newer competitors green with envy. Formerly the Egon Ronay Gold Plate Hotel of the Year and more recently the only hotel outside London to receive the English Tourist Board's Five Gold Crown Award, it is a member of the prestigious by-invitation-only Relais et Châteaux group and holds a coveted Michelin star for its Marryat Restaurant—not to mention Michelin's five-red-turret salute to the hotel itself. Tributes not only to the Skans but also to managing director Robin Hudson, who, it would seem, never sleeps—he's always around, always available.

So what's the Skans' secret? Simple enough, really—a passionate dedication to the pleasure and comfort of their guests, one which manifests itself in so many very appreciated ways. There's the chauffeur-driven Jaguar that meets you at Heathrow, the warm welcome by name at the door, the decanter of sherry in every room, the bedside tins of biscuits and chocolates, the monogrammed slippers and plush robes, flowers in the bathroom, selected books on bedside tables, and the aplomb with which they handle the periodic landings of their clients' private helicopters. Then there's their carefully handpicked staff, who to a man (or woman) seem to be clairvoyant. You need only think about having a drink in the drawing room when a waiter appears, or you need only begin to feel restless when chauffeur/guide par excellence, Geoff Gates, suggests a jaunt to nearby Stonehenge, Salisbury or Winchester.

Which is not to suggest that there's nothing to do at Chewton Glen, except relax in the lap of luxury. Quite the contrary, no matter what the season. Outdoor and indoor pools are at your disposal, along with one outdoor and two indoor tennis courts, a fully equipped gym, sauna and steam rooms, a par 3 9-hole golf course (another ten full-scale courses are within a 12-mile radius), and a putting green are at your disposal on the hotel's 70 acres. If your sporting tastes run to the field variety, Chewton Glen's location on the edge of the historic hunting grounds of the ancient New Forest make for easy accessibility to clay pigeon shooting, deer stalking, fox hunting, game shooting and fly fishing. An ancient forest called "New"? It's ancient *and* new because it was created by William the Conqueror's depopulation of the area to provide a royal hunting ground.

While we appreciate the historical and environmental significance of the government-managed forest, it doesn't occupy much of our attention when we're at Chewton Glen. We're more lounge lizards than sportive animals, and the hotel offers plenty of opportunity to exercise our predilection toward plopping somewhere with a good book. There's Masterman Ready for one. It's our favourite room at £390 a night with its large balcony overlooking the conservatory and lush lawns. Here, as everywhere in the hotel, Brigitte Skan's exquisite taste reigns supreme. A transcendent profusion of colour, apricot and peach in this instance, are her trademark. And the decor, like the entire hotel, is a constantly evolving work in progress.

The Skans, in their neverending quest for perfection, are constantly adding to, improving upon or refurbishing Chewton Glen. Fortunately, they can be trusted. You don't have to worry that they'll tamper too much with the seductive charm of the split-level coach-house suites. Reached either by a covered walkway from the flagstone courtyard punctuated by a fanciful fountain or from the main house, each suite has its own secluded garden and balcony off the bedroom. Suites can be had for £320. Other rooms, such as The Poacher with its nice view of the swimming pool, start at £205 and go to £250.

Admittedly, it's hard to tear yourself away from any of them, as all have such distinctly charming character above and beyond their names, but more delights await in the public rooms. The Elphinstone Suite offers conversational groupings of sofas and armchairs where you can lounge by an open fire while enjoying the talents of the resident pianist after dinner. Before dinner, the Marryat Bar beckons. It embraces you in a riot of reds and blues peppered with antiques and copies of the author's books. There, the estimable François Rossi, a 20-year veteran at Chewton Glen, demonstrates he can hold his own against London's best mixologists. Even they might blanch at a request for a Mint Julep. Not François. The official drink of the American Confederacy is a Chewton Glen tradition. Captain Marryat brought back the recipe from one of his trips to the States.

Tempted though we might be by François' rendition, we generally keep our palates clean with a glass or two of champagne. Chef Pierre Chevillard deserves that "sacrifice." Every night he and his team of 18 assistant chefs make sure the Marryat Restaurant lives up to its reputation and keeps its Michelin star, not to mention the award from Egon Ronay. Focusing on the freshest local ingredients, he goes light on the butter and cream but long on imagination. Witness a combination of Aylesbury duck and duck foie gras wrapped in fresh pasta and served in a *light* cream sauce or a fillet of seabass served with a white wine and butter sauce, infused and garnished with red currants. For hors d'oeuvres, we were impressed by a tartare of salmon with avocado and flavoured with tarragon and layers of flaky pastry, young salmon and spinach topped by a delicate horseradish sauce. Doesn't sound so light to you? Worried about what four or five days of such feasting will do to your figure? Don't. Pierre's menu also covers truly Spartan territory, where there's not a speck of fat or cholesterol in sight!

While hotel guests and locals alike flock to the restaurant for Pierre's food—starting at £32.50 for a three-course table d'hôte including tax and service—the ambience rates high praise, too. Predictably the decor manages to be stunning yet warm and comfortable—rich pumpkin-colour walls set off by dark green banquettes and crisp white linens. Did we mention the wine list? We should, it's one of the best in Britain with more than 400 choices. But then you wouldn't expect anything less from the Skans and the little bit of heaven they've created just two hours' drive from London. Just another bit of heaven that is Chewton Glen. ❦

Cliveden

Taplow   0628-668561
Berkshire SL6 0JF   (FAX) 0628-661837

Home to a prince of Wales, three dukes and four generations of the Astor family, Cliveden has been an important thread in the fabric of Britain's social and political life for three centuries. Today, 325 years after the 2nd Duke of Buckingham commissioned architect William Winde to create a mansion "overlooking ye Thames," it continues its preeminence as one of the country's most expensive hotels and one of its best. Moreover, Cliveden has the distinction of being England's only stately home (as opposed to country house) hotel. Of course, this, coupled with the fact that Cliveden has been enormously successful since opening its doors to paying guests in 1986, begs the question of whether the next round of redecoration of London's finer hotels will be themed by the traditions of Britain's stately homes—they've already done the country house theme!

In any event, Cliveden is beyond stately. It is magnificent, restored to its original splendour by a private company which includes the Honourable John Sinclair who acts as general manager here. The company leases the 376-acre estate from the National Trust which have been in possession of it since 1942 when the Astor family donated it as a national treasure. During the intervening years, before 1986 when it was entrusted to Blakeney Hotels, the house, which had witnessed the first performance of "Rule Britannia," hosted Queen Victoria and entertained the likes of Rudyard Kipling, Lawrence of Arabia, Bernard Shaw, Lord Curzon, Henry James and Winston Churchill, had slowly deteriorated to the point of being almost unrecognizable. The Astor family continued to live here until the 3rd Lord Astor died in 1966—two years after the chance meeting of Christine Keeler and John Profumo at Cliveden's swimming pool brought down the Macmillan government. It was then leased to

Stanford University and by the time the Blakeney people got hold of it, the house was barely furnished and badly in need of a facelift.

Painstakingly renovated, Cliveden is now resplendent in its Edwardian decor, which approximates that of the golden age of the Astor regime. We suspect the scions of William Waldorf Astor, New York's largest landlord when he acquired Cliveden in 1893, would also approve of the level of service, which is staggering unless you, too, were to the manor born— from the uniformed footman who parks your car, to the maid who offers to unpack for you, to liveried waiters who respond to the ring of wall buttons placed throughout the house, the service is attentive in an unobtrusive sort of way and deferentially efficient. From the moment you arrive, the entire staff knows who you are, addressing you courteously by name, and knows in which of the 31 rooms you are staying. Should you forget either bit of information, your name is inserted in a little frame on the door of your room. Convenient for them and for you to know where your fellow guests are.

There's no registration desk, as such. Rather, you are invited into the imposing, lavishly carved wood-panelled great hall by Michael Holiday, the butler (manager), Cliveden's answer to Hudson of *Upstairs, Downstairs* fame. There, in the presence of 16th-century suits of armour and a superb portrait of Nancy Astor by John Singer Sargent, you will be asked to fill out a card with the basics. It will be the last thing you sign until you check out, no matter how many cocktails you enjoy in the intimate library, how many meals you partake in the grand terrace dining room, how many horses you ride, and how many hours you spend cruising on the Thames on any of Cliveden's Edwardian boats. Of course, many of Cliveden's myriad amenities are included in the room rates—the minimum of £200 you'll spend for a double entitles you to a full English breakfast in the rococo French dining room, which shimmers with ornate gilding on the wall-panelling taken from Madame de Pompadour's Château d'Asnières near Paris. It'll also allow you access to swimming and tennis, both indoors and outdoors, as well as squash, croquet, the saunas, the steam room, the gym, the billiard room and the video library which services the VCRs in each room.

One of our favourite activities here is walking the extensive grounds, with the collection of sculptures that is considered one of the finest in the country. Suggested routes and the approximate time it takes to walk them are mapped out in an informative brochure, which, together with the audiotape commentary by Robert Hardy, makes the days of Lady

Astor come alive. Even a predictable spell of Britain's rainy weather need not dampen your strolling ambitions—there's an ample supply of Wellington boots and giant umbrellas at your disposal.

But the beauty of Cliveden is that you don't *have to* do anything. Just being there, experiencing a lifestyle that exists in few other places in the world is entertainment enough. And you can certainly be forgiven for holing up for days on end in any of the beautifully appointed rooms. Each is named for a notable individual connected with Cliveden and is decorated accordingly, complete with pictures of the esteemed personages in their respective rooms. The Lady Astor is a picture of feminine perfection in soft pastel colours accented by an abundance of fresh flowers. A baronial fireplace, flanked by French doors opening onto a private terrace, dominates the conversational grouping of plush sofas and armchairs. As in all the rooms, a silver tray is loaded with decanters of various libations and the huge bathroom is decked out in Floris toiletries. A night spent in these opulent digs makes you feel like royalty, presumably the kind with money, given the £465-a-night pricetag.

As you might imagine, some rooms like the Mountbatten are more masculine in tone, though a pretty, well-lit vanity tucked away in a corner of this large, light and airy chamber is indicative of habitation by the fairer sex. Elaborately carved wooden wall panelling rises from the geometric print carpeted floor to a ceiling awash in plaster swirls and rosettes. A raised platform nestled in a bay window enthrones a table and chairs, perfect for a rousing game of cards or a romantic tête à tête over a glass of sherry. The Mountbatten, designated a junior suite, goes for £345; while full suites, like the blue and green brocade Prince of Wales, go for £440 to £465 a night.

There is good reason, however, to venture forth from any of the enthralling lodgings—a meal in the elegant terrace dining room which, with its trompe l'oeil marble colonnade, once served as Cliveden's principal drawing room. Open to nonresidents, it serves lunch and dinner in undeniable style, made uncommonly comfortable by high-backed, tapestry-covered armchairs. Both à la carte and fixed-price menus are offered, the latter being a choice of three or four courses—£27 and £32 respectively—at lunch and a five-course £41.80 extravaganza at dinner. All prices include mineral water, coffee, tax (but not service) and a contribution to the National Trust, which we think is a very nice touch. The food, self-styled as modern English, is beautifully presented and often imaginative.

And the cheese board is out of this world, baffling in its abundance of alternatives.

Speaking of which, you do have the option of taking over Cliveden in its entirety for the ultimate house party. From £8,300 a day during the winter season to £10,950 during the summer, you and your guests have the exclusive use of the premises. You can even throw a gala dinner party for as many as 150, followed by a cabaret and dancing in the Great Hall. The charge for that particular extravagance is a matter between you and Paul Sinclair.

During the course of the negotiations, he'll no doubt remind you, "Those things which are the ultimate in life have two things in common—they are not cheap and they are good value." Cliveden is certainly both and only 25 miles west of central London, easily accessible by car or train, and only 20 minutes from Heathrow. 🦃

The French Horn

| Sonning-on-Thames | 0734-692204 |
| Berkshire RG4 0TN | (FAX) 0734-442210 |

At the end of a village so picture perfect that Hollywood movie producers have used it as a set, sits a long, peak-roofed, vaguely Tudor white stucco building of undetermined age. The family seat of the effervescent Emanuels, The French Horn is a hotel and restaurant of bountiful country charm, just a stone's throw from London—45 minutes by car, 22 minutes by rail from Paddington Station, plus a 10-minute taxi ride. If you're playing weekend tourist, spend the day on Saturday at nearby Windsor and the night at The French Horn. Stick around long enough for brunch on Sunday, and then wind your way back to London via Henley.

A cross between a quaint inn and country house hotel, The French Horn has been a fixture for weekend jaunts for generations and their heros, from John Wayne to Paul Hogan, thanks in large measure to the Emanuels who originally found gastronomical fame and fortune with Wheelers. Patriarch Ronnie, a devilishly good-looking gentleman with warm dancing eyes, bounces among his guests dispensing goodwill— we'd settle for the glorious gold French-horn-shaped cufflinks he always wears. But he won't part with them, not even for his son Michael who's reduced to wearing replicas in silver. Michael's just as dashing as his dad, primed to take over the family business if Ronnie will ever let him. It took a broken leg, the result of a skiing accident, to persuade Ronnie to invite Michael on board.

But he was well prepared, having studied in France "with everyone from Bocuse to Vergé," and today the menu reflects Michael's classical training. The food is familiar, often deceptively simple and always properly prepared, and it is garnished with a bit of theatre in the manner it's served. The waiters act as entertainers, carving meats and finishing dishes tableside.

Actually, you're struck by the theatricality of The French Horn long before you get to the table. The entrance, where you're warmly welcomed by Ronnie, Michael or maître d' Manuel Gonzalez, opens into a contrived castle-like chamber that could be the set for an Errol Flynn movie. The delicious aroma of assorted fowl roasting on rotating spits over an open fire fills the air, while tapestries, a large collection of antique copper, and crests painted on the wooden beams lend additional touches of medieval grandeur. The heavy, red velvet-covered furniture would be out of place and ugly anywhere else, but here, like all the other affectations, it conspires to create a fetching ambience.

For Sunday brunch, our favoured meal at the Horn, the lounge is crowded with chummy regulars who shout amiable greetings to one another as they peruse the menu. Most have a pretty good idea of what they're going to order. Even though the à la carte and fixed-price menus change every three months, the locals can always count on staples like roast rack of lamb, prime rib, Aylesbury duckling roasted on the spit, and chateaubriand. The wine list presents more of a dilemma—it is one of the most complete listings of the great vintages to be found anywhere in Britain. The red Bordeaux are particularly impressive, including a 1949 Chateau Latour for £1,500 and a 1945 Chateau Margaux at £1,950. If the 200-plus choices prove overwhelming, Martin the sommelier, can be relied upon to direct you to an excellent and reasonably priced bottle—a 1985 Côtes du Rhône at £11.50 or a 1980 Chateau Vignelaurie, a fine wine from Aix-en-Provence for £16.50.

After wrestling with the food and wine decisions, you have ample time to enjoy a cocktail and eavesdrop on the animated conversations surrounding you before being taken to your table. When you make your reservation, be sure to ask to be seated in the room overlooking the trellised terrace and the river beyond. The view of the water rushing under the willows and round the bend in the river that graces the site is splendid— and unadulterated. The Emanuels own both shores of the Thames so there's no chance of unsightly new construction mucking up the vista. And because the land downriver is theirs as well, the Horn is the only restaurant on the Thames allowed floodlights to take advantage of the view at night.

There's a stately Regency look to most of the rooms of the large Wedgwood blue-and-white restaurant, except for the terrace-oriented one that takes on a rustic appearance. The ceiling is covered with vines that weave in and out of the round skylights, which bathe the room in a dramatic painter's light. But your attention is soon, if temporarily, distracted from the surroundings by the arrival of the first course. While we generally prefer to order à la carte here, we couldn't during our last visit resist the description of the Cocktail de Crevettes for £26.50, inclusive of tax and 10 per cent service, on the Sunday lunch menu. One of us just had to have the "baby prawns snoozing on shredded lettuce and covered with a piquant sauce." Good choice, as was the fillet of beef topped with a cream of truffle sauce that followed. From the other à la carte, the £7.80 scallops wrapped in bacon, cooked in a Benedictine sauce and served on a bed of chopped spinach was a delightful precursor to the thin slices of veal, sautéed in butter laced with brandy, and covered with a white wine, mushroom and cream sauce for £10.50.

It's worth feigning interest in dessert just to watch the waiter deftly negotiate the giant sweets and cheese trolleys through the tables. But to really test his mettle, indulge in a port or brandy from the titanic liqueur cart topped by a tower of cigar boxes.

Should you take our advice about a weekend outing, you have a choice of one of the ten rooms upstairs or the suites in the former staff cottages across the road. As far as we're concerned, it's a toss-up. The main building offers picturesque chintz rooms off hallways filled with the comforting tick of lots of handsome clocks, while the cottages boast duplex accommodations with fireplaces. Room 7, above the main dining room, features a glamorous pink bathroom accented by brass fixtures, a built-in vanity and a little terrace overlooking the river—all for only £95 for two, including a full English breakfast, service charge and VAT, £85 if you're flying solo.

Even more of a bargain are the duplex suites at £120 for two and £100 as a single. The gas-fueled brick fireplaces and engaging mix of traditional and modern decor make them charming. The upstairs bedrooms nestled under the eaves sport world-class bathrooms and another fireplace. Each has a separate entrance from a terrace facing the river and a back door leading into a communal corridor that culminates in a well-stocked kitchen.

There can be few more agreeable places from which to explore the Thames basin west of London or to grab a quick lunch if you're passing through on a weekday. Actually, with selections like herring roe on toast and duck pâté, followed by grilled local pink trout and steak-and-kidney pudding, the three-course executive business lunch served in such a special atmosphere is worth the trip in and of itself at £14.90.   🍷

Gidleigh Park

Chagford   0647-432367
Devon TQ 138HH   (FAX) 0647-4322574

Are you willing to drive three-and-a-half hours south of London for peace and quiet, splendid gardens and possibly the best Yorkshire pudding in Britain?

We certainly hope so, because Gidleigh Park, a 1920s mock-Tudor house in Devon, is such a refuge of welcome and comfort, you'll instantly feel at home.

Set on 40 acres of magnificent secluded grounds, Gidleigh Park overlooks the north River Teign, within Dartmoor National Park. We were glad we had packed some good walking shoes and riding boots, for the moor is best seen on foot or horseback. The hotel will gladly send you off on a stallion or mare, with gourmet picnic in hand.

However, you may not make it to the moors, as the fresh flowers, antique porcelain, crackling fires and deep-seated, chintz sofas in the cosy living rooms bid you welcome with their own spectacular views.

In the late 1970s, Gidleigh Park was purchased by Americans Paul and Kay Henderson, who spent some £1.3 million renovating their remote country home. Each time you return, you'll see new furnishings, pictures and gardens, as the owners are constantly working toward Mr Henderson's goal: "to create a hotel that offers good food and wine, peace and quiet; a place that I would want to stay in, and that I could recommend to my friends."

Judging by the Hendersons' awards—1988 Cesar, Most Sumptuous Country House Hotel, and 1990 Egon Ronay Guide, Hotel of the Year, they have achieved their goals.

One reason, certainly, is their staff, who have the unique ability to be natural, friendly and unstuffy, even when their hotel is grand, famous and, yes, expensive.

The 14 bedrooms have been decorated by Mrs Henderson in antiques and English and Egyptian fabrics, and have all the modern amenities you'd expect, like colour television and direct-dial telephone. Mrs Henderson has thoughtfully added dressing tables with three-way mirrors, spacious closets, potpourri and full-size bottles of Crabtree & Evelyn toiletries in every room. Don't plan on sneaking the toiletries into your luggage, however; just enjoy as much as you want while you're there!

Of the 14 rooms, we think the best are Rooms 1, 2, 4, 5, and also 9, the Hydrangea Room. The floral fabrics are in beige and cranberry, with antique tables and chairs. A nice touch is the elegant reading lamps beside the bed for late-night reading.

Charges vary from £200 to £315, depending on size, and this includes a four-course dinner, morning tea or coffee in your room and Continental or cooked breakfast. The garden and park views are free.

You may want to stay in a sweet two-bedroom thatched cottage just next to the main house called the Pavillion. It has the same quality of furniture and fabrics, but it offers a little more privacy for one or two couples.

Gidleigh Park doesn't take reservations for one-night stays for the high season, but it certainly does for two or more. We think a three–five day stay is perfect. Because the hotel is always busy, you need to book about five months in advance of the time you want to visit.

There's certainly enough to keep you quite entertained for many days, with choices of tennis, croquet, fishing, golf, or riding. Lots of guests come to loaf around, to read and to take long, leisurely walks.

After all this exercise, you'll be quite delighted to turn yourself over to the gourmet talents of chef, and managing director, Shaun Hill.

Shaun is a chef with a sense of humour who often wears black-and-white-striped socks with his chef "whites" and always has a smile on his face. When *The Michelin Guide* took a star away from him in 1990, Shaun just smiled and said, "Well, everyone's entitled to their opinion."

We certainly didn't agree with *The Michelin Guide,* but then neither did the respected and much-loved food critic, Fay Maschler. She wrote a lengthy piece in *The London Standard* blasting away at the book—bravo, bravo, Fay. We do agree with you, Shaun is a brilliant chef.

If for some bizarre reason you don't get to Gidleigh Park, then by all means write to have a copy of Shaun Hill's *Gidleigh Park Cookery Book* sent to you. The truth is we tried to get Shaun to come home with us, but this is a man who loves where he is and what he's doing. This is also a man who oversees eight chefs for only 14 rooms.

He turns out robust creations of fresh fish and garden vegetables that attract diners from miles around. While you're in the dining room, take a look around, and you'll see guests who have driven an hour or two for the pleasure of having dinner at Gidleigh Park.

What Shaun Hill can do with country cooking! We loved his scallops with lentil and coriander sauce, delicately spiced with cardamom. And his Yorkshire pudding and homemade truffles are divine. Dinners are priced at £42, including VAT.

The wine list that goes with this scrumptious food has received numerous awards, including a Grand Award from *The Wine Spectator* in 1984, and the first British Wine Cellar of the Year award from Egon Ronay.

Although it seems endless and includes Californians, Jaboulet Rhones, top-class Italians and old champagnes, Mr Henderson has starred his recommendations to make it easier for you to select just the right wine for your meal. Wine prices begin at £17, including VAT, and go up quite steeply.

If you wish to pamper yourself in unostentatious luxury, then do make the trek out of London to the wilds of Dartmoor, down the single track lane, lined with huge granite boulders and trees, to one of Britain's loveliest of country homes.   ❧

Le Manoir aux Quat' Saisons

Great Milton	0844-278881
Oxford 0X9 7PD	(FAX) 0844-278847

What is it about this reference to the calendar-year's seasonal changes that invariably spells *first class?* Think about it. In New York, the restaurant Four Seasons has long inspired worship by the food faithful; while the Four Seasons hotels win raves internationally. London has got its own talk-of-the-town Four Seasons restaurant, with its newly polished Michelin star—a rare anointment among hotel eateries, but then it *is* in a Four Seasons Hotel, the Inn on the Park. And in the suburbs, if you count Oxford and its environs as such, there's yet another example of Four Seasons' success potion, Le Manoir aux Quatre-Saisons.

Lest you sniff that the French translation is a little *de trop*, you should know the establishment comes by it honestly. Raymond Blanc, the visionary creator of Le Manoir hails from Gallic territory and, in fact, the structure traces its origins to a 14th-century Norman nobleman.

The bulk of the present house, however, was built toward the end of the 15th century. As local legend has it, its builders were so intent on their work that no noise, other than the steady tapping of trowel and chisel and the clanking of rope and pulley, could be heard during the period of its construction. Today, while the 27 acres of this most luxurious of country house hotels afford plenty of sought-after solitude, you're likely to hear the hum of conversation punctuated by laughter as guests make use of the swimming pool and tennis court or congregate in the lounge before a meal. Certainly, you'll hear the clatter of dishes and the tinkling of glasses, as dining is a major activity here.

You see, Raymond not only owns the place but also cooks for it, and he was voted European Chef of the Year in 1989. What's more, Le Manoir boasts two Michelin stars—no mean feat. Remember this is Britain *and* this is a hotel. But it is certainly a restaurant-driven hotel. Raymond, described by one critic as "an extremely accomplished and brilliant cook, with a very original mind," has become quite the celebrity and, at only 43, a possible successor to Albert Roux's culinary crown. Regular television appearances, a best-selling cookbook and a weekly recipe column keep him and his beloved Manoir in the public eye. Consequently, reservations for the restaurant made two weeks in advance are an absolute must. As for any of the hotel's 19 rooms, plan on making arrangements at least five weeks before the date of your intended stay. Maybe more. Raymond has already accepted one reservation for New Year's Eve in 1999!

We couldn't imagine thinking that far ahead until we sat down to our first Le Manoir meal. Though tempted by the £52 eight-course menu Gourmand featuring gustatory goodies like a mosaic of chicken wings and vegetable pâté splashed with a honey vinaigrette, a chervil-infused asparagus mousse, and wood-fire grilled medallions of beef, reason prevailed. We opted for the three-course version at £24.50. And, typically, it was a decision split right down the middle—one of us savoured the thinly sliced fillet of lamb, resting on a bed of artichokes and green beans, dressed in its own cooking juices; while the other dove into a delicate mousse of squab livers, served in a port and tomato sauce. Then we went for the roasted medallions of monkfish, masked with herbs and breadcrumbs and topped with meat juice, and the boned leg of Bresse chicken, stuffed with a light mushroom mousse and served with a rich sauce of wild mushrooms. There was little room left for dessert, but we couldn't resist the warm raspberries nestled in a biscuit, flavoured with a dash of kirsch and knapped with a vanilla and raspberry sauce.

Now, if the prospect of the 45-minute jaunt back to London after such a meal seems daunting—it should. The restaurant does not subscribe to the eat-and-run theory. If you come for lunch, you're here for the afternoon. And you'll be ready for a nap when you finally finish—the portions are gargantuan.

So take our advice and plan to spend at least one night here. It's far from hazardous duty. Each of the 19 rooms has a distinct and somewhat extravagant personality—winsome window treatments, loads of pillows, lots of antiques and gold-plated bathroom fixtures. The 10 original rooms in the main building are named after the flowers that bloom in such abundance in the extensive gardens. We were taken with Mimosa, predictably a cheerful symphony in yellow. The four-poster's enveloping canopy and drapes, which can be drawn to enclose the bed, make it very difficult to get up in the morning. Make it your "problem" for £220, including—as do all the prices—VAT and service. And Le Manoir throws in a Continental breakfast.

Another room we adore is the Gallica Rose, all done in lush pink-and-green floral fabrics that surround a magnificent solid brass bed. Lovely antique mint green and peach chairs and sofas are arranged so you can look onto the garden; that is, when you're not soaking in the whirlpool tub. But for us, the most stunning aspect of the room was the fact that the vanity set on the dressing table was actually sterling silver! You couldn't begin to replace it for the £350 nightly charge for the room.

Perhaps the most fascinating of the rooms is Hollyhock, which for £250 comes complete with a ghost—or, at least, a ghost story. It seems that the room has been haunted ever since the deaths of Oliver Cromwell and his horse. You see, the dreaded Cromwell expired here after being thrown from his horse. Lady Cromwell was in such a state about the whole affair that she shot the horse, only to incur the wrath of the locals. She fled their scorn, whereupon the furniture in the Hollyhock room took to moving about of its own accord. Things became so bad that the room was officially exorcised in the early '80s; and now you can sleep there in peace—if you dare.

Still, if it's romance you seek, ask for the Michael Priest Suite, which occupies the 16th-century dovecote. In all its frilly finery, the duplex resembles nothing so much as the top of a wedding cake. Actually, given its privacy quotient and decor, it's ideal for honeymooners. The dormer-beamed ceiling of the second-floor bedroom rusticates the flying white doves that hold up the canopy over the bed and the pink-and-white-striped cabana that serves as a closet. The interior details worthy of Jayne Mansfield continue in the bathroom downstairs, where you'll find a four-footed bathtub adorned with more billing and cooing doves.

It really does look like a movie set. But then the whole place does. No wonder Hollywood so often comes to roost for a few days. Mel Gibson, Jeremy Irons, Charlton Heston, Dudley Moore—all have stayed here. But the proof of the pudding, as they say, is the patronage of Michael Caine—a liver of the good life if ever there was one.   🍒

Ston Easton Park

Ston Easton	0761-21631
Bath	(FAX) 0761-21377
Somerset BA3 4DF	(Toll-free from U.S.) 800-544-9940

Just eleven miles south of Bath and Bristol is a grand country home where anything can happen, and usually does. One summer during the Bristol Balloon Fiesta, for example, one of the hotel guests brought over four hot-air balloons and pilots from France. Off they all went, champagne in hand, sailing over the Somerset countryside into the sunny blue morning sky.

Another day, we spotted badgers and foxes padding past the house. You just never know what will happen next at Ston Easton Park.

When Peter and Christine Smedley purchased the house in 1978, they were really just looking for a home for themselves. They fell in love with Ston Easton Park and, after extensive repairs and refurbishing, opened it in 1982 to guests. Lucky us.

Their very first year, Ston Easton Park was awarded the Egon Ronay Gold Plate for Hotel of the Year.

The Palladian-style house was built in 1740 and contains some of the most exceptional architecture and decorative features of its period. It is set in an utterly romantic landscape, created by Humphry Repton in the

18th century. We loved watching the River Norr which flows through the gardens.

As you step inside, you feel a sense of history everywhere. The Saloon is probably the finest room in Somerset, featuring grisaille paintings on canvas, Corinthian columns and a frieze of shells and floral garlands encircling the walls. The magnificent ceiling contains an ornamental oval with the eagle of Jupiter descending out of the sun, surrounded by lightning. It's a perfect room for stimulating conversation or daydreaming!

The Library, richly decorated with mahogany bookcases, brass grille doors, a marble fireplace and Italian paintings, is an equally perfect place to curl up with a good book.

One of the wonderful traits about Ston Easton is that amidst all this splendour are homely touches, such as the family photographs. You'll even see Lucy, the Smedleys' dog, roaming around. You really do feel that you are a guest in the Smedleys' own home, as indeed you are.

The staff of 70 for only 21 rooms will all go out of their way to coddle and please you. General manager Kevin Marchant is so attentive and sensitive to your every need; no request is too small. In his quiet, dignified way, he takes care of everything.

Mrs Audrey Gill, the head housekeeper, knows every remedy for every emergency, whether it's removing stains from clothes, sewing on lost buttons or fixing a broken shoe. Angus Hooper, the gardener, can take a single lily bulb and turn it into a whole garden! Pam Savage, one of the receptionists, is a very talented artist who designs the wonderful witty Christmas cards that go out every year around the world from the Smedleys. And Annie Oakes bakes scones, breads and biscuits for which you'll give up your diet.

Speaking of food, much of it comes straight up on a wheelbarrow from the Victorian kitchen garden: lots of vegetables and local fruits. There are always daily specials and the chef will even serve you a boiled egg and buttered toast in bed, if that suits your mood.

The clientele here are people who want peace, luxury and beautiful surroundings. Stanley Marcus has found his way here, as have Evelyn and Leonard Lauder. And if you do, you won't regret it.

May to September are the busiest months, and you need to book four to six months in advance. Although Christmas is off-season, it's a fun time, with a great mix of Brits and Americans.

The bedrooms were done by British designer Jean Monro, who did several rooms at the British Embassy in Washington, D.C. Her speciality in 18th-century interiors is evident in the beautiful antiques in every room. Yet the rooms have a warm feeling about them, not at all like hotel rooms.

Each room has beautiful china and porcelain accessories, and luxurious fabrics in calming colours. The new marble bathrooms have wonderful Penhaligon shampoo and bath oil toiletries. For a little midnight snack, biscuit tins filled with home-made cookies are at your bedside.

The Master Bedroom, one of our favourites, has a very inviting original Chippendale four-poster bed and a spectacular view of the Norr River valley. There are lovely antique bedside commodes, a dressing table and a chest of drawers over which is a magnificent carved mirror. We loved the two porcelain parrots (made by the Marchioness of Aberdeen, Anne Gordon) which match the fabric of the room. This room goes for £265 per night.

The Chinese room has twin beds, with draped Chinese fabric hanging from a gilt carved wood coronet. The oriental wallpaper surrounds you with birds and flowers and gives the room a cheerful feel. It's on the second floor, giving you a wonderful view across the park. This room is £220 per night.

If you're feeling energetic, there are three very good 18-hole golf courses within 15 miles of the house. Or you can play croquet or tennis, jog or bike, or take a morning horseback ride.

You might want to explore Bath, which has excellent shopping, the Roman baths and the Pump Room for tea. Or go to Wells and see the moated Bishop's Palace.

And since this is the home of cheddar cheese, you might want to visit the cheese farm close by.

Of course, you may just want to sit in the house library and catch up on your reading, or walk in the flower gardens.

We hear that Angus has planted asparagus and is also growing passion fruit in one of the glasshouses. Surely you'll want to drop by Ston Easton Park and have a taste, English country style.   🍇

Woburn Abbey

Woburn   0525-290666
Bedfordshire MK43 0TP

There are a number of stately homes—houses really built by Britain's noble families as showcases for their wealth and power—which make worthy day-trips from London: Blenheim, the seat of the dukes of Marlborough, as well as the birthplace of Winston Churchill, and Castle Howard among them. But when we feel the urge to immerse ourselves in a day of history and culture, we head for Woburn Abbey.

An hour's jaunt by car or rail, the 400-year-old home of the dukes of Bedford rates preferred status on several counts. To begin with, Woburn Abbey is the birthplace of "the stately-home business." But when the current Duke of Bedford first opened it to visitors for fun and profit in 1955, the practice was considered quite unorthodox. More important, it is a treasure chest of paintings by Gainsborough, Lawrence, Reynolds, Van Dyck and more—one of the most impressive and important private collections in the world. The long gallery boasts the famous Armada portrait of Queen Elizabeth I by George Gower. When you envision the red-haired "Virgin Queen," it is most likely you see this representation of her as Empress. And the main dining room doubles as a museum dedicated to the works of Canaletto, with 21 views of his beloved Venice gracing the walls.

Even more intriguing than the artwork is the structure itself. Its history dates to 1145, when a Cistercian monastery was founded on the site. In 1547, Woburn Abbey was bequeathed to Sir John Russell, the future 1st Earl of Bedford, as part of Henry VIII's wealth. Since the original building had been partially destroyed by fire just before Henry's dissolution of the monasteries, Sir John did not embrace the Abbey as the family seat. Rather, it was the 4th Earl who, in the early 17th century, embarked upon its restoration to make it habitable. His improvements, thought to be designed by Inigo Jones, included a two-storey wing on the north side, as well as a fantastic grotto fashioned in a marine motif which remains one of the Abbey's principal attractions.

By 1732, parts of the building were again in serious need of repair, and the Palladian architect Henry Filcroft was commissioned by the 4th Duke (as opposed to earl—the Russells had come up in the world) to rebuild the west side of the building. The result was the magnificent series of state rooms, meant for the entertaining of royalty, that enchant visitors today. The Abbey was essentially completed toward the end of the 18th century when Henry Holland added the east wing.

There is so much to see, so much to discover. More than we can possibly do justice to here. But we do have a couple of don't-miss-under-any-circumstance rooms that we simply must rant and rave about—the Chinese Room and the Flying Duchess' Room. The exquisite hand-painted wallpaper of the former is of Chinese origin, circa 1753. A continuous river landscape flows around the room, its colourful birds, plants and trees painted with incredible accuracy. The 18th-century Chinese export on display in the room is equally awe-inspiring.

Speaking of awestruck, that's what we always are when we consider the story of Mary, the wife of the 11th Duke—grandmother of the present Duke, great-grandmother of the Marquess of Tavistock whose attractive family currently occupies the Abbey. Mary learned to fly at the tender age of 60. Hence her enduring nickname as the "Flying Duchess." Not only did she learn, but like everything else she did in life—nursing, painting, bird-watching, ice-skating and photography—she excelled. Mary set two flying records: one to India; one to South Africa. Her charming room is filled with memorabilia from her extraordinary life. It's a warm friendly place, where you can almost feel the effervescent presence of the irrepressible Flying Duchess.

Other chambers of note include the spectacular Reynolds Room, where all the portraits, including his own, are by Sir Joshua Reynolds. Then there's the lavish Queen Victoria's Bedroom, with its elaborately decorated ceilings, glorious silk wallhangings, and superb collection of 17th-century Dutch and Flemish paintings. Yes, Virginia, the diminutive queen *did* sleep here and did so on the suitably majestic four-poster bed—six feet long and seven feet wide.

Invariably, after a visit to Woburn Abbey, we're hit with an all-consuming craving to redecorate our homes in the style to which we would like to become accustomed—filling them with fine English and French antiques. Fortunately, we don't have to fight the yearning. Those clever Russells (still the family name after all these years), the folks that brought London the original Covent Garden, have thought of everything. There's an antiques centre on the property, thought to be the largest such showcase outside London. Some 40 shops are represented, selling furniture, porcelain, paintings and prints, silver, and glassware. The only limitations are your imagination and budget.

Our final rationalization for choosing Woburn Abbey over all its stately competitors addresses a subject close to our hearts—food. Where else can you get such a large dose of culture *and* sit down to a fine meal? Yes, the Russells have covered the gastronomic angle as well by engaging the Roux brothers to oversee their delightful restaurant called Paris House. Open for lunch and dinner, Paris House would be noteworthy even if it weren't situated on the Abbey's 3,000 acres or housed in such an architectural gem. The black-and-white timber "high Tudor" structure was originally built in 1878 for the Paris Exhibition. After serving its purpose as an attraction there, it was dismantled and reassembled at the Abbey to enhance the grounds.

Today, Paris House serves up some of the best food to be found outside London, courtesy of the talent of on-site chef Peter Chandler. His imaginative dishes are truly representative of modern French classic cuisine without being nouvelle or too cutesy. The three-course £23 fixed-price menu for lunch and dinner might include such delectables as a mosaic of vegetables topped by a green sauce or a rich casserole of snails and mushrooms among the appetizers. The main-course listing has been known to boast a surprisingly successful fillet of pork with banana in a ginger sauce, as well as more conventional leg of lamb with tomatoes and basil. Any one of the desserts—from raspberry soufflé to one of Peter's house sorbets—is a fitting finale. Just as dinner here is the perfect way to end your day at Woburn Abbey, try the Abbey's Flying Duchess Pavilion (aka the coffee shop) for an appropriately light lunch.

CHAPTER THREE

Restaurants

*London's new role as gourmets'
dining destination*

There is, believe it or not, more to British cuisine these days than shepherd's pie, warm beer or bangers and mash. It may not be so very long since self-styled gourmets stopped taking a grin-and-bear-it attitude toward London dining. For much of recorded time, they'd counted on suffering through meals of overcooked meat, vegetables boiled to mush, and thick tasteless gravies. Their tales of culinary woes were reliable subjects for communal commiseration wherever sophisticated travellers gathered. No longer. World-class dining has become another of London's many attractions.

The epiphanal event, no doubt, was the appearance of a red Michelin for Britain. The oh-so-very-grudging acknowledgment by that touchstone of French haute cuisine that there was something in Britain worth putting between those famed, hard red covers was the first hint that change was in the wind. The fabled Gallic tasters from across the Channel had finally decided they could indeed find a meal in London that was worth at least a detour.

Today, there are even meals worth voyages unto themselves.

Of course, for those of us with less sophisticated palates, the situation was never so bad as the jaded gourmets would have it. Fresh and flavourful salmon from Scottish rivers, rich steak-and-kidney pie, delicate Dover sole, and roast beef served with Yorkshire pudding were but a few of the city's traditional delights.

But it's only been during the last decade or so that the creative cooking of some London kitchens, like those of Albert Roux and Anton Mosimann, brought Michelin inspectors from Paris, followed, as day the night, by the world's gourmets.

Former disciples of these and other chefs have fanned out across the city, establishing outposts of culinary excellence. In the process, they've generated a renaissance in English cooking, capitalizing on the potential of customary staples by preparing them with innovative twists. Or, more often, they've used brute force. Like the dictatorial Nico Ladenis who might single-handedly be credited with the education of the British palate to the joys of eating duck breast rare by literally shoving it down people's throats.

Not to worry, no matter of force could convince a respectable Brit to consider venison topped with kiwi—and, while it's true some menus get a little carried away with rapturous descriptions, for the most part the emphasis is on fresh ingredients, clean, crisp flavours...and hefty prices. If you haven't blown your £1,000 before tea, you're likely to succeed *during* dinner at many a fashionable eatery.

Except at weekends, when most are closed—mute testimony to the natives' penchant for country retreats. In fact, you could starve in the West End or the City on Saturday and Sunday if it weren't for pubs and hotel restaurants, both of which deserve your patronage—the former for their convivial and affordable authenticity, the latter for their convenience and surprisingly good food. Moreover, neither embraces the abhorrent practice of charging a cover, a particularly annoying affection of many a London dining establishment. We don't understand it. If the restaurants need that extra couple of pounds to cover the cost of the "complimentary" bread, why not just add it onto the menu prices?

After all, they have no trouble factoring in the VAT—almost all restaurant prices include tax, and many include a service charge which tends to hover in the 12 per cent range. But it's not necessarily what you think. Most, sometimes all of it, goes toward the cost of linen and breakage, not to the staff. If you want to ensure that your waiter or waitress is rewarded, it's necessary to leave a tip—yet another dent in your £1,000 a day!

One thing that won't cost you a farthing is reservations; and you don't have to leave home without them. Plan ahead and call the London Restaurant Hotline, toll-free from the U.S. at 1-800-937-4634, to make sure you reserve a seat at the city's most sought-after tables.

Annabel's

44 Berkeley Square	071-629-3558
London W1X 7RT	(FAX) 071-491-1860

It's a nice idea naming things after a loved one—yachts, restaurants and the like. But in an age of serial monogamy, it may not be all that practical. Things have a way of lasting a lot longer than relationships, and it's such a nuisance changing the registrations, licences and letterhead. Of course, you can always let the name stand as a memorial to a love long lost. And for our late-night dining pleasure, there is no better example of such a tack than Mark Birley's Annabel's, the private club he named after his wife in 1963.

These days the energetic beauty who inspired Mark to create London's chicest nightclub is married to Jimmy Goldsmith, but the place and the name remain the same. And it's still not unusual for her to sweep down the stairs to the panelled hall where reception manager Ted Racki holds sway with the help of three assistants. They treat every guest like royalty (in fact, many are) but Lady G. rates extra-special attention—the club still bears her name, and Mark is the first to admit that she had a lot to do with the club's instant success. As a warmly vibrant and very unself-conscious hostess, she managed to imbue the atmosphere with that of a rollicking private party. It's an atmosphere that has continued to thrive despite that fact that the original core membership of 600, nearly all friends of the Birleys, has now swelled to 8,500 and counting.

Mark still accepts application for membership. Be prepared to rustle up at least two, but preferably three, current-member sponsors who will write long, glowing letters about you and to ante up a £250 initiation fee along with the yearly dues of £500. You had better also plan on waiting a while to be accepted. Depending upon the strength of your sponsors, it could take as long as two years.

Whatever the wait—it's worth it. Annabel's is just as special, just as unique and just as beautiful as the woman it was named after. First and foremost, this is truly a private club with a capital *P*. No easily obtained temporary memberships for out-of-towners here. If you don't belong, the only way you get in is to be in the company of a member who signs you in with Ted and who is not only responsible for your bill but also responsible for your behaviour! Furthermore, the press is never allowed to cross the threshold, though photographers tend to lurk outside to get their pictures of Di, Fergie and company on girls' night out.

What's more, the food is fantastic, made all the more so by the drop-dead gorgeous room it's served in. Dramatic vaulted ceilings are supported by great shiny brass columns which reflect the artwork covering the walls and the riotously festive colour scheme—green upholstered banquettes and chairs snuggle up to pink draped tables dotting the bright green and red Stewart tartan carpet. The clientele is just as colourful. Of course, we can't name names—it just isn't done here.

But one name you should know is manager Louis Emmanuelli, the famous Louis who has acted as maître d' since Annabel's first opened. Word has it that he never forgets a face. Certainly, he manages to keep everyone happy, no matter how long heels have to be cooled at the bar before getting the table he promised. In all fairness, no one ever really feels stranded at the always busy bar. There are so many entertaining diversions to occupy your time—kicking up those chilled heels on the tiny dance floor, for instance. This is one place where everyone dances, often well into the wee hours—of course, no one gets here until 10 P.M. with 11 being prime dining time, though the doors open at 9.

Alternatively, you can hang out in the main sitting room. Cosy yet lively in its daffodil yellow, it's the sort of room that demands spirited discourse. Still, you don't have to join the party. There are all sorts of nooks and crannies throughout the club where you can hole up in solitude or with a few intimate friends. One such place is the wine cellar, lined with floor-to-ceiling wine racks and complete with a copy (hung over the mantel) of Velasquez's portrait of King Carlos II on horseback, which was painted by Mark Birley's father. It's a perfect room for entertaining in grand style, which is the only way to go here—a *hamburger* is £17, breaking the record set by New York's 21 Club at $24.50.

Actually, menu-wise, Annabel's borrows more than just hefty prices from 21—first-rate chicken and corned beef hashes (£16 and £16.50) and the delicious steak tartare (£19) look and taste very familiar. Don't get the wrong idea, Annabel's does venture into less prosaic territory with a rich wild mushroom risotto at £16 and grilled foie gras with lentils for £20. And that's just for starters—literally and figuratively.

Among the main courses, we like the unusual langoustine soufflé laced with mustard at £20 and the market-priced seabass with olives and capers. Throw in what in London passes for a Caesar salad for £10, along with the £3 cover charge, and you're looking at a likely dinner tab of £100 for two. You're also looking at a night to remember.

L'Arlequin

123 Queenstown Road   071-622-0555
London SW8 3RH   (FAX) 071-498-7015

Once upon a time, London's gourmets would never dream of venturing south of the Battersea Bridge in search of sustenance. Indeed, one can make the correct assumption that many of them had never been out to Queenstown Road for any reason. But the advent of the original Chez Nico changed all that, and now the area has become as familiar to sophisticated eaters as Mayfair. In fact, quite a few folks who used to power lunch at Le Gavroche now do so at L'Arlequin—right next door to Nico's former premises, which by the way, now houses Cavaliers. Imagine, two Michelin-starred restaurants on one street of this once unprepossessing neighbourhood!

Actually, L'Arlequin has been heralded as one of the finest examples of French cooking and service anywhere in London. Egon Ronay declared it Restaurant of the Year in 1989, and *The Times* cited it as the best among the French contenders that same year. Such accolades result from the tireless dedication of Christian and Genevieve Delteil, the husband and wife team that owns L'Arlequin.

The Delteils named their establishment after the travelling troubadours who entertained the courts of the Middle Ages with their lyrical stories—an acknowledgment that their charge as the proprietors of a restaurant was to put on a show as captivating as those of their medieval predecessors. But to our way of thinking, the name is, however inadvertently, an invitation to either one of these attractive young restaurateurs to tell their own fascinating tale.

It seems that Christian stopped off in England en route to the U.S. and what he thought were gastronomic streets paved with gold. His intention was to learn that strange native language—English. He did that and more, finding a new home and a partner in life in the charismatic Genevieve. Since Christian and Genevieve were both working at Le Gavroche and staying in the same bed-and-breakfast, they were thrown together morning, noon and night. Taking a hint from fate, they dutifully fell in love and the rest, as they say, is history. Christian refined his cooking skills at the Connaught and Chewton Glen before opening L'Arlequin over nine years ago. Needless to say, he never made it across the Atlantic.

Here, in their own little garden of Eden, a 50-seat pale-green dining room with a view of the world courtesy of the quaintly primitive murals and the large windows of the former shopfront, Christian and Genevieve put on a daily show that has the critics raving. It's a show based on Christian's versatile imagination which defies classification of their restaurant as classical, nouvelle or anything else. He changes the printed à la carte menu seasonally but exercises his considerable creativity, cooking "what I feel like," with a daily fixed-price menu at midday. He also devises special additions to the à la carte offerings every day, for both lunch and dinner.

Unquestionably, the £18.50 pricetag, inclusive of tax and service, for the set luncheon represents outstanding value, with such treats as pigeon salad with mushrooms, followed by medalions of veal with Christian's rich homemade noodles, and a delicious dessert. Hard to beat. And many folks settle for it because the staff is careful to offer the daily menu before mentioning the much pricier alternatives. Nice touch. But you know us, money is seldom a major consideration, especially when it comes to food. So we always make a point of reviewing all the options and often wander into à la carte territory even at lunch. Our respective palates just can't resist dishes like a terrine of sweetbreads and lobster, and cabbage stuffed with a veal forcemeat, both £8.50. And if truffles are in season, it's likely Christian will feature them in a daily special. He might use them to top his divine noodles, for instance, for £15 or so, depending upon the current state of the truffle market.

All main courses are served with exquisitely prepared vegetables or a green salad, and range from the sublime braised turbot with red peppers to the classic roast lamb rubbed with olive oil and thyme at £20. All prices include tax. You're on your own where service is concerned, but it's likely you'll be generous because service, under the direction of Genevieve, is superior.

At night, Genevieve herself acts as hostess which is one reason we prefer L'Arlequin at dinner. The room sparkles with her personality, and its low-key decor is brightened by the truly glamorous crowd that replaces the power-lunch bunch. Also, the attractive lighting sets off what may be the most subtly elegant flower treatment in town—lovely little orchids floating in winsome crystal vessels. Just another element of Christian and Genevieve's standing-room-only show. Figure on a couple of day's notice for seats, lunch or dinner, Monday to Friday. Saturday and Sunday are dark (read *closed*).

The Bombay Brasserie

Courtfield Close   071-370-4040
Courtfield Road   (FAX) 071-835-1669
London SW7 4UH

Many people make a strong case for the Bombay Brasserie as London's best bet for Sunday brunch. But you couldn't prove it by us. We've never been able to get a table for the wildly popular £12.95, tax inclusive, buffet despite the restaurant's grand scale. It seats 118 and has been known to serve 250 or more on Sunday afternoons. But having enjoyed many a dinner here—it's a little out of the way for lunch unless you're planning a day at the Victoria and Albert Museum—we are fully prepared to subscribe to the best-bet theory of the brunch's many regulars who only call when they *don't* plan on taking their customary tables complete with their pet waiters.

What's the draw? Well, the price is an obvious factor—it represents outstanding value. This British outpost of the swanky Taj Hotels group tenders an extensive range of authentic dishes reflecting the cosmopolitan character of Bombay, where India's diverse customs, lifestyles and traditions converge. Here, according to the menu, you'll find "the sumptuous cuisine of the Moghul Emperors, wholesome Panjabi fare, the earthy delights of the Tandoor clay ovens, the fish dishes of Goa's golden coast, the robust cuisine of the northwest frontier. . .and more in an environment with the ambience of an age gone by." All true. In fact, the Bombay Brasserie is one of London's most imposing restaurants, with the lofty ceilings of the palatial 1920s main dining room, and the glowing charm of the adjacent conservatory. Murals evoke the days of the Raj as does the haunting sepia-toned portrait of an Indian noblewoman on the menu.

But there's another element which makes the restaurant such a favoured Sunday destination—so many of London's other fine eateries are closed. The dearth of choices is even greater for Sunday evenings. But once again the Bombay Brasserie comes through. It's open Sunday night, just as it is every night of the year, taking orders until midnight.

Reservations for dinner are a good idea and tables can usually be booked at 24 hours' notice—ask to be seated in the conservatory. We make a habit of arriving half an hour early for cocktails in the large, very attractive lounge, as this is one of the few bars we actually choose to languish in before dinner. It's a treat to settle into the plush cushions of the bamboo furniture and soak up the gracious colonial atmosphere of the handsomely shuttered room, dominated by a huge ornamental fireplace crowned by a colossal gilt-framed mirror which soars to the ceiling. If you're on the wagon, try a class of chaas, a sweet yet spicy yogurt drink.

Once seated at your table, the large menu is presented with ceremonial flourish. At this juncture, we've seen many a face fall as its five pages can be overwhelming. Don't be shy or skeptical about asking for direction from your waiter, even if he obviously isn't of Indian origin, which many aren't. The last time we dined here, a delightful Frenchman answered our questions with unfailing accuracy and made excellent suggestions, the zesty crab Malabar as a £4.95 starter among them. Made from fresh flaked crab sautéed with spices and grated coconut, it's the perfect complement to the sweet and sour sev batata puri—small, crisp biscuit-like puris topped with cubes of boiled potatoes, onion, green chili and coriander leaves covered with a date and tamarind chutney for £3.50.

In keeping with Indian custom, all main courses are accompanied by a potato preparation, a vegetable of the day and a lentil dish. You're not likely to leave hungry. And don't bother saving room for dessert. They are expensive relative to the rest of the meal and tend to feature demon lychee nuts which are sickeningly sweet. But we've never run across a failing elsewhere on the menu. We're especially fond of the tender lamb cooked with dried apricots in a spicy red masala and garnished with crispy straw potatoes for £8.50. And the fish curry and rice, with its generous chunks of fresh fish simmered in a tangy curry sauce made from coconuts, is justifiably Goa's most famous speciality, also £8.50.

For vegetarians, the restaurant is nirvana. A whole page of the menu outlines complete meals as well as side dishes which allow vegans to assemble dinner according to their individual tastes.

Wine connoisseurs may be less satisfied—the list is modest in terms of size and selection. There is, however, compensation in the fact that the prices are equally unassuming. Indeed, all prices here are admirably restrained, considering the superior quality of the food and ambience. They include tax, but not service. A 12.5 per cent gratuity is added to the bill and there is a minimum of £15 per person at dinner. Experience dictates you'll spend more like £20 each for a feast fit for a maharaja.

Bibendum—Restaurant and Oyster Bar

Michelin House   071-581-5817
81 Fulham Road   (FAX) 071-823-7925
London SW3 6RD

"Nunc est Bibendum"—now is the time to drink—claims the massive stained-glass window dominating this airy, light-filled establishment. It might just as well proclaim "now is the time to gawk," as gawk you certainly will at the eye-popping decor of this restaurant that occupies the former touring office of the 1911 edifice built to house Michelin Tyre's British operation. Everywhere you look, the interior, designed by Conran's Design Group (yes, of *the* Conran's, as in shop, which is also lodged in the restored landmark building), takes advantage of the corpulent form of Bibendum, the Michelin Man.

His rotundness is reflected at every opportunity—specially designed Bibendum china, glasses, vases and ashtrays. Rimmed Bibendum detailing is evident on the bar and in the lighting fixtures—even the tables were created to feature a Bibendum bulge. They all bask in the colourful glow of stained-glass windows that also boast Bibendum images. Adapted from early 20th-century Michelin advertisements rendered by a poster artist named O'Galop and an intrinsic part of the building's original composition, they have a stylish wit about them that has survived the decades. The "Nunc est Bibendum" window depicts the Michelin Man raising a champagne glass laden with sharp objects, suggesting the (relatively) easy repairability of his company's then revolutionary pneumatic tyres.

Of course, the windows are at their best during the day, which is just as well, because so is the restaurant they grace. Granted, chef Simon Hopkinson's menu is larger, more varied and more ambitious in the evening than at lunch, but it also allows more room for error. Bibendum is open seven days a week and, as dedicated as we know Simon to be, he can't possibly be on site all the time. The simpler, but no less interesting, daily luncheon menus are easier for Simon's assistants to cope with in his absence. During our last visit we began our feast (no nouvelle nonsense here—portions are generous) with a sublime watercress soup and rare grilled tuna served cold with a sauce of lime, olive oil and pickled shallots. Flavourful roast wild duck with cranberries and a grilled veal chop topped by a superior béarnaise sauce followed. Then we sat back in the notably comfortable chairs with their unconventionally draped covers designed by fashion's darling Jasper Conran, who's also Sir Terence Conran's son, to relish the rich choice of desserts. We singled out a sinful pecan pie and a delightful crême brulée. Ours was a flawless meal consumed in the presence of friendly, informally attentive waiters, all for a fixed price of £19.50 each and only one or two days' notice required for a reservation.

It may take one or two weeks to get a dinner reservation, no matter how much you plead with maître d' Graham Williams, and the meal will certainly take a bigger bite out of your budget. With appetizers like escargots at £15 and a ballotine of foie gras for £18, coupled with £17 roast pigeon with cabbage, bacon and juniper or grilled fillet of veal with mozzarella and sage at £15, you'll certainly spend £60 for two on the à la carte menu. This would include dessert, but not wine which tends to be on the dear side. There's precious little available for under £30.

If you take our advice and opt for lunch, don't do it before one o'clock. The eclectic crowd, made up of ladies who lunch (Bibendum is so convenient to the fashionable little boutiques on Brompton Cross), businessmen and literary types, doesn't show up until then. By the same token, don't even think of dinner here before eight.

In either case, plan to arrive a little early so that you can take time to appreciate the architectural marvel, even oddity that is the Michelin Building. Designed by a company employee, it is an extraordinary departure from contemporary architecture, a completely unique structure built, more than anything else, to express Michelin's exuberant, innovative and very successful advertising campaign—one that reflected the imaginative entrepreneurship and vivacity of the company's founding siblings, Edouard and Andre Michelin.

Its ebullient, tile-clad façade had long endeared the building to Terence Conran, as it had to his friend Paul Hamlyn, head of Octopus Publishing Group. When, in 1985, they learned Michelin was prepared to sell, they were both in need of additional space for their burgeoning businesses, and they both wanted to open a restaurant. The Michelin Building could serve all three purposes, so they bought it and painstakingly restored the structure to its original, albeit somewhat quirky, grandeur. Consequently, today the building is rededicated to activities of which the Michelin brothers would wholeheartedly endorse—design, marketing, publishing, food and wine.

The Blue Elephant

4–6 Fulham Broadway   071-385-6595
London SW6 1AA   (FAX) 071-386-7665

Remember when the themed restaurants, like Trader Vic's, seemed special, even genuinely exotic? The Blue Elephant, London's premier Thai restaurant takes that legacy one step further to resplendent authenticity. The tawdriness of its somewhat questionable neighbourhood is forgotten once you step through the restaurant's unprepossessing portals. You're greeted by a delegation of bowing beauties in blue silk, draped in traditional Thai fashion. The fleeting impression that you've walked onto the set of yet another revival of *The King and I* is one shared by all first-timers. However, the fantasy is dispelled by the one sour note in the Blue Elephant's otherwise completely entrancing siren's song—the hostesses' gentle insistence that you alight in one of the rattan fan chairs in the lounge to consume one of the restaurant's cocktail concoctions. You know the kind—heavy on the fruit juices, light on the alcohol and embellished with flowers or paper fans.

In all fairness, the lounge is a lovely place to get acclimatized to the lush tropical environment which is the antithesis of London generally and Fulham Broadway in particular. It's like being in a fragrant, flourishing garden enhanced by antique sculptures and museum-quality beaded wall-hangings, glittering with intricate designs in gold thread. So don't begrudge the obligatory wait too much, just stick to conventional libations.

When your table's ready, you are escorted across a bridge over a lily pond into what appears to be a real Thai village. It is, more or less, authentically constructed of imported teak and furnished with regional antiques. A series of Thai "houses" surround a central marketplace with a babbling brook and waterfall. Certainly, such an ambitious design could have been tacky, but mercifully it's not. Instead the effect is spellbinding, the man-made splendour overshadowed only by that of the incredible flowers which are flown in weekly from Thailand.

The owners of this second location in a fledgling chain—the first Blue Elephant opened in Brussels in 1981—are rightfully proud of their establishment. Partners Manat Suyannupakon and Thaviseuth Phouthavong are usually on hand, doling out courteous hospitality in tune with their confident philosophy that once people come here, they'll return again and again.

Certainly that has been our experience. We never tire of the opulent atmosphere and the multi-dimensional flavours of the food. Five chefs contribute their specialities to the comprehensive menu, indicative of the fact that Thai cooking is an individual art, with recipes handed down through generations by word of mouth—no known printed recipes were in existence prior to World War I. The food, none of it tainted by the use of monosodium glutamates, is exquisitely presented—melons serve as salad bowls and each dish is garnished by elaborately carved fruit and vegetables. In fact, the restaurant employs two full-time food sculptors.

If your hunger is acute, order the Royal Thai Banquet Menu at £28 per person, including tax and the £1.50 cover charge. It's an extravagant repast which allows you to taste a variety of the chefs' specialities, as several dishes make up each course of the five courses. The menu is especially appropriate for large parties, which comprise a fair amount of the Blue Elephant's business. The layout is so conducive. Any one of the houses can accommodate 20 to 60 people—the entire restaurant seats 250, enormous by London standards. But it seems much smaller, made intimate by all the private enclosures. Even the fan-shy Richard Gere finds a necessary degree of seclusion here. Whether you're one, two or 40, you'll be comfortably ensconced at blue-and-white draped tables set with gleaming brass service plates and bamboo-patterned cutlery.

Should you elect the à la carte route, don't miss the lightly grilled marinated scallops served with a spicy sauce for £5.95, or the £5.25 vermicelli salad laced with chicken and prawns tossed in a lemon and fish sauce dressing. Naturally, the chicken and pork satays, £6.25 and £5.75, with their peanut sesame sweet-and-sour sauce, are state-of-the-art, as are the £4.75 spring rolls. For those who expect and like Thai food to be fiery, try the searing stir-fried pork with chilis, garlic, green peppercorns and lemon grass for £7.50. The stir-fried chicken with pineapple, baby corn and cashews at £8.50 is a suitable choice for less adventuresome souls. And no one should pass up a bowl of tom yam koong, Thailand's favourite soup—a clear broth with spiced prawns—for £6.75.

For a wide-ranging taste of Thailand, without getting involved in the banquet menu, try the £7.95 Pearls of the Blue Elephant, a selection of all-time favourites, followed by the royal platter for £14.25. Described as a "wondrous variety of main courses showing Thai cuisine at its most alluring," it miraculously lives up to the hype as an harmonious blend of flavours and textures. It may look overwhelming when first delivered, but Thai food is low-fat and light. So even if you consume every morsel, you can order dessert with temerity. Indeed, this is the only purveyor of Asian cuisine where we recommend you do so. The £3.25 coconut flan is superb and the large selection of fruit sorbets can be a refreshing finale to an impressive meal, made unforgettable by one charming parting gesture—as you leave each woman in your party is presented with a beautiful flower.   ❦

Boulestin

1A Henrietta Street   071-836-7061
London WC2E 8PS

Designated by *The Times* as one of London's most expensive eateries (ranked third among that august group), Covent Garden's best does have a lot to offer for its outrageous prices. For instance, there's the legacy of Marcel Boulestin, described in gastronomic terms as one of the most influential men of his age—a declaration backed up by *The Times'* assertion that this "most French of Frenchmen...has become almost a British national institution."

By inclination more an interior decorator and writer than a chef, Mr Boulestin's disastrous dealings with those professions forced him to hone his cooking skills to feed himself (he couldn't afford restaurants) and, eventually, others. He supported himself by catering dinner parties when his services as an interpreter for the British were no longer required after World War I. As a result of the success of his parties, he was persuaded to write a book titled *Simple French Cooking for English Homes,* a triumph in contrast to his earlier literary efforts. Indeed, his publisher commissioned a second cookbook, and his friends encouraged him to open a restaurant. He did so in Leicester Square, where his was considered the only genuine French restaurant in London.

Success was guaranteed by its unique status, by Boulestin's pioneering of an à la carte menu in a city full of restaurants offering only a table d'hôte version, and by the fact that his books were very popular. Indeed, the only sour note in this rags-to-riches scenario was the fact that the Restaurant Français, as it was succinctly called, did not have a liquor licence. A nearby pub served as the restaurant's bar—waiters scurried back and forth fulfilling customers' orders for alcoholic libations.

By 1926, the practice had become a bit old and Boulestin was open to the suggestion of a competitor (with a licence) to join forces to start a new restaurant near the Royal Opera House. Restaurant Boulestin made its auspicious debut in October of that year and was quickly adopted as a suitably glamorous haunt of London's café society. Habitués included the likes of Lloyd George, the Aga Khan, Hilaire Belloc, Sir John Gielgud and Virginia Woolf. Things haven't changed much in 65 years. The salon-like cellar restaurant (recently refurbished) is still sumptuously beautiful—fountainesque deco chandeliers, marble columns, soft shades of salmon everywhere, velvet armchairs, crisp white damask laden with oversized cutlery, and a fascinating collection of animal portraits. There is still an inordinate number of cooks most definitely *not* spoiling the pot—12 people toil in the kitchen for a full house of 80 patrons, which helps explain appetizers priced as high as £15.75. And the crème de la crème still hang out here. When Parliament is in session, everyone from Maggie Thatcher on down the political totem pole shows up for lunch, though chef/manager Kevin Kennedy says it's just as well the former prime minister is not a regular with a capital *R*—her entourage takes up too much room! Unburdened by bodyguards, Fleet Street lawyers and brokers along with Lord Sharp, Lord Young, Sir John Junor (who virtually owns Table 5 and will never sit anywhere else) and Sir Geoffrey and Lady Howe, enjoy leisurely and often impromptu lunches. They—and you—need only reserve in the morning by calling the engaging Greek maître d' who answers to the name of Andreas.

Dinner is another story in terms of reservations and clientele. It's necessary to book two to three days ahead to experience Boulestin at its most festive and rub elbows with Princess Diana (sans Charles who, it seems, seldom ventures into public restaurants—clubs are more to his taste), Princess Margaret, members of the Rothschild family and Lord Rothemere with his indefatigable Lady Mary, also known as "Bubbles."

The unabashed Frenchness of the food is another Boulestin tradition that hasn't changed with the passage of the decades. The dapper Kevin Kennedy imaginatively adheres to the heritage of Escofier, while bowing to the fact that times have changed. His menu states that any of the main courses can be simply grilled and accompanied by grilled tomatoes, mushrooms, straw potatoes and a watercress salad. Fair enough. But at a minimum charge of £35 per person at either lunch or dinner, we want fancy food. So we tend to go for the likes of the roasted pigeon at £15 and the salade de homard at £14 for hors d'oeuvres, though we have been known to select the comparatively modest-priced terrine de canard for £7.25. In any case, we can't resist the two most expensive entrées— the £16.75 tournedos and the £17.50 selle de venison. The £7.25

cheese tray never disappoints, nor does the like-priced selection of desserts, such as the luscious grapefruit mousse doused with orange liqueur. Naturally, the wine list keeps up with the food in terms of quality and price. And the service, doled out by white-aproned waiters, is meticulous.

Bottom line, Boulestin consistently delivers an impressive meal in a luxurious setting without being stuffy (despite the breathtaking bill). In fact, consistent with the restaurant's calmly civilized air, Kevin doesn't even insist on ties for gentlemen. But making a jacketless appearance is not advised.   ❦

The Capital

22 Basil Street	071-589-5171
London SW3 1AT	(FAX) 071-225-0011

We've heard Nina Campbell's decoration of this perpetually chic little restaurant, which also happens to be the dining room of its equally chic parent hotel, described as "gentle." We call it unfortunate—a wall of rose-and-cream-striped curtains, ruched to within an inch of their life, looks sloppy, and the tufted brown velour banquettes are beyond-belief bad. It's all just so strangely bland, not at all what we've come to expect from Nina. Certainly, we can't imagine it's the sort of thing the charmingly flamboyant Fergie had in mind when she engaged Britain's most famous interior designer to decorate her new home. But maybe that's the point, maybe that canny Scot, David Levin who owns the Capital, didn't want the decor to compete with the food for attention. There is, in fact, no comparison—the food presented by Philip Britten is spectacular.

Philip, a young Van Johnson with his movie-star redhead looks, arrived three years ago to take over a restaurant which has proved to be a training ground for superstar chefs—Langan's Richard Shepard and Turner's Brian Turner are but two of the Capital's alumni who have gone on to greater glory. Of course, Philip wasn't exactly an unknown when David lured him here with a remodelled kitchen, which, like the rest of the hotel, looks a lot better than the dining room. He trained under Anton Mosimann at the Dorchester and, during his sojourn at Chez Nico, earned a Michelin star in his own right. Since taking over the Capital, he's regained the star that disappeared upon the departure of his predecessor. The smart money says more stars are in his future here.

It also dictates that reservations made weeks in advance, for both lunch and dinner, are a necessity. There are only 35 seats, and we've never seen any of them empty. We've known of guests of the hotel who declined to book a table when they made their room reservations and who stayed days without ever being able to get a meal (other than breakfast, *maybe*) in the restaurant. This, despite all the best efforts of the Capital's laudable concierge.

As much as we appreciate the relatively reasonably priced lunch menus—£18.50 and £21.50—which change daily, we really prefer the Capital in the evening. In the first place, the room looks better at night. Clever lighting lends a little much-needed sparkle, and we do love the tiny nook of a bar for an apperitif. Somehow in this snuggery, with its elegantly etched mirror panels reflecting the golden patina of the "antiqued" wood panelling, even those brown banquettes are less offensive. Certainly, they're a comfortable perch from which to survey the fashionably dressed crowd to develop a consensus within your party.

You see, if you're in the company of like-minded or like-appetited souls, you may wish to partake of one of the two £46 prix fixe dinner menus. Six-course marathons, they've been known to consist of such gustatory delights as light langostine and tomato bouillon, beignets of foie gras with apples, sole and leek on a fondue of watercress and champagne, and a terrine of ceps, artichokes and foie gras. That's just for starters. Then there's the enticing possibility of roasted partridge with chestnuts in a juniper sauce or fillet of lamb knapped with a sauce of girolles and served with a confit of garlic, followed by orange sorbet and topped off by a prune and Armagnac soufflé. To assure an equitable and timely distribution of food, Phillp strongly suggests that these menus be taken by all guests in a party; hence the need for an early consensus.

If your gang is like ours, it's impossible. But rest assured that the à la carte selections are every bit as tempting. We were recently bowled over by a wild mushroom timbale, glazed with juniper and claret for £12, and the lasagna of asparagus, smoked salmon and hollandaise sauce at £13.50. We stayed struck with the delicate baked fillet of seabass in a thyme and orange sauce, and the heavenly veal sweetbreads and kidneys served with button onions and glazed with port—both £20 and tendered on oversized plates which enhanced their already extraordinary visual appeal. Still, we have to admit we were sorely tempted by the steamed fillet of brill served in a light champagne and watercress sauce at £19 and the ballotine of duck stuffed with foie gras and rilletes and sauced with ceps for £17.50 . . . which brings us to the *real* reason we prefer the Capital for an evening's repast. This is clearly a place for serious dining, for agonizing over decisions and the leisurely savouring of the final selections, for the comparing of notes and tastes with fellow diners. That's all part of the fun, and there's simply never enough time at lunch.   🌰

Le Caprice

Arlington House	071-629-2239
Arlington Street	(FAX) 071-493-9040
London SW1A 1RT	

With the exception of a six-year, much-lamented hiatus, Le Caprice has been a star in London's restaurant firmament since 1949. During the post-war years, under the supervision of Mario Galatti, it became popular as one of the few places where you could get a good meal after 9:00 P.M. Le Caprice became the stomping grounds of the theatre crowd, and Hollywood hung out here, too. Mario became one of the city's first restaurateur celebrities as he rubbed shoulders with heads of state and commerce throughout the 1950s and early 1960s. But the dawn of the 1970s brought serious competition from the trendy trattorias that sprang up all over town. Mario retired, and the restaurant limped along for a few years without him, finally closing in 1975 until its resurrection in 1981.

Le Caprice owes its second coming to the debonair Jeremy King and Chris Corbin. Veterans of such popular haunts as Joe Allen and Langan's, they determined to re-create the legend of Le Caprice as an elegant brasserie with a clubby aura. They've achieved their goal— witness the fact there's often a two-week wait for luncheon reservations during the week, even at the bar. Dinner's the same story. So if you want to experience Le Caprice on short notice, consider Saturday lunch when the demand for the restaurant's 70 seats tends to ebb.

So what's the big deal? The winning formula at Le Caprice is impeccable service and clever food at moderate prices. The sophisticated white and grey interior doesn't hurt either. Perhaps a tad bright for our taste, the room is nonetheless captivating, with its smashing black-and-white photographs by David Bailey, sleek black lacquer-framed bentwood chairs, mirrored columns and crisp white linens. The clubby atmosphere is attributable to the diners, who all seem to be very much on their own turf here, rather than to the decor. Once again the playground of the powerful, Le Caprice makes them comfortable with a nonchalant attitude toward their celebrity—no calls to the newspapers about who was seen dining here and when. No photographers are allowed on the premises, and Jeremy and Chris (one of them is always on hand) do their very best to keep the press from lurking outside the door.

They don't name names either, but suffice it to say a meal here is almost assuredly accompanied by the sighting of a famous face or two. If not, chef Mark Hix's food will more than compensate for any disappointment. On the light side, the cuisine draws from French, Italian, American and Oriental influences. Appetizers include Bang Bang Chicken—smoked and shredded, served in a peanut butter and sweet chili pepper sauce—for £4.50, and grilled squid with marinated peppers for £6.50. The caesar salad (£3.75 as a side, £5 as an entrée) is about the best in town, as is the £9.75 steak tartare. We hear the £8 salmon fishcake, served on a bed of spinach and topped with a sorrel sauce, is a perennial favourite among regulars, but we prefer the juicy grilled salmon fillet with tomato and basil for £9.75. And the £4 mousse des deux chocolats (as in white and dark) is, as they say, to die for.

Prices include tax but not service nor the £1.50 cover charge, which we find less bothersome than usual at Le Caprice. After all, where else can you get a bottle of perfectly respectable house wine for £6 (Italian, red or white) and order until midnight seven days a week? ❦

Cecconi's

5A Burlington Gardens   071-434-1509
London W1X 1LE

We've heard of three-star restaurants, we've even been to our share, but a three-king restaurant? Cecconi's is the first we've come across. The designation stems from the fact it hosted three monarchs in the same evening (not an easy feat in these democratic days)—the King of Denmark, the King of Jordan and the King of Greece. Okay, so we're stretching it a bit in terms of recognized royalty, but the Princess of Wales has lunched here on more than one occasion and no one of any consequence questions her future queen status.

In any case, none of these majestic personages shows up for the decor. There isn't any to speak of. The restaurant was once the site of a Rolls-Royce showroom, and it shows—floor-to-ceiling windows barely dressed with champagne-coloured curtains dominate the visual scene. People come for the food, which, in a city overrun with Italian restaurants,

stands out for the exemplary service and for the dignified, discreet atmosphere they're assured by owner Enzo Cecconi. A 14-year veteran of
Venice's famed Cipriani, Enzo opened in London in 1978 and was immediately embraced by a wealthy, sophisticated clientele who recognized him as (almost) one of their own with his clear blue eyes, Bulgari
watch and impeccably tailored suits.

Besides being beautifully groomed, he is the consummate restaurateur, no task too demanding, no detail too small to command his attention. One day we walked in during that limbo period between lunch and
dinner. The waiters were taking advantage of the break in the action by
setting up for the evening meal, and Enzo was . . . well, this most elegant
of men was vacuuming. It seems one of the boys on cleaning detail had
been a tad careless, missing a spot or two. When we arrived, Enzo was
showing him how to be more precise in his vacuuming pattern—how to
be meticulous enough to pass Enzo's scrutiny.

Enzo's just as fussy about his kitchen, demonstrated by the reliably
high quality of the food it presents. The pastas are made fresh daily and
should not be skipped (pass on the appetizing but not terribly interesting
antipasti if you're counting calories). Try the cannelloni Cecconi, a magnificent rendition of this traditional dish for £8.20. Either of the risottos,
vegetable or fish, is terrific for two at £16.80 and £18.60. For main
courses there are some tempting choices in the fish category, but we
tend to stick with the *carni* here. We're especially fond of the veal dishes,
notably the tart and tasty £11.80 veal piccata and the tender veal chop
served in a mushroom cream sauce for £14.80. The homemade ice
cream at £4.90 is the best of the sweets, and we're always intrigued by
the £3.70 selection of cheeses.

Typical of Enzo's commitment to service, though, you don't have to be
confined to the menu, which usually boasts two or three daily specials.
The kitchen will do its best to cater to any culinary whim, and no one
sniffs in distaste if you just want an appetizer portion of carpaccio, a salad
and a glass of wine. Enzo's smart enough to know that on your next visit
you're liable to be hungrier and indulge in a full meal, bound to cost £80
for two at either lunch or dinner (same menu) with an average-priced
bottle of wine. With one of the many exceptional bottles on the wine
list, the tab can escalate considerably. But no matter what and how much
you order, you're subject to a £2.50 cover charge. If you're seated in the
back room to the right, you won't mind because you'll be surrounded by
a fascinating group of international movers and shakers, as well as some

stunning women who may or may not be among the former. Enzo depends on their presence to ornament the non-decor. "It's the women that add the beauty," he claims; "I don't need fancy decor, they make up for it."

On the other hand, if you're placed in the front, the cover charge adds insult to injury. This is the area for unknowns. Still, don't be too hasty to leave in a huff. Getting a table, any table, at Cecconi's can be the kind of chore that tests the mettle of the city's best concierges—the restaurant is only open from Monday through Friday, and the demand is high. So as a first-timer, forgive Enzo the indignity of the front room and look forward to your next visit when you might, just might, gain entrance to the inner sanctum.   🦋

Chez Nico

35 Great Portland Street	071-436-8846
London W1 N5DD	(FAX) 071-436-0134

There's no question about the fact that this is indeed the domain of Nico—Nico Ladenis, holder of two Michelin stars and the 1988 Chef of the Year Award. The restaurant is a reflection of his very strong personality, one that does not easily suffer fools or modifiers of his cuisine (both are part of the same subspecies in Nico's view). This is not the place to order the sauce on the side. Nico simply will not serve it that way. By the same token, he is of the strongly held opinion that there is only one way to prepare meat—rare. Any request for a deviation from that standard is met with disdain. Even the use of salt and pepper is discouraged. And heaven help the boor who indiscriminately pours either without having had so much as a bite.

Fortunately, we think hot pink meat is just right, and we only use salt or pepper under the most dire, most tasteless circumstances. So we get along just fine with Nico, as does a legion of fans that keeps his 48-seat restaurant so busy that it's necessary to reserve two weeks in advance for the prime dining hours—1:00 P.M. for lunch, 8:30 to 9:00 P.M. for dinner. Folks such as Andrew Lloyd Webber, Sir Terence Conran (who's got his own pretty good eatery in the popular Bibendum), and *Daily Telegraph* owner, Conrad Black, are addicted to Nico's wizardry in the kitchen. His prowess makes this one of the best restaurants in town, where flavours are powerfully distinct, the service, overseen by wife Dinah-Jane and daughter Isabella, is first rate, and the presentation breathtaking.

Each dish, framed by simple white china with just the faintest hint of a decorative border, resembles a well-lit still-life masterpiece. No romantic, dim lighting here, Nico wants to be sure you see what you're eating. Actually, it's a tough call as to which is better served, the eye or the palate. Certainly, both are titillated by either of the fixed-price menus at lunch and dinner—one seems to stimulate the other. The £27 (including tax and gratuity) three-course luncheon will even thrill your wallet. It's a relative bargain with choices like a hearty fish soup or roast lamb salad, followed by duck breast in a Beaujolais sauce or salmon sautéed with a seasonal selection of vegetables, and capped off with one of Nico's sinful desserts—we recommend the light and luscious lemon tart.

For richer and more expensive fare, there's the £40 two-course menu, also inclusive of tax and tip. Add £8 for dessert. It's worth throwing cholesterol and budget caution to the wind and pay the £3 supplement for the terrine of foie gras served with a small leek and truffle salad. The turbot enrobed in a potato crust is an excellent complement. And a bottle from the extensive wine list completes the memorable, if pricy meal—there are only ten selections for less than £20. Most wines populate the £50 to £100 neighbourhood.

At dinner, Chez Nico truly becomes a special-occasion sort of place with a £40 menu. High rollers are reflected everywhere in the deco-esque mirrors, but they're not necessarily recognizable. People come here to eat not to be seen, which is just as well, as Nico refuses to feed items to gossip columns or allow the paparazzi to lurk outside. It's old, secure money dining here on delicacies like a pigeon hailing from Bresse in garlic cream sauce with red cabbage, and medallions of sweetbreads infused with herbs and served with sautéed mushrooms. Again, dessert adds £8 to the bill, but who's counting when you dive into a superb chocolate mousse accompanied by a pear sorbet? But do count on the cost of a babysitter. Children in dignified restaurants is another thing Nico feels strongly about—he doesn't like it.

But in all fairness, we should make it clear that Nico has made a valiant stab at creating a less forbidding restaurant, titled appropriately enough, Very Simply Nico. A self-described Parisian brasserie, the 47-seat restaurant tries hard to be informal. Still, asking for ketchup could have gotten you thrown out by chef Tony Tobin, who had paid his dues at Nico's side for five years. Now that Tony's left, we're not quite sure what the policy is on tampering with your food at the earthier, more reasonably priced piece of the Nico legend. It may be worth a visit to its Rochester Row site, close to Parliament, to find out. 🍃

Christophers

18 Wellington Street   071-495-0808
London WC2

New York has lately been a prime market for British exports, notably one Andrew Lloyd Webber and/or Cameron MacKintosh musical after another, as well as successful outposts of Floris and N. Peal. So London's recent embrace of an old New York tradition—the steak house—is very gratifying. Christophers, as in Christopher Gilmour, son of financier and former cabinet minister Sir Ian Gilmour, is modelled after Manhattan's legendary Palm, the city's preeminent purveyor of massive steaks and monster lobsters. In fact, it was the lack of a decent-sized lobster (he'd been hooked during ten years of futures trading in the U.S.) that prompted Christopher to convince some equally deprived like-minded souls to back him in the venture—his papa, international social historian and playboy Taki, journalist Charles Glass and our pal, the self-described "modest, self-effacing restaurant consultant" and PR wiz Alan Crompton-Batt among them.

With that kind of muscle behind it, not to mention a sound idea that fills more than a perceived void, Christophers is bound to be a long-running hit. The restaurant's execution of the city's first authentic Caesar salad is enough to endear it to us. And then there are those lobsters, flown in daily from the chilly waters off the coast of Maine where they grow them large, tender and sweet. Of course, we're talking about market price *and* what it will bear, but then lobster is always in a class by itself.

As for the other component of this high-class surf and turf affair, the steaks are American corn-fed beef (another London first) that are large, well-marbled and aged to melt-in-your-mouth perfection. The 10-ounce New York strip is a winner at £11.50, and if you like oysters, try the carpetbag version—8 ounces of prime stuffed with three oysters for £14. It's one of our favourites and is seldom seen, even in the U.S. Likewise, soft-shell crabs are not a staple of London's menus, so it's a special treat to find these seasonal delicacies here at £5 each.

In the starter category, we've already addressed the merits of the Caesar salad, £3.95. There's also a respectable Waldorf salad complete with apples and walnuts, also £3.95. And the £3.50 Oysters Rockefeller can't be beat, while the clam chowder, another steak-house basic, should not be ignored at £8.50.

Even the decor draws upon the American prototype. Caricatures of the investors and regulars decorate the walls just as they do at The Palm and Broadway Joe's, another venerable New York steak house. But that's where designer Emily Todhunter, who was responsible for New York's former nightspot of the moment Au Bar and who just happens to be of special significance to Taki, drew the line. The rest of her transformation of the former Inigo Jones' design has a very clean, contemporary look— no sawdust on the floor or tin ceiling.

There is, however, a fixture at the door, which even The Palm cannot lay claim to—a parking attendant. Christophers has joined the growing number of London restaurants and clubs that offer valet parking. It may be a bit of an affectation at other locations, but here in the heart of Covent Garden, where the parking situation is dismal at best, it borders on a necessity.

Naturally, in so hot a spot, reservations are equally vital, which is not to say that if you're suddenly stricken with a craving for red meat, you shouldn't give Christophers a spur-of-the-moment shot. You just might get lucky.   🍇

Clarke's

124 Kensington Church Street	071-221-9225
London W8 4BH	(FAX) 071-229-4564

We'd heard so much about this unique London restaurant, invariably described as "Californian," that we were under the impression that owner/ chef Sally Clarke did indeed hail from the West Coast of the U.S. We were wrong. Sally was born and raised on English soil. Even so, she has done time at Michael's in Santa Monica, the spawning ground of so many other successful restaurateurs. And her one-menu-a-night policy was inspired by Alice Waters' fabled Chez Panisse in Berkeley, California . . . sort of.

It seems that since she was a teenager working for a flourishing catering company in her native Guildford, Sally has fantasised about running a restaurant like a home where it would be "like cooking for my family."

Her ideal restaurant would not rely on a fixed menu or even a fixed shopping list, but would take advantage of whatever market purchases were fresh or particularly good on any given day. Sally describes her first visit to Chez Panisse as a "revelation" that such a restaurant was indeed possible—never mind that success in laid-back Berkeley and considerably more staid London are two entirely different propositions.

Her sex didn't help. There are even fewer serious female chefs in Britain than there are in the U.S. During Sally's year-long search for a space in which to turn her dream into a reality, agents often patted her on the head and suggested she open a wine bar instead. Determined, she persevered, finally finding a site and a sympathetic bank manager. Clarke's opened in 1984, paving the way for all the other eateries that would follow, which flaunt food more decorative than the environment.

That is not to suggest that Clarke's is in any way unattractive. Quite the contrary. It's simple, peach-hued decor positively sparkles with the ingenious use of natural light. And yes, something about the crisp freshness of the place, something about light, plank floors and bentwood-style chairs enlivened with a flirtatious green-and-bone-coloured cane weave, and the full view of the kitchen from one of the dining rooms does say "California."

So does the food. Most meats and fish are grilled, and absolutely everything is homemade, including the oatmeal biscuits to go with the nightly offering of British cheeses. Then there's that novel menu, which despite (or perhaps because of) its somewhat bossy approach (i.e., you eat what you are served) draws a very broad clientele—Virgin Records rockers rub elbows with aristocratic matrons, while reporters from the *Daily Mail* and *Evening Standard* compare notes with local antique dealers.

Open for lunch and dinner with Sally doing yeoman's duty as head chef and hostess throughout, the restaurant is at its purest form for the evening meal. At lunch Sally waffles a bit on her fantasy—there are choices, albeit very limited, and a fixed price of £18 for two courses and £20 for three, inclusive of service, tax, and coffee, tea or infusions. But at dinner what you see is what you get, unless you have a verifiable allergy to the evening's submission or you swear you're a vegetarian. In both instances, Sally will make allowances. Otherwise, sit back, relax and enjoy. If you find it much too nerve-racking not to have to decide anything other than the appropriate wine from the extensive list (heavy on the Californians, of course), entertain yourself by reading what diners will be eating the next night. . . or what they had the evening before. Each night, Monday to Friday, it's a different story. Sally takes a much-needed break at weekends, although she does spend much of them planning the following week's menus. All printed on a single page.

Since Sally claims every dish stems from an idea, usually a new one, and the word *recipe* doesn't exist in her vocabulary, nothing described here may ever again see the glow of the single candle on each table. Three facts are certain, though: the price is £30, inclusive; reservations made two to three days ahead are a necessity; and the food will be good, assuming you like that sort of thing. . . whatever it is.

Since tripe is about the only food known to man we can't stomach (and we've never seen it on any of Sally's menus), we're always happy with our pot's luck. One recent Monday evening, she treated us to fresh salmon marinated in dill and served over fennel, artichoke and red onion, all topped with a dill-mustard sour cream sauce. A boned, herbed veal chop grilled with a startlingly good red wine and tangerine glaze and accompanied by roasted baby potatoes with garlic and shallots followed. The cheese course and an Italian-style baked pear with mascarpone cream topped off the completely satisfying meal.

Other highlights of the week included Tuesday's breast of corn-fed chicken filled with sage and served over pumpkin and chestnut, as well as Thursday's grilled salmon with red onion wings, roasted red peppers and aioli.

Should the need for freedom of choice prove irrepressible, stifle it by wandering into Sally's shop "& Clarke's" right next door. There you can agonize to your heart's content over the nice selection of California wines, along with Sally's homemade vinegars, oils, breads and other delicacies.   ❦

Deals

Harbour Yard	071-823-3198
Chelsea Harbour	(FAX) 071-589-0936
London SW10 0XD	

Time was, not so very long ago, that you had to make the trek to Chelsea Harbour to get a Deals' deal. No longer—the boys who brought you the original hot, hip and happening hangout have replicated the formula, sans river views, in Soho. Still, sticklers for authenticity, we like the Chelsea Harbour archetype better. After all, shouldn't a place that looks like a cross between a legitimate salty seaside fish house and a sanitized outlet of a seafood restaurant chain be on the water?

Not that the menu has much to do with fish, except for the Dealers' Choice fish of the day or the prawns, which you can have one of two ways. We like them as D.I.Y. Deals, especially when we're with our gang. The *D.I.Y.* refers to "Do It Yourself," as in cook your own meal according to the ancient Korean custom of using a hot ceramic stone. Very hot! This puppy is heated to 360 degrees and then brought to your table. It's a fun communal exercise to watch those huge £8.90 Pacific prawns cook, turning from their super-fresh blue to a tasty pink. There's even more fun in store when you insist that your buddies share the wealth and order the chicken pieces at £6.50 and fillet of beef pieces for £7.80, which can also be cooked in this manner.

Actually, fun and food are what this place is all about, and the appeal is broad enough to attract a crowd almost as eclectic as the menu. At lunch, construction crowds mix amiably with Chanel-suited business-women. Later, young and old "chic-sters" crowd into the large wooden booths, which are surprisingly comfortable and offer a fair degree of pri-vacy (although there's no escaping the deafening sound system). In any case, you don't want too much privacy, because this is prime people-watching territory.

Even the owners eat here—Lord Linley (as in Viscount, the furniture-designing son of Princess Margaret and Lord Snowden) and his some-what less royal cousin, Lord Lichfield. They created Deals as an eatery with a variety of cuisines, so that a group of friends can eat there and all be assured of finding something to their individual tastes. Hence the Ko-rean cooking gimmick, along with Thai curries, Chinese spring rolls, Greek salad and a big dose of Americana.

The Dealsburgers are terrific at £4.95 for a plain one accompanied by baked potato or chips and £5.50 for the au poivre and teriyaki versions—two more countries heard from. But for us, the best deal is the £7.80 spareribs. Crispy on the outside and chewy as you bear down on the bone, they're a sizzling, sloppy sensation. Add the killer homemade coleslaw for £1.20 and you are transported to hog heaven.

And the best news is that you can take advantage of Deals take-away service and retreat to truly private quarters to make a pig of yourself. You can even do it any day of the week, as the restaurant is open all seven of them from 11 A.M. to 11 P.M., but you'd be robbing yourself of the pleas-ant company of the staff.

This United Nations of waiters is an extremely attractive articulate lot. Hailing from all over the world, they manage to be friendly without being intrusive or presumptuous. On our last visit we were waited on by a very handsome young man from Capetown who, in a deep seductive voice, informed us he was enjoying earning a living at Deals before "heading up to Oxford to study law." We guess he was earning a pretty good living at that. The place seats about 200 and is usually packed. Prices include tax but not service, although a "discretionary" 12.5 per cent is added to the bill. No doubt Michael was used to having a few more discretionary percentage points tacked onto that—Deals is so much fun, that you just can't help feeling benevolent toward your fellow men, especially those who have served you so well.   🍒

Drones

1 Pont Street	071-235-9638
London SW1X 9EJ	(FAX) 071-491-2477

Back in the long gone but not lamented days when you couldn't get a decent hamburger in London, when Wimpy's offered the only, not very accurate facsimile, several pals got together to rectify the situation—if only for their own edification. David Niven, Jr., David Gilmore, George Roberts, Bob Carrington and Nicky Kerman were in desperate need of a good burger. Furthermore, they wanted to savour it in a casually convivial atmosphere, where fellow burger aficionados could feed their habit well into the evening. Unable to find such a place, they invented it when they opened Drones in 1972. Instantly institutionalized as a breakthrough on the culinary scene, it was a success from the start.

Of the founding five, however, only Nicky really had the stomach for restaurateuring. So, in 1973, he bought out the others. Two years later he faced the devastation caused by a fire and wondered if he, too, were burnt out. But he and Drones rose from the ashes to even greater success—much to the relief of the world's professional tennis players who, during Wimbledon, had come to count on Drones to fulfil their burger fantasies. Drones is a particular favourite of John McEnroe, Bjorn Borg and Ivan Lendl.

In all probability, they appreciate not only the large juicy £8.40 hamburgers or the first-rate £10.50 chopped steak, but also the sophisticated, sassy crowd that frequents this chic greenhouse full of plants and trelliswork. The mosaic-like antique quilts that cover one wall do nothing to deaden the noise, which is considerable. But no one seems to mind it nor the fact that the tables are precariously small and uncomfortably close together. Indeed, it almost seems that because of the noise and the tight quarters, everyone is having a jolly good time. Yes, that could be Jack Nicholson's distinctive laugh you hear through the chatter—he never fails to stop in when he's in town.

To make sure you get in on the fun, call Manolo for reservations. A day in advance should do on most days, but for the very popular Sunday dinner, call by Thursday. In any case, ask for the front room—it affords the best and most interesting eavesdropping possibilities. And believe us when we tell you it's worth listening; there's lots of gossip about who did what the night before with whom (we didn't have the nerve to ask if the name Drones referred to the original owners or to the clientele). Even if you don't know the players, it's likely you'll recognize a name or two (or think you did, same score on the titillating scale), and the details are fascinating.

If the atmosphere sounds exciting, but you don't subscribe to the meat-and-potatoes theory of dining, don't despair of finding gastronomic rewards here. The fresh, imaginative salads are standouts in a country where people still speak of the "salad season," and the seafood selections are stellar. We love the grav lax for £5.95, the grilled Dover sole at £15.90, and the £12.90 salmon sautéed with oysters in their natural juices, served with a cream and mushroom sauce.

The menu is the same for lunch and dinner. We tend to prefer lunch here (the gossip is so much fresher). Either way, you're talking a minimum of about £45 to £50 for two, including a bottle of wine from the lower end of the very respectable wine list. Should you be in the enviable and always aspired-to position of having someone else pick up the tab, take note of the connoisseur wine list on the back of the menu—select the Chateau Petrus 1975 at £350 and prove that you can declare rank amongst the drove of drones. 🍒

Emporio Armani Express

| 191 Brompton Road | 071-823-8815 ext. 35 |
| London SW3 1NE | (FAX) 071-823-8854 |

When it comes to a fast bite at midday, nothing beats a pub lunch for solid, satisfying food at a gratifying price. But if you're into chi-chi, you might find the atmosphere a tad too pedestrian—in which case this café on the first floor of Giorgio Armani's Emporio Armani may be for you. It's self-consciously under-designed for the fashionable who like to feast fast. Its matte-finished hardwood floors complement the hard gleaming wood tables and the blue upholstery of the booth benches. The fact that all the seating is in those comfy booths lends some warmth to a room that otherwise comes dangerously close to being very cold.

On sunny days, the row of paned windows overlooking Brompton Road ensures lots of bright, cheerful light and an endless parade of people worth watching. During rainy weather, concentrate on the television monitor, where you can watch the video of the latest Armani collections. You might also take a good look around—on our last visit we spotted designers Bruce Oldfield and Margaret Howell. Even if no personalities are peopling any of the booths, it's invariably a very attractive crowd, deserving of your perusal. After all, besides its own parent emporium, Armani Express is right in the middle of some of the world's best shopping, just a stone's throw from Knightsbridge, Beauchamp Place and Sloane Street.

Reading the menu won't intrude on your people watching. It's short and to the point, with a nice assortment of light pastas and salads. We're fond of the homemade ravioli stuffed with a sublime mushroom mixture for £8 and the carpaccio crowned with artichoke and sprinkled with fresh parmesan at £9.50. The £8.50 insalata tropicale, assorted seafood with avocado and fruit, is another good choice. For dessert, the tiramisu looks appropriately gooey for £4. We can't attest to its taste because we categorize the Italian version of trifle with the English as dreadful. But the affable manager, Nick Larrett, assures us it's good and that it's made right on the premises. The ice-cream cake with a cup of espresso poured over it for £4 is much more to our liking.

Late in the day, a light-snack menu is available. And, of course, you're always welcome to pop in just for a cup of espresso or cappucino, as long as you do it during store hours—10:00 A.M. to 6:00 P.M., Monday to Saturday. ❦

The English Garden

10 Lincoln Street	071-584-7272
London SW3 2TS	(FAX) 071-581-2848

The first time we strolled into the English Garden we were both struck with the same thought—the Box Tree. Malcolm and Colin Livingstone's little jewel of a restaurant reminded us of the Box Tree, Manhattan's most unabashedly lavish romantic restaurant. Both occupy townhouse settings in essentially residential neighbourhoods and, in fact, are done up to look like private homes, albeit very fancy ones worthy of the pages of *Interiors,* which has waxed poetic about both. But the resemblance goes beyond the decor, which admittedly stops just short of being too precious: both benefit from the benevolent dictatorship of their owners (who even know each other), and they both serve very fine food, indeed.

They even share the not-so-envied reputation of being tourist traps, a reputation somewhat deserved by the Box Tree. It is outrageously expensive, and we don't know any natives who actually go there, certainly not on anything that could be considered a regular basis. On the other hand, the English Garden, while not cheap, is not an arm-and-a-leg relative to other restaurants of its ilk. Furthermore, it attracts a clientele of frequent diners made up of neighbourhood types, as well as banking and insurance folks who like to throw private parties there. They don't want to be surrounded by colonials oohing and ahing at the quaintly cosy beauty of the place with its fabric-covered walls highlighted by marvelous dried-flower arrangements as artwork, multiple fireplaces and candlelit tables.

Consequently, the Livingstone brothers are careful to keep a balance between locals and tourists, which is to everyone's benefit. Actually, the last time we visited, we seemed to be the only foreigners—unusual in so highly rated a restaurant, which along with its sister property the English House was a forerunner in the renaissance of English cooking. Here you'll find what Colin describes as "fancy nursery food," which is at once familiar and exciting. As he points out, there's a fine line between how homelike the food can be and "what is not considered good enough" for dining out in an elegant restaurant.

But to satisfy the clientele, he and Malcolm manage to keep just the right equation on a menu that changes seasonally. Not that they're the ones actually doing the cooking—that is left to the chef. Rather, Colin says that he and his brother are "good at picking up dead flowers and plumping up pillows." They're also extraordinarily charming hosts who make you feel very welcome. Usually, it's Colin who's on hand here to escort you up the narrow staircase to the top-floor sitting room, where you can indulge in a cocktail as you study the menu or the marbled ceiling. It's a good system. You don't feel as though you're in a holding-pen bar, and you get to take a peek at most of the English Garden's series of small dining rooms on the way up.

Each is lovely. But we're partial to the one you don't see—the conservatory at the rear of the ground floor. Back in 1981, when Malcolm and Colin took over the building, it was a lean-to. They have transformed it into a glass-domed wonderland which would have tickled Alice's fancy. What better place could there be to nestle into as you contemplate succulent home-cured boar with horseradish cream at £6.50 or a subtle, light mushroom custard filled with various wild fungi and served hot with a Madeira cream sauce for £8.75? True to the nursery-food school, liver is on the menu, and it's divine—you don't even have to ask for it rare. It comes that way and is just as tender as it can be, accented by a tasty onion marmalade for £12.50. Now, we realize liver isn't everyone's cup of tea, but who could resist homemade sausages accompanied by a black currant relish at £7.75 or scallops of beef with oysters, served in a stout (as in Guinness) sauce at £15.25?

If you eschew red meat, don't despair. You'll find chicken and fish on the menu and maybe a vegetarian dish like the unique and yummy artichoke-and-custard pudding topped with melted cheese for £8.25. Speaking of puddings, if you have a taste for trifle, we hear the English Garden's is one of the best. Of course, we never touch the stuff, opting instead for the brandied mincemeat wrapped in crisp filo and served with clotted cream. It's just as sinful as it sounds, and so rich it serves two very nicely for £5.

Lunch is a deal here at £13.75 for three courses, including tax but not service. However, you are cheated out of the romance that evening brings to the English Garden. Still, if you're in the neighbourhood, you can't do much better at that price for a filling meal of wood pigeon and pheasant salad tossed with a red currant vinaigrette followed by a fish pie topped by creamed potatoes and ended by a selection of regional cheeses.

As for reservations, for either lunch or dinner plan on a couple days' notice.

Four Seasons

Hamilton Place   071-499-0888
Park Lane   (FAX) 071-493-1895
London W1A 1AZ

We'll never forget the day word first leaked that the Four Seasons, the signature restaurant of the much-acclaimed Inn on the Park, was about to be anointed with its first Michelin star. As luck would have it, we were dining at the Four Seasons, and the usually tranquil atmosphere was charged with electricity as the tom-tom drums of the restaurant community's rumour mill spread the news throughout the staff. The waiters were literally bursting with pride, dying to tell their customers but never presuming to do so. We were only let in on the secret by virtue of Vinicio, the debonair maître d', who knew it was our business to know such things.

In any event, even if the starring of the Four Seasons had been shouted from the rooftops, it is unlikely the lunchtime crowd would have evidenced much surprise. Of course, they would have understood what a singular honour it is for a hotel restaurant to be so recognized by the picky folks at Michelin, but in their book the Four Seasons had long been a winner, worthy of very regular patronage—the business people who frequent it at lunch often do so two or three times a week.

The less loyal social butterflies alight at night, but they all come for the same thing that earned the restaurant the star, the stylish but resolutely unfussy cooking of Bruno Loubet who has held sway here since 1988. During that time he has developed quite a reputation for his "Cuisine du Terroir," which he learned to love at his mother's table in Libourne, a village in the fabled countryside of France's Bordeaux region. Indeed, he developed such an early respect and appreciation for food that he wanted to be a chef for as long as he can remember. By the age of 12, Bruno was working in a pâtisserie, and he continued to pursue his dream through college, apprenticeship at restaurants in Brussels and Paris, and a stint in the French Navy, where he became head chef for the Admiral's table.

Bruno's 1982 move to London to work at Gastronome One in Chelsea proved providential. His fondness for real food relying on the freshest (but not most expensive) ingredients and combinations of flavours with a proven historical reference, rather than the ridiculous concoctions of so many of his contemporaries, began to attract attention. The *Good Food*

Guide named him "Young Chef of the Year" in 1985, and he was on his way to stardom, despite not having paid his dues with the Roux brothers.

Having secured Bruno's services in a bid to elevate the already enviable standing of the Four Seasons, Ramon Pajares, the general manager of the Inn on the Park, decided to give him a new, grander setting for the presentation of his culinary efforts. Ramon banished the handsome if boring cream-and-beige decor in favour of a more striking grey and pink scheme, which basks in the remarkable light afforded by the giant windows overlooking the Inn's private garden and Hyde Park beyond. The exciting contrast of deep pink tablecloths and a black-patterned carpet, softened by an abundance of exotic foliage, mirrors the exhilarating, boisterous quality of Bruno's cooking—turnip ravioli filled with wild mushrooms, slightly smoked fresh salmon served hot on creamed potatoes with veal jus, and roast saddle of rabbit with sun-dried tomatoes and braised vegetables.

Nowhere is he more inspired than with his nightly Dîner Surprise menu—four courses, including a glass of dessert wine, coffee, tax and service for £40—which may or may not include any of the above. It is always and absolutely a complete surprise. No amount of bribing will induce your waiter to reveal its offerings. So, if you hate surprises, stick to the printed à la carte menu, the same for lunch and dinner. There you'll find delicacies like a warm prawn salad with crispy vegetables in a delicate coral dressing for £18 and a celeriac tarte tartin flavoured with black truffles at £9.75 as appetizers. For the second course, though we know Bruno has a fine way with fish, we tend to stick with the meat selections where his country roots are put to best use. The £21.50 roast breast of wild duck in an unusual tangerine and brandy sauce is a must, as are the roasted sweetbreads glazed with Madeira and truffles and served with a rosemary infused sauce for £21.

As you might imagine, the desserts are the stuff that dreams are made of—goodies like white chocolate mousse in a thin chocolate leaf served with candied fruit ice cream, and paper-thin puff pastry topped with warm apples flavoured by honey and thyme.

Clearly not for the calorie conscious. But in keeping with the Four Seasons Hotels and Resorts' policy of tendering spa cuisine for those so inclined, there is a selection of "alternative" dishes. And if you're budget conscious, try the restaurant for lunch when a fixed-price £23 menu is offered, inclusive of tax and service. Better yet, take advantage of the

Four Seasons as one of the very few restaurants of this calibre open on Sunday, and indulge in the £25 supper. It's an ideal way to end the week-end, or begin the week.

We like to come early and stay late, watching the natural light fade on the fresh flowers that adorn every table, while ensconced in one of the rounded banquettes that occupy the corners of the large rectangular room. And, yes, we know the tables in front of the windows are considered prime, but we like the banquettes better. They're so very comfortable. Besides, they offer an excellent vantage point from which to ogle the beautiful collection of decanters displayed throughout the restaurant—souvenirs of the general manager's worldly wanderings.

Just remember that whenever you choose to dine here, the decision cannot be made at the last minute. Reservations should be made at least 48 hours in advance.   🍒

Gay Hussar

2 Greek Street   071-437-0973
London W1V 6NB

Opened in 1954 the name of this perennial Hungarian favourite predates any sexual connotation of its name. If anything, the interior of the narrow, circa 1836 house it occupies is a vintage study in machismo—smoke-darkened walls, rough-hewn wood banquettes softened by red velvet upholstery, tables simply set with heavy hotel plate and crisp white linens. Just the sort of clubby place where the hearty-eating and heavy-drinking mostly male clientele feel at home.

At lunch the restaurant is considered a cheaper version of the Savoy Grill. The three tiny rooms—each on its own floor—are always crowded with politicians, mostly from the Labour Party, attended by the usual flotilla of journalists. They, in turn, have a following of writers and publishers, whose books constitute the principal decoration in a proud display over the miniscule service bar in the street level dining room. Whatever their profession, most stick to the £14.50 three-course meal (including tax), seldom even bothering to look at the à la carte selections. The set menu has a gratifying number of choices, as many as 20 main courses in fact. The list of appetizers is shorter but only just, including such central European treats as chilled wild cherry soup, pressed boar's head pâté, mixed vegetable and sausage salad, pickled herring, Hungarian bean soup and more.

The inventory of entrées runs the gamut: chicken pancakes in paprika sauce, Hungarian goulash, baked minced veal with savoy cabbage, smoked sausage doused with paprika, and succulent roast goose, served with red cabbage and Hungarian potatoes are typical highlights. As for dessert, they're all good—it's a tough call between the chestnut purée, poppy seed strudel and the lemon sweet cheese pancakes.

If you're unfamiliar with Hungarian food, ask your waiter for advice. Most have been here for decades and are therefore well-versed in the cuisine. Our favourite, Stephen, has been here since the restaurant opened, and Albert, whose Lilliputian domain is the first-floor room up the one-person-wide stairway, has been here for 31 years. At 75, this distinguished-looking gentleman continues to perform his duties with the same theatrical flourish which once attracted Adolf Hitler's attention. He has a number of devout followers who will sit only in his room. Indeed, most midday frequenters of the Gay Hussar feel very strongly about one room or the other (the third room is used for private parties like the one Lord Callaghan, the former prime minister, was hosting the last time we lunched here) and have territorial rights to certain tables. And, in fact, most daily diners have territorial rights to their "own" tables.

Consequently, reservations for lunch are a must. Manager John Wrobel, whose portrait graces the menu, says you can often get away with calling a day ahead, but 48-hours notice is a safer bet. Dinner's an altogether different proposition—it's easier to get a table and the atmosphere is less power-charged. In fact, it gets downright familial, which seems only right and proper given the comforting nature of the food. As John points out, the food reminds him of his grandmother's cooking, even though she was Polish. And, indeed, its gusto somehow reminds you of everyone's grandmother's cooking. Of course, in John's case, it doesn't hurt that head chef Lazlo Holecz is Polish, too.

At dinner, it's à la carte only from a menu that follows the fixed-price menu's lead—the choices are myriad. Try the £4.05 vegetable and sausage salad or the goose and pork pâté at £3.15 as an hors d'oeuvre. The classic wiener schnitzel at £12.50 and the £11 medallions of pork cooked with diced bacon, onions, potatoes and green paprika are excellent entrées. And two like-minded people can't go wrong with the Transylvanian mixed grill served on a wooden platter for £29.

Again, desserts are worthy of consideration, especially the £3.80 walnut soufflé and the raspberry and chocolate cake for £3.50. But be sure to keep a mental tally of what you're spending (around £30 each for the whole nine yards and a bottle of wine), unless you have an American Express card—it's the only credit card the restaurant takes. If you're caught short of cash, you'll have to work it out with John. Now, we're sure he'll make every effort to minimize your embarrassment, but why put yourself in that position in the first place?   ❦

Le Gavroche

43 Upper Brook Street	071-499-1826
London W1Y 4EB	(FAX) 071-409-0939

Le Gavroche is to London what Lutece is to New York—a temple of the best French haute cuisine at equally "haute" prices. It has more Michelin stars than any other place in town, three to be precise. However, for our minimum of £45 per person at dinner, Le Gavroche has it all over its counterpart in the U.S. in the decor department. It's sumptuously beautiful, a sea of muted rose and moss green which manages to be both extremely feminine, yet thoroughly masculine and absolutely dignified.

This is definitely a place where one is expected to worship food. Still, there is a warmth here due in large measure to the gnomish joviality of maître cuisinier de France, Albert Roux. Arguably the best French chef in Britain, certainly the most famous, Albert's easy manner and ready smile belie his deadly serious pursuit of perfection, from the finest ingredients to the most lavish of table settings. True, he's not as omnipresent as he used to be, because he's travelling quite a bit these days—business, don't you know. But his indelible stamp remains, most notably and importantly in the kitchen, where son Michel now reigns supreme, except, of course, when papa's in town. Indeed, since Michel is truly his father's son when it comes to culinary artistry, we can't quibble too much about Albert's frequent absences.

He deserves a break. He's been cooking since the age of 14 when he began a two-year apprenticeship at the Patisserie Lecler, St Mande, Seine. Albert first came to London to work in the kitchen of Lady Astor and ended up cooking for the French Embassy. Meanwhile, his brother Michel also embarked on the road to chefdom at age 14 and soon found himself in the employ of Cecile de Rothschild. Having practised their craft and learned the elegance ropes from two of Europe's most gracious households, they were ready to open their first restaurant in 1967. Today, the Roux brothers are the proud possessors of more of those Michelin stars than most any two restaurateurs around—Michel operates the legendary Waterside Inn and Albert, along with lovely wife Monique, has opened a small hotel next door to Le Gavroche, which is a winner in the luxury sweepstakes. (See Fortyseven Park Street in the hotel section.)

Now, while the restaurant is owned by Albert, the man with the real power here, the man you'll want to make your new best friend, is Silvano Giraldin. As maître d' he decides who gets a table, when and where. It's a thankless job, with all those high-powered business tycoons so anxious to do their deals here at lunch and all the fashionable socialites wanting to be seen at dinner. Necessarily, Silvano runs a tight ship, and you'd best play by his rules if you want to sample Le Gavroche's supreme French cuisine. Start by calling three to four days ahead for lunch, a full week for dinner, and make sure to reconfirm the day before. If you don't, your reservation will be given away. Ditto, if you're half an hour late and haven't called. When a meal at Le Gavroche is on your agenda, portable telephones become more than an affectation. They become a necessity, due to London's all-too-frequent traffic snarls.

So what's all the fuss about? Well, at lunch Le Gavroche offers what may be the city's best gastronomical bargain—a £27.50 four-course menu full of difficult choices. Fortunately, dining à deux, we each got a taste of everything—the mussel and escargot salad in a parsley-laden dressing, as well as the terrine of duck and foie gras made crunchy with pistachios for a first course. Then there was the picture perfect "pave," as in diamonds (menu writing has become an art form in itself), of cod resting on a potato mousseline knapped with a lobster sauce, and the lamb sautéed with lentils and sage. Next came cheese for one of us, a pear soaked in red wine for the other, and we both delighted in the pretty little petits fours served with coffee.

For dinner, there's that £45 minimum, which is a moot point if you opt for the seasonal and aptly named menu, exceptional for £55, inclusive of service and tax. But at least two people in your party have to order it, so if you're à deux, stick with the à la carte menu in order to taste as many of the kitchen's offerings as possible. It's changed twice a year, and there are always intriguing daily specials like ravioli stuffed with ceps, and woodcock, "perfumed" with truffles for £21.30. Indeed, novel combinations are the kitchen's trademark—the cuisine may be haute here, but it is far from predictably classic. Take the £18.80 pear flan served with coquilles St Jacques as an hors d'oeuvre, or the "symphonie" of poached seafood in a lobster sauce on a bed of fried celery as an entrée for

£27.50. More traditional, but still benefitting from the innovative Roux interpretation, are the roast duck for two at £50.60 and the veal kidneys with three mustards for £26.50.

The bottom line is that you're in for at least £70 a person with dessert and a simple wine, but you're also in for an evening that approaches perfection...that is, unless your party is on the large side or you prefer to pay with American Express. We know of one gentleman whose greatly anticipated dinner was tarnished at the start when his nine guests were divided between two tables, and ruined when he tried to settle the bill (in excess of £1,000) with American Express. Yes, they *take* the card, they just don't like to accept it. In this case, leave home without it! ❧

Green's Restaurant & Oyster Bar

| 36 Duke Street | 071-930-4566 |
| London SW1Y 6DF | (FAX) 071-930-1383 |

When Simon Parker Bowles decided to switch careers, he sidled into a new profession for which he was uncommonly well prepared. As a wine merchant, he knew all about a major profit centre for most restaurants and had spent a great deal of time in various dining establishments. Actually, too much time in the heyday of nouvelle cuisine. He often left unsatisfied. It was 1970, and Simon yearned for a restaurant that served good basic English fare accompanied by fine wines, particularly champagnes. So he opened one.

The original Green's offered a substantial selection of cold foods and wine—oysters, smoked fish, roast beef and ham platters. You could graze at Green's before the term had been coined. You still can in the clubby bar which now serves as the entrance to a more formal Green's, the result of a 1984 expansion. It seems that when the shirt shop next door became available, Simon couldn't resist the temptation to expand upon his hugely successful concept and open a restaurant that served hot, as well as cold sustenance.

As such, the new improved Green's is great. But we still love the panelled booths in the bar. We settle into their comfortable privacy to chow down on a little of this and a little of that, washed down with a bottle of their commendable private label, non-vintage champagne—£20 for a bottle, £40 for a magnum. In the "this and that" category, we like the hearty £4.50 Scotch eggs (one of only three things in this world that should ever be referred to as "Scotch," and a person hailing from Scotland is not one of them). The chicken liver pâté laced with port and dotted with green peppercorns for £4.50 is another favourite, along with the kipper pâté at £4.50. And if we visit between September 1 and April 30, we never fail to order Green's special Irish oysters, £13 for a half dozen.

When we venture into the handsome restaurant proper, boasting more booths (larger than many efficiency apartments) and well-spaced tables, we're always impressed by the attractive crowd sizzling with high-powered vibrations—Green's gets more than its share of members of the royal family and other assorted aristocracy. They enjoy the civilized atmosphere that ensures they won't be disturbed by the curious or the merely rude. No one bothers business moguls like British Airways chairman Lord King, or show-biz heavyweights such as Andrew Lloyd Webber, Dustin Hoffman, Albert Finney and Steve Martin.

The sophisticated clientele is much more interested in chef Beth Coventry's classic British cuisine. She creates a daily à la carte menu that complements Green's standards—first-rate fish cakes served with a parsley or tomato sauce for £7 or bangers and mash (read sausages and mashed potatoes) for £7.50. There's an interesting bit of trivia attached to the very flavourful bangers served here. Called Porkinson's, they're made by a concern founded by the late world-famous photographer Norman Parkinson. As for the daily specials, you're likely to find a soothing £3.50 warm cheese tart or cream of vegetable soup at £2.50. Follow either with a scrumptious steak, kidney and mushroom pie for £8, or a £9.50 roast lamb fillet enlivened by garlic and grain mustard and a red currant sauce. You'll understand why we think Green's is (British) nursery food nirvana—albeit an up-market one at £65 to £70 for two with a bottle of the house champagne.

And the good news is that Green's is one of the few non-pub establishments in this tony neighbourhood that's open at weekends and for Sunday lunch. Not that we have anything against pubs, quite the contrary in fact, and neither does Green's. Indeed, Simon encourages convivial evening gatherings in the bar where stockbrokers and secretaries mingle in a very pubby fashion—everyone seems to know everyone else, as is the case in the club-like atmosphere of the dining room. But it's an easy enough club to join. Just pick up the telephone and call general manager David Vickerstaff to book a table. If you'd prefer the bar's lighter provisions and want a booth, you'd best reserve that, too.   🍃

Grill St Quentin

2 Yeoman's Row   071-581-8377/6064
London SW3 2AL

The St Quentin phenomenon marches on (see Restaurant St Quentin) with this dining addition—or rather expansion. The grill incarnation of the very prosperous chain that concentrates on French components was already established and immensely popular. So popular in fact that it quickly outgrew its original site. A former parking garage and health club capable of seating 150 proved more suitable than the former location, just down the street, and opened as the "new" Grill in November 1989. But change of venue aside, no one's tampering with what made the old Grill such a success in the first place—"a simple menu of good value and quality grilled fish and meat," according to managing dirctor, Didier Garnier.

A stickler for authenticity—all the staff and most of the ingredients are imported from France—Didier wanted the look of the Grill to approximate that of his beloved Parisian bistros. So he took interior designer Kate Osborne on a field trip to the French capital—her first—to effect the desired results. Kate must be a fast learner, because the Grill is comfortably reminiscent of La Coupole, without being a direct copy. And like its inspiration, the stylish simplicity and the clean lines of the interior match the clear flavours of the food.

Given its location close to Harrods and the other thriving businesses of Knightsbridge and Chelsea, it's not surprising that lunch is the hot ticket here. Crowded to the point of bursting at the seams by 1:00 P.M.— don't even think about showing up without calling a day or two ahead— the restaurant is, nonetheless, a cheery reassuring midday haven. This probably has a lot to do with the intriguing colour and texture combinations. The palest of yellow walls take on authority with a dabbled appearance resulting from careful "rag-rolled" handpainting. Silvery sky blue velour covers the banquettes which are divided by commanding columns—wood surrounds define the lower half; arresting blue and gold marbelizing, the upper. And, of course, there's plenty of gleaming brass and mirrors to reflect the attractive countenances of Roger Moore, Simon Callow, the Duchess of Kent and the ubiquitous Michael Caine.

We wonder if they're as addicted to the pommes frites as we are. Served with all the grills and main courses, they are nothing short of sensational—McDonald's, move over. Besides the fries, we're partial to the Grill's £3.20 version of fish soup and the stuffed artichoke at £4.10. While the plats du jour are often tempting, we can't ever pass up the potted duck, done to perfection for £8.60. Which brings up an interesting point. While the young staff are enthusiastic and friendly, their English is often less dependable than their service. Consequently, the menu thoughtfully offers a French/English guide to ordering meat. This is a far cry from Chez Nico; no one here will throw a fit if you ask for your £8.50 leg of lamb "bien cuit" (well done), but these kids are French and therefore innately sensitive to such issues—you get away with just dampening their spirits.

Matters of cuisine protocol aside, we also usually opt for the tender smoked chicken stew for £8.50, leaving plenty of room for dessert—cheese in this instance, as Didier's selection lives up to the Grill's 1989 award for Best Cheese. Make sure you sample the bread as well—Didier won a best award for that, too. He should also be honoured for good sense for his policy of no cover charge. A 12.5 per cent service charge is added to the bill, but according to the menu it's not obligatory.

Bottom line, including the tax that's factored into the prices, lunch tends to cost less than £20 per person. Expect to pay closer to £25 for dinner when you're likely to indulge in more food or wine. Of course, it's a fine line between the two here because the menu remains constant, and the restaurant remains open, all day from noon to midnight, Monday to Saturday. In fact, to avoid the lunch bunch, we've been known to combine the two meals at supper in the 5:00 P.M. neighbourhood. It makes for an early evening, but allows for a full day of constructive activity. Another one of life's little trade-offs.　　　　　　　　　　　　　　　　❦

The Guinea

30 Bruton Place   071-499-1210
London W1X 7AA

As a denomination of British currency, the guinea no longer exists—as a purveyor of food and drink, The Guinea is omnipresent, on Bruton Place at least. There's The Guinea as pub, The Guinea as restaurant, and then there's the Guinea Grill. But our interest lies principally with the restaurant, and in passing with the pub—the adjacent Guinea Grill is in no way associated with either, simply taking advantage of the reputation of the former and the history of the latter. There has been an ale house on the land now occupied by the pub since King Charles II first introduced the guinea coin.

That The Guinea restaurant is, in fact, a grill room which is entered through the lounge of The Guinea public house further muddies the waters for first-timers. But for the legions of regulars who count on The Guinea for a simple, satisfying meal in a comfortable setting, there's no confusion. Princess Margaret, Elizabeth Taylor, Charlton Heston and Frank Sinatra nod to the locals as they stroll through the pub, heading straight for the astounding display of fresh meats and seafood that marks the entrance to the restaurant. There, they make their selections and instruct the grill chef, Antonio, on how to prepare them. Then they place themselves in the solicitous hands of Vincenzo, the maître d' who generally seats them in the garden room off to the side. The appellation stems from the fact that the room occupies what was once the back yard of the property and, in fact, once sported some rather dreary plastic flowers strung across the skylights.

These days, it looks like the rest of the restaurant, comfortably sophisticated with wooden wainscoting meeting pale yellow dappled walls decorated with tasteful prints. An ornate antique mantle clock serves as focal point, but we haven't the foggiest notion about whether it actually works. Here, you don't watch that or any other clock—The Guinea is a time-honoured bastion of civilized, leisurely dining where the waiters are less formally stiff than at other, similarly exclusive institutions, where the food is always good, and where the menu never changes.

This is the restaurant of choice for the cognoscenti in search of a succulent steak cooked to perfection—rump cut priced at £12, sirloin for £15, and fillet at £19, each garnished with grilled tomato, mushrooms and watercress. We usually spring for the tasty £1.95 fries and balance the meal with vegetable starters—an artichoke dressed with a tangy vinaigrette for £4.50 or fresh asparagus topped with a piquant hollandaise sauce at £9.50. All prices include tax, but not the £1.25 cover or the 12.5 per cent service charge which are automatically added to the bill. And what's a steak without a good bottle of red wine? So count on driving the bill up by as much as £269.50 for a 1947 Savigny les Beaunes Burgundy, or as little as £7.75 for the house red from the large and very international wine list.

Naturally, reservations are advisable, but the situation here is usually fluid, since going to The Guinea is often an impromptu decision induced by overindulgence in the city's temples of haute French and Italian cui-

sine. Furthermore, if you show up and Vincenzo is unable to accommodate you, there's always the pub to retreat to for a perfectly respectable
and predictably simple repast. And isn't that what you came for?   🍒

Hard Rock Café

| 150 Old Park Lane | 071-629-0382 |
| London W1Y 3LN | (FAX) 071-629-8702 |

You've seen the T-shirts on tight young bodies all over the world—the
distinctive feel-good logo emblazoned across the front, or back. Now experience the originator of the Hard Rock phenomenon. Yes, this chain
devoted to the best of American down-home cooking has its roots in
London, where Isaac Tigrett of Jackson, Tennessee, opened the first
Hard Rock Café on June 14, 1971. Twenty years later, it remains a mecca
for believers the world over in the company's "Love All—Serve All"
motto.

Yes, the music is too loud, and you suffer the glare of popping flash-
bulbs from dozens of tourist-held cameras, but the food is good, the
prices reasonable, and (until Cleveland, U.S., got in the act to revitalize
its stagnant downtown) it was the site of the planet's only rock-'n'-roll
museum. Actually all the Hard Rocks are chock full of what Sotheby's
calls the "largest collection in the world of musical memorabilia." Much
of it is on permanent display as the decor of each of the restaurants,
while some very special pieces like Keith Richards' five-string guitar and
B.B. King's legendary "Lucille" go on tour throughout the chain.

Most of all, the Hard Rock is fun. There's an ardent energy that even
infuses the inevitable queues. Once seated at a red-and-white check covered table in the cavernous room—shoot for one of the elevated sections
to the right or left of the centre pit—the sociable waitresses decked out
in '50s diner best (right down to pert little triangular caps) make you feel
right at home. Despite the constant clamouring for a table, they give you
ample time to wade through the not inconsequential menu and are likely
to offer unsolicited opinions on your selections. They won't quibble if
you order any of the world-class burgers—£4.95 for a third of a pound
sans topping, to £6.25 for a half-pound "down home double burger" with
any combination of cheese, bacon and barbecue sauce—served with
large, crispy fries and a salad. We have, however, noticed them arch an
eyebrow at a request for the fruit and avocado salad with cottage cheese
for £7.

Somehow, it's just not a salad sort of place. Head for the Hard Rock to satisfy a hearty, though not necessarily healthy, craving for hickory smoked ribs at £7.95, accompanied by creamy cole slaw and fries. Finger-lickin' good, as is the £6.20 "pig" sandwich, the old southern delicacy of "pulled" (read shredded) pork served on the Hard Rock's homemade ice-box bread.

This is also the place to go when you're having guacamole withdrawal. We've been known to sit for as long as our eardrums can stand it in one of the oversized wooden booths of our favourite section, known as "F," consuming several £3.25 orders of their excellently spiced rendition, our gusto encouraged by a first-rate margarita or two (or three). Strung along the Old Park Lane side of the room, "F" is relatively bereft of the gold records, autographed pictures and concert posters that litter the restaurant, but it sports a window wall that broadens the people-watching possibilities. If you get tired of the eclectic crew inside—from jeaned gawkers to business-suited regulars—you can peruse the passing parade on Piccadilly.

Open seven days a week from 11:30 A.M. to 12:30 in the morning, the Hard Rock is always a safe, sure bet for a satisfying meal, as long as you're armed with cash—no credit cards accepted.   🎐

Harry's Bar

26 South Audley Street   071-408-0844
London W1Y 5DJ   071-491-1860

Mark Birley is a great one for naming successful clubs after people—his ex-wife, himself and Harry MacElhone. Harry MacElhone? You know Harry. Or at least you know his bar, the first of the world's many Harry's Bars which opened in Paris in 1911. Harry not only invented an institution still going strong under the ownership of his son (which in turn spawned the most famous Harry's Bar, the one in Venice) but also introduced the hot dog to Europe and is credited with inventing the Bloody Mary and the sidecar.

So as usual, Mark knew what he was doing when he teamed up with James Sherwood, the head of Sea Containers who put glamour back into travel with the Venice-Simplon Orient Express, to open his third private membership club. James didn't want to call it Harry's Bar, but Mark persisted, knowing the name signified a rich tradition of good food, drink and camaraderie—just the equation to make Harry's Bar the unqualified success it has been since the day it opened.

Of course, it's much more patrician than its Parisian predecessor. Here, green Fortuny fabric and marbeled wainscoting take the place of smoke-stained panelling on the walls, graceful wooden chairs made comfortable by plump chintz-covered pillows fill the seating void created by the too occasional stool, and crisp white damask covers tables that are bare in the City of Lights.

After all, this is a bar (read restaurant) frequented by royalty. Harry's counts King Hussein of Jordan as a member. King Constantine of the Hellenes is one, too. And it's not unusual to see Princesses Margaret and Michael dining here, though it might cause a bit of a stir if they were doing so together. Then there is royalty of the show-business kind like Sean Connery, Roger Moore, Cubby Broccoli (the producer of their collective 007 movies) and David Frost.

They fill up the former wine merchant's shop daily to indulge in the excellent fare produced by chef Romano Resem's kitchen. The Italian menu reflects James Sherwood's original intention of venturing into the London restaurant game with a Venetian eatery called Cipriani after the legendary hotel he owns, which was named after the family that founded it who *still* own the Harry's Bar off St Marco's square. Talk about things coming round full circle!

At any rate, the food is as much a draw as the panache. No less an expert than the dapper chronicler of royal activity, Nigel Dempster, claims it's the best Italian food outside Venice. Both lunch and dinner are served here by the unfailingly courteous (all Polish) waitresses. We prefer lunch, partly because the light of day makes it easier to read the captions of the valuable collection of Peter Arno cartoons. Since *The New Yorker* has long been our favourite magazine, this little touch of home-grown humour makes Harry's Bar especially lovable to us. It's even enough to make us forgive the £2.50 cover charge on top of prices which range from £13 to £19 for pasta and £19.50 to £23 for main courses, *not* including service.

For appetizers we tend to stick with the tried and true: flavourful prosciutto with melon and avocado for £14 and carpaccio dressed with a green sauce at £14.50. If we're of a mind for pasta, the ravioli stuffed with mushrooms and topped with a fresh tomato sauce infused with rosemary is usually our choice for £14. Otherwise, we head straight for the £20 veal piccata and the £19.50 delicately sautéed salmon. And we virtuously skip dessert in favour of an order of steamed vegetables for £6.

Not surprisingly, there's a list of top-drawer Italian wines to complement the food. Consuming a bottle at lunch is not our usual style, but at Harry's, it's hard to resist, considering the serene surroundings of people *and* decor. Wine is an integral part of that Harry's Bar equation that makes a meal here such a jolly good time.   🍎

Hilaire

68 Old Brompton Road   071-584-8993
London SW7 3LQ

We've dogged Dustin Hoffman's steps through most of the best restaurants in New York and London, and he's never steered us wrong. Any place good enough for Dustin is good enough for us; but in the case of Hilaire, he goofed, not because he went there, but because he didn't. You see, when we left this pretty little shop-front restaurant, feeling all warm and fuzzy as a result of the excellent food and service, we happened upon a taxi driver who asked us rather pointedly how we had liked it. After obligingly listening to our enthusiastic babbling, he told us that just the night before he had brought "an American movie star" by, who had asked him to drive on after taking a rather cursory glance at the unprepossessing exterior. The poor man must have thought we were daft when we burst into uncontrollable giggles at his confirmation of our speculation whether the star in question was our old pal Dustin.

Since we have it on pretty good authority that he's no snob, our guess is that Dustin was less concerned about the look of the place than he was about the fact that the eight tables on street level are in full view of all passing foot and vehicular traffic—which is considerable given the restaurant's chic location. He must have envisioned a meal made miserable by curious fans. He shouldn't have been so hasty in his assessment of the dining logistics. Had Dustin got out of the taxi and gone in, he would have discovered that Hilaire boasts a downstairs dining room where the possibilities of privacy are compounded by the presence of two very secluded booths.

He also would have been treated to the sunny greeting of Jenny Webb, whose husband Bryan has been Hilaire's chef for the last three-and-a-half years. Now the engaging 30-year-old Welshman is also the owner, having persuaded Jenny they should sell everything they owned to purchase the place in early 1990. Good on you, Bryan—we're sure it was the right decision. Hilaire is such a charming, intimately manageable restaurant, just the right sort of place for a young couple to cut their entrepreneurial teeth. Indeed, under the Webbs' patronage, the establishment's always respectable business has improved to the point where reservations should be made three to four days in advance.

The food is happily more contrived than the decor, which is invigoratingly guileless, without being stark. Pale yellow walls with more than a hint of green in them are unadorned, except for elaborate Victorian wall sconces. Two ceiling fans in the ground-floor dining room further enhance the 19th-century solarium effect. Bryan has made noises about smartening up the look, but his kitchen duties have thankfully kept him too busy. We like it just the way it is, finding it just the right setting to savour his ingenious cuisine.

Bryan's menus change daily depending upon the market's best offerings, but one thing you can count on is an abundance of appetizers. At times we've been so hard-pressed to choose that we've asked for and got a couple of tiny portions as pre-appetizers—just a sampling of scallops sautéed with wild mushrooms before moving on to deep-fried calves' brains served with baby sweet corn and a Thai dip, and a selection of terrines accompanied by a tartly sweet onion chutney. At lunch, such dishes topped off with a little bit of cheese might just about do us. But at dinner, our favourite meal here, we do justice to the £27.50 (including tax but not service) menu, working our way through it right down to the scrumptious desserts.

The night of our encounter with the taxi driver to at least one star, we delighted in the pancake of fish with wild mushrooms and the roast rabbit and wild rice in a creamy mustard sauce. Then there was the pièce de résistance—the fan-sculptured pear resting in a bed of vanilla ice cream in a pastry shell, the whole sitting in a pool of chocolate sauce. The trio of chocolate desserts—mousse, ice cream and pastry knapped with a darkly rich hot fudgy sauce—wasn't bad either.

The bottom line is Dustin missed a winner. His loss, your gain.

Ken Lo's Memories of China, Chelsea

Harbour Yard   071-352-4953
Chelsea Harbour   (FAX) 071-351-2096
London SW10 0QJ

Ken Lo has been reminiscing for the last eleven years at his very popular
Ebury Street establishment in Belgravia, but the spry 77-year-old's recol-
lections are even better articulated at Chelsea Harbour. To begin with,
the riverside location is very impressive and has a particularly poignant
association for Ken—he grew up in southern China on the banks of the
Ming River. And the giant pagoda-like Belvedere Tower at the heart of
the Chelsea Harbour development conjures up additional echos of his
childhood.

Furthermore, the food offered at Chelsea Harbour constitutes a gastronomic tour of China, rather than a representation of a specific
region—the North in the case of the Ebury Street restaurant. Ken notes
that regional distinctions are beginning to disappear, even in China. Consequently, he feels it's very authentic to "amalgamate dishes from all over
the country into a single menu." And if ever anyone was capable of devising a mouth-watering Chinese menu, it is Ken Lo. He's written over 30
Chinese cookbooks—more than "any other man alive." Indeed, his best-
selling books are credited with the more sophisticated appreciation of
Chinese food which set the stage for the establishment of "serious" Chinese restaurants, as opposed to the typical neighbourhood carry-out emporiums.

One of the first such serious establishments was the eponymous Mr
Chow's. At first glance, the tony Knightsbridge eatery would seem to be
Ken's major competitor. But he claims otherwise. Ken points out that Mr
Chow is seldom around these days, while Ken's beaming presence is felt
in both his restaurants. Pictures of him and wife Anne ("the one with the
business sense") with happy guests line the wall opposite the bar at Chelsea Harbour—guests like Marlon Brando, Michael Caine and Joan Collins. Ken says the infamous Nico drops by and has proven to be not as
picky an eater as he is a chef. He chuckles that, "We throw any old thing
at him."

Somehow we doubt it. But we certainly understand Nico's enthusiastic
consumption of Ken's memories in a setting reminiscent of a waterfront
hotel in Hong Kong. Walls of windows allow unrestricted views of the
river and the yachts in the marina. And the glamorous white grand piano

in the bar lends a dash of oriental decadence to a decor otherwise under-statedly luxurious in blond wood, royal blue and gold. There's even a lit-tle hotel marketing savvy in the manner in which the restaurant is divided into two levels, offering two distinctly different dining experi-ences.

The ground level is essentially a Chinese brasserie where dim sum, sa-tays, Chinese Moslem barbecues and Ken's new "Long Life Salads" are produced with rapid-fire precision by a team of chefs operating in an open-to-view kitchen. The selection of dim sum is a particular treat. This is the first place the delectable savouries, the Chinese equivalent of the Spanish tapas, have appeared outside Soho. Goodies like deep-fried prawns, onion pancakes stuffed with tasty mince-meat and steamed beef dumplings at £2.20 each have made weekend dim sum brunch at Chel-sea Harbour a London family tradition.

Upstairs, the atmosphere is more formal. The menus draw upon the cuisine of the five main culinary regions of China and feature dishes as diverse as long-cooked meats and barbecues from the Silk Road and freshwater fish dishes from the lower Yangtze. The one typical element of this unique restaurant is the extent of those menus—the number of choices is staggering. We've been known to take the easy way out and go for one of the set menus—£27 with soup, £23.50 without. Big fans of the hot-and-sour variety, we generally opt for the former, though it's hardly necessary to ensure appetite satisfaction. The meal can more properly be described as a feast, with several dishes appearing on the ta-ble for the starter and main course—which explains the two-person mini-mum for these menus.

A recent sampling began with poached prawns, an assortment of dim sum, and seasoned pork choplettes resting on a bed of crispy seaweed. Piquant onion and ginger flavoured lobster played the role of "major dish," followed by the soup. Then came the "main courses," accompa-nied by fried rice—steamed seabass, crispy hot and spicy shredded beef, and stir-fried mushrooms. Fresh fruit salad and sweet/sour sorbet served as a refreshing dessert.

If you would rather go the à la carte route, don't miss the deep-fried oysters with seaweed for £5.80 or the Peking smoked fish for £5.50 as appetizers. You should also give serious consideration to the £9.50 Mon-golian barbecue of lamb as a main course. Better yet, forget our advice and consult the waiters. But you should take our counsel where reserva-tions are concerned—call 24 hours in advance. ❦

Kensington Place

201-205 Kensington Church Street	071-727-3184
London W8 7LX	(FAX) 071-229-2025

Named *The Time*'s Restaurant of the Year for 1989, Kensington Place may seem comfortably, though somewhat surprisingly familiar to urban Americans. Yet, it was awarded the honour, in part, because it is so very unique in London—a large, loud, theatrical, informal, boisterous, not-necessarily comfortable restaurant serving better-than-good food at modest prices. New Yorkers will recognize it as a "downtown" sort of place, while Los Angelenos could easily imagine it sprawling along Melrose.

So, when you've had enough of hushed temples of haute cuisine, of rich wood panelling and ornate crown moulding, when you can't bear to see another waiter whipping a silver dome off a preciously arranged plate, performing the ubiquitous "Voilà!" service, Kensington Place should be your next stop. What a relief to wander into the exhilarating high-tech din, where all pretension on the part of patrons and staff alike is checked at the door! Indeed, at Kensington Place you're privy to an unusual sociological observation, what *The Times*'s Jonathan Meades describes as that of "British people conducting themselves *in public* without self-consciousness, stiffness."

Which is exactly what that dynamic, not to mention handsome, duo Simon Slater and Nicholas Smallwood had in mind. Having made their mark on London's restaurant scene with the very successful, albeit fairly conventional, Launceston Place, they determined to open another "Place" (which seems to be their lucky word) that would break all the rules in terms of decor, ambience, service and food. According to Nick, their aim is "to serve the best possible food in contemporary surroundings with the minimum of fuss." They've accomplished their goal, on all fronts.

Let's start with the interior, which is very much a family affair. Designed by the husband–wife team, Julyan and Tess Wickham, its two most outstanding features are the lily-pond mural on the back wall painted by Julyan's brother Mark and the controversial Pola chair, named after the Wickhams' eldest daughter. Dubbed "deliciously uncomfortable," the chairs in metal and wood with their exaggerated horseshoe backs seem destined to be singled out by the Metropolitan Museum of

Art for the functional beauty of their construction. Their fluid lines are complemented by boldly modern architectural features like lots of metal piping that provides a commanding framework for the bar and the towering wall of windows that fronts the restaurant.

The combined effect is exciting and almost unexpectedly appealing, engendering the sense of occasion that pervades here. There's an unconventional and uncontrived cordiality, which is encouraged by the staff's informal yet proficient approach to their responsibilities. They participate in the fun, without being ingratiating—none of that, "My name is Robert, and I'll be your waiter" nonsense. "No fuss, no muss" seems to be their credo, which suits chef Rowley Leigh's food just fine. A Roux brothers' alumnus, his cooking doesn't require gimmicks to make it impressive—its variety and scope take care of that.

A lunch menu's appetizers might include a ploughman's plate of assorted salami for £8, potato salad with a difference—truffles—and the winning combination of griddled foie gras with a sweetcorn pancake, both at £9. Main courses are equally eclectic—£8 broiled tongue with horseradish sauce, to noisettes of monkfish with mussels and saffron at £9.50. Even the £12.50 set lunch reflects the unusual balance of Rowley's menus. A choice of squid and yellow pepper or warm chicken liver salads is followed by a decision between grilled tuna with salsa verde and beef Danube with olives. His approach is creative without resorting to promiscuous flights of food fancy. And best of all, the prices are of a bargain-basement nature, despite the tony Kensington location. Two can feast on less than £50 even at dinner, and that takes a healthy bar bill into account.

Impossible in such a smartly casual eatery you say? Au contraire. Start out with either the chicken and goat cheese mousse with olives or the vinaigrette of red peppers with anchovies for £4 each. And the remarkable duck and sweetbread stew accented with Girolles for £12.50 or the red mullet with citrus fruits and olive oil at £9.50 and you're up to £30 for two. Splurge on a couple of à la carte veggies like the £1.50 red cabbage with chestnuts and the £1.25 mashed potatoes, and you've got plenty left over for dessert and a bottle from the sensibly priced wine list.

Open seven days a week, the restaurant is a neighbourhood haunt at night, taking orders till 11:45 P.M., while lunch has a sophisticated commercial tone—lots of media and film folks cutting their next deal or discussing production schedules. Reservations four days in advance are advisable for either meal, especially if you've got the popular 1:00 P.M. and 8:30 P.M. time slots in mind. But the restaurant does seat 100, so the situation is often, shall we say, fluid. Call Grahme Edwards to discuss the options, and request a window seat or one of the tables in the centre.

❧

Langan's Brasserie

Stratton Street	071-491-8822
Piccadilly	(FAX) 071-493-8309
London W1X 5FD	

Langan's is, in the immortal words of Gilbert and Sullivan, the "very perfect model of a modern major" brasserie—large, loud and brassy with a menu to match. It's also very reminiscent of Manhattan's famed Mortimer's, ostensibly an informal, neighbourhood restaurant but in reality an unofficial club where the uninitiated (read unregular or unfamous) need not apply. To show up at Langan's as an unannounced, unanticipated unknown is to get lost in a sea of regulars, to languish at the bar for an hour or so and then, finally, to be consigned to a seat in Siberia, the upstairs dining room.

You'll fare better with a reservation, assuming you've had the foresight to speak to one of the three operators taking them at least two days in advance. Alternatively, apply to your concierge, whose probable acquaintanceship with restaurant manager Graziano Oregano may ensure you a proper welcome. Don't misunderstand. The Langan's folks don't really mean to be so forbidding, it's just that they've got an extraordinarily popular restaurant on their hands, one generally filled to its considerable capacity with regulars, many of whom are celebrities. Sightings of Sean Connery, Roger Moore, Louis Jourdan, Victoria Principal, Barbra Streisand, Eddie Murphy, Joan Collins, Donald Sutherland, Joan Rivers, Shirley MacLaine and, of course, Michael Caine are common.

Of course, Michael Caine? Usually, it's *of course,* Dustin Hoffman. Well, this truly is a place Michael can call his own. He and Peter Langan opened the joint back in 1976. Four months later, Richard Shepherd signed on as chef, and the rest is history. Langan's has been an ongoing, unqualified success, despite the unfortunate passing of Peter in 1988. A lot of it has to do with the breezy café atmosphere, which remains somewhat of a novelty among London's notable dining establishments. The handsome, long mahogany bar and bright main dining room bustle with the congeniality of a crowd comfortably familiar with its surroundings. Table-hopping and cross-room salutes abound, both at lunch and dinner. Big business is conducted during the midday meal, while the evening hours are strictly social.

The oversized menu boasts the countenances of the founding partners in watercolours and, in its composition (both of food and of style), reflects Langan's rather amazing hodgepodge of an art collection that quite literally covers the walls. Oils by David Hockney rub shoulders with photographs by David Bailey, and watercolours sidle up to prints. Likewise, cream of celery soup is cheek to jowl with spinach soufflé topped with an anchovy sauce, while black pudding with kidneys and bacon is juxtaposed with poached fillet of salmon in a leek and champagne sauce.

Our favourites among the starters include the crab mousse with green pepper chutney for £4.25 and the £3.95 oyster mushroom salad. For the main course, we've been very happy with the traditional roast beef and Yorkshire pudding at £10.75 and, having had an unfortunate experience or two with skate, we were pleasantly surprised with the deep-fried rendition, accompanied by a tasty tartare sauce for £7.95. Naturally, desserts run the gamut from a £2.95 rice pudding to a £3.95 crème brulée. Regardless of your preference for basic or for chi-chi, you'll be charged a £1 cover, and a 12.5 per cent service charge is automatically added to the bill.

While the menu is printed daily, in deference no doubt to the many regulars who show up for lunch *and* dinner several times a week, there is one perennial specialty which should not be missed—Langan's interpretation of bubble and squeak, a time-honoured English dish designed to use up leftover potatoes and cabbage. Basically, we're talking about a potato cake stuffed with cabbage, which is lightly floured and then fried to crispy perfection. At £1.80, with a tossed salad for £1.95, it makes a terrific pub-like lunch. Be sure to wash it down with some wine to keep your waiter from getting testy. Meals are meant to be reasonable here, but not quite that reasonable!

Launceston Place

| 1A Launceston Place | 071-937-6912 |
| London W8 5RL | (FAX) 071-938-2458 |

There we were minding our own business, chatting with Anthea Moore Eade in her charming children's wear shop, when we noticed a gentleman with the lean good looks of a British rock star peering intently through the window. At first, we thought he had an uncommonly keen interest in kiddies' clothes, until we realized that *we* were the object of his attention. At first we were flattered, then hopeful, when Anthea, who obviously knew our tall, not-so-dark but definitely handsome stranger, signalled for him to come in. But our fantasies faded as the conversation ensued. It became apparent that, as the owner of the restaurant across the street, his entrepreneurial instincts had been aroused by the sight of two "obviously American" (whatever that means) women, pen and pad in hand, interviewing Anthea. If we were journalists, he wanted to know the who, what, where and the how of getting in on the promotional action. Seems a glowing review in *Gourmet* a couple of years ago had improved his business immeasurably.

Once informed of the nature of our project, he invited us over to his place in the very obvious hope that we might include it in the book. We'd like to think that, through our extensive contacts constantly working for information, we would eventually have gotten around to Launceston Place without this chance meeting. But maybe not. This is very much a neighbourhood boîte, albeit a very smart one, echoing its environs, which is exactly what Nick Smallwood and his partner Simon Slater set out to create. They didn't want to be chi-chi. They didn't intend to devise a "definitive restaurant." Instead, according to Nick, they wanted to offer "good food at good value."

Easier said than done. But Nick knew something about food and value from his days as the first manager of the Hard Rock Café. And he and Simon had the business acumen to select the perfect site for their first venture (they've since opened Kensington Place)—a former three-wheel-car showroom in a neighbourhood where people have the disposable income to eat out often. Indeed, since Launceston Place opened five years ago, it has become an extension of many a local's dining room. It's booked solid every single night, turning most of the 50 seats twice. Neighbourhood restaurant or no, you should reserve three days in advance for such popular time slots as 7:30 and 9:30 P.M. At lunch, you can usually drop in unannounced, but you'll have plenty of company in this cheerful eatery that has the look of a dressed-up tea room, full of captivating little nooks and crannies.

Noteworthy art adorns the pale yellow walls which are set off by white-coloured tablecloths. Casually arranged flowers decorate the tables as do the diners, who are an attractive lot. Princess Di finds it convenient to her home, and our infatuation with Nick was tempered when he pointed out "the head of Warner Brothers." Since it wasn't Steve Ross, he wasn't the *head* head, but whoever he was, he ought to put himself in pictures.

Interestingly enough, this gentleman was, by choice, sitting in what could be considered the establishment's Siberia, the little triangular sky-lit room tucked away at the back. Once the ladies' room of the Italian restaurant that occupied the site for 30 years, it is now the room of choice for those who wish to see, but not be seen. From this snuggery, diners can observe goings-on in the lively main body of the restaurant where less circumspect diners prefer to sit—unless they're of the older variety who tend to book the front room with its comfortable banquettes.

Nonregulars shouldn't be picky. Anywhere you sit, you'll be well fed and served. Nick's almost always around to make sure of it. Simon does similar duty at Kensington Place. And then there's that issue of value, which the set menu most assuredly is—a bargain even at £12.50 for two courses, £14.95 for three. It's available at lunch and for dinner until 8:00 P.M. After that, it's strictly à la carte—not hazardous duty when you consider most of the entrées are in the comfortable £10.25 to £12 range.

The fixed-priced menu changes daily, with offerings like Jerusalem artichoke tart or potato pancakes topped with salmon eggs and sour cream, followed by grilled mackerel accompanied by a zesty soy-based sauce or a hearty beef stew. Among the à la carte selections, which change monthly, we found the terrine of leeks and langoustines sublime at £6.50. We also liked the unusual vinaigrette of smoked eel for £4.75. And the £10 wild mushroom risotto was nothing short of divine, as was the nage of shellfish with a pungent aioli for £9.00.

Some "neighbourhood" restaurant! But then this is some neighbourhood populated by sophisticates who, we suspect, would just as soon maintain Launceston Place as theirs, which is why we might not have stumbled across it had Nick not been so inquisitive, not to mention insistent. We're certainly glad he was and hope that our endorsement of his restaurant is just as effective as *Gourmet's*.

Leith's

92 Kensington Park Road   071-229-4481
London W11 2PN

Compared to many of her restaurateuring comrades, Prue Leith discovered her passion for food relatively late in life—not until she was 19, when she hit Paris and found French cooking infinitely more fascinating than the French history she was there to study. The Cape Town born dynamo made up for lost time. Now, as the head of a gastronomical empire with sales over £6 million and some 250 employees, she can probably buy and sell most of her competitors.

After learning the basics of French culinary traditions as an au pair and refining her technique at the Cordon Bleu School, Prue first set up shop in London in 1962 with a small outside catering service. She would cook dinner for housewives in their homes for £3 a pop. By 1969, Prue's small enterprise had become Leith's Good Food Ltd, which these days caters to the likes of the English portion of the Orient Express and Kensington Palace.

That same year she opened Leith's, which remains a popular fixture on London's grand luxe restaurant circuit. Elegantly ensconced on the ground floor of three Victorian houses strung together, Leith's has a lot going for it. To begin with, you can usually get a reservation for any night of the week, including Saturday and Sunday, with only a day or two's notice. The refreshingly straightforward Prue thinks all the fuss about reservations weeks in advance is rubbish, so she won't even allow manager Nick Tarayan to take them. Then there's Nick himself—one of the most charming dispensers of hospitality we've met in quite some time. He has an amazing facility for remembering not just his customers' names, but their food and drink preferences as well...which leads us to Leith's other most outstanding feature, a special menu for people with a special preference—namely, vegetarians.

Flexibly priced at £21.50 for two courses, £28.50 for three and £32.50 for four (that's appetizer, entrée, cheese course *and* dessert), the vegetarian menu is an entirely separate entity, not an appendix as in at most places. Choices include a sublime double Stilton and walnut mousse or cream of pea soup, followed by spinach, tomato and oriental vegetable flan or potato, shallot and eggplant cake topped with a garlic beurre blanc. Finish off your healthy indulgence with the selection of English cheeses (unless, of course, you opted for the Stilton mousse) and/or with desserts from a trolley that resembles an Old Master still-life.

As you might imagine, the regular menu is equally tempting. Prue plans both of them, which change seasonally, with Nick and head chef Alex Floyd. Yes, Prue is indisputedly in charge, but she has the catering company and the cooking school to attend to, not to mention her successful books to write. So Alex tends to the chef's chores at Leith's, which is just fine by fan Sir John Gielgud.

A lifelong carnivore, he sticks to dishes such as pheasant with foie gras and cracked wheat in a wild mushroom sauce or wild boar and venison casserole with bread-and-bacon dumplings. He might also start out with first courses from the massive, virtually irresistable hors d'oeuvres trolley—seafood and coriander salad, gravlax with dill sauce, and celeriac with smoked chicken salad are but a small sampling. And again, there is the knock-out assortment of new and traditional British cheeses, as well as the dessert cart. The pricing strategy follows that of the vegetarian menu. It depends on the number of courses desired and is inclusive of coffee, service and tax—two courses for £31, three for £38 and four for £42.50.

If you go for the whole nine yards, you'll appreciate that the formal but friendly service is never rushed, and neither are you. There's plenty of time to relax in the plush burgundy and grey chairs or banquettes, while you chat *privately* with your companions. Prue has been very generous with her table spacing—the three understated beige dining rooms, enlivened by mirrored "window" panes and decorative white moulding only seat about 80. The entire atmosphere is one contrived to encourage the leisurely dining necessary to truly appreciate the exceptional food served here. Attention to detail is all-important, from the fresh produce which is grown at Leith's own farm, to the picture-perfect presentations at which Alex is a master.

Where you won't spend much time is in the tiny bar at the entrance. Prue doesn't like her guests to become anxious or impatient, so reservations are strictly honoured. But as you pass through, sneak an olive marinated in oil, herbs and garlic. Like everything else at Leith's, they're divine.

L'Incontro

87 Pimlico Road	071-730 3663/6327
London SW1W 8PH	(FAX) 071-730-5062

L'Incontro—the encounter—sounds like the title of an Alfred Hitchcock thriller and looks every bit as stylish in its deceptive simplicity. Lacquered uplit deco columns break up what would otherwise be the pre dictable monotony of a mirrored wall, while striking body-contoured green suede chairs lend both form and substance to the seductive ambience. This is, after all, a restaurant dedicated to the noble cuisine of Venice, that most romantic of all cities. Just in case you don't get it—either the name of the restaurant or the origin of the food—remarkable black-and-white photographs of Venetian encounters of the intimate kind focus attention on the softly lit walls. Indeed, the only direct light cleverly hits the centre of the tables, which makes all the pretty people who hang out here look even prettier—Joan Collins, Shakira Caine, Sean Connery, Steve Martin and Victoria Tennant and our own dearest Dustin Hoffman.

Open since September 1987 on antique shop happy Pimlico Road, L'Incontro is an offshoot of the great Santini, also owned by Gino Santin who is a stickler for details. One we're especially fond of is the complimentary presentation of scrumptious garlic-toast quarters topped with a wee bit of cheese and tomato that take the edge off your appetite while you're sipping a cocktail or two. Then there's the practice of delivering *two* side plates, discreetly stacked, with £8.50 orders of plump mussels in a white wine, tomato and garlic sauce. When the first inevitably fills with discarded shells, it is quickly cleared to reveal uncluttered territory. Seems obvious. But how many times have you had to wave an empty shell in front of a waiter's face before he removed an overloaded plate, only to have the flow of the meal interrupted while you waited for the arrival of a new vessel?

Besides the sensibly served mussels, we like the Venetian speciality of fish mousse served with polenta as an appetizer at £8.50. And if prawns are laid out on the mountain of crushed ice on the counter by the entrance, they're probably a speciality of the day—order them. At dinner, we tend to go the whole hog and follow our antipasti with some of the restaurant's excellent homemade pastas, like the tagliatelli in a wild mushroom sauce or the potato gnocchi with fresh tomato and basil, both

£8.50. Whether we pasta or not, we can't resist the £19.50 grilled langoustine with lime as a main course. Make no mistake, these are not the spiney flavourless creatures that pass for lobster in warmer climes—these babies are flown in fresh every day from Inverness, which in our book make them Maine lobsters with a Scottish accent. And speaking of importing, maître d' Marcello tells us that one of the secrets to the butterlike grilled calves' liver is its Dutch pedigree. Tulips yes, but liver? Whatever, it's delicious at £12.50.

With prices including tax and the obligatory cover charge of £1.50 added to the bill, along with a 12 per cent service charge, you're likely to spend £30 to £35 per person at lunch and £40 to £45 at dinner. Both estimates include a nice bottle of wine from the heavily Italian list. And you should know the menus, including the specials, are identical—the difference is that people—including ourselves—tend to eat more in the evening. The other variation is the length of time one should allow for a reservation. For lunch you can get by with a call the day before. But for dinner, allow three. And if you like to dine to the tinkling of the ivories ask for the downstairs room which is graced nightly by a talented piano man. On the other hand, if your object is to see and be seen, insist on the main room on street level. Either way, you can enjoy a L'Incontro encounter seven nights a week, and/or every day for lunch except Sunday.

🍎

Ma Cuisine

| 113 Walton Street | 071-584-7585 |
| London SW3 2HP | (FAX) 071-584-2664 |

If you have a hankering to sample the delights of one of London's smallest and most romantic restaurants, take advantage of modern technology and fax ahead for reservations. *Ahead* is the operative word here, it takes as many as three or four months in advance to secure one of Ma Cuisine's 32 seats. While you're at it, request tables 6, 8 or 9 if you seek privacy, or table 10 if snuggling in a cosy booth is your idea of romance. Of course, there are last-minute cancellations, so don't write off dining here if you hit town on the spur of the moment. Call Lucien Celentino, who will make every effort to accommodate you. And if he can't, no one can. This is a man whose devotion to his business gives new meaning to the term "chief-cook-and-bottle-washer"—as a proprietor/chef he's done it all since opening this French provincial snuggery 16 years ago.

Yes, we did say French. Yet your assumption that Lucien is Italian is absolutely correct. He hails from Naples, the progeny of a mixed marriage—Italian father, French mother. But it wasn't a matter of Lucien being tied to his mama's apron strings that explains the paradox of his current establishment. Rather, it has to do with the fact that as a teenager he went to the kitchens of two of Cannes' better restaurants—Chez Moi and Felix's. Lucien discovered he had a flair for French food, and has been consumed by the perfection of its preparation ever since.

He goes to considerable lengths to ensure that his cuisine is worthy of the pains his customers go to just to get reservations. The wee hours of every morning, except Sunday when Ma Cuisine is closed, find him at the market making his purchases for the day. By 4:00 A.M., he's at home catnapping for three or four hours. Then Lucien's off to the restaurant to get ready for lunch, save Saturdays when it's dinner only. Lunch or dinner, he constantly darts between the kitchen and dining room, tasting everything and chatting with everyone. He's truly in his element here, clearly a happy soul.

Even on his day off, Lucien's usually at Ma Cuisine cooking up a Sunday dinner for friends who act as guinea pigs for his culinary experiments. Once perfected, they may end up as one of the ten daily specials that supplement the à la carte menu, which is revamped annually. But one dish is inviolate, a perennial favourite of regulars—la mousse brulée. It's a scrumptious concoction of caramel mousse in a crown-like nest of brandy flavoured wafers, the whole topped by a luscious caramel sauce to create an unforgettable taste sensation. At £3.50, it is by far and away the most popular item on the menu.

Still, a meal it's not, merely the reward for having the good sense to be here in the first place, the good sense to savour the delights of the fork-tender roast pork, served with a Drambuie sauce for £9.25, or the hearty £9.70 boned leg of chicken roasted with garlic, tomato, and sherry vinegar. As for starters, we like the lobster consumé accompanied by ravioli filled with a light vegetable and lobster mixture at £5.30, and the wild pigeon pâté laced with Armagnac for £5.95. And we have been known to order the £5.25 baby Dover sole cured in a dressing of citrus fruits, mustard and a hint of mint.

Generally speaking, you'll spend £50 to £60 for two including wine, unless you share Lucien's infatuation with Armagnac. He stocks some very special bottles, prizes he's secured at auctions or estate sales which he frequents with his pal Salvatore from the bar at Dukes. Fortunately,

Salvatore's a brandy aficionado, so they don't have to compete for the best vintages and can celebrate their finds over a friendly drink of very fine, usually very expensive wines. These boys don't fool around—Lucien sells a glass of 1893 Armagnac for £72.25. The 1918 vintage is a relative bargain at £48.75. Not so a glass of the circa 1750—Lucien says the price is available upon request so you know it must be astronomical. Less costly but equally fortifying is his selection of vintage ports—as little as £10.15 for a glass of one dating from 1967.

In fact, Ma Cuisine is an ideal post-theatre retreat for a light supper or dessert, coffee and a glass of one of Lucien's precious wines. The restaurant is open late, its soft tones of beige and brown bathed in the glow of candlelight; and the very professional staff is unruffled by virtually any request, whatever the hour. Most have been here forever and with a clientele that includes the Prince and Princess of Wales (together—we did say it was romantic), the Queen Mother, Margaret Thatcher, Tony Curtis, Faye Dunaway, Clint Eastwood, Peter Ustinov, Madonna and, of course, Dustin Hoffman, they've heard it all.

They've witnessed everything, too. Lucien loves to tell the story about the evening he randomly sat two couples next to each other and forged an unexpected reunion. It seems the two gentlemen had been school chums in Sweden, but one had emigrated to Canada, the other to the United States. They hadn't seen each other in 20 years until they found themselves at Ma Cuisine. So happy was their experience that—on the spot—they scheduled their next get-together for three years to the hour hence. They've got a table for four booked at 8 P.M.

Monkeys

1 Cale Street   071-352-4711/5120
Chelsea Green
London SW3 QT

You remember the three monkeys—see no evil, hear no evil, speak no evil? At Brigitte and Thomas Benham's little restaurant, there's a fourth monkey—eat no evil. You'll see no evil in this intimate two-room wood-panelled establishment. Probably, you won't hear much evil, or anything else for that matter—Monkeys caters to a rather subdued crowd. And the food is such that you will eat no evil. So there's certainly no evil to speak of here.

What *is* here is a tiny restaurant that seats just 45, where rather serious folks come to dine on food that exudes a simple grandeur. Thomas does the cooking, while Brigitte charmingly oversees the front-of-house chores, an interesting division of labour, since she's French and he's just as English as English can be. But it works. Brigitte's eyes justifiably light up with pride when she talks about Thomas' prowess in the kitchen, especially with game, his passion. Indeed, during the season (mid-August for grouse to the end of January for partridge) a substantial portion of Thomas' menus is devoted to it, including a critter or two we've never even heard of.

We use the plural when it comes to menus, because Thomas changes his every eight to twelve weeks. So regulars, like the Bruce McAlpines, Robert and Sandi Lacey and the *Daily Mail's* favourite chronicler of royal romances, Nigel Dempster, are never bored. They may, however, be disappointed when house specialities like the £10 hot foie gras salad are not offered. This is one of Thomas' triumphs, a dish that foie gras fanatics never fail to fawn over.

Regardless of its specifics, the menu is always divided into three sections—two fixed-price groupings at £19 and £30, along with the à la carte selections. The nineteen pounder is a bargain and should definitely be considered if you're operating on a budget. It consists of three courses with choices like a spinach and potato salad laced with sautéed salmon, and grilled fish of the day with a scallop velouté or fried calves' liver with limes, topped off by an assortment of cheeses. We throw budgets to the wind when we visit Brigitte and Thomas. We head straight for the à la carte section for that foie gras salad or the foie gras terrine at £10. Entrée-wise, we've savoured the succulent £16.50 fried monkfish with lobster sauce and found the roast Bresse pigeon with fresh lentils tough to beat at £18.50. Should you follow our lead and deal only with the à la carte side of the menu, you can count on spending about £70 for two, not including wine.

Twenty-four hours' notice should get you a reservation for either lunch or dinner (we suggest dinner), but don't plan on calling on Friday for Saturday. They're closed at weekends, except, perhaps, for a special private party, like Victoria Lockwood's bachelorette bash held here behind drawn curtains to thwart the paparazzi. It would seem that the new Viscountess Althorp, otherwise known as Di's brother's bride, has better taste in restaurants than in wedding gowns. Her sable-trimmed, gold brocade costume was declared a fashion faux pas by the British press.

But we imagine they, and she, will get over it. After all, her sister-in-law's gown wasn't exactly an unqualified success, and Diana's now considered one of the world's best-dressed women.

Typically discreet, Brigitte and Thomas have no opinion on the matter. Rather, they imitate their restaurant's namesakes—never seeing, hearing nor speaking evil of Victoria or any other of their very discerning clientele.   🍇

• *Morton's*

28 Berkeley Square	071-499-0363
London W1X 5HA	(FAX) 071-495-3160

Founded by an American in London, Peter Morton, in 1970, this private dining club, superbly located on the north side of Berkeley Square, has recently benefitted from the revitalizing effect of new ownership. Directors Andrew Leeman, Howard Malin and Simon Lowe believe in hands-on management and are always around to ensure Morton's offers superior food, service and ambience.

Individual annual membership fees are £275. Couples can join for £375 per annum and corporate memberships are available for £400. But, should you hail from across any of the waters that surround Britain, you can enter this particularly refined sanctuary for as little as £35 for a two-week membership. And by presenting yourself, with passport and cash in hand, at the door of the circa 1823 manse that is Morton's, you avoid the lengthy written application process. Should you opt for a full-fledged overseas membership, it's £150.

If we're in London for a week or so, we always join up. The extended hours—last dinner orders at 11:30 P.M., the bar bustles till 3 A.M.—and the virtual guarantee of a reservation make it worth every bit of that £35. In fact, the spectacular saloon on the main floor, with its 45-foot-long mahogany bar has often been a lifesaver after a night of carousing. It serves savoury snacks like Welsh rarebit for £3, chicken satay for £3.75, scrambled eggs laced with smoked salmon at £7.50 into the wee hours, and a £5.50 hangover-banishing cheeseburger. The food and the room's sophisticated comfort and 1920s flair hit the proverbial spot if one has frolicked to excess.

When we're not into cavorting and simply want to enjoy one of chef Julian Jeffrey's excellent meals, we head for the stunning dining room upstairs. Its soaring ceiling adorned with ornate moulding and its French doors, extravagantly draped in flowered silk, framing a sweeping view of the square, make a suitably stylish setting for the young, singularly attractive crowd—lots of models and other members of the fashion industry cognoscenti. It's a tough call as to whether the people or the extraordinarily large and absolutely exquisite dried flower arrangements are more worthy of a good long look. Either way, the abundance of mirrors adorning the muted yellow walls ensures their collective beauty is properly reflected.

As for the food, it's English cuisine for the 1990s—sweet red pepper soup served with garlic-infused croutons for £3, quail egg tartlet topped with hollandaise sauce for £3.50, and braised leeks on a bed of bacon and Stilton at £3.75. Such comely comestibles are complemented by a tender £7.25 loin of pork with an apple and fennel stuffing, classic roast rack of English lamb for £9.75, tasty veal kidneys served over wild rice and glazed with grain mustard sauce at £8.50, and medallions of veal capped by a lime and ginger sauce and accompanied by a leek soufflé carrying a £10.50 pricetag. Don't forget the £1.50 cover charge or the gratuity which is not included.

The menu changes quarterly, so that even daily dining club members are unlikely to suffer from any ennui. Indeed, in our considerable experience, there is never anything that comes close to approaching dull about Morton's. It's an invariably lively, friendly place that eschews the reputation for pretentiousness of London's clubland. ❦

Mosimann's

11B West Halkin Street	071-235-9625
London SW1X 8JL	(FAX) 071 245 6354

The Swiss-born son of a restaurateuring family of modest means, Anton Mosimann claims to have been born with a wooden spoon in his mouth. If so, he's traded it in for one fashioned in 24 carat gold, courtesy of this breathtaking dining club that bears his name. Housed in a circa 1830 Scottish Presbyterian church, Mosimann's is by far and away the most visually spectacular such enterprise in this or any other city—the most divinely successful transformation of a religious edifice into a secular one that we've come across.

Certainly, Anton deserves a great deal of the credit. He's responsible for the stunning new staircase that leads to the balcony, now home to the bar and the unique glass-fronted 2,000 bottle wine "cellar," where guests may sample before ordering. But the eccentric Mrs Oakley Maund must be paid her due as well. She's the one who in 1923 first had the building deconsecrated and turned it into a private home—it's her soft yellow fleur de lis patterned wallpaper that Anton has carefully re-created. Since her death, the former church has passed through a number of hands, becoming the Belfrey Club in 1945, which it remained under several regimes until Anton got hold of it in 1988.

Their union has truly been a marriage made in heaven, the one-time church proving to be the ideal showcase for Anton's thoroughly modern, healthful and creative cooking. He maintains that food (and life) should be "an experience of happiness, serenity and joyful giving." Mosimann's members consider these words gospel, and happily ante up the initial fee of £600 and the £400 annual dues. At least male Mosimann's members do—ladies who lunch here are charged £150, but that's all they do unless they show up in the evening with a fully franchised (read male) member. Whatever your sex, you've got to be proposed by one member and seconded by another to join the 1,500 lucky souls who have the right to consider Anton Mosimann their private chef.

Actually, despite the relative youth of his club, Anton's talents have long been deemed the possession of a privileged few. For the twelve years that he reigned supreme at the Dorchester, where he earned and kept two coveted Michelin stars, the hotel's restaurant became the haunt of regulars who delighted in Anton's trademark "Menu Surprise"—a sort of gourmet potluck affair. Seven courses employing the best of the day's market offerings were presented to the eager diners, each taken on faith in Anton, as no printed menu or verbal announcement revealed the meal's contents. Indeed, the restaurant became so popular that people started planning their stays at the Dorchester for those rare dates when a table was available.

The Menu Surprise tradition continues at Anton's club for approximately £65 per person, as does his patented contribution to healthy eating, Cuisine Naturelle. Noted by a small "cn" next to the price, you can feel very virtuous by ordering such items as salmon sashimi with sesame seed and warm tea-smoked chicken with red lentil salad, both £14, or barbecued salmon with herb noodles at £17.50. Actually, you can feel pretty good about any dish from Mosimann's menu—the emphasis is on simplicity, on the preparation of the most perfect ingredients money can buy in ways, according to Anton, that are "best suited to them...so as to bring out their colour, flavour, succulence and natural goodness." So while you don't need a lot of time to pore through lengthy menu descriptions, you are invited to make your selections over an aperitif in the lush bar overlooking the main dining room. Should you get bored waiting for your table, turn your attention to the walls where you'll find Anton's large collection of old menus displayed—it's fascinating to contemplate what was considered a fashionable meal at the dawn of the century, the narrative of what was served at the coronation of Edward VII, for instance.

When your first course is ready, maître d' John Davey will escort you to your place in the remarkable dining room, where the term "cathedral ceiling" takes on a rather literal meaning. Here, interrupted only by handsome exposed beams, it soars three storeys above the widely spaced tables. Double rose windows bathe the room in a festive light during the day, and still work their magic at night, thanks to a state-of-the-art, computerized lighting system.

As if this room weren't enough to make Mosimann's a serious contender in the most sumptuous surroundings sweepstakes, there are four enchanting private dining rooms—The Tiffany, The Wedgwood, The Gucci and the Alfa Romeo. That they each have a very distinct personality is indicated by their names and is confirmed by the fact that Anton had the brilliant idea of asking each company to actually decorate "its" room. The results are nothing short of smashing. The club's destiny to grace the glossy pages of the world's interior design magazines already assured, Anton went one step further with a Chef's Dining Room. Through a specially designed window, guests can witness the workings of his kitchen, reputedly the most efficient and modern in the city.

If you figured getting a gander at the place is worth the price of admission, you figured right. But the food isn't overwhelmed by the decor and is ultimately the reason Mosimann's has been such a success. It even brings couples together, *married* couples that is, for lunch—the only restaurant we visited that claimed such a feat. During our girls-only visits, we've enjoyed several of the house specialities marked by the club's striking "M" logo—ravioli with feta cheese and a heavenly salad or "symphonie" of seafood, £8 and £8.50, followed by the unlikely sounding but very good £12.50 fish cakes topped by a parsley sauce, and chicken teriyaki at £12.50. Chicken teriyaki? We know, but trust us, you haven't lived until you tried Anton's version *and* it's even a "cn" selection.

At dinner, the prices go up and some richer dishes are in evidence. We're especially fond of Anton's way with terrines—the leek and mushroom number doused with hazelnut dressing was lovely at £9, as was the

£9.50 terrine of Scottish salmon in a coriander vinaigrette. Then there's the maître d's way with steak tartare which we can't resist at £21. And the turbot and salmon strudel with a sherry wine vinaigrette is just as good as it sounds, also £21.

The bottom line is if you frequent London town and can pay the piper to join Mosimann's, do so. If not, on either count, be relentless in your pursuit of a member who will spot you to a guest visit.

The Neal Street Restaurant

26 Neal Street   071-836-8368
London WC20 9PH   (FAX) 071-497-1361

If you're a mushroom addict, head straight for this Covent Garden eatery. We guarantee you'll be in mushroom nirvana. After all, the Neal Street Restaurant employs the only full-time mushroom hunter in Britain. Most mornings, Gennaro Contaldo scours the British countryside in search of the edible fungus in all its glorious varieties: chanterelles, oyster mushrooms, ceps and the tricky honey fungus, which is poisonous raw but safe and delicious when cooked.

He's dispatched on his daily quest by owner Antonio Carluccio whose obsession with mushrooms was eloquently chronicled in *A Passion for Mushrooms*, which instructs the novice in the fine arts of finding, identifying and cooking the little darlings. Apparently, the lust for mushrooms is a global phenomenon—Antonio's book has so far been translated into five languages.

When he's not writing (he's also the author of *A Taste of Italy*), Antonio is overseeing in the restaurant's kitchen which has been his domain since 1980. But the establishment has only been one he can truly call his very own since June 1989 when he bought it from brother-in-law Sir Terence Conran. Presumably, the transaction had some impact on Antonio's and Terence's respective bank accounts; however, few differences in the restaurant itself are perceptible to the public. Sir Terence's signature, clean interior design, remains intact, down to the dramatic Hockneys and Stellas that lend colour to the white brick walls. And the publishing and advertising heavies who work in the area continue to treat Neal Street as their private canteen at lunch. Still, they don't seem to mind the occasional assault on their territory by Prince Andrew, Placido Domingo, the BBC's Terry Wogan, and in days gone by, Sir Alec Guinness. They'll be equally gracious with you, assuming you've had the foresight to call a couple of days in advance to make sure you can get a table.

Ditto for dinner, especially for post-theatre dining for which the restaurant is particularly popular, not to mention convenient. But never on Saturday or Sunday, when it's closed; and don't even think about having a mushroom fix before curtain. Antonio doesn't start serving the evening meal until 7:30 P.M.

Of course, you can always get around that by chowing down at a late lunch—the menu's the same all day—and call it dinner. Whatever, you'll spend £75 to £90 for two including service and tax, along with an unpretentious wine, and you're sure to have an outstanding culinary experience, thanks to Antonio's fearless approach to food. He loves to experiment, playing with creative combinations of ingredients until he finds something he likes—always with an eye toward discovering yet another way to showcase the delicate flavours of his beloved mushrooms. Which is not to say that if you have an aversion to them you should avoid Neal Street. Antonio has an ecumenical attitude. He does do dishes without mushrooms; he even features dishes that aren't Italian, like home-cured gravlax for £9.00 and grilled Dover sole at £15.00.

Still, it's a crime not to partake of Antonio's passion, to delight in the seasonal specialties—St George mushrooms in April, oyster mushrooms in May. You can hit the jackpot from September to November, when as many as 50 different kinds may be featured. We can't resist the rich £7 wild mushroom soup or the intriguing international merger of truffles and shiitake mushrooms for £12. Then there's the fillet of beef with a sublime sauce of ceps and the medallions of venison topped by a savoury fungi concoction, both priced at £16.

Yes, we share Antonio's ardour and consequently heartily endorse the one physical improvement he's made to the place—Sydney Noland's painting entitled *Adoration of Mushrooms*. It hangs in a place of honour, just to the right of the entrance, where it seems to proudly proclaim the restaurant's orientation. Antonio traded "food for life" with the artist to obtain this striking visual representation of his personal philosophy—we think they both got a good deal. 🍄

Ninety Park Lane

Grosvenor House   071-409-1290
Park Lane   (FAX) 071-493-3341
London W1A 3AA

When our pal Vivian Appell, an extraordinarily sophisticated woman whose excellent taste can normally be relied upon, told us we could not write this book without including *the* restaurant at the Grosvenor House hotel, we thought we'd finally caught her in a lapse of good judgment. Of course, a hotel restaurant will always do in a pinch—like so many hotels in London we imagined, it simply disproved the old adage that such establishments should be avoided at all costs. But worthy enough to stand on its own, to be touted as a destination? We doubted it.

Naturally, Vivian was right, and we couldn't have been more wrong. Ninety Park Lane, named after its address, has been the site of some of the most splendid meals of our collective lifetimes. And, indeed, it is generally acknowledged by those in the know as one of the finest restaurants in London. That, at the moment, Ninety Park Lane is Michelin starless attests, we suspect, to that organization's ongoing prejudice against restaurants of a hotel nature (the Four Seasons being a very notable exception). It may also have something to do with the fact that some gourmets grumble about the expense of a meal here. Expect to spend in the neighbourhood of £140 for an à la carte dinner for two, assuming you steer clear of the Chateau Petrus 1945 tagged at £1,750 which was still languishing in the wine cellar when last we checked. (The bill for lunch is lowered significantly only if you skip wine altogether and/or order the £25 menu du jour.)

But for dinner that £140 is a bare minimum. It's easy to top the £175 mark if you indulge in the £62.50 Menu Louis Outhier accompanied by an appropriately refined wine and capped off with a brandy or two. Higher still if you aspire to the £35 glass of 1893 Armagnac from the tall silver liqueur trolley. Too rich even for our tastes—the Armagnac, that is, not the menu. Indeed, the Outhier menu is one extravagance we cannot resist, if only to salute the entrepreneurial cunning of this most prolific of chefs. The man's everywhere—everywhere it would seem but the three-star L'Oasis on the French Riviera. Though closed for several years, it was the source of his original fame, if not fortune. The fortune is coming from his executive chef status, which he has raised to a new art form, plotting the course of world-class restaurants from New York to Boca Raton to London.

It's great work if you can get it. Breeze into town, plan a few menus, work with the hands-on chef for a few days, take a lot of credit, check back in every so often for quality control purposes, and move on to the next enterprise in an expanding stable of restaurants. Louis has done a nice, even exceptional job elsewhere, but as far as we're concerned Ninety Park Lane is the jewel in his toque.

To begin with, it's uncommonly pretty. You've heard of country house hotels *(ad nauseum)?* Well, this is a country house restaurant—subtly furnished with antiques and paintings from Lord Forte's private collection. They bask in the glow of an assortment of lamps, strategically stationed around the long, low room. The look is further enhanced by the use of sofas, endowed with decorative pillows, instead of banquettes and by rectangular or round tables only. Not a standard restaurant-issue square four-top in sight. And the noise level, thanks to the gilt trimmed wood wainscoting which alternates with fabric-covered wall panels, is just loud enough to remind you there are other guests at this house party, but not at all intrusive. In fact, it adds to the sensory appeal of the place. There's a festive buzz that puts you into a celebratory mood the moment you cross the threshold. Make that thresholds—two entrances grace the premises, one directly from Park Lane, the other from the hotel.

Either way, you're greeted by the effusive Sergio Rebecchi, who solicitously inquires how you would like the evening to proceed. Would you care for an aperitif in the lounge, or to go straight to the table? Usually, when given the choice, we head straight for our assigned seats, but not at Ninety Park Lane. If the 80-seat restaurant is the living/dining area of an elegant country house, the lounge is the library—just as warm and cosy as it can be with a welcoming fire in the winter and lively conversation year round. There are few more delightful experiences than sipping a glass of champagne in its gracious intimacy, wallowing in Sergio's ministrations while studying the menus. You have three choices: the à la carte, the £35 four-course gift to vegetarians named the Menu Potager and the Louis Outhier.

But as we said, as far as we're concerned, there's only one option—the seven-course salute to Louis. Of course, it means settling in for the evening, and we wouldn't have it any other way. What's the point of going to such a sumptuous restaurant, if you're operating on an eat-and-run timetable? Just sit back and let the luxury wash over you. Allow yourself to be charmed by the attentions of the formal but not forbidding waiters, like the devastatingly handsome Salvatore, one of the two Catanzano brothers who work here. And enjoy speculating about who might be occupying the curtained alcove so often reserved for members of *the* family, while you relish the dainty but delectable offerings from the chef.

They whet your appetite for an unforgettable meal, served on china specially commissioned from Royal Worcester, that might start out with fresh foie gras served on a truffle jelly, followed by ethereal poached scallops in a feather-light vegetable broth flavoured with a delicate dry sherry. Next, you might be treated to an unusual lobster gratin in a casserole with mustard seeds. Then it's time for a little palate-cleansing vermouth and grapefruit sorbet succeeded by luscious medallions of lamb knapped with a rich port sauce. Goat cheese topped with lightest virgin olive oil and a chive purée precede the finale of desserts presented on the three-tiered English-folly wedding-cake of a mahogany cart.

If this all seems like too much of a good thing, the à la carte selections are equally seductive. Among the hors d'oeuvres, we highly recommend the sautéed langoustine layered with spinach and pasta in a cognac butter—just as sinful as it sounds for £21.50. As for main courses, Louis Outhier's Riviera roots are evident in the magic worked with seafood. The seabass encased in pastry served in a Choron sauce laced with freshly chopped tomato is a house speciality for two, at £25 each—*if* you know enough to call and place the order well in advance. The tricky dish is no longer regularly featured on the menu. Fortunately, there are plenty of lovely alternatives, such as the £24 lightly poached scallops and vegetables infused with white port. And while it's definitely not from the briny deep, if venison is on the menu, order it. The last version we had was glazed with a blueberry sauce and accompanied by a duxelle of celeriac and wild mushrooms.

In case you missed the point, let there be no mistake that dining here is quite a production. The restaurant definitely subscribes to the theory that its activities are a branch of show business; nevertheless, the shows can be produced to accommodate the schedules of the real world. The £25 luncheon menu can be served and consumed within an hour. Seems a pity to rush the Ninety Park Lane experience, but if that's the only way you can fit it in, do it.

One Ninety Queen's Gate

190 Queen's Gate	071-581-5666
London SW7 5EU	(FAX) 071-581-8172

In the 1980s when food critics talked about London's standing as a culinary capital, they talked about Menage à Trois, the original grazers' paradise with its elaborate (but skimpy) starters, fanciful desserts, and self-styled policy of "no intercourse." In the 1990s, they're talking about One Ninety Queen's Gate, an elegant eatery for those in search of hearty food made of robust ingredients and served in large portions. Surprisingly enough, in both diametrically opposed instances the critics are talking about chef Anthony Worral-Thomson, the former rugby player whose beefy hands certainly seem to have a firm grip on the pulse of food fashions.

We tend to believe that he's really more comfortable in these solidly Victorian surroundings than in the rather precious atmosphere of Menage à Trois. Originally meant to be a dining club for members of the Restaurateurs' Association of Great Britain, One Ninety Queen's Gate is overseen by that group's flamboyant president, Roy Ackerman. Happily, it has evolved into a hybrid, part of the public domain until 11:30 P.M., when it becomes the private preserve of Britain's greatest chefs— Boulestin's Kevin Kennedy, Langan's Richard Shepherd, and the brothers Roux. Here they relax and unwind after their nightly chores, eating and drinking until the 3:00 A.M. closing.

Even during the public hours, there's a friendly, clubby aura about the restaurant, despite its occupancy of the bottom two floors of a rather imposing stucco mansion. The dimly lit ground-floor lounge—all wood panelling, comfortably padded mahogany bar, oil paintings and enveloping chairs—is the site of lots of animated conversation. Downstairs there's nothing basement-like or pretentious about the richly curtained, uncommonly pretty butter-yellow dining room, further distinguished by good Matisse prints. At lunch its 60 seats are filled by an amiable crowd made up of regulars from this residential neighbourhood, members and lots of other folks in the food business, from reviewers to wine merchants.

The three-course luncheon menu changes daily, while retaining a set price of £13.95 for members and £16.15 for nonmembers, including tax but not service. Compared to the enormous hand-written dinner menu, its typed single sheet is easy to decipher and, in deference to members who tend to prefer simple, hearty fare, features lots of earthy dishes like charcuterie with homemade pickles and chutneys and chicken pot pie. Typical of Anthony, the menu also displays a sense of humour. One day, it offered grilled baby chicken with chips and sauce rouge. The sauce turned out to be ketchup, ceremoniously presented in its familiar Heinz bottle. We half expected the waiter to proffer the cap for a sniff, before leaving it on the table!

For dinner, the lights are lowered and the candles lit to cast an enhancing hue over the decidedly glitzy clientele—Francis Bacon, Peter Blake, rocker Mark Knopfler and Britain's dean of restaurant public relations, Alan Crompton-Batt. Plan on a leisurely meal. A good twenty minutes are spent reading the menu, not because there are so many choices, but because each dish is an original made of novel combinations which take some consideration. At least the pricing structure is uncomplicated— £24 for a starter and main course; £29.50 for starter, main course and "pudding" (Anthony Worral-Thompsonese for dessert). Tax is included, but you're on your own in the service department. Tack on a very average bottle of wine from the 18-page list and you can count on spending £80 to £100 for two.

On our last visit, after a careful perusal punctuated by a chuckle or two, we chose "A Terrine of Leeks, Lentils and Liver [foie gras, actually] with Hot Potato Cakes" and "A Jellied Rockpool: Shellfish and Vegetables set in a ginger scented Lobster Jelly." Both descriptions were sources of amusement, but they proved accurate and delicious. We followed them with two equally long-winded dishes—"Oven roasted, pine-encrusted Fillet of Sea Bass served on Artichokes and Sprouting Wheatgerm with Extra Virgin Olive Oil" and "Stuffed Saddle of Venison sitting on a bed of Haggis with a Pepper Sauce and three Vegetable purées." Editorially, we feel compelled to tell you that the seabass was coated with pine-*nuts*, and haggis is a green three-legged creature that inhabits the highlands of Scotland. . . okay, it isn't. But trust us, you don't want to know what it is. Just take our word for it and try the Scottish national dish, in this or any other incarnation. You should also know that both these main courses were predictably memorable.

Since the portions are so generous, we tend to skip the puddings, as tempting as they read: "A Thin Hot Tart of Apples and Prunes served with Apple Sorbet and Prune and Armagnac Ice Cream"; "Feuillets of Pear and Carmelized Nuts served Hot with Caramel Ice Cream and Bitter Orange Sabayon"; or "A Terrine of Chocolate with a Honey Basket of Pistachio Ice Cream and a wicked Chocolate Sauce."

However long you linger, you'll feel like Cinderella at 11:30 P.M. It's time to leave the ball, so that all the prince charmings of chefdom can frolic in peace, away from the "punters"—those annoying diners who insist on asking about the *exact* recipe for a favourite dish (as if there were one!) or who request that one ingredient or another be eliminated to suit their sensitive palates. Not that you would be so gauche, of course, but you may be the refreshing exception in a world full of punters.   🍒

Overtons

4–6 Victoria Buildings	071-834-3774
Terminus Place	(FAX) 071-491-2477
London SW1V 1JP	

Just across the street from Victoria Station, Overtons (founded by Horace Overton who was Queen Victoria's gamekeeper) has long been the first stop of British travellers returning from the Continent—Dickens used to count on it to settle his stomach after a difficult Channel crossing. Since crossings are no less turbulent these days, we still follow his lead and belly up to the white formica counter (some things *have* changed since Dickens was last here) in the white-tiled oyster bar on the first level and order some succulently sweet shellfish—£9 for six native oysters, £7 for the same number of Overtons' specials. We usually wash them down with a half bottle of champagne. Indeed, one of Overtons' most endearing qualities is its respectable list of wines by the glass and half bottle. We're partial to the dry and slightly lemony Lanson Black Label at £9.75.

Other gastronomical goodies are available in the bar, including full meals—scampi sautéed in garlic, olive oil with tomatoes, anchovies and olives served over rice for £11.20 and poached skate with capers and lemon served with buttered potatoes for £9.65. But we think the bar is most conducive to some seafaring grazing. Besides the oysters, we like the large selection of hors d'oeuvres, including mussels marinière at £4.75, smoked salmon for £6.80 and a delicious £4.20 lobster soup.

For more serious dining, head upstairs to the restaurant proper, a series of small rooms which are a vision in green—dark green velvety banquettes and drapes, sea-green walls accented by white moulding and pale green panels and enlivened with colourful Lautrec-like prints. The menu is a little more extensive here and even bows to the non-fish-eating infidel with three pretty pedestrian meat dishes—lamb cutlets, calf's liver with bacon, and steak, all in the £8 to £11 neighbourhood. Typical of Overtons, they're simply prepared but are certainly not representative of the kitchen's forte. The scrumptious Dover sole is more like it. Poached in white wine and served with a lobster sauce laced with prawns and brandy—at £12.95, it's a dish of which Overtons is justifiably proud.

Having been in business for over 125 years, Overtons certainly has a handle on how to run a good old-fashioned fish house. It's a simple enough formula, but one few others follow—fresh fish daily, prepared without guile and served in comfortable surroundings at a fair price. Of course, its location doesn't hurt either. Right in the middle of a bustling commercial area, it's convenient for many a business lunch and the restaurant's proximity to the Apollo, Victoria Palace and Westminster theatres make it an ideal pre- or post-performance spot. Indeed, Overtons claims theatre suppers as a speciality and structures serving hours accordingly. Orders are taken from 5:30 to 10:45 nightly, except Sundays when the restaurant is closed and—not so coincidentally—most theatres are dark.   🍷

Overtons St James's

5 St James's Street	071-839-3774
London SW1 AIEF	(FAX) 071-491-2477

Since there are two Overtons, we guess they could be considered a chain. But we prefer to think of them as a pair—"chain" suggests more blatantly commercial establishments like the ubiquitous Wheeler's. One of Wheeler's outlets is forever etched in our memory as the site of an incredible scene involving a waiter whose command of the English language was too rudimentary for him to comprehend our request for no mayonnaise with the cold assorted seafood platter, and a kitchen that couldn't grasp the concept. We never did get what we wanted, or rather we continued to get what we didn't want! At any rate, we've never experienced any such frustration at either Overtons.

The admirable ability to cope with special requests aside, the St James's Overtons is very different in character from its older sibling. It has a more sophisticated tone, reflected in the prices and in the decor which, with its knotty pine panelling, fireplace and abundance of artwork reminds us of the bar/lounges of New York's and Washington's

Jockey Clubs. While the menus of the two restaurants are by no means duplicates, there is some overlap of dishes, and in each instance the cost at St James's is slightly higher than at Victoria.

The difference probably has a lot to do with their respective locations. This Overtons, after all, is just around the corner from Christies in an area replete with art galleries, not to mention St James's Palace. So when the restaurant was renovated in 1988, it was done with a potentially posh clientele in mind. We say "potential" because prior to the much-needed restoration, this was a somewhat dreary, sleepy place, not the haunt of the tony set that it should have been. Now, however, it's a bustling, bubbling bastion of urbane art dealers and collectors, some of whom, of course, are very serious people—like Rupert Murdoch, who finds the booths in the front room just right for a private conversation about his next media maneuver. In fact, the St James's Overtons has become so upscale that it has taken to charging a cover—£1.50 per person at lunch and dinner.

As mildly irritating as the cover may be, it's a small price to pay for the privilege of partaking of such a fine array of fish. Oysters are a must here at £12 for six of the Imperial variety, as is the £4.20 crab and sweetcorn soup. We've also found the traditional cockney dish of jellied eels at £4.40 a tasty appetizer. The seafood platter with fresh fish selections, shellfish, crab meat, prawns and lobster (mayonnaise optional) is another winner at £14.50. Then there's the terrific £16.60 turbot, poached with asparagus and scampi served in a glazed Parmesan cheese sauce. And we adored the oyster pudding, a special during our last visit, that is essentially a steak and kidney pie spiked with oysters.

The imperturbable maître d' Louis has been here for 25 years, taking the changes in decor and clientele in stride. Consult with him about a reservation. We suggest that if an Overtons lunch is in your future, don't take it before 1:00 P.M. Otherwise, despite Louis' attentions, you may feel a bit lonely here. Still, if you do lunch early to miss the afternoon hordes, it's easier to get a good look at the artwork, which, primarily by English and Scottish artists (Nicholas Healy Hutchinson, Viola Patterson and Alexandra Haines among them), is worthy of your perusal.

La Poule au Pot

231 Ebury Street   071-730-7763
London SW1 W84

Our native friends are pleasantly surprised when we mention our fondness for this slightly off-the-beaten-track French provincial charmer. Ditto, David Hopkins, the suave general manager of the Ritz. La Poule au Pot is one of his favourites, too, but one he tends to consider the private preserve of locals. Suitably sophisticated locals, of course—witness his own penchant for the place and its location near Sloane Square. But there's nothing self-consciously chi-chi about the restaurant which, when it opened in 1962, was one of the first informal beachheads of French regional cooking in the city.

Which is not to say that La Poule au Pot lacks atmosphere. Quite the contrary, in fact. In an era when brightly lit minimal decor is the norm for newer, more trendy establishments, the mélange of dark wood, exposed brick, pots of blooming plants, private nooks and crannies, and baskets everywhere, all profiting from soft candlelight (at first glance seemingly the only source of illumination), is downright disarming. La Poule au Pot has atmosphere to the max, making it an ideal haven during one of London's rainy nights.

Indeed, we last sought refuge here after a devastating hurricane had brought the city to a virtual standstill. After a harrowing day—the constant whine of sirens had evoked visions of wartime London—manager Marc Faillat's reliably warm welcome was a god-send. We nestled into a high-backed wooden banquette, ordered copious amounts of the house's respectable red table wine and dove into bowls of restorative onion soup at £3.95. Once rejuvenated, we sat back, took a real look at the familiar menu, and further raised our spirits by flirting with our handsome waiter. They're all very easy on the eye here and are possessed of Gallic charm which they exercise with good-natured abandon. In between shouting instructions to the kitchen, ours nattered away about running over to Paris the next day to get his hair cut.

Shouting? Well, we did say it was informal. Indeed, the communication between the waiter and the chef resembles that between waitresses and a short-order cook in a roadside diner. They solicitously take your order, then, still at the table, shout it in code to the kitchen. The only difference is that here they do it in French. Oddly enough, rather than shattering the atmosphere, the practice enhances it—you feel as if you're dining en famille.

And, indeed, Marc enjoys playing the host, brokering introductions between his patrons, with varying degrees of success. The night of the killer hurricane, he hooked us up with a fellow countryman of ours whose demeanour lent new meaning to the term "Ugly American." Quickly realizing his mistake, Marc ushered the boor away and spent the rest of the evening hovering apologetically, and protectively, while we consumed our meal.

Having taken the edge off with the soup, we opted for two somewhat more glamorous hors d'oeuvres, the flavourful salmon pâté and the sensational braised endive, both £4.95. Escargots at £5.45 are another good bet, but be forewarned that they are very much of the country classic variety, i.e., heavy on the garlic. And it is tough to resist the £5.45 creamy coquilles, complete with coral-coloured roe. As for the main course, we always feel compelled to order la poule au pot at £11.95, but somehow never do. We're too taken with the rabbit in mustard sauce for £10.95 and the magret de canard at £12.45.

Desserts are not a strong suit here—stick to the £3.55 crème brulée or the £3.50 selection of cheeses. Better yet, skip it altogether and cap off your appetite with the delicious bread accompanied by a light, sweet, first-press olive oil for £1.30—it tends to arrive whether or not you ask for it. And rest assured you will be charged for it, just as you'll be charged the £1.30 cover. Tax is included in the prices, but the 12.5 per cent service charge is not. All of which makes the set three-course luncheon a bargain for £11.95, with wine charged by the glass at £1.50.

Bargain or no, however, the restaurant is not nearly so appealing by the light of day. Atmosphere is the name of the game here, and you have to go at night to get the full effect.   ❧

The Red Fort

77 Dean Street	071-437-2115
London W1V 5HA	(FAX) 071-434-0721

Time was when London's Indian restaurants were reliable distributors of good cheap eats. Plenty of those tacky curry palaces still exist, but the trend is toward upscale and authenticity. Witness the success of the

Bombay Brasserie and of the Red Fort, owned by the enterprising Amin Ali, which several of our pals say is the best Indian restaurant in town.

If that's so, it's due to the diligence of Amin who emigrated from Bangladesh with his family when he was 16 years old. His parents returned to their native land after a year, but Amin remained, supporting his English studies as a waiter at an establishment allegedly devoted to the cuisine of the subcontinent. He was "shocked and disappointed by the food we had to serve...I'd never come across anything like it at home." He explains that what passed for Indian food in this country was primarily of British invention, relying on basic Indian ingredients but not traditional techniques. Shortcuts were employed to facilitate mass production, which accounted for its being inexpensive—legitimate Indian cooking is time-consuming and not particularly economical.

Amin was convinced the British people would enjoy his country's real food, if only they had the opportunity to try it. He was determined to give them a chance. And with a group of like-minded friends, he raised £80,000 to open the Last Days of the Raj in 1979. It set a new standard for authentic north Indian food. Another restaurant on Tottenham Court Road followed in 1981, but Amin didn't really hit the big time until he opened the Red Fort in 1983. Named after the red fort built in Delhi 300 years ago by the Moghul emperor Shah Jahan, the man who gave the world the Taj Mahal, the restaurant is decidedly up-market. Simply decorated in soothing neutral tones highlighted by grape purple, as opposed to the expected red, and a profusion of plants, it's located right in the middle of oh-so-fashionable Soho. As such, it attracts an interesting clientele at lunch—MPs and lawyers, enlivened by personalities from nearby Channel 4 and ITV. At dinner it can be overloaded by tourists, but many locals enjoy intimate meals in the romantic little room downstairs.

Lunch or dinner, call a day ahead and be prepared to sample dishes you may never have heard of before, dishes that are the result of Amin's thorough research of his country's history and culture during the years of the Moghul Empire. They represent the best of Indian, Pakistani and Bangladesh influences, prepared by time-honoured methods. Try the tandoori quail as a starter, which Amin first introduced to London here. The quail, cooked in a clay oven, is first marinated in yogurt with garlic, ginger, cumin, and tumeric and sells for £4.50. The aloo patishapta—a pancake stuffed with delicately flavoured potatoes and carrots—is almost as good. And the £3.50 minced-meat filled pastry served with a lightly spiced tomato sauce should not be ignored.

If you want to get an overview of Amin's philosophy of the subcontinent's cuisine, order the thali, a set meal for £12.50, featuring three meat dishes, one vegetable, a yogurt-and-cucumber salad, rice and leavened bread. The only problem with it is that it doesn't include our Red Fort favourite—succulent king prawns cooked in onion, garlic, coconut milk and cream for £10.95. To quench our desire for heat, we ask for the lamb cooked with onions, ginger, peppers and fresh chili. At £6.50 it fulfils its promise of being one of the hot dishes.

Stick to the fruits, sorbets and ice creams for dessert. They add £2.50 to £3.75 to the tab, including tax. The management tacks on another 15 per cent for the admirable service. It's the same deal for the Sunday buffet lunch served from noon to 3:00 P.M. It's a bargain hunter's dream at £10.95, even with the obligatory service charge.   ♥

Restaurant St Quentin

243 Brompton Road   071-589-8005
London SW3 2EP

No, there's nothing wrong with your eyesight. You're not seeing double. There are indeed two shop fronts displaying the St Quentin logo strung out along a brief stretch of Brompton Road, just west of Harrods. And there's a third tucked around the corner on Yeoman's Row—a restaurant, a grill, and a patisserie, each dedicated to showcasing different aspects of the food and service customarily found in Paris. All are spawned from the success of the original Restaurant St Quentin, opened in 1980.

Inspired by the traditional brasseries of the 19th century, the restaurant is a mecca for London's large French community. The French feel right at home in its leather banquettes, where they consume familiar dishes and are served by an authentically Gallic staff. Make no mistake, the eatery is equally popular with the city's English citizens who appreciate its casual yet smart atmosphere and hearty French fare, not to mention the fact that it's actually open on Sunday—as well as on every other day of the week. People like Princess Margaret and Mark Thatcher (Maggie's son) depend on it as a desirable weekend destination when so many other good restaurants are closed.

Because of its proximity to the exciting shopping prospects on Beauchamp Place, we like St Quentin for lunch and often go for the £11.90

daily menu—a four-courser that might include a choice of fish soup or salad of smoked fish, followed by fillet of trout in a crème sauce, or roast leg of lamb served with flageolet beans, succeeded by a cheese course, and topped off by a scrumptious dessert. Alternatively, the à la carte menu features hors d'oeuvres like homemade rough country pâté and smooth salmon mousse with a shallot and butter sauce, both £3.90. The main courses, be they poisson or viande, are accompanied by potatoes and are priced in the narrow range of £8.40 to £8.80. There's also a cover charge of £1.30 per person and a service charge of 12.5 per cent which is described as being "at the discretion of the customer," i.e., you're invited to increase it should you feel your waiter or waitress is deserving.

Our preference for lunch here aside, the restaurant is generally busiest at dinner, which is served until midnight from Monday to Saturday, until 11:30 on Sundays. Again, you can go either the table d'hôte or the à la carte route. At £14.90, the three-course menu is a steal and always presents tempting treats like leek terrine knapped with a truffle vinaigrette and robust lamb casserole laced with seasonal vegetables.

But being frugal means skipping the duck liver encased in a port jelly for £8.80 or the raw salmon marinated in olive oil and lime juice at £3.90—something we find virtually impossible to do. Once plotted, our à la carte course continues with the unique £9.10 curried monkfish pie and the roast breast of duck complemented by a luscious béarnaise sauce for £8.80. Or, when feeling particularly familial, we order the rack of lamb pour deux at £19.60. No matter what the choice, there's still that £1.30 couvert, which we must admit is less bothersome at St Quentin than at some more pretentious establishments—the prices are relatively moderate, and we like to think our £1.30 each covers the cost of the bread shipped fresh daily from France.

Indeed, despite having been recently purchased by the very properly English Savoy Group, St Quentin imports most everything from its metaphorical motherland—food, wine, staff and style. It truly is an hospitable French outpost in the heart of London's West End.

River Café

Thames Wharf	071-381-8824
Rainville Road	(FAX) 071-381-6217
London W6 9HA	

We relearned two important lessons with this one—never believe everything you read, and always trust the hall porter (read concierge) of a good hotel. You see, we'd read lots of good things about this three-year-old establishment, raves, in fact, in usually reliable sources like *Gourmet* and *European Travel & Life*. Consequently, while we were surprised by the hall porter's disparaging tone as he summoned a taxi to Dukes to take us to the very out-of-the-way location, it did nothing to dampen our enthusiasm for what we were convinced would be a memorable evening. It was, but not an especially pleasant one.

The first disappointment was the much-touted view—there wasn't one to speak of, despite the floor-to-ceiling wall of window on the river side of the restaurant. At night there really isn't anything to see, and even during the day a waist-high wall at the end of the admittedly attractive riverside garden separates you from the water.

Worse, the service was on the slow and sullen side. There was what is described in the vernacular as a lot of "attitude" on the part of the staff—which they may have adopted in deference to the fact that one of the chef/proprietor partners is formerly of Nell's, the once chic New York nightspot. The final blow came when we proffered an American Express Card and were told the restaurant didn't accept it. Fair enough, except that when we made the reservation, we had specifically asked about their policy vis-à-vis Amex and were informed the restaurant took it, "but preferred not to." Well, in this instance *we* preferred to use it and did not take kindly to the blunt, not to mention dishonest, refusal. Upon threat of stiffing her, the indignant waitress finally processed the paperwork, and we fled for the taxi which the manageent had (atypically) graciously ordered.

As for the food—it was fine, even very good, but not worth the £8-ish ride from St James's and the aggravating staff. And the menu, which changes daily for lunch *and* for dinner, was one of the most difficult to read we have ever encountered. After several passes at it, we finally settled on the extremely tasty fresh ravioli stuffed with ricotta and spinach in a butter, sage, and Parmesan sauce for £6, and the intriguing £5.75 grilled salt cod knapped with a fresh tomato and basil sauce. Both satisfying choices, we followed them with pan-roasted partridge stuffed with fresh thyme and served with grilled polenta and sautéed wild mushrooms at £23 and the char-grilled seabass resting on a bed of artichokes braised in garlic and accompanied by a salad of white chicory and fresh basil for £17.50.

So one expectation was fulfilled. As advertised, the kitchen excels in honest northern Italian cooking, ostensibly inspired by Richard Rogers' grandmother. No, not the composer of *The Sound of Music* (that's Rodgers), but the architect of the Pompidou Centre in Paris...and of the River Café. You see, Richard, who converted a group of deserted warehouses into the complex that shelters the restaurant, is married to Ruth Rogers, one of the aforementioned chef-proprietors. Rose Gray is the Nell's veteran. It's Richard's Italian mama who taught Ruth how to cook and is therefore credited with the restaurant's predilection for grilled meats, fish and vegetables. Of course, it doesn't hurt that Rose—the one who brought some previous restaurant experience to the table—lived in Tuscany for four years! But the mother-in-law story is a better one, especially in an eatery that is so much the product of familial contributions.

Richard is responsible for the appealing minimal decor—high barrel-vaulted ceilings meet white-washed walls, trimmed in red and blue. Cane-backed and seated chrome chairs nestle up to black formica tables disguised with white linen, which in turn is covered with white paper, presumably to simulate a casual café appearance. The single decoration is a large, colourful, modern painting that dominates one wall and is changed regularly—always the work of Ruth's sister, Susan Elias. The effect is one of relaxed contrivance, which is perfectly pleasant if not the *Interiors* marvel we had expected.

Was ours an off night at the River Café? Possibly—maybe Ruth and Rose's insistence that the waiters and waitresses come in early to help with the food preparation has begun to wear a little thin. But the taxi driver on the way back to the hotel told us he'd picked up a lot of people at the restaurant and that, more often than not, it was clear they had been disappointed.

Still, the 60 seats are almost always occupied. Reservations are a must, and despite our feelings about the place, we do recommend you give it a shot for lunch during the warmer months when they set up tables on the terrace, overlooking the pretty, sculpture-studded garden. It is, after all, one of those restaurants everyone has heard of, so your tales of woe or wonder are guaranteed to be fodder for good cocktail conversation. 🍋

San Lorenzo

22 Beauchamp Place   071-584-1074
London SW3 1NH

San Lorenzo is so trendy, so often cited in food and social columns that newcomers to London may be under the impression that it opened only a month or two ago. In actual fact, Lorenzo and Mara Berni opened this perennially chic conservatorial concern way back in 1963. Early on it may have been considered a bit of a hideaway, but no longer—anyone who is anyone shows up here at one time or another. Nor is San Lorenzo any longer London's absolutely best Italian restaurant—the competition has heated up in the last 28 years—but it's still a contender.

The garden-like setting, brimming with plants and dominated by a two-storey high tree, and the relatively reasonable prices (read *no credit cards*) make it an enduring favourite with the locals. They also appreciate the fact that no one gets huffy if you order just an appetizer and a glass of wine, spending (with the £2 cover) only £10 in the process. Lorenzo and Mara know it all comes out in the wash—on your next visit, perhaps you'll go whole hog and rack up a whopping bill. Would that all restaurateurs exhibit such good common sense!

Most of the regulars prefer the three rooms on the ground floor with their tile floors and rattan chairs. The front one is further enhanced by a humourous Jonathan Routh mural. (If you like his work, check out the gallery that represents him upstairs.) Light pours through the glass roofs which open up during the summer months, bouncing off the energy that always permeates the atmosphere here. But for quiet private conversations or a romantic rendezvous, we prefer the room upstairs. Wherever you sit, rest assured there is no Siberia here—under the Bernis' watchful eyes, the food and service is superior throughout the restaurant. We're particularly happy to see Tiziano, Gian-Lucio or Domenico approach our table, as they've all been here forever and are adept at remembering our favourites. Even if they're not on the menu which does change frequently, they'll remind us of favourites like the £7.50 garlic-laden spaghetti with fresh mussels and the grilled fresh sardines at £6.50. The kitchen can usually rustle them up, and you can always count on the dreaded tiramisu being one of the homemade sweets for £4.50. We're told it's out of this world—we just keep it off the table and order the £3 crème brulée or one of the freshly made ice creams instead.

Among the pesca and carni, the poached cod with hollandaise sauce and the spicy Italian sausages served with beans are excellent tried and true choices, both priced at £11.50. The kitchen also has a way (actually several) with calves' liver and veal for £1 more.

To get a reservation for either of the lunch seatings—12:30 and 2:15—you'd best call a day or two ahead. Likewise, for the 7:45 and 10:15 dinner seatings. Reservations are taken by whoever answers the telephone. You're just lucky if you get Mara, not because she's got more authority than anyone else save hubby Lorenzo, but because she's such a warm charmer, whose love for people and food is abundant. . .and evident.

❦

Santini

29 Ebury Street	071-730-4094/8275
London SW1 WONZ	(FAX) 071-730-0544

"They" say more business is conducted during lunch at Santini than is done all day long in the City. We guess that means there's only 70 serious players in town, because that's all this jewel of a restaurant, opened in 1984 by Gino Santin, seats—and there's only one seating from 12:30 to 2:30 P.M., so there's plenty of time to mix business with pleasure, while being pampered by a staff of 35.

What's the appeal to London's business biggies? There's that incredible staff-to-diner ratio for one, which ensures irreproachable service. Gino, born and bred in the hotel and restaurant industry, hires only professionals who take pride in their work—no sullen "I'm just passing through" aspiring whatevers here. The low-key decor is another factor—its terra-cotta floors and pale iceberg lettuce coloured walls trimmed with three bands of earthy hues could be a prototype interior for a stress reduction centre. The calming effect stops short of putting you to sleep, courtesy of stunning photographs of Gino's beloved Venice by Sylvio Roiter, and the energy generated by the high-profile karmas of Lord Hansen (credited with leading the power pack to Gino's door), the head of British Petroleum, and Lord King from British Airways. And, of course, the food is spectacular.

But the real secret to Santini's extraordinary success—we dare you to try to get a reservation for lunch or dinner with less than a week's notice—is Gino's passion for perfection. Trained virtually since birth in the art of hospitality by his inn-keeping family, and a graduate of one of Europe's most difficult hotel schools, Gino is a master of both the front and back of house activities—he can't be conned (or cowed) by a finicky chef or a pompous maître d'. He knows the business from top to bottom and insists that everyone involved in his restaurants (Gino also owns the delightful L'Incontro) meets his exacting standards, standards which ensure his sophisticated, international clientele return again and again. They know Gino doesn't take them or their expense accounts (we're talking about £100 for two, lunch or dinner) for granted. "I have no guaranteed clientele. I work at it all the time. The point is I have to give them the maximum value for the money they're spending. I use the best quality ingredients, the most professional in staff and offer superb surroundings," he states.

Consequently, dinner is just as popular as lunch here, although the glamour quotient improves considerably. Santini is a favourite of Prince Charles and of Fergie, his fun-loving sister-in-law. Whenever Robert Trump is in town, he dines here, as does Frank Sinatra who once ate here four out of the five nights he was in residence. Queen Nor of Jordan, Queen Beatrix of Holland, Roger Moore, Liza Minelli, Don Johnson, George Hamilton, Andrew Lloyd Webber and Shirley Temple Black may not be quite so fanatic about their Santini fixes, but they're here often enough to be considered regulars.

And when they can't enjoy Santini first-hand, we bet they get a dose second-hand via Gino's cookbook *La Cucina Veneziana*...make that third-hand, as we imagine most of these folks have cooks who faithfully follow the Italian cooking gospel according to Gino. It's a doctrine that depends upon the rich traditions of Venetian cuisine, but draws inspiration from other regions, too. Gino is fond of reminding his patrons that it wasn't until 1861 that all the very separate, culturally and politically distinct city-states of the Italian peninsula were united. In his view, there is no such generic entity as Italian food; rather, there is a series of regional culinary legacies that can be employed to create exciting dishes like fillet of beef in a cream, brandy and Dijon mustard sauce. One of our favourites among Santini's carni, it sells for £15.50.

As for the pesci, we like the £10.50 monkfish cooked with green peppers, tomato and garlic and the seabass in a tantalizing herb sauce for

£19.50. For starters, we favour fresh tortellini with ricotta and spinach at £9.50, and skewered Mediterranean prawns in a garlic and butter sauce for £11.50. And this is no place to skimp on the wine. The list is over 100 strong, ranging from a refreshing soave santi '87 for £12 to a rather profound £475.75 bottle of Chateau Latour Paulliac Medoc Premier Grand Cru '59.

All prices include tax, but when calculating what you're likely to spend add in a £1.50 cover per person and a service charge—and don't forget to add £4.50 for a slice of the chocolate mousse cake which is absolutely better than sex, safer too. ❦

Scotts

| 20 Mount Street | 071-629-5248 |
| London W1Y 6HE | (FAX) 071-491-2477 |

If there's one thing we like better with our champagne than oysters, it's caviar. At Scotts we can indulge ourselves in both—the venerable Mayfair restaurant's oyster bar doubles as a caviar counter, offering sevruga, oscetra and beluga along with tasty complements like buckwheat blinis and smoked salmon. There's also an intriguing selection of "frozen" vodkas for those who find that liquid lightning gives them more kicks than champagne. Always on the look-out for a deal, we have been known to forego our preference for the bubbly and order the special of 50gms of golden oscetra and a shot of Finlandia for £39. And should you believe in the seductive powers of caviar, you might be interested in Scotts' takeaway service.

Once a rather moribund place a bit past its prime, Scotts owes its rejuvenating touches, like the caviar bar and a stylish interior, to Nicky Kerman, who follows New York's McNally brothers' credo of developing a good formula and sticking with it, using it over and over and over again. But for our dining money, Nicky's restaurants seem somehow more substantial, and while his help may be less decorative than that of the divided McNally empire, they also have a less annoying attitude problem. Indeed, at Scotts, they couldn't be more unobtrusively attentive, and we've encountered few more charming (not to mention movie-star dashing) maître d's than Tino Paissoni. Call or fax him at least two days in advance for either lunch or dinner. If you want to graze in the oyster bar, almost a separate entity with its own entrance, Michel Tahar is the man to talk to.

It's always a dilemma for us to decide whether "to restaurant" or "to bar" at Scotts. Having agonized over that, we are further distressed by the question of lunch or dinner. The menu's the same, but the crowd changes dramatically. Scotts is home to one of London's more potent power lunches—few women on the premises, which we, of course, consider a plus. On the other hand, the atmosphere gets very glamorous in the evening. The lights dim (by 30 per cent from their lunchtime setting, thanks to Nicky's superb computerized system), the peachy walls glow, the fine collection of handsome 19th-century English primitive paintings takes on a new depth, and Scotts becomes a sumptuously luxurious restaurant, dressed with very pretty people enjoying pretty, perfect food—Linda Evans, Warren Beatty, Elizabeth Taylor, Charlton Heston, Shirley MacLaine, Robert Wagner, Julie Andrews, Peter O'Toole Michael and Vivienne Appel and Faye Dunaway to name just a few.

Of all the Kerman eateries, the menu here is the most ambitious, and with the notable exception of Drones, caters most effectively to carnivores. Scotts' meat dishes are worth the price of admission, particularly the £15.50 beef fillet sautéed in butter and served with a foie gras, Madeira and truffle sauce, and the saddle of lamb, also sautéed in butter and topped by a wine and tarragon sauce for £16.30. Still, fish is really the focus. We love the scampi tossed in a spicy curry sauce and served over rice with a selection of "boys" (those nifty little munchies-like peanuts and raisins served with curry) at £15.70. We were also especially taken with the £13.90 coulibiac of salmon. A chef's special the last time we visited, it's a Russian dish of salmon, spinach, mushrooms and rice encased in a delicate dough which is baked to a golden brown and knapped with an ethereal white wine, cream, parsley and butter sauce. If they're featuring the coulibiac when you stop by, order it.

We also recommend the ogen melon at £6.50 as an appetizer. Besides being deliciously sweet and juicy, this little melon is so cleverly presented—the top is cut so that you can partake of the fruits and then reassemble the melon. As for dessert, the £3 crème brulée (large enough for two) should not be missed.

Any way you slice it, assuming you skip the caviar which will add £38 to £95 to the tab, you're talking about £85 for two with a moderately priced wine.

Sheekeys

28–32 St Martin's Court   071-240-2565
London WC2 N4AL   (FAX) 071-491-2477

Sheekeys may best be described as London's answer to New York's Sardi's—they're both in the heart of their respective city's theatre districts, both decors depend heavily on theatrical images, both have red banquettes and both claim the patronage of stars of stage and screen. But for our pre- or post-theatre money, Sheekeys has it all over Sardi's. Here, dim lighting is atmospheric (rather than a disguise for dinginess) and the food is worth the visit, whether you have theatre tickets or not.

Established in 1896 on the delightful, pedestrians-only St Martin's Court, where its bold, glossy exterior signs act as a beckoning beacon, Sheekeys has been famous for fish ever since. Indeed, until recently, the menu offered nothing but seafood. Now, for landlubbers, there's a grilled sirloin steak for £9.90. We're sure it's just fine, but there are certainly better places for beef in London. Take our advice—if you can't stomach fish, go elsewhere or, better yet, learn to like it.

After all, it would be a shame to skip the opportunity to rub shoulders with the likes of Sir John Gielgud, Dustin Hoffman, Sir John Mills or Albert Finney on any given evening. And it would be a crime to miss Sheekeys' winning ways with fish. The £17.90 grilled or steamed lobster, the poached salmon for £11.80 and the grilled halibut at £13.50 are exceptional. They're also a good choice for the uninitiated. Save the £9.95 stewed eels and mash or the £7.80 grilled plaice for fish fanatics, who should also take note of the sweetly delicious native oysters when in season. And if it's on the menu, make sure someone orders the fish pie. A house speciality, it's a selection of fish and shellfish poached with white wine, mushrooms, tomato and basil, topped with creamy mashed potatoes grilled to a lovely golden brown for £9.95.

The lunch and dinner menus are interchangeable and, if they look familiar, it's because the graphics bear an unmistakable resemblance to those on the menu of another venerable fish house, Overtons. Small wonder, it seems that Nicky Kerman, whom we first met as one of the founders of London's hamburger heaven, Drones, owns both establishments. At any rate, Sheekeys' lunchtime clientele is less recognizably theatrical than at dinner—more publishing and producing folks. But for either meal, you'll spend about £60 for two with a bottle of wine from their refreshingly reasonably priced list. As for reservations, you'd best call Pasquale two days ahead for pre-theatre dining. Book for 6:30 to allow for a leisurely meal and request the front room, our personal favourite because of the fascinating photographs of stage legends from the 1930s to the 1990s lining the walls. Rest assured, there's nothing really wrong with the other three connecting rooms. Each is cosy and attractive, with art nouveau sconces, impressive antique mirrors and walls decked out with lots of pretty prints. It's just that we like to star gaze out front.

We've also been known to perch at the bar by the entrance. It's smothered in theatre posters, from seasons past and present, which are changed with some degree of regularity. So in addition to being a great place to grab a light snack (or full meal), Sheekeys' bar is usually a current, pictorial representation of what's playing on London's stages.   🦋

Stringfellows

16–19 Upper St Martin's Lane	071-240-5534
London WC2H 9EF	(FAX) 071-437-3423

"That's Cynthia Lennon," we screeched.

"Well, of course it is," responded our host. Easy for him to say. It's business as usual at Stringfellows where rock-'n'-roll icons have been hanging out since Peter Stringfellow—a pied piper if ever there was one—opened this glamorous, shimmering black glass and brass club in 1980. But for us, who had spent our early adolescence jealous of Cynthia because she was married to *him,* the oldest, sexiest, most experienced Beatle, it was the apogee of the evening to watch her approach— we marvelled at the fact that, right down to the long blond hair, bangs and glasses, she didn't look any different than she did those many years ago.

Peter jumped up to greet her with a big hug—no air-kissing for this craggy teddy bear of a man with his mane of blond hair—and made introductions all round, never hesitating over a name. (It's no coincidence that his trademark butterfly, worn as a gold earring, is most definitely a social one!) Then, after ushering Cynthia and her party to their table, he was off like a shot to embrace another regular night-crawler. When Peter's in town, holding court at his large round table, dead centre of the dining room, being at Stringfellows is almost like attending a terrific pri vate party where the host makes an Herculean effort to make sure you and everyone else have a jolly good time.

Of course, few hosts have so much to work with—Peter's genuinely warm hospitality is further extended by a phalanx of gorgeous waitresses outfitted in pink leotards and tutus, and his presence is made known throughout the splendiferous space via the miracle of close-circuit television. Every so often, he grabs a mike, hits his mark at one corner of the bar area (reputedly one of Europe's greatest sites for pretty people meeting similarly blessed types), and cajoles his guests into having a good time.

Few need much persuasion. The monster sound system programmed by savvy DJs keeps the downstairs dance floor crowded from 11:30 P.M. until closing, its plexiglass surface alive with colourful cavorting lights and occasional blasts of atmospheric fog. It's all frenetically fun, invigorating *and* enervating.

Upstairs, the street level is for quiet pursuits, chatting at the long bar or dining on cuisine worthy of a first-class restaurant, which Stringfellows definitely is, in addition to being a dance palace. No fewer than 10 chefs labour to execute the extensive menu, under the guidance of Nick Biberovic who has been with Peter from the beginning. We find the £8.50 paper-thin seared beef excellent with its light sesame oil dressing, and the ravioli filled with duck and spinach, which is bound by a sweet red pepper sauce, is just as tasty as it sounds at £7.50. We've also been known to dive into the selection of seafood, including prawns, shrimp and crabmeat, served in a giant shell—accompanied by a glass or two of champagne. It's a meal in itself for £17. Or, you can always take a cue from the Arab princeling who "owns" the table next to Peter's and order beluga caviar at £40 an ounce!

We've never been disappointed by the £16.50 Dover sole here, while the lamb, seasoned with rock salt, rosemary and garlic, filled with a chestnut and red onion stuffing and served with a light jus sauce is a real winner for £16.80. And the £17.50 house speciality of a butterflied fillet of beef, pan-fried in butter and knapped by a rich Boursin cheese sauce laced with wild mushrooms certainly warrants Peter's pride. Since the portions are on the large side, we seldom venture into dessert territory, although the £8 assortment of exotic peeled fruits is a sight to behold, easily enough for two to enjoy.

A £2 per person cover charge and a 15 per cent gratuity are tacked onto your bill, but if you're dining you won't be assessed the admission charge—£8 on weeknights, £15 at weekends. Of course, if you're a member, there's no entrance fee in any case, here or at Peter's other clubs in Beverly Hills or at Miami's Coconut Grove. And if you don't have the star power of, say, a Rod Stewart, Morgan Fairchild, Mickey Rourke or Cybill Shepherd, one of the three levels of membership will ensure you get through the velvet ropes in the first place. . . although a dinner reservation is equally effective. For Friday and Saturday nights Peter recommends booking a week in advance. And although Stringfellows opens at 8:00 P.M., don't settle for anything before 9:30. If you do, you, the waitresses and the easy-listening trio will be the only folks in the place.   ❦

Tall Orders

676 Fulham Road   071-371-9673
London SW6

For once the reality lived up to the hype. Dubbed by the *Sunday Times* as what "could be the most influential restaurant of the nineties" and described by eminent food writer Sir Clement Freud as a "haven of culinary originality and excellence," Tall Orders became an instant sensation when it opened in January 1990. We wondered if it could possibly satisfy our expectations. . . and we had a long time to ponder that question as it's way out on Fulham Road. Mercifully, the restaurant fulfilled the tall order of living up to its reputation.

First and foremost, it truly represents a unique concept in dining devised by the energetic Nick Gill, who earned a Michelin star during his tenure at Hambleton Hall. Every dish on the menu is £2.95 and is not categorized as appetizer, entrée, side dish or dessert, except in your own mind. Mix and match at will, knowing that Nick is keen on his being healthy food. You construct your own tall orders—the name comes from the novel mode of service whereby the savoury dishes are delivered in a dramatic stack of Chinese steam baskets. It's very entertaining to watch the waiters balance their trays of towering baskets as they wade through the throng at the bar and negotiate the tight quarters of the dining area.

Indeed, if we have a complaint about Tall Orders, it's about the cramped layout. The bar jutting out into the middle of the fresh-looking blue-and-white restaurant takes up a lot of room, forcing the patrons in the 100 seats to eat cheek by jowl. Nobody seems to mind though. Actually, neither did we, once we realized that part of the fun is sharing the discovery of the contents of each basket with your neighbours. The room is filled with "oohs" and "ahs" as the mixed crowd—young, old, chic and less than chic—open the lids, starting at the top and working their way down to the bottom of their stacks. Their order is determined by the kitchen, so until the end you're never sure what comes next. It's like opening a series—the menu recommends three to six—of gifts, each presented in pretty bowls nestled in the baskets.

We shared six and felt like we had indulged in a bacchanalian feast, the remnants of which are depicted by the massive mural which is the room's principal decoration. The containers may be Oriental in nature, but the food mirrors French, Italian and Moroccan influences. We sampled the spinach tortellini with smoked salmon, cream and lemon, and then turned our attention to delicious sliced meatballs with just a hint of a crunch. Next came crisply fried mushrooms and onions which we dipped in a flavourful chili mayonnaise, followed by salmon carpaccio with guacamole. Whole prawns cooked with coriander, ginger and garlic were a nice preamble to the finale, which was Cotechino sausages sitting on a bed of lentils and roast peppers. We didn't bother with dessert, although there are plenty to choose from. In fact, you can satisfy even the most demanding sweet-tooth with the Pudding Club, one of their "skyscrapers"—ready-built towers, consisting of six storeys selected by Nick with an eye to their complementary characteristics. For vegetarians, there's the Emerald Tower, and the Multistorey is a selection of the day's specialities—all the skyscrapers are £12.90.

We favour building our own stack because it necessitates entreating the uncommonly handsome waiters for guidance. Ours, one Sam Morney by name, was a dead ringer for a masculine Michael Jackson and hailed from Midland, Texas. While he's *really* a model and singer, he did an admirable job of impersonating a terrific waiter. Sam was sort of our seventh present for the night!

So, if you're an adventuresome eater, exercise your tastes at this restaurant that takes the 1980s concept of grazing to the next level. Just make sure you don't miss the £1.20 warm loaves of homemade bread served with light, fruity olive oil or garlic pesto mayonnaise. Obviously, meat-and-potatoes types need not apply.

La Tante Claire

68/69 Royal Hospital Road	071-351-0227
London SW3 4HP	(FAX) 071-352-4071

Generally considered one of Britain's most gifted chefs, Pierre Koffmann came to prominence via a somewhat circuitous route. He put his time in with the Roux brothers (an apprenticeship which seems to virtually ensure a place in the country's culinary hierarchy) and may in fact be their most famous "graduate." He was not, however, overwhelmed at an early age by a compulsion to cook. Sure, he loved to eat and was not above helping his mother. But in terms of future career, it was certainly not love at first bite.

Instead, he tried studying what he describes as "industrial vocations" in his native Gascony in southwest France, only to discover they tended to dampen his fun-loving spirit. He found out that cooking school had more holidays, and the rest is gastronomical history. While a number of Britain's chefs are described as Roux brothers alumni, few have actually worked for both Albert and Michel. Pierre, who looks a little like a large Wolfgang Puck with a beard, exercised his talents at both Le Gavroche and the Waterside Inn before opening La Tante Claire in the late seventies.

Unlike most new owner-chefs, Pierre never experienced the anxiety of grappling with a negative cash flow nor the uneasy wait to be canonized by a fawning press. The night he opened, 36 of his 40 seats were taken, and La Tante Claire has quite literally been full ever since. If an 8 P.M. dinner reservation is the object of your desire, call the engaging Enga four weeks in advance. For lunch, plan a couple weeks ahead. A word to the wise—there's almost always room after theatre, except at weekends when Pierre takes a welcome rest. Indeed, since he mans the kitchen in the company of only one other chef and without benefit of an army of sous-chefs, he may well wonder if he traded in those industrial vocations for another form of drudgery. He admits that it's "not a very romantic way to operate," but it assures that no one ever walks away from his cheerfully sophisticated little eatery disappointed. His hands-on approach also had a lot to do with the restaurant's receiving (and keeping) its coveted status as a Relais et Châteaux, one of only two restaurants in Britain so designated.

Lunch at La Tante Claire is a choice between two fixed-priced menus at £23.50—such as ravioli stuffed with lobster floating in resonant bouillon, followed by roasted rabbit and topped off with cheese or a Chinese pear served in a sorbet laced with other exotic fruits. The flavours are aggressive, the combinations creative without being silly and the presentation a beautiful melody, each course presented more dramatically than the last. Pretty heady stuff and relatively modestly priced, but lunch is not our meal of choice here.

True, during the day the windows facing the quiet residential Chelsea street shed a chipper light across the primrose yellow room making the chairs, fashionably draped in bright yellow fabric, look like daffodils dancing round white cloth-covered tables. And we do mean "round"— there's not a square top in the room, which adds to its softly comfortable appeal. And we suppose that same light allows a better look at the large colourful pieces of modern art which in their ingenious lucite frames comprise the primary decor. But La Tante Claire is a bit out of the way for lunch, unless you've been playing Sloane Ranger at nearby Sloane Square, which may explain Princess Di's frequent lunches.

Rest assured she has to make reservations well in advance, just like anyone else, though Pierre confides it's always done under a pseudonym. And he says the tabloids' headlines about her tendency toward anorexia are nonsense—"I don't know what she eats at home, but she eats plenty here." Moreover, he's happy to report he has had the pleasure to serve more than the occasional romantic dinner à deux for the princess and her allegedly estranged prince.

We think the royal couple have the right idea. At night the well-bred intimacy of La Tante Claire drips with glistening romance. Besides, over dinner, you have the time to truly savour what is most definitely très haute, if not always classic, French cuisine. Consider the ragoût of oysters, asparagus and truffles at £8.50 or the £17 incandescent langouste ravioli in a tomato and basil sauce as starters. Then dive into the epitomy of Pierre's cooking, a mixture of the traditional and the modern, a twist on the conventional. He transforms the old peasant standby of pot au feu with lobster and duck confit for £29. And his tried-and-true pied au cochon, a £21 menu staple since the beginning, is made aristocratic with morels and sweetbreads.

Clearly it's not difficult to hit the £40—tax and service included—per person minimum. You've got it locked with a drink or two, and wine easily takes you over the top. But at least there's not a supercilious cover and the consistently extraordinary food keeps you from begrudging the prices or the wait for a reservation.

Thai Pavillion

42 Rupert Street	071-287-6333
London W1V 7FR	(FAX) 071-587-0484

Considered most authentic of London's growing community of Thai restaurants, the Pavillions (this one in Piccadilly and a sister establishment in Dulwich) are, ironically enough, enterprises owned by an extremely good-looking couple, neither one of whom is from Thailand. Ameer and Chantal Khasru hail from Bangladesh and France, respectively. But they lived in Bangkok, where they developed a profound respect for Thai culture and food. When they moved to London, they missed both and decided the only solution was to open a restaurant where they could immerse themselves in the traditions of their adopted country. Enter the Dulwich-based Thai Pavillion in 1987.

Despite its somewhat out-of-the-way location, the restaurant was an immediate hit, and its success spawned the opening of the Piccadilly Pavillion in November 1989. Since the Rupert Street restaurant is right in the middle of the theatre district, it has become our favourite of the two. Actually, its whereabouts is not the only reason for our preference—the interior has a lot to do with it as well. The narrow 19th-century building was a challenge to transform into a restaurant, but the Khasrus have done an admirable job with the use of Thai artifacts. Of particular note are the extraordinary tapestries on the walls. One, shimmering with gold threads on black silk, depicts all the signs of the zodiac in incredible detail. Ameer, who brought it from Thailand as he did the rattan chairs, cushions, dishes, napkins and placemats (not to mention the chef), figures it's about 80 years old. Equally spectacular is the 19th century wall-hanging which represents a royal Thai procession in ground mother-of-pearl, jewels, silver and gold on brown silk.

They are truly breathtaking, as is the food. But not because it is unbearably hot, a common misnomer about Thai cuisine. Yes, it can be spicy. More often than not, however, it's an extremely refined blend of Chinese and Indian influences which results in a subtle layering of flavours. If you're not familiar with the cuisine, you may find the menu's cursory explanations unsatisfactory. Never fear, all the waiters are Thai and will happily elaborate. They'll also help you negotiate a hotly or mildly spicy route, depending upon your inclination.

With or without their guidance, don't miss the satay, which you've undoubtedly encountered on the cocktail party circuit. Order it here for £4 and you'll find out how all those bits of barbecued beef, chicken or pork skewered on bamboo shoots and served with a scrumptious peanut sauce are *supposed* to taste. On the less routine and hotter side, we like the Tord Mun Pla—a £3.75 deep-fried fish cake with a refreshing cucumber sauce. Given the prices and the portions, you might want to wash down the hors d'oeuvres with Poa Teak, which is best described as Thai bouillabaisse, £7.20 for two. Or you might contemplate some "yum," defined as traditional Thai salads of meat, seafood or fruit with either cooked or raw vegetables and flavoured with a variety of dressings. There are ten to choose from, ranging from £4 to £6.50.

And speaking of choices, wait until you get into the main-course action of the menu! There are 51 tempting dishes, divided into six categories—curry, stir-fry, vegetable, egg, rice and noodle—most in the £5.25 to £8 neighbourhood. The seasonal seabass curry in a memorable sauce at £19.50 and the lobster and pineapple curry at £15.50 are the most notable exceptions. We tend to concentrate on the curry and stir-fry categories, wandering into the vegetable and rice listings for a complementary dish or two. By following our lead, you'll spend about £25 per person, including a reasonably priced bottle of wine, tax and service. At lunch, sans wine and assuming that any more than two courses in the middle of the day will put you to sleep, you may have trouble making the £12 per person minimum.

In fact, if you're hunting a bargain, head for the former cellar, now home to the fixed-price Eternal Lunch, actually a Thai salad bar with endless supplies of soup and rice, all for £10. The other alternative is the newly inaugurated satay bar on the ground floor. It's a Thai version of the Spanish traditional tapas bars where you sip and snack. Here you'll spend approximately £6 to £9 for a couple of Thai snacks and a cocktail, depending on what it is you order to drink.

Feel free to drop into the bar or pop in for the Eternal Lunch, but for the complete, à la carte Thai Pavillion experience, you'll need to make reservations for the pretty bone-and-blue dining room upstairs. Don't balk at the thought of its traditional Thai seating—the floor cushions have thoughtfully been provided with backs to make it comfortable for Westerners to sidle up to the low tables. Generally speaking, you can get one of them with a few hours' notice.

Toto's

Walton House   071-589-0075/2062
Walton Street
London SW3 2JH

There is something Emcrald City-ish (in a high-tech, terra-cotta and
glass sort of way) about the entrance to the restaurant—it's certainly startlingly incongruous on this otherwise charming cobblestone mews. Beyond that and the name suggesting the proprietorship of Dorothy's little
mutt, there is nothing else about Toto's to suggest the classic yarn, except that they both benefit from a great deal of enduring (and endearing)
personality and style.

Once the bacherlorette digs of Lady Clementine before she married
Lord Churchill, this private home turned Italian eatery has a chequered
history as a dispenser of hospitality. During World War II, it did duty as
an after-hours officers' club. In the 1960s it became the Jacaranda Restaurant in honour of the giant, several hundred years old tree that dominates the terrace. In 1983 it was purchased by Antonia Trapani, who is
responsible for its current incarnation as one of the very few stylish London dining establishments open for lunch and dinner seven days a week.
As such, it attracts a very cosmopolitan crowd who appreciate the consistent quality of the food and service. Manager Mario Endrighi has been
here since Toto's opened, as have most of the staff. Maître d's Walter and
Pino "dress" the four levels of the restaurant beautifully, showing
regulars—such as Faye Dunaway, Ringo Starr, Lauren Bacall, Cubby
Broccoli, Al Pacino and Rod Stewart—to the downstairs dining room in
the winter and to the popular terrace in the summer. Privacy seekers like
Madonna prefer the mezzanine overlooking both the miniscule, Sibe-
rianesque front room as well as the main dining chambre. There, they
can watch the usually bustling scene unobserved.

Wherever you sit, you can't help being struck by the singularly engaging decor. It is at once light and airy, courtesy of high ceilings and lots of
windows, and comfortingly cosy, seating only about 90. The abundance
of hanging and potted greenery coupled with the redwood trim and
bentwood chairs summons visions of California—an impression that is
mercifully tempered by the massive ornate mantelpiece that occupies
the back wall and the enormous, remarkably sophisticated floral arrangement that possesses what passes for the centre of the meandering interior.

As for the food it, like the restaurant, is light yet soothingly satisfying. The printed menu is in force all day long, but there are lots of dishes in the kitchen's repertoire that never appear on it. So be sure to consult with Mario or his assistant about what's available. On our last visit, they steered us toward the unlisted spaghetti with fresh lobster, and we always ask Mario for the salad he created for la Dunaway—lots of greens capped with French beans, asparagus tips and tiny slices of mozzarella. Heaven!

In fact, Toto's is one of our favourite places for a moderate lunch (in terms of price, despite the £2 cover charge, and calories).

Besides Faye's favourite, we adore the £15 crab salad and the mixed seafood insalata for £10.50. We've also found taking Toto's up on their seafood risotto for two at £14 happily solves the luncheon dilemma. And best of all, we can usually pop in at a moment's notice as so many ladies do . . . which may explain why, if truth be told, we like dinner at Toto's even better than lunch. With the lights down low and the candles lit, it takes on a romantic glow which is ever so flattering to all the pretty patrons, including the men who seem to eschew the light of day here.

For dinner, plan to reserve a day in advance and to spend from £30 to £35 a person including wine, cover and tax, but not service for meals consisting of a pasta and meat or fish course. We like the Tagliolini verdi gratinati—very fine, very fresh green "angel hair" noodles in a creamy white sauce topped with Parmesan cheese for £6.50. Also £6.50, the Trenette alla Ligure—linguini in a riveting pesto sauce—is an equally good choice. And you can't miss with either the sweetbreads simmering in brown butter and capers or the sweetly sautéed calves' liver served with polenta, both £11.

Again, if nothing on the menu is quite what you had in mind, talk to Mario. As he claims, if it's Italian, his kitchen will produce it.   🍇

The White Tower Restaurant

1 Percy Street   071-636-8141
London W1 PEOT

The site of London's premier Greek restaurant, Number 1 Percy Street, frames a charming little corner of the city near Russell Square. The cheerful blue-and-white tiled entrance with its awning and well-tended flower boxes has been greeting a devoted clientele for almost 30 years. In fact, about 80 per cent of the customers can be designated as regulars.

The aromas floating across the dining room from the kitchen along with the prices on the menu are your first indication of the secret to the White Tower's continuing success. And George Metaxas, the heart and soul of the operation, promises the recent sale of the restaurant will not change anything. It better not, or else there's likely to be a riot.

Of course, it's *un*likely that anyone would be so foolish as to tamper with the decor which is refreshingly modest. Colourful plates decorate the walls, and the tin ceiling testifies to the age of the congenial room that seats only 70. Because of its size and popularity, it's best to book a table two to three days ahead for either lunch or dinner, Monday to Friday. The restaurant is closed on Saturday and Sunday, which is too bad for weekend history buffs—the British Museum is nearby, and this is the perfect place to eat after a few hours of artifact perusal.

Actually, it's occurred to us that George persuaded one of the museum's curators to write his menu. This is one of the few ethnic restaurants where you can trod unfamiliar territory with temerity. The descriptions of the dishes are lengthy and are as fascinating as they are informative. Rest assured, you will not be subject to an unwanted or unpleasant surprise as you work your way through a menu which can best be portrayed as Larousse meets Zorba. All the classic Greek dishes—moussaka, taramosalata and dolmadkia—are represented, but executed with a refined finesse unusual in such hearty "peasant" fare. And there are divinely light creations as well, like the escaloppini zacharoff—sweetbreads and escalops of veal sautéed in butter and finished off with a squeeze of lemon for £11.25. As George points out, such straightforward cooking necessitates only the freshest, highest quality ingredients, and he wouldn't have it any other way.

He's proud of his food and downright boastful when it comes to his wine list, which is fairly priced and surprisingly diverse. In addition to a pleasant selection of Burgundies and Bordeaux, there's a large selection of clarets and several Greek wines. We're partial to the Domaine D'Ahera, a dry red from Cyprus that sells for £9.75 and is a perfect complement to our favourite dish here, the Aylesbury Duckling Farci à la Cypriote. At £13 (including, as all the prices do, tax but not service), it also results in our favourite description:

> "These aristocrats of the poultry world, specially reared
> for the White Tower, are prepared for the table before
> they are eight weeks old. (After that they grow their

'second feathers' which means they are not 'ducklings' any more!) Broad as they are long, they weigh between 5½ and 6½ lbs. . .just right for two hungry people. Stuffed with the famous bougourie of Cyprus, chopped almonds and ducks' livers and roasted to a crisp brown turn in the oven, this is the dish to gladden the happy gourmet's happy heart!

What did we tell you? How can you resist? Actually, most people don't— the duckling is a perennial favourite here, so book it along with your table.

Still the £10.25 moussaka should not be ignored. Neither should the meats grilled over a charcoal fire. We highly recommend the Shashlik à la Russe, a succulent marinated lamb shish kebab complete with mush-rooms, tomatoes and onions on the skewer.

As for what the menu calls "introductory dishes," we always order the mixed pâtés—the lemony smoked cod mixture known as taramosalata and the White Tower's rendition of chicken liver pâté called Diana—for £4.50. A pot of each is placed on the table along with some olives and hot toast. It makes for a communal start to the meal and gets us over our pique about the one pretentious element of the restaurant, the £2 cover, spelled "couvert" on the menu. Zorba would never have stood for it!

❦

Wiltons

55 Jermyn Street	071-629-9955
London SW1 6LX	(FAX) 071-495-6233

Wiltons has been around since 1742, and we do mean around—the res-taurant has claimed three different locations during its illustrious career, all within the boundaries of St James's. Its various owners, including the current Savoy Group management, have always appreciated the fact that the historic district is the haunt of the hearty-eating business people who are traditionally the lifeblood of an establishment like Wiltons, one "noted for the finest oysters, fish, and game."

No doubt about it, Wiltons is an old reliable, even though it has only been at this address since 1984. With every move, many of the original interior features like the fine collection of piscatorial pictures, the ornate Chinese embroideries and the high-backed banquette seats have been incorporated into the new premises. Furthermore, some of the menu offerings are sacrosanct. For summer, Monday always means sausages and mash; Tuesday takes on Irish stew; while Wednesday features fresh scallops. On Thursday it's liver and bacon and, of course, Friday is fish day. Actually, every day is potentially fish day at Wiltons, as there's always plenty on the menu, from smoked wild (as opposed to farmed) Scottish salmon for £12.25 as an hors d'oeuvre or £19 as a meal to lobster newburg starting at £28.50. During the winter months, look for other seasonal daily regulars.

And then there are the oysters—or at least there are for eight months of the year. Wiltons remains faithful to the old edict of oysters only being fit for eating during the *r* months, September to April. During that season Wiltons goes through a lot of them. Pat, the head oyster shucker of 25 years' standing, figures he alone is responsible for opening some 55,000 oysters annually. At £13.50 or so for six, Pat's operation must be quite a profit centre! Indeed, one of his predecessors, the legendary Jimmy Marx who ran the oyster bar before World War II, has been immortalized at the site of his former toils—a portrait of "The Guvnor," as Marx was affectionately known, hangs in the bar, testimony, no doubt, to his contribution to Wiltons' balance sheet.

As pleasant as the bar is with its cosy little sofas and always tempting display of seafood, we prefer the secluded booths in the dining room toward the rear. At dinner, their plush green velvet seats, made even more inviting by pretty yellow pillows and their unrivalled privacy, courtesy of floor-to-ceiling wood and etched-glass dividers, make for a romantic rendezvous. Still, in search of same, we have been known to ask manager Robin Gundry for a very visible table at lunch when Wiltons is almost entirely populated by men—men like Sir James Goldsmith, Sir Geoffrey Sterling, Albert Finney, the Duke of Devonshire and David Frost.

As fond of us as Robin is, he's hard-pressed to promise us anything since we don't really rate as regulars, while 90 per cent of his luncheon crowd does. They join him several days a week and therefore needn't book at least a week in advance as the rest of us must. Regarding reservations, it's the same story at dinner, although there are many more couples taking advantage of the flatteringly dim lighting and those snug booths. For either meal, plan on spending at least £45 a person including tax and the £1 cover, but not service. There's also a minimum of £12.50, which is no problem if you order the two ounces of royal beluga caviar for £110.

The daily specials address the game issue. On our last visit, saddle of hare with a pepper sauce for £18.50, roast partridge at £22 and grilled pheasant at £17 were among the enticing options. We usually consult the waitresses about the relative merits of each offering. Mercifully, they've never steered us wrong. Any duplicity from these nannylike creatures (an illusion studiously enhanced by starchy white uniforms) would be nothing short of unbearable. In fact, we find ourselves taking extra care to finish all our vegetables before daring to ask about one of the yummy nursery desserts—bread and butter pudding, baked jam roll and rice pudding.

The waitresses, like the restaurant they serve so well, are comfortingly familiar and always so reliable.

Zen Central

20–22 Queen Street   071-629-8103/8089
London W1

Lawrence Leung didn't set out to be a restaurateur. He studied to be an economist and dabbled in films, but since opening his first Chelsea eatery in 1983, he seems destined to inherit the mantle of Ken Lo (Mr Chow abdicated long ago) as king of London's Chinese hosts.

Zen Central, located in the heart of Mayfair, is the latest and most sophisticated of Lawrence's three popular restaurants in London—the others being the original Chelsea Cloisters Zen and ZenW3 (as in the NW3 postal code for Hampstead). But the Zen empire stretches far beyond even London's extended environs, as far as Hong Kong where Lawrence now owns two Zens, and to Montreal where Zen is the toast of the town.

All but the first Zen have been designed by Rick Mather, who makes these high-profile Chinese restaurants glamorous without being glitzy, fashionably minimalist but with soul. Zen Central is his best effort yet. The single long room warmed with a muted grey and mauve carpet is cleverly broken up by the curvature of the ceiling, enhanced by recessed lighting. Decoration is relegated to the one mirrored wall with its arresting etched glass sculptures by Danny Lane. The rest is sleekly functional. Large, well-spaced round tables, surrounded by surprisingly comfortable steel-framed black leather chairs, are set with oversized silver service plates, a soup spoon and a pair of chopsticks—that's it. If you require more, you'll have to ask.

Of course, you'll be graciously accommodated, but in a restaurant where at least half the clientele is Chinese (always a good sign) you may want to adopt a "when in Rome, do as the Romans do" approach to dining—usually the tack taken by the likes of Lord Grade, Roger Moore, Lord Charles Churchill, Richard Harris, Dustin Hoffman and his British counterpart in the eating-out sweepstakes, Michael Caine. In any case, you won't have to ask the waiter to hold the monosodium glutamate. There isn't even any in the kitchen. And one look at the food will tell you this is no ordinary Chinese restaurant. The natural-looking viscosity of the sauces is testimony to the lack of corn flour as a shortcut thickener, and the vegetables are not subjected to dousing with copious quantities of soy sauce. But you don't have to wait for the food to notice the difference—the menu says it all. Ignoring territorial boundaries, it combines the best of Peking, Szechuan and Cantonese styles to create a "nouvelle" Chinese cuisine—one that even encompasses influences from other Asian countries. "We only serve what we like," says Lawrence.

We only eat what we like. So we eat here a lot—as in often and in volume. We graze through the four pages of appetizers (designated as hot, dumplings, wrapped and cold), enthusiastically consuming such delicacies as crunchy sesame prawn toast for £4, yam packet filled with spiced crabmeat at £3.80, chopped oysters seasoned with green herbs and wrapped in lettuce for £4, and the raw salmon and scallop salad for £4.

Despite the pointedly placed spoon, we usually skip the soup and head straight for the main event—crispy aromatic lamb served with spring onions, cucumbers and pancakes for £12, prawns sautéed in a unique spinach sauce at £8, or barbecued breast of duck flavoured by a Chinese herb marinade for £6.50. And we're still trying to work our way through all of Zen Central's choices when it comes to the preparation of seabass and Dover sole, £14 and £12.50 per pound, respectively. There are five, including sole steamed with black bean sauce and sole deep-fried with sweet and sour sauce.

Whatever we choose, we order side portions of the quick-fried seasonal vegetables for £5 and, possibly, the £4 Singapore noodles.

The menu promises that after sampling Zen Central's delights, you will understand "something of the heights to which Chinese cooking can soar." This is one restaurant that unequivocally delivers on such a lofty assertion. And one more thing you should know—it is open daily for lunch and dinner, making it a weekend mainstay. For Sundays, in particular, be sure to call a couple of days ahead for a reservation.

CHAPTER FOUR

A Sudden Yen

Nothing that a few pounds—sterling and otherwise—couldn't satisfy

*L*ondon may not be Paris for its capacity to satisfy carnal desire nor New York for its "city-that-never-sleeps" qualities. But there's a lot to be said for that quintessentially British resourcefulness of the gentleman's gentleman. Hard to conceive of Jeeves not being able to provide just about anything at any hour of the day or night. That's London for you. Willingness to satisfy...in style. There are the flowers that might have come from the formal country garden—an enchanting nosegay or a "palaceful" of exquisite arrangements. There are the meals assembled from the food halls of Harrods or Fortnum & Mason or the tiny specialty shops that for centuries have been "purveyors to the Crown" of their finest Stiltons, the most carefully aged port wines or the single malts that are the nectar of the Scottish highlands.

Above all, there is the whole range of establishments that are blessed with the Royal Warrant—suppliers to the Crown and their offspring of the finest that the British Isles have to offer. This is not to say that the Crown has a lock on quality. There is an entire mosaic of firms with pedigrees dating back centuries who've never been graced with a royal foot crossing their thresholds.

It's all here, and often for considerably less than your £1,000, before or after tea.

PURVEYORS OF FINE FOODS & DRINK

André Simon

14 Davies Street   071-499-9144
London W1Y 1LJ

Among connoisseurs of wine, André Simon is reputed to have possessed one of the most sophisticated palates the world has ever known. For less well-informed fanciers, the master's name has been immortalized by a mini-chain of shops founded by his son. Of the three, our favourite is this petite emporium in the heart of Mayfair, right off Berkeley Square. It's a fun place to explore, to find wonderful wines that you've never seen before and probably have never read about.

Indeed, André Simon's buyers specialize in unknowns, especially those from Burgundy. Many of the wines of this region are overshadowed by their chateau-bred cousins from Bordeaux. Yet there are some real gems from lesser-known producers, and this group of oenophiles prides itself on merchandising wines that are not sold anywhere else in London.

Consequently, as wine becomes just a profit centre to multinational conglomerates, André Simon conserves the personal touch by maintaining relationships in the wine districts. They've actually found a Sancerre made by brothers in France who still seal their bottles with wax!

Treasure hunts are always intriguing, and you can invariably go on one here. André Simon always has a wonderful selection of bin ends to pore through, and then there are all those unique, exclusive wines like the delightful Bourgogne Rouge Pinot Noir 1986 for £6.85 a bottle. And the collection of white burgundies is indicative of the time and energy put into selecting them. A total of five weeks is spent in the region annually by the André Simon buying team. On average, they visit eight growers a day, tasting 10 wines at each stop. Out of these 400 or so, they buy or reserve no more than 20.

The range and variety of champagnes, including the 1985 Duetz Blanc de Blanc that we can never get enough of at £25.85, is properly intoxicating. A bottle of the 1962 Kruge for £138 makes for a memorable gift or celebration, but we're willing to bet that, in most instances, the

£20.65 Pommery will suffice. And, if you experience any moments of in-
decision, the alert but relaxed staff will help you out. Otherwise, they'll
let you explore in peace to your heart's content.   🍎

Berry Bros. & Rudd

3 St James's Street	071-839-9033
London SW1A 1EG	(24-hour service) 071-930-1888
	(FAX) 071-839-1841

Should you, upon entering Berry Bros., wonder, "If this is a liquor store,
where are the bottles?", you won't be the first. . . or the last. Unquestionably, the shop looks a great deal more like the setting of a Dickens' novel
than it does a purveyor of wines and spirits. Where you would expect to
find walls lined with modern fixtures full of colourful bottles, you find instead wood panelling darkened by the patina of age, a giant set of scales,
Victorian high desks and original wheelback Windsor chairs.

Berry Bros. comes by its ancient ambience honestly. Number 3 St
James's, just a step away from the palace of the same name, has been occupied by a single family or its close associates "in the trades" since the
1690s. They started out as grocers to the aristocratic neighbourhood—
hence the sign of the coffee mill outside—but gradually removed themselves from the greener aspects of that noble trade to concentrate on the
sale of alcoholic beverages. In actual fact, it is likely they were involved
with them from the beginning, as it was not uncommon for 17th-century
grocers to deal in wine. In any event, the ground floor of the shop has
changed very little since 1765, when the Beau Monde first adopted the
practice of being weighed on its scales.

Originally installed to weigh sacks of coffee, tea and sugar, the scales
gained notoriety as the conscience of such weight-watchers as Lord
Byron and Beau Brummel. Nine leather-bound volumes are filled with
the names of the famous and infamous, Berry Bros. customers all, who
have been weighed here over the years—Charles Lamb, Napoleon III,
A.J. Balfour, John Nash, Lord Melbourne, Gertrude Lewis, Michael
Redgrave, Anthony Eden, Laurence Olivier, Vivien Leigh, the previous
Aga Khan and several generations of Rothschilds.

But the scales' tales pale in comparison with the wines and liquors sold
here. The inventory, while virtually invisible in the shop, is in fact
enormous—cellars stretch beneath St James's Street, and the firm's
warehouse outside London houses some 200,000 cases, plus another

20,000 of customers' stock. The wine list alone, including port and brandy, comprises some 146 fascinating pages. Maps of the world's great wine-producing regions (excluding California) are accompanied by explanations about what separates them from the pack. The character and history of most individual wines is detailed, and each is designated "ready to drink," "ready but will improve," or "for laying down."

If ever you wanted to start a cellar, this is the place to do so. Not only will the expert, though surprisingly young, clerks advise you on how to develop and maintain a respectable cellar, but also they will arrange to store your wine for you. Should you opt for the latter, you will be supplied with an annual stock list and information on when your wines should be drunk. You can even ensure that your descendants' palates are properly attended to by laying down bottles for future consumption. Put aside a bottle at a time, if you like. Your beneficiary will be notified of the gift and sent a stock report once a year.

As for your own education, as well as gratification, you might want to start with some of their sampling cases, specially selected and priced wines offering a variety of taste sensations. The red wines of France, composed of three bottles each of Bordeaux, Beaujolais, Rhone, and a French "country wine" from Cahors, is a particular value at £76.25. In actual fact, case lots, whether of the staff's choosing or yours, are the way to go here. Berry Bros. is not really the sort of place you pop into for the odd bottle of wine on the way to a dinner party—not that you wouldn't be courteously accommodated. It's just that Berry Bros. is set up to deal with serious buyers and reward them accordingly with incrementally increased discounts, depending upon the number of cases purchased. The firm is, after all, the official supplier of Buckingham Palace.

Still, if you're in search of an exceptional bottle for a special person or occasion, don't hesitate to darken their door. Berry Bros. will be delighted to fill in the blanks on the list where it says "prices on request" for such connoisseurs' choices as a 1985 Chateau Latour, Paulliac, a 1975 Chateau Haut Brion, Graves or the grandaddy of the Sauternes, a 1982 Chateau d'Yquem. As for us, we'd be thrilled with a bottle of 1966 Quinta do Noval port for £31.50.

Charbonnel et Walker

28 Old Bond Street   071-491-0939
London W1X 4BT   (FAX) 071-495-6279

The connection between Charbonnel et Walker and the royal family may
be closer and older than the firm's current appointment as Queen Elizabeth's official chocolate makers would indicate. Legend has it that Mademoiselle Charbonnel, one of the leading chocolatiers of her day, was
rather friendly with that legendary lothario Edward VII. He met her in
the City of Lights, when he was still Prince of Wales and the bane of his
prim-and-proper mama's existence. It was at the prince's invitation that
Mademoiselle Charbonnel set up shop on Old Bond Street in 1875.
Only a romantic story? Perhaps, it has never been verified. But is it just a
coincidence that today Charbonnel et Walker is resplendent in royal blue
and located at Number One, The Royal Arcade?

Regardless, the company, which was recently purchased by the energetic Allan Bacher, declares that it makes "probably the best chocolates
in the world." With Allan at the helm, we suspect that eventually there
will be less waffling involved in that claim. Ambitious, he plans to maintain the high standards that have made Charbonnel et Walker internationally famous—their mail-order business, especially to the United
States and the Far East, is astounding. The chocolates continue to be
hand finished in the firm's own factory in tony Tunbridge Wells, still
made according to the founder's recipes in the original Victorian moulds.
Furthermore, they continue to be packed in the firm's trademark handmade boxes, many replicas of frivolous Victorian designs covered with
velvet or satin. Still, Allan sees expansion as the key to the company's
future. He has already instituted "The Chocolate Drink," which he describes as "really excellent and real chocolate," as well as truffle sauces in
a variety of scrumptious flavours, and flakes of chocolate packaged in
plastic bags so that they "can be put straight into the microwave or boil-
ing water and then the chocolate squeezed out by cutting the corner—no
mess or waste!"

We can't wait to try all his chocolate-based products. The very thought
of ice cream slathered in one of those truffle sauces sends us into a fren-
zied state of anticipation. You see, we already know Charbonnel's truffles
are out of this world, especially the strawberry ones. Created for
Wimbledon and only available from September to Easter, they stand out

in all their creamy white glory—white chocolate mousse enrobing white chocolate truffles infused with just the right amount of strawberry liqueur. Sensational. Even more so when packed in one of the pretty floral theatre boxes, known as such because of the fashionable Edwardian practice of snacking on chocolates while watching thespians at work. Today, oval-shaped boxes filled with your choice of goodies sell for as little as £6.50 for a quarter pound to £15.50 for a pound. Should you care to, you can go as high as £47 for one of these. Or you could indulge in the charming silk hat-shaped boxes. And we think the chocolate champagne bottles filled with truffles at £25 make terrific hostess gifts.

Obviously, the packaging is as important as the contents. Indeed, many Charbonnelics order large boxes constructed to their design specifications to coordinate with the decor of a room and then have them refilled on a regular basis. But the real speciality here is the boîtes blanches—gorgeous white boxes filled with the sweetest of all possible messages. Solid chocolate letters spell whatever you want them to—from £28.50 for one-and-a-half pounds, including 15 letters/spaces, to £165 for ten pounds, with as many as 50 letters. Ask to have the letters foiled to really drive your message home as one gentleman did, not too long ago, when he proposed by boîte blanche. The next day, the object of his desire came in to order a one-and-a-half pounder emphatically stating "YES!!"

For real emergencies, when you want to say it with chocolate *fast*, take advantage of the Charbonnel's courier service, which operates directly from the shop's factory, depending upon your order. The ever accommodating manager, Betty Foxton-Morris, will make this or any other shipping arrangement for you.   💘

Hobbs of Mayfair

20 South Audley Street	071-638-1230
London W1Y 5DJ	071-638-1231

We think it's sweet that Marion Cartwright and Sara Hughes call themselves grocers, albeit "London's most exciting" grocers. Somehow, neither they nor their ever-so-smart basket-laden, marble-and-glass-countered emporium bears any resemblance to your neighbourhood grocers. Theirs is not a store you pop into for basics. Rather, Hobbs of Mayfair is a gourmet shop, par excellence, complete with esoteric commodities like quails' eggs at £2.50 per dozen. Indeed, more often than not, Hobbs is described as London's Fauchon. But the somewhat coy insistence on the term *grocers* is clever—it makes Hobbs seem more down to earth than it really is and suggests that it's accessible and user friendly, which certainly is true.

Chalk one up to Sara, the marketing maven of this partnership. She's also responsible for the distinctive blue-and-gold-labeled bottles, jars and cannisters that bear the store's logo. But to a great degree, Marion is responsible for what's inside. She's got the nose for food and is an accomplished chef. It is Marion who discovers the products and refines the recipes for others, destined to be slapped with those imperial-looking labels. Every packaged comestible in the place, with the notable exception of the quite respectable selection of wines and champagnes, is exclusive to Hobbs.

Goodies like parsley relish, honey-glazed almonds and a range of uniquely flavored £7.95 vinegars—orange and clove, raspberry and mint—line the shelves from floor to ceiling. They are cheek-to-jowl with 11 varieties of jams and marmalades, along with three types of honey, all priced from £2.75 to £4.95.

They form a dramatic backdrop to the display counters, loaded with cheeses, pâtés, pies, hams, breads and pastries. But as far as we're concerned, the hottest Hobbs items are the gift baskets. They bring tears to the cook's eyes, filled as they are with delectable ingredients—the stuff that can lend zip to the most pedestrian of larders. "Condiments of the Connoisseur" at £52 is a case in point. Bottles of caper-and-dill olive oil and cucumber-and-dill vinegar are bundled up in a Shaker-style wooden box with jars of mixed peppercorns, garlic and honey; savoury peach cooking sauce; a one-pound bag of wild rice, a three-ounce packet of sun-dried tomatoes and a 30-gram bag of dried sage.

Naturally, Hobbs is also a whiz with hampers. But leave it to Sara and Marion to come up with a novel twist. In addition to the delectable but nonetheless conventional day-at-the-races picnics, they've come up with the most spectacular special-occasion "hamper" we've ever seen. Actually, it isn't even your run-of-the-mill wicker number that is consigned to the back of the hall closet as soon as you've eaten your way through its contents. Instead, we're talking about an exquisite hand-stitched canvas-and-leather valise filled with a bottle of Krug Champagne, 250g of oscetra caviar, a box of white champagne truffles, two crystal champagne glasses, two horn caviar spoons, two crisp damask napkins, and a worsted wool damask rug. Can you imagine anything else more divinely decadent for £500? We can't. Yet there's the practicality of the handsome weekend-getaway-sized suitcase (not to mention the glasses, napkins and rug) when you've finished celebrating. Some grocers! And, yes, Hobbs does ship anything that legally can be shipped to just about anywhere in the world.   🥄

John Milroy Limited

3 Greek Street   071-437-0893/2385/9311
London W1V 5LA   (FAX) 071-437-1345

If you have the impression that we're not the type of gals likely to belly up to the bar at Dukes (or the Stafford, or the Westbury) and ask for a Scotch and soda, or Scotch and anything else for that matter, then you're right. The rough edges of the blended swill commonly known as Scotch is not to our taste. But on a jaunt through God's country (i.e., the Scottish Highlands), we discovered the pedestrian variety's aristocratic smooth and silky cousin—single malt Scotch whiskey. While the regular Scotch may be a product of as many as 40 more or less (mostly less) wonderful stills, each single malt is the product of a single distillery and proudly bears its name on the label—much like French châteaux vintage wines. Aged to perfection, single malts, like fine wines before them, have developed a fanatic international following. And Milroy's is their mecca.

Back in 1964, when John (known as Jack) Milroy first translated his family's pub-keeping experience into a retail liquor operation, he was primarily a wine merchant, selling only four single malts. Meanwhile, back from the diamond mines in South Africa, his brother Wallace was becoming the world's leading expert on malt whiskey. Their complementary career paths converged—Wallace joined the business, and now the shop carries some 220 different malts. Since Wallace is usually off lecturing on the finer points of sniffing and tasting his beloved single malts, Jack oversees the shop along with wife, Velma.

A big, burly, bearded Scot with a devilish twinkle in his eye (you know he'd look divine in a kilt), Jack is more a gracious host than a shopkeeper, pouring "wee drams" of his precious amber liquors for his guests. As you taste, he talks, filling you in on the relative merits of all the malts he has to offer. Jack says that every distillery producing single malts is represented in his shop, but because "there are so many permutations, there must be vintages we don't have." That may be, but we doubt anyone has ever seriously found fault with the selection. Furthermore, there are malts available here that can quite literally be found nowhere else because of Milroy's penchant for purchasing casks and bottling them. For instance, the brothers own a Balvenie dating from 1957, which they bottle and sell for £2,500 per bottle. At that price, it doesn't exactly walk out the door. Still, Jack says they sell at least a bottle a week—mostly to the Japanese.

For those of us to whom the pound isn't play money, John tells us there are plenty of good choices for around 100th of the price. Take an 8-year-old Glen Garioch for £15.15, which Jack describes as a "very pleasant, daytime malt." For sipping later in the day, Jack likes Royal Lochnagar—12 years old and £18.50. He also recommends the £21.75 Pheasant Plucker, while slyly noting that "if you drink too much, you might get the name wrong!"

After dinner, Jack suggests a snifter of 25-year-old Glenfarglas for £35, instead of brandy or Armagnac. An even more exciting substitute is the 18-year-old Glenmorangie, a £27.75 newcomer on the market from a distillery heretofore famous for its decade-old malt.

As Jack continues his tour through his wall of malts, he becomes increasingly enthusiastic, especially when he gets to those he feels "separate the men from the boys"—his favourites. There's the very gutsy 16-year-old Lagavulin for £18.70 and the 15-year-old Laphroaig at £22.75. Presenting an even greater challenge are several cask-strength malts to which no water has been added. Consequently, they're about 60 per cent alcohol, priced from about £22 to £35, and are gaining in popularity. Relatively new, they make great presents for aficionados. But if you really want to make an impression, go for the 50-year-old Mortlach for £499.

And throw in a copy of Wallace's *Malt Whisky Almanac* at £5.95, *the* single-malt bible. Instructive, it's also very practical—brandish it at any of the distilleries and Jack claims you'll get extra-large measures of the already generously poured samples. 🍎

Justin de Blank

42 Elizabeth Street	071-730-3721
London SW1W 9NZ	(FAX) 071-730-9050

Most of us have speculated about what we would do with a sudden windfall, the parting largess of the proverbial "rich uncle." Yachts, jewelry, cars, planes, and other frivolous squanderings generally come to mind, but not to that of Justin de Blank, a jolly gentleman of Dutch extraction who "by chance" was brought up in France. When his uncle died and left him £6,000, Justin knew judiciously what to do with it.

At age 40, he was ripe for a change and had long observed that food shopping in London was a bit of a bore, with the notable exceptions of the fabled food halls of the major department stores. Why, he had wondered, did his adopted city not have the small speciality food shops which made shopping such a delight in France? Justin, along with pal and future partner Robert Troop, even made a survey of the range of foods available in London. The results? The average French town of 10,000 had a better selection of goods than one of the world's great capitals.

With Justin's uncle's legacy as a stake, they quit their day jobs and transformed the cramped quarters of a former boutique into a gourmet food shop, full of enticing tins and bottles of what they thought would be exciting comestibles to the sophisticated Belgravia shopper. Their assumption was partly correct. But it became clear that what Justin now calls "hamper goods" were not enough to attract a steady clientele. Justin and Robert began shopping Covent Garden—still then the vegetable market Liza Doolittle would recognize—in the wee hours of the morning to import fresh fruits and vegetables to Elizabeth Street. As a way to control waste, they turned a corner of the stock room into a kitchen and recruited a woman to make salads, quiches and cooked dishes. The Justin de Blank formula was beginning to emerge—a combination of those fancy "hamper" goodies, fresh produce, cheeses, meats and prepared foods laid out in abundant, opulent displays on deceptively simple and self-consciously inelegant plywood and scaffold-pole shelving. Still the only firm in the city with shop kitchens capable of turning out fresh food daily, Justin de Blank's is a formula that has fostered a very successful fine food retail and wholesale business which has expanded into catering—de Blank Restaurants services a number of London's major museums and operates the General Trading Company's café, which is rapidly becoming a popular luncheon spot.

While there are now three Justin de Blank shops, the original Elizabeth Street site, which has benefitted from several enlargements, remains the flagship. Always crowded, it is considered a Godsend to a neighbourhood heavily populated by affluent singles and resident/tourists—several U.S.-based banks rent flats for their executives in neighbouring Chester Square. Obviously, the prepared foods are very popular, and Justin keeps them that way by maintaining high standards of quality, but not a set menu. The offerings are constantly changing. So customers, as yet undecided about their plans for the evening meal, make it a habit to pop in on the way home from work to see what's what. On any given day the selections might include lasagna, moussaka, barbecued chicken drumsticks, chicken Florentine, and beef casserole, ranging in price from £5.00 to £8.00.

In fact, you can walk away with a complete meal worthy of entertaining a very important person. There's a respectable collection of wines, a terrific assortment of cheeses, and the bread from the shop's own bakery is unrivalled, witness Justin de Blank's appointment as bakers to the Queen. If you prefer biscuits with your cheese, pick up the popular wheat wafers from the Isle of Wight at £1.45 for a 150-gram packet.

Take-away desserts are equally delectable. Again, the offerings differ from day to day, but chocolate mousse, lemon and lime mousse, chocolate fudge cake, and a lovely Greek orange and almond confection for £4.20 a pound are typical.

With 24 hours' notice, you can leave the arduous decision-making process up to the young extroverted staff by ordering a picnic hamper. Excluding wine, hampers run about £100 for an elegant repast for four, plus a £60 deposit to ensure you return the basket, cutlery, china and glassware. Delivery is free within central London. On Derby Day and during Wimbledon, Justin de Blank trucks scurry all over the place delivering their extravagantly packaged but all-so-edible cargo.

For those who actually care to sully their hands with cooking, check out the meat department—particularly the sausages. A plaque on the wall proclaims Justin de Blank supreme sausage maker at the National Sausage Competition in Harrowgate. Add one of their delectable custom-blended sausages—£2.50 a pound for the small, £2.10 for the large—to your classic English grill or to spaghetti sauce for an extra-special taste sensation. These days Justin de Blank has become almost as famous for sausage as for bread; they make and sell at least a ton a week. And if you're in charge of bringing home the bacon, check out the unusual varieties featured here—Rolled Ayrshire at £2.45 a pound and Suffolk Streaky for £2.90.

Yes, indeed, Justin has turned his well-invested £6,000 into a food-based fortune. Still, his is anything but a life of leisure. The competition in the fancy-foods sweepstakes has heated up since his pioneering days.

So he continues to work long hours, often upwards of 12, for six to seven days a week to keep his formula in fine fettle. And it shows. 🦫

Partridges

132–134 Sloane Street	071-730-0651/7102/7103
London SW1X 9AT	(FAX) 071-730-7104

Like other capital cities, London is a mecca for those who wish to escape the provincialism of the hinterlands. And yet, the very same people who flock to the Big City in search of urban excitement often become its most severe critics, bemoaning the lack of a sense of community, as well as mourning the traditions of quality, pride and service they took for granted in the "old-fashioned" village shops. For them, Partridges is a haven, where the neighbourhood converges to get in a little shopping amidst the good-natured gossiping and where an amazing assortment of first-class products (over 7,000 different lines) is sold with pride by a staff committed to providing exemplary service.

The fact that this paragon is conveniently located on one of London's most fashionable shopping streets in a large modern space is somewhat of a paradox, although certainly a happy one for those who appreciate the wonders of this true English grocer's. No hoity-toity gourmet shop, this is a grocery store that stocks as its logo claims "good things for the larder" as well as basics—esoteric items, such as olive oil flavoured with truffles, share shelf space with the more pedestrian Welch's Grape Jelly, for instance.

Director Herbert Ventham, a lifelong veteran of the grocery trade, feels that today's food retailers need to be renaissance men: "food broker, wine merchant, cheesemonger, fruit and vegetable specialist, patisserie person, delicatessen craftsman and, on a more ethereal level perhaps, culinary advisor, translator, negotiator, private detective and even, occasionally, confessor." Partridges and its staff fulfil all these functions, which is why it has become such a beloved institution in such a short period of time. The Shepard brothers, John and Richard, created it in 1972 and maintain it very much as a family business, despite the fact that Richard now has other pressing obligations—he has become a Member of Parliament for Aldridge/Brownhills in the West Midlands. Indeed, the staff is part of their extended family, as many have been at Partridges from the beginning and have become institutions in their own right.

Take Mr Ashby, in charge of Partridges' best-selling item, smoked salmon. At the tender age of 85, he continues to slice it enthusiastically and precisely, drawing customers from miles around. Then there's Phyllis Hutt, the cheese lady and the proud possessor of national awards for the displays of over 300 varieties of cheese on her counter. And so many others who make this such a hospitably friendly place to pick up a sack of potatoes or some perfectly prepared beef Wellington. Not as glamorous as Fortnum & Mason, it is also not as stuffy and decidedly not overrun with busloads of tourists.

The shop has taken one cue from that most famous of food stores, though, and developed a bang-up hamper business, particularly popular at Christmas when Partridges publishes a glossy catalogue brimming with basketed goodies. The Sovereign Hamper at £385, plus shipping and tax, is nothing short of mind-boggling, stuffed with items too innumerable to mention. Suffice is to say that it contains everything from a magnum of Brut Souverain Champagne Henriot and a bottle of 10-year-old MacCallum single malt scotch to a 6-pound loin of pork and a 15-pound turkey to a box of Mondose Praline Liqueur Chocolates. The £185 Sloane is a little more manageable with highlights including a 2-pound Christmas pudding, a tin of vichyssoise, a cooked ham, a bottle of Dry Sack, a Stilton and a box of Walker's shortbread.

The hampers, like the store that assembles them, have something for everyone in the way of food and wine, especially those seeking solace from an all too impersonal world, but who still demand what we've come to describe as modern conveniences like the acceptance of credit cards and the ability to shop seven days a week, from 8:30 A.M. to 9:00 P.M.

❦

Paxton & Whitfield Ltd

93 Jermyn Street	071-930-0250/0259
London SW1Y 6JE	(FAX) 071-358-9556

In London, when wits are faced with a camera and asked to say cheese, they're likely to utter "Paxton!" The two are virtually synonymous here and have been since 1826 when Harry Paxton first joined Sam Cullum's family cheese business, one that dated back to 1797. Not long after Harry signed on, his pal John Whitfield joined the fold, and in 1853 the firm officially became Paxton & Whitfield. But most people refer to it simply as Paxton's, and everyone who's ever bitten into one of its superb

Stiltons, knows it to be *the* purveyor of the world's finest cheeses—some 250 to 300 varieties, mostly of British and French origins.

Of course, given the shop's long history, the Gallic cheeses at Paxton's are relative newcomers. It was the best of British cheeses that firmly established the company's reputation, particularly that most noble of English cheeses, Stilton. Reputedly created about 300 years ago by a farmer's wife in the village of Stilton, the British challenger to Roquefort and Gorgonzola as the world's greatest blue has long been associated with Paxton & Whitfield. Only six companies produce the cheese, often reserving their finest examples for Paxton's. Uncut Stiltons are available as a whole 16- to 18-pound cheese, or as a baby version of approximately 5 pounds—£3.75/lb and £22.50 each if you pick them up at the charming, circa 1674, Jermyn Street premises. If you want either one of them packaged and sent overseas or across the Channel, you're talking about £6.90/lb or £45 each.

As official cheesemongers to the Queen Mother and to Queen Victoria before her, Paxton's is accustomed to satisfying an exacting clientele and has come up with a number of inventive ways to do so. The shop's sleek black trucks whirl around the city, filled with tempting delicacies like the popular Best of British packs. One, Pack A, offers a 4-pound cheddar and a 10-ounce earthenware jar of Stilton at £37 for UK consumption or £54 for export, including packaging, delivery or postage. The other, designated as Pack B, serves up a 5-pound junior Stilton, plus a 2½-pound baby Cheshire for £51 or £72.

Unfortunately, Paxton's most creative efforts, like the Port and Stilton Packs and the glorious picnic baskets overflowing with comely comestibles cannot be sent beyond the borders of Great Britain. . . which is not to say they can't be physically carried across, but that's your business, isn't it? In any case, they make terrific treats while you're here and *very* impressive gifts, too. We've scored a few points when we've arrived bearing a parcel boasting five-year-old "late bottled" Offley port and 10-ounce jar of Stilton, all for a £34 pricetag.

While we've certainly been known to depend upon the excellent prepackaged goodies that Paxton's offers, we do like to pop in and immerse ourselves in the often long and always tasty process of making our own selections. The seductive aroma alone is worth a visit. It and the visual stimulation of the extraordinary assortment of cheese so artfully displayed overwhelm your senses. Eventually, though, the head clears and you take a good look around, at which point you notice the rows of cured hams hanging from the rafters. Curious, until general manager Debi Frost submits that some argue that Paxton's is just as famous for hams as it is for cheeses. Indeed, if you ever thought ham was ham, period, Paxton's will persuade you otherwise. The shop carries a variety, each distinctly different while still being the product of traditional, centuries-old curing processes and techniques. It is here that we discovered the aristocrat of hams, the Bradenham, named after Lord Bradenham, who developed his noble marinade in 1781. After curing, a Bradenham, is cloaked in successive coats of spices, juniper berries and molasses; then it's left alone for several months while the flavours blend to yield a delectable taste sensation. A whole ham, about 12 to 16 pounds costs £5.40/lb. You can also order a half; add £5 for postage in the UK only.

As if the cheeses, the ports (not to mention the fine range of clarets, Burgundies and champagnes) and the hams weren't enough, there are any number of complementary items to be found here—an extensive selection of charcuterie, biscuits, pickles, chutneys, preserves and the like. It all adds up to one-stop shopping of the gourmet kind.   🍒

FLORISTS

Caroline Dickenson

Landsdowne House   071-491-9494
55 Berkeley Square   (FAX) 071-491-9406
London W1X 6AN

Whether you're looking for an ultra-simple vase of peonies or dramatic tiers of hydrangeas, you'll find the pure and pretty blooming alongside the exotic and unusual at Caroline Dickenson's.

We first ran across Caroline's stunning floral arrangements in her Grosvenor House store. Every time we passed the giant windows lining the hotel's driveway, we stopped to stare and marvel at her winning way with flowers. Soon, we found our way to Caroline's Berkeley Square branch located in the Saatchi & Saatchi Building. The stern, medieval, grey stone-faced building provides an ideal backdrop to Caroline's trademark bright, brilliantly clashing red, pink and orange flowers—all displayed in unusual containers. Caroline uses fabric to dress up terra-cotta pots and actually weaves it into the arrangements. She also uses shells to decorate ceramic pots. There are swathes of luxurious materials everywhere, and even a few upholstered chairs for weary customers.

Caroline's floral art is highly prized for private homes, weddings, balls and VIPs—very important parties. For Grosvenor House, she always places huge fabric bows on the hotel's Christmas trees and incorporates musical instruments into lyrical orchestrations of blooms and greens. As far as she's concerned, virtually any object is fair floral game.

Caroline's unique talent has enabled her to build a high-profile clientele. Lord McAlpine used to send baskets of Caroline's flowers to Mrs Thatcher to wish her good luck before a vote in Parliament; now he sends them just because it gives him and Maggie pleasure. Tom Stoppard finds her arrangements theatrical, while Yves St Laurent and Giorgio Armani think they make an appropriate statement of thanks to big-spending clothes horses. And Estée Lauder eschews Caroline's cherished colours in favour of her masterfully arranged white blossoms.

With 17 employees, Caroline has the flexibility to shuffle staff between the two shops, depending upon the level of business at each. She feels that personal service is the most important part of her business and works hard to give her clients what they want, even though "they usually don't know what they want," or at least have a difficult time articulating it. Consequently, Caroline's routine visits to clients' homes to see how they are decorated comes in handy. Her personal knowledge allows her to make sure the flowers she provides complement the decor. Such attention to detail is very important to Caroline—she wants to make sure the style and colour of the arrangements are harmonious with their destined environment. But whatever the composition, Caroline tends to use lots of foliage, pussy willows, ivy and mosses.

Sounds expensive? Not necessarily. You can cut a bunch of cut flowers for as little as £15. Then again, you can drop £42 in an instant if you're in the mood for a dozen magnificent long-stem French roses. Arrangements start at £20, but many regular customers think nothing of plopping down £100 or more. For a charity ball or wedding, the prices can escalate into the tens of thousands, fast!

Of course, Caroline can't be in two shops, countless homes and any number of hotel ballrooms at the same time. So you may not have the pleasure of meeting this handsome blond lady whose charming directness translates so beautifully into her creative efforts. Never mind, all of her arrangers have her art down to an exact science. Still, we've developed a particular fondness for the saucy Rosi Tansley, who's a whiz at adapting whatever you had in mind into fabulous floral fantasies. 🌿

Kenneth Turner Ltd

19 South Audley Street	071-355-3880
London W1Y 6BN	(FAX) 071-495-1670

As a boy growing up in County Down, Northern Ireland, Kenneth Turner became fascinated with his grandfather's garden. His interest grew into a passion, one he's been sharing with the world since 1972 when he opened his first shop on Brook Street. Home to what is called the "Turner Treatment," his new location, next to Thomas Goode on South Audley, turns out the most incredibly imaginative examples of the English style of flower arranging—a mode that originated with the late Constance Spry's inventive use of country flowers and unconventional items like tomatoes and cabbages.

Whether it's filling an order for a nosegay or gratifying the Duchess of Kent's request to "get rid of the gilt" in Kensington Palace by camouflaging it with flora, the Turner Treatment means an out-sized abundance of fragrant colour. For the Duchess of Kent, Kenneth hung flowers from everything in sight. Roses enveloped gilt chandeliers and climbed up the gilt stairwell, while the floor was dotted with hundreds of potted birch trees. Yet, it all seemed to grow naturally in the palatial environment. The fact that Kenneth is not only a floral decorator but also an educated horticulturalist explains his flair for producing uncontrived-looking floriated designs. Indeed, his career stemmed from wanting to do something "more theatrical" than lecturing on the fine points of horticulture. So he went to work for the fashionable London florist Pulbrook & Gould, where he refined his skills to the degree that he's variously described as an artist, a horticultural inventor and a latter-day Turner.

Since starting his own business, the Turner touch has been felt worldwide. He has loads of clients in the U.S., as well as in the Middle East and Japan. We're talking about people like Lord Snowden, Jackie Onassis, Jack Nicholson, Mick Jagger and George Harrison. He's always flying off to fulfil their floral fantasies. For a party, prices can range from £2,000 to the stratosphere, plus expenses. And given the sort of fantasies he deals with, we suspect that more often than not prices soar into that out-of-sight category. Take, for instance, the time Kenneth created a tropical garden for Claridge's by ripping out carpets, "planting" bamboo and fruit trees, and devising waterfalls where none had flowed before . . . or the occasion of Courvoisier's launch of its *Book of the Best* which prompted him to use grapes and leaves as the medium to sculpt giant snifters . . . or the Renaissance masked ball replete with swirling dry ice adding to the mystery of topiaries, garlands of ferns and pillars of black grapes adorning a palazzo on the Grand Canal in Venice.

Of course, individual arrangements are considerably less pricy. In Kenneth's frequent absences, his assistant Jeremy Jeffcoat (known as "Jeff") and store manager Bronwen Careless (leave it to Kenneth to have staff with delightfully eccentric names) will help you determine the perfect floral orchestration to send for a little thank-you or a big celebration, starting at about £40. Should you wish to send a touch of Turner a little farther afield (i.e., outside central London), consider one of the shop's extraordinary dried arrangements, starting from £125. We were mesmerized by a still-life guaranteed to dress up even the most pedestrian of kitchens with its clever combination of dried flowers and wheat with artichokes in a glorious basket for £450.

Indeed, we can think of few better treats than those from Kenneth Turner.   ❦

Oasis Artificial Flora

194–196 Walton Street   071-584-9519
London SW3 2JL   (FAX) 071-581-3499

Okay, we know you think that anything artificial in the way of greenery is just too tacky for words. And we imagine that you've tried to get over this fake phobia, because real plants can be such a nuisance and have the unfortunate habit of dying, while the artificial varieties are so practical. We know all this, because we felt exactly the same way until we ran into Michele Sigg and her amazing facility for making immortal silk, polyester and plastic look just like the real thing. Proof of the pudding is the fact that the business she founded nine years ago has been a phenomenal success in a country of dedicated gardeners, who have long sniffed at their Continental neighbours' penchant for fabricated flora.

Michele's shop is testimony to her skill. Minus the cloying, humid heat and peaty smell, it resembles nothing so much as a glorious greenhouse, where any number of species flourish in abundance. Baskets of colourful cut flowers—tulips, poppies, lilies, chrysanthemums, daffodils, orchids and roses—vie for your attention with exotic shrubs, and trees—

bougainvillea, palm, cactus and mango—and with a seemingly endless inventory of bushes and other plants. The price list is eight pages long! Delicate, handmade silk flowers imported from France, Italy, Thailand and China start at £1.20, plus tax. Flowering plants like petunias are priced from about £9, plus can go to £21.50 or so for azaleas, depending upon size. As for trees, count on *at least* £40 and as much as £415.70 for an eight-foot-tall ficus. Remember, these are quite literally lifetime investments—washable and so extraordinarily lifelike due to the unique process of photographing real leaves and then transferring the print onto fabric. The leaves are then coated with a protective formula that keeps them from fading or losing their shape. Oasis' trees can be "planted" indoors or out.

When Michele's not out combing the English woodlands for the branches and tree trunks to which she grafts silk and polyester leaves, she presides over her little green empire from a large fan-shaped rattan chair and glass table supported by four stately stone lions. From there, she can gaze at the enchanting wall mural of a palladian folly, shrouded in classic English mist. We suspect it's while losing herself in the painting's intriguing depths that Michele dreams up some of her more spectacular creations.

And she's been called upon to do some pretty serious dreaming, like the complete landscape environments she's often asked to create for offices, hotels and restaurants. Recently, Oasis softened the edges of a multi-storey glass and chrome atrium by decorating nearly inaccessible balconies with lovely creepers trailing over the side, and by designing a 20-foot ficus which now dominates the whole area. Whatever maintenance or rejuvenation is required is routinely provided by Michele's competent and caring staff, one of the many services that makes Oasis so popular with corporate and private clients alike. Ever notice all the incredibly fresh-looking plants and flower arrangements that adorn the hallowed halls of Harrods? They're a prime example of Oasis' work, and yes, those are real flowers that are mixed in with the fabulous fakes—the clever juxtaposition of nature and man-made flora is one of Michele's trademarks.

An arrangement, plant or tree from Oasis Artificial Flora may be one of London's best souvenirs—with very little tender loving care, it'll last forever, convincing all who encounter it that you have the very greenest of thumbs.

Pulbrook & Gould Ltd

Liscartan House   071-730-0030
181 Sloane Street   (FAX) 071-730-0722
London SW1X 9AS

Thirty-three years ago, when "floral decorators" were simply florists and mostly women, Susan Pulbrook and Rosamund Gould set up shop in a tiny basement. Their flawless taste and talented hands quickly put them on the road to success, a route which led them to their present location, set back off Sloane Street in a delightful mews. There, the firm (now minus Rosamund and plus Susan's sister-in-law, Sonja Waites) reigns as the grande dame of London's society floral decorators.

The spacious shop, made to look even more so by the clever use of mirrors and marble, produces lavish arrangements for clients like Princess Alexandra and the très chic Capital, as in restaurant and hotel. Pulbrook & Gould did the flowers for the fabulous *Upstairs, Downstairs* series and the memorable *Duchess of Duke Street*. Unfortunately, most of the work is done out of sight in the basement, where Susan's 40 elves have ample space to create their floral masterpieces.

Still the beloved domain of the energetic Susan, otherwise known as Lady Pulbrook, the shop is breathtaking in its abundance of colourful flowers and lush foliage. Exotic, hothouse varieties are not Pulbrook & Gould's pampered favourites. Rather, the shop tends to produce highly original orchestrations of heartier stuff, much of it "home-grown" in the private gardens of the verdant countryside—gorgeous roses so much more vibrant than their never-seen-the-light-of-day brethren, as well as garden raised hydrangeas, sweet peas, geraniums and other posies.

If you're a do-it-yourselfer, call in an order for your choice among the abundant selection of fresh-cut flowers. There's no minimum charge for them to be delivered. But if your floral artistry is anything like ours, let Susan's staff exercise their expertise and put together an arrangement for you, starting at £25. Should you truly wish to make a statement, however, plan on spending more like £70 to £100, which is not to say that you can't make an impression for considerably less. Make someone's day with the presentation of a bunch of mixed English anemonies for £3.50.

If you want to make someone's week, try surreptitiously photographing one of that person's better vases and send (or fax) the picture to Lady P. She and her staff, all of whom serve a rigorous apprenticeship before being turned loose on client orders, will compose an arrangement perfectly suited to the container. Indeed, Pulbrook & Gould maintains a file of many of their regulars' inventory of flower vessels. Therefore they can send over designs to complement any one or all of them on virtually a moment's notice.

CHAPTER FIVE

Shopping

If it's not here, it has probably been bought by the Japanese

*I*t may be a trifle redundant to proclaim that, above all else, shopping in London is civilized...but it is. There is, after all, the tradition that begins with "bespoke," and runs all the way to silver and gold. Savile Row curves easily into the Burlington Arcade which dumps out in Piccadilly and New Bond Street. Along the way are establishments that have been supplying the British nobility since before the pilgrims first landed at Plymouth Rock, before the colonials decided to chuck the tea into Boston Harbour, before the redcoats burned Washington. When you can fill orders and ship your wares to an empire on which once the sun never set, you can certainly satisfy the demands of a mere Park Avenue matron or a Wall Street tycoon.

If there's a touch of the supercilious from some of the "sales assistants," who'd be called clerks on the U.S. side of the pond, they deserve their apparently pumped-up title, and for generations have been earning the right to look slightly down their supremely aquiline noses. They offer unfailingly polite, respectful, interested and totally unflappable assistance. Note the word *offer.* They're not pushy, and once it's made clear that you wish to browse in peace, they'll leave you alone until—and *if*—you need them.

Our guess is that you will need them, if only to figure out the real cost of that Victor Edelstein gown or Tommy Nutter suit—unless you can work out the complexities of subtracting out the dreaded Value Added

Tax. If you're "purchasing for export," you're entitled to a rebate of 15 per cent. Sometimes you can negotiate it out of the price up front, but more often it is racked right up there on your bill—where it probably stays. After all, by the time you've received the cheque from the British government, you've already spent it.

Speaking of negotiation, the usual rules apply. Don't try it at Harrods or Fortnum & Mason, but you've got nothing to lose at smaller owner-operated establishments. In fact, the more expensive the goods, the more likely you'll find a Monty Hall prepared to play "Let's Make a Deal." But never forget that England has long been described as a nation of shopkeepers, and they haven't been at it for centuries without learning a thing or two about turning a profit.

And if they've been graced with a Royal Warrant, they're certainly unlikely to be turning their profit by supplying members of the royal family. Given the House of Windsor's well-documented penchant for parsimony, it's certain that concessions are made on the part of management in return for the privilege of displaying the royal imprimatur. Never mind, these royal Good Housekeeping Seals of Approval serve as a magnet for attracting new business and maintaining old. And the fact that the royals are based in London assures that the very best—from braces to boots—is available here.

London's commercial emporiums provide the necessities for the greatest show the world has ever known—the British Royal Family. But with more than 1,900 Royal Warrants currently issued, you can't depend solely on that list as a guide. Moreover, the protocol of royal life decrees a certain style, a look that isn't for everyone—a good reason for our road map to spending your £1,000 before tea.

For Men

Bates—Gentleman's Hatter

21a Jermyn Street   071-734-2722
London SW1Y 6HP

Apparently, the folks at Bates don't entirely believe in truth in advertising. Their sweet little turn-of-the-century shop is awash in wonderful old hat boxes, but alas, today Bates' very proper and always stylish hats are delivered in plastic bags. Then there's the matter of Binks, a regal-looking tabby cat who serenely surveys the scene...from a glass case. It seems his soul departed this earth back in 1926.

Nonetheless, this firm, founded in 1902 by George Samuel Bates, does live up to the promise of the large grey top hat that swings over its portal. Bates supplies gentlemen of the world with an astonishing array of headgear. Geoffrey Bates (George Samuel's great-nephew) oversees a hat fancier's nirvana, especially for those of the male persuasion, though ladies are certainly welcome and many are regular customers. The catalogue of "traditional English headwear" profiles 24 styles—just the tip of the iceberg. Bates carries many more styles and stocks 2,000 to 3,000 of the popular flat cap alone. With its deep back, long bill and narrow sides, it's ever so natty—the perfect golfing, hunting and convertible riding hat at £29.50 in tweed, about £40 to £45 in cashmere.

One gentleman friend of ours looks particularly dashing in his Bates racing hat. Made of fur felt, which Geoffrey tells us is making a comeback in terms of popularity, its narrow brim is accented by a grosgrain ribbon, and it sells for £58. It comes in a variety of colours, but most gents we know prefer the sable mid-brown. The sable description is apropos, since this hat's felt is not of ordinary wool. Rather, it is made of specially processed rabbit fur—divinely soft to the touch.

For Sherlock Holmes fans, there's the classic tweedy deerstalker for £36, and for Fred Astaire freaks, or those just determined to make an entrance for a very special evening, there's the black polished fur felt top hat at £188.50. The bottom line is that at Bates there's a hat for just about every head.

And if the shop doesn't have it, it'll be made to order. Should you wish to match a favourite suit, sports jacket or coat and can secure enough fabric from your tailor, Bates will custom-make a hat in whichever of their styles you choose. It will cost you the same as the price for the stocked version, but you'll have to wait at least six weeks. Naturally, Bates will ship anywhere in the world, so your custom chapeau is bound to catch up with you.

Now, if we could just get Geoffrey to expand his staff's exemplary efforts to please to the point of parting with some of those vintage hat boxes. They would make such chic storage units for myriad things, even hats!

Dege Savile Row

10 Savile Row	071-287-2941
London W1X 1AF	(FAX) 071-734-8794

The first thing you should know about this respected 126-year-old tailoring concern is how to pronounce the name. It's *D*, as in David, double *E*, *GE*, deege... or Dege.

The second thing is that while the shop is visually indistinguishable from many others on "the Row," its management, in the guise of president Michael Skinner, is definitely different. A descendent of William Skinner who first joined forces with the Dege family in 1900, Michael is an aggressive dynamo, intent on spreading the gospel of Savile Row bespoke tailoring throughout the world. Michael's a born salesman "and proud of it." He's not content, like many of his tailor brethren, to wait for clients to come to him—he doesn't trust them, either. "To see someone jumping into a Rolls... with rubbishy clothes is sacrilege. So we have to persuade the pop stars to have clothes to match their cars. There's still a lot of money in this world, and my job as a tailor is to chase it and convince those who have it why they should buy top-class clothes."

Thanks to Michael's global wanderings, the firm holds the Royal Warrant of the Sultan of Oman, producing many of his country's majestic ceremonial uniforms. Dege has also made uniforms for Crown Prince Harald of Norway and the Crown Prince of Bahrain, and has designed uniforms for the bulk of Saudi Arabia's military forces. In case, you hadn't guessed, uniforms are a bit of a specialty here, so you can imagine the attention paid to detail. It takes 30 yards of gold cord, intricately stitched and draped, to properly adorn the ceremonial uniforms for officers of the Yeoman of the Guard, the Queen's bodyguard. Dege is the only firm in the world authorized to do it.

But military attire is certainly not the whole story here. In fact, Dege is further differentiated from many of its neighbours by its emphasis on bespoke tailoring for ladies of a sporting nature. Joanna Lumley has her shooting knickers made here. And Malcolm Plews, who acts as tailor to the distaff clients, has been persuaded to make the most cunningly chic, traditional yet feminine tuxedos you've ever seen. For men's custom tailoring, David Cook, the sales director, is the gentleman to see. Even if you don't order anything, you'll enjoy listening to his seemingly endless fund of stories.

But there's a price for perfection, not only in terms of money but also in terms of time. Dege cutters take at least 37 measurements for a three-piece suit. Afterwards, they put a standard jacket on the client and spend the next 30 minutes or so mucking with it, pinning here, marking there. Then they take a few photographs, so they have a lasting image. A month later, a basted version of the garment is ready for a first fitting, another month for the second. Three months after the measurement-taking you'll be ready to strut your stuff in a Dege-made suit. Once the shop has your records on file and has worked with your figure, the process can be condensed to about six weeks.

There's no break on the price, however. Three-piece suits start at £1,090, whether you're ordering your first or your tenth. For cashmere, plan on spending at least £2,000. Sports coats run about £675, double that for cashmere. And top coats range from £975 to some £2,500.

In the instant gratification (and less expensive) category, there's a terrific selection of natty Scottish tweed and cashmere caps, perfect for a lady or gent's country hacking. You should also take a look at the beautiful cashmere ties at £59.50. And if nothing else, Dege's is worth a visit just to see the pattern cutters practising their craft. Their workroom at the back is within view of the shop.   🍂

Doug Hayward

95 Mount Street   071-499-5574
London W1Y 5HG   (FAX) 071-499-5574

A friend of ours has a real love-hate relationship with his valet, a very forbidding gentleman without whom our pal cannot exist, but with whom he finds life difficult. Quite frankly, his servant terrorizes him with unrelenting disapproval of virtually every aspect of his life. Or did, until we introduced his valet to the delightful Doug Hayward, tailor to the aristocracy of the theatrical and heralded persuasion. One look at Doug's tiny shop, which resembles nothing so much as a very proper gentleman's dressing room, and our friend's "valet from hell," as he's affectionately known, became a pussycat, purring the praises of his employer's formerly despised friends who had the good sense to bring him here. He began to muse about the marvellous new wardrobe that would be his to maintain. Suddenly, all was right with the world and a new, tranquil contentment has settled over our buddy's household.

Needless to say, our friend can't imagine being (and in any event wouldn't dare be) dressed by anyone but Doug these days. Indeed, valet happy in tow, he makes weekly treks to Mount Street to explore the depths of the massive chest of drawers at the front of the shop. Doug is forever changing the merchandise stocked here, so there's no telling what goodies will be discovered. More accessible, are the £85 cashmere scarves casually draped over wall pegs, ready to be pulled off and wrapped around customers' necks. The ties, neatly displayed on racks and selling for £35 are equally inviting to the touch, and the cupboards, filled with brilliantly coloured sweaters—about £100 for lambs' wool and £330 for two-ply cable cashmeres—make a mesmerizing mosaic of the walls.

Sink into the comfy paisley sofa and let Doug or the estimable Audie Charles act as *your* valet, showing you the contents of what you can't help considering your very own dressing room.

Actually, despite Doug's proprietorship, you're better off relying on Audie, the consummate saleswoman—Doug has a disconcerting habit of quoting two-year-old prices. His turf is really the back room where the actual tailoring is done. It's almost a clandestine operation, as there is nothing about the shop window or the front room to indicate the presence of a genuine bespoke tailor of considerable talent. People don't just stroll in off the street on impulse and ask to have a suit made. They've been referred—or they've asked Michael Caine or Roger Moore about the source of their soft sartorial silhouettes.

Doug has one of those never-met-a-stranger personalities that puts new clients at ease, none of the Savile Row, we're-doing-you-a-favour by deigning to make you a suit attitude from him. Before showing you any of the thousands of fabrics he keeps on hand, Doug chats with you in a seemingly aimless, albeit very pleasant, manner. But there's a method to his madness and in no time at all he's accurately assessed your lifestyle and made decisions about how you should be dressed to suit it. After taking your measurements, he'll expect to see you in about ten days for the first fitting. Of course, if you're only in town for a week, he'll rush it a bit. Doug's very keen on attentive, indulgent service—he even cuts your first suit himself to ensure that it's flawless.

And it's Doug who makes the corrections after that first fitting. Generally speaking, he requires two more to meet his exacting standards, but again, he'll work around your schedule. In any event, you'll spend about £1,000 for a wool suit and up to £1,750 for a cashmere blend. Sports coats tend to hang out in the £750 neighbourhood, and custom-made trousers can be had for £250.   🍂

Foster & Son

83 Jermyn Street	071-930-5385
London SW1Y 6JD	(FAX) 071-439-3803

There have been a lot of Foster boys since Foster & Son first opened its doors for business in 1840—four generations' worth, in fact. Chester Foster, part of the most recent crop, just retired. But not before he'd passed on the generations of experience to Terry Moore, who has been an important element of the operation for more than a quarter century.

In fact, if you're intent on a pair of Foster's made-to-order shoes, you're going to have to consign yourself to his hands, as he's the chap in charge of measuring. There you stand in your stocking feet on the well-worn measuring book as Terry traces them and takes very precise measurements. Then comes the fun part; you're immersed in leathers of every conceivable colour and texture and shown the dozens of styles available. Don't be afraid to choose a toe treatment from one, the heel from another. The shoes, starting at £700, are custom made just for you—Foster's expects you to order exactly what you want. The staff will take care of the rest.

But it's a lengthy process, this handmaking of shoes. After Terry takes your measurements, it'll be about three months until the fitting. And rest assured, there *will* be a fitting or you needn't bother ordering in the first place. From Foster's perspective there's just no other way of ensuring that the shoes fit perfectly—despite the skill of the "closer" who stitches the top part of the shoes and the "maker" who completes them on the wooden replicas of your feet, called lasts.

After that initial fitting, your superbly crafted, hand-stitched, all-leather and divinely comfortable shoes will be finished in a month. You can dispense with the fitting process for any future orders. And you can bet that there will be future orders—custom handmade shoes are an addiction. Terry, his eyes twinkling, claims that "most of our customers have one pair of shoes always in the works."

It's easy to do. Once fabricated, each clients' last is kept "forever . . . or at least 20 years," whichever comes first, we guess. So, if Foster's clients see a pair of shoes anywhere in the world they simply must have, all they have to do is send or fax a picture, and voilà! Eight weeks later they're the proud possessors of the custom-made version.

If you don't have the patience or the pocketbook for Foster's bespoke shoes, you can still take advantage of the shop's nearly two centuries of practising the art of shoemaking by purchasing a ready-made pair. They cost from £150 to £250. The difference in quality and price comes in the manufacture—these are "bench made," which means they're the result of machine *and* hand work. There's no comparison to their hand-made brethren, but they'll do in a pinch.   ❧

Gieves & Hawkes

| 1 Savile Row | 071-434-2001 |
| London W1X 2JR | (FAX) 071-437-1092 |

It's fitting that the stately townhouse sitting at 1 Savile Row is home to Gieves & Hawkes, arguably the grandfather of London's tailors and cer-tainly the most far-flung, with outposts as far out as Tokyo and Hong Kong. You see, the house was built in 1732 by the 3rd Lord Burlington, who was married to Dorothy Savile. The street takes its name from that connubial connection.

Today, Gieves & Hawkes is synonymous with Savile Row for an inter-national clientele who subscribe to the theory that shopping there is the mark of a gentleman. On a street otherwise ostensibly dedicated to suits, Gieves & Hawkes stands out for its comprehensive selection of sports clothes, shirts, sweaters, ties, shoes, luggage and complementary accessories in addition to the ubiquitous suits, both ready-to-wear and bespoke. In fact, the firm brought off-the-rack clothing to Savile Row, an innovation in 1922 which met some resistance from the old guard. No longer. The wide range of choices and prices allow gentlemen to enjoy Gieves & Hawkes' quality throughout their lives—the young man who can only afford £300 for a suit can look forward to the day when he can spend £800, and work his way up to his first custom-made two-piecer for about £1,200.

Along the way he'll be in good company. Mikhail Gorbachev has been known to purchase ready-to-wear suits here, and someone's been send-ing Gieves & Hawkes' ties to George Bush for years; but, of course, the staff is too discreet to reveal the identity of the president's generous inti-mate. At the bespoke level, we're talking about an eclectic group, includ-ing Michael Jackson, George Benson, Viscount Althrop, the Duke of

York and the Prince of Wales—those dashing uniforms Prince Charles and Prince Andrew wore at their weddings were made for them by Gieves & Hawkes.

In fact, the firm, founded in 1785, was originally a naval and military tailor. So renowed was Gieves & Hawkes for its adherence to the principle that no gentleman should be guilty of distressing his colleagues or friends by appearing manifestly incorrectly dressed, that cadets entering the Royal Naval College were regularly reviewed by Gieves' staff to ensure they were properly outfitted. The naval officer technically responsible for this task readily deputed it to Gieves & Hawkes. He gratefully acknowledged they knew the Admiralty Dress Regulations better than he did.

Years later, when the legendary Charles Laughton stopped in to enquire whether the shop had made uniforms for a certain Captain Bligh, he was shown the original ledger in which Bligh's measurements and specifications were recorded. Needless to say, when Laughton portrayed the infamous captain in *Mutiny on the Bounty,* his uniform was accurate down to the tiniest detail.

Details are still important here, and there's still a member of the Gieves family around to make sure they're attended to. Robert Gieve, himself a qualified tailor, represents the fifth generation. He's also a cutter, the person who takes your measurements for a custom-tailored suit and who consults with you about which fabric and style are best suited to your lifestyle. Don't be shy about asking for him if you're visiting the second-floor bespoke department. But not to worry, if he's not available. Any of the six superbly trained cutters will take expert care of you, seeing you through the four to five fittings and eight or so weeks it takes to make sure there will be no droop at the shoulder or hollow in the back of the jacket.

Actually, the entire staff are comfortingly knowledgeable and just as elegant as the store they represent. There's such a clubby atmosphere here, reinforced by the den-like reception area, complete with fireplace and elaborate mantel, leather Chesterfield sofas, magazines and newspapers scattered over a coffee table and large, glass-enclosed cases displaying a captivating collection of toy soldiers, worthy of even the late great Chairman Malcolm's attention.

Beyond, stretch two rooms of ready-to-wear and accessories, the second soaring two stories to a vaulted skylight and graced by an ornately balustraded mezzanine. It was the library of the original house and once served as the site of Dr Livingstone's lying-in-state before his burial in Westminster Abbey. It still houses precious cargo, Gieves & Hawkes off-the-rack suits, while the front room boasts such treasures as four-ply cashmere sweaters for £425, French-cuffed shirts ranging from £55 to £95, and £50 hand-sewn leather gloves. There's also a superb assortment of braces—suspenders—at £25 to £45, and their cunning little knotted silk cufflinks make marvellous gifts for £5 the pair, as do the line of Gieves & Hawkes fragrances and aftershaves starting at £19.

The ground-floor is home to the extensive shoe department. All last-made shoes, most are crafted entirely by hand, are priced from £250. But the pièce de résistance of this level is, of course, the bespoke department with its high ceiling, painted the most remarkably beautiful shade of blue, set off by white mouldings. It's a lovely, inviting room meant for spending the extended periods of time required of the custom tailoring.

And speaking of time, it stands still in Mr Gieve's office which doubles as the firm's museum. There, artifacts from over 200 years of tailoring are proudly displayed—such items as an early catalogue, complete with hand-stitched fabric samples, an example of the nearly extinct detachable collar dating from 1908, a Gieves Sock Brace Attachment that fed down inside trouser legs to act as garter to socks, and a turn-of-the-century sea-chest, evidence of the days when the company was almost considered a department of the Admiralty.

You're welcome to visit the museum whether or not you're in the market for a bespoke suit—just as you're welcome to use the shop's exemplary dry cleaning service, Lilliman & Cox, even if you don't yet own a stitch of Gieves & Hawkes. The holder of three Royal Warrants, the service is just what you'd expect from an establishment as particular about everything as Gieves & Hawkes. And, oh yes, the shop cleans ladies' clothes too.   ❦

Harvie & Hudson

77 & 96–97 Jermyn Street	071-930-3949
London SW1 6JE	071-839-3578
	(FAX) 071-839-7020

In business since 1949, Harvie & Hudson is a youngster compared to many British family firms. Nonetheless, in just over 50 years it has become a significant force in the very competitive arena of English shirt-making, with three bustling locations—the third is on Knightsbridge.

Naturally, we favour the Jermyn Street shops because the ancient avenue is the historic home of the industry—thus the oft-used term "Jermyn Street quality" (or lack thereof) when assessing the merits of a shirt.

Much of Tom Harvie's and George Hudson's early success was based on carrying a large inventory of ready-made shirts in an era when made-to-measure shirts (and ties) were still the norm. These days, the second generation of family management, Jeff Harvie and brothers Derek and Howard Hudson, is serving an increasing demand for bespoke shirts. But, just as savvy as their dads, Messrs Harvie and Hudson haven't lost sight of the business' origins. They maintain one of the largest stocks of ready-to-wear shirts in London in sizes running from 14¹/₂″ to 18¹/₂″. Sleeve lengths are finished to customers' exact measurements, free of charge, in two days. They cost £57.50 in cotton, £67.50 in Sea Island cotton, and there is a range of silk ties at about £30 designed to be perfect complements.

Traditionalists at heart, we really prefer the custom-made interpretations. The fit is so flattering to any figure, and you're in such good company—the Aga Khan, George Segal and Tony Curtis. They've all been measured by Roy Woodhead or Kerry Ford and have agonized over the astounding selection of fabrics. All are designed by the firm's own creative team and woven exclusively for Harvie & Hudson by David and John Anderson of Scotland, whose company dates to 1822. And all are on display at 77 Jermyn, where the whole back wall, floor to ceiling, is stacked with bolts and bolts and bolts of fabric. The choice is staggering, especially the first time out, even overwhelming, given Harvie & Hudson's hallmark of wide colourful stripes. The only approach is to settle into one of the imposing throne-like antique chairs as the fabrics are presented, and take comfort in the fact that you don't have to settle on one. There's a four-shirt minimum at £95 each for cotton and £130 each for the Sea Island variety.

Regardless of the size of your initial order, Harvie & Hudson will only cut one and use that as a guinea pig. It'll take from three weeks to a month to fashion that first sample for a fitting—we're talking about time-honoured construction here, hand cutting and hand-operated sewing machines. Then it's another three weeks to complete the order once the original is approved by you and the tailor. Monogramming doesn't lengthen the process, but it does add £4 per letter to the cost. As trivia buffs, we were interested in Derek Hudson's assertion that 99 per cent of his clients prefer their initials embroidered over their hearts, though some Americans remain wedded to the notion of them stitched on the cuff.

While Harvie & Hudson is essentially a male preserve, women have discovered their terrific long-sleeve nightshirts. We're just mad about them—men's shirts have always been our sleepwear of choice, for a number of reasons—and the shop will shorten the sleeves, same deal as for the regular ready-to-wear shirts. We find it such a delicious thought that the devastatingly attractive "RJ" (Robert Wagner) sleeps in these. He has a particular £79.50 made-to-order version. We generally settle for the ready-mades at £69.50.

While RJ may conduct his business with Harvie & Hudson in London, he doesn't have to. Third-generation representatives Richard Harvie and Andrew Hudson are regularly dispatched to various cities in the U.S. to set up shop in hotel suites where they invite customers, new and old, to review "recent designs and discuss personal styles and suitable fabrics." Call or fax to find out when the Harvie & Hudson road show might be passing your way.   ❦

Henry Poole & Company

15 Savile Row	071-734-5985
London W1X 1AE	(FAX) 071-287-2161

Henry Poole's managing director, Angus Cundey, would like to claim his firm's tailoring lineage is longer than any other on Savile Row. He's traced Henry Poole's father to a family of tailors hailing from Shropshire, which was in business when old man Poole left for London in 1806. So Angus imagines the Pooles were cutting and stitching as far back as the middle-to-late 18th century. But until he can back up his supposition with archival evidence, Gieves & Hawkes has him beat in the oldest-tailor sweepstakes with a recorded charter dating from 1785.

Never mind, Angus has other Henry Poole horns to toot. Namely, the tuxedo can be certifiably traced to a smoking jacket the firm designed for the Prince of Wales (later Edward VII) in 1861. It seems the prince adopted the short jacket in lieu of more formal tails for private dinners at Sandringham, his country estate. The Poole people liked what they came to regard as the "dinner jacket" look and thought it deserved more public exposure. Among an enviable client roster that included J. P. Morgan, Henry Frick and a healthy assortment of Vanderbilts, Mellons and Whitneys, the company dressed one Evander Berry-Wall, a man of considerable sartorial splendour. He owned some 500 outfits and was known to change clothes at least six times a day. Eager to show off what he had been convinced was the latest from London, he donned a Poole-made dinner jacket and confidently strode into the ballroom of the United States Hotel in Saratoga. There, he was the only gentleman not wearing the obligatory tailcoat and was ordered to vacate the premises by the hotel's indignant manager.

That might have been the end of the revolutionary look had Henry Poole not had another clotheshorse client, one who had the good sense to debut his dinner jacket at the country club his father had founded at Tuxedo Park. Eyebrows were raised, but Griswold Lorillard was on his own turf that October of 1886. His temerity was widely reported in the social press, and his jacket became a sensation. Originally known by a number of names—call coat, compromise coat, go-between coat—it finally, irrevocably became the tuxedo.

Today, Henry Poole still makes tuxedos, starting at £1,200, and maintains its ties to the U.S.—40 per cent of its clients are Americans seeking the perfect posture that Henry Poole suits seem to impart. They bestow a military bearing upon their wearers that seems to be particularly attractive to professional men who have probably never seen a day of active duty—lawyers, doctors and accountants. No specifics, though. Angus smiles a tad thinly when he says, "We just don't like discussing our living clients." Dead ones are okay, however. And Angus does allow that, over the years, Henry Poole has made clothes for someone in every country in the world.

Despite such claims and the associations with the ubiquitous penguin suit, there's nothing stuffy about Henry Poole, nothing intimidatingly grand about the shop. Rather, it's a comfortable, friendly place where you sink into one of the four large leather chairs, surrounding an ordinary-looking coffee table, to make fabric selections. It takes about six weeks, two fittings (three if your posture really is bad) and £1,000, plus tax if you're a native, for a three-piece suit. Two-piecers start at £985, and no matter how many pieces, you're looking at close to £2,200 for one in cashmere.

Besides being old and on Savile Row, Henry Poole meets another important criterion of a real bespoke tailor. Everything is made in the shop's workrooms occupying the basement and the second and third floors. Well, *almost* everything. It turns out that the waistcoat maker works at home, and a couple of the trouser makers toil at abodes about five minutes away. Still, the bottom line is that nothing is contracted out—Angus is too particular about the quality.

You see, it's not just his firm's reputation that's on the line, it's his family's. When Henry Poole died, he had no direct heirs, so he left the business to his cousin, Samuel Cundey—Angus' great-grandfather.   ❧

John Lobb—Bootmaker

9 St James's Street   071-930-3664/3665
London SW1A 1EF

When we first spoke to the very dignified John Lobb, great-grandson of the founder of this esteemed company, he was politely dubious about our project, protesting that "you cannot buy anything here for £1,000." He meant there's nothing that inexpensive—the minimum price for a pair of bespoke shoes at John Lobb is about £1,100. As delicately as we could, we suggested he lighten up and understand that the title of our little book is meant to be amusing, not literal. Besides which, we already knew that his family's firm produces what many a shoe maven insist is the world's best, let alone priciest, footwear.

Once he understood what we were about, this gentleman (his patrician features remind us of Prince Philip whose warrant the shop holds) couldn't have been more gracious as he guided us through his Santa's workshop of a store. As you step through the well-trodden vestibule, you're assaulted by the sights, sounds and smells of dedicated craftspeople—men and women carving the wooden lasts which serve as accurate models of clients' feet. They work in a space open to the showroom which occupies the length of the shop. The opposite wall is lined with three massive, seemingly ancient vitrines which showcase the artistry of John Lobb, both old and new. The middle one is essentially the company's museum, displaying such artifacts as Queen Victoria's last, which John somewhat ruefully admits Lobb's didn't make; the prototype for the Wellington boot; and samples of the work that consistently won major prizes at the global exhibitions so popular during the second half of the 19th century. Upstairs in his mezzanine-level, worn-shoe of an office with windows overlooking St James's and the interior of his domain, John traced the firm's history to Sydney, Australia, circa 1849. There, the original John Lobb, forced off his family's Cornish farm by an injury which made him unfit for hard labour, started making boots for miners during the Australian gold rush. They were distinguished by their hollow heels—secret hiding places for stores of the results of the miners' labour. His business thrived to the point where he could return to his homeland with enough of a stake to set up shop in Regent Street. It was a sweet victory, since just a few years earlier he had wandered the streets of London in despair, turned away by every bootmaker in the city—a particularly depressing blow, when you consider that at the time bootmaking was the third largest trade in London. It's no wonder then when he secured the Prince of Wales' Royal Warrant, the plaque proclaiming his endorsement was one of the largest ever displayed!

Since John's death at the end of the 19th century, the business has been passed down through three generations, and the current John Lobb tells us that one of his three sons is already taking a stab at the business. And quite a business it is, with an international reputation so strong that 80 per cent of the production is for export. In fact, John Lobb's fitters make an extensive tour of the U.S. twice a year, and Hermès on the Faubourg St Honoré in Paris acts as a Continental outpost.

Wherever your measurements are taken, the process is the same. Armed with the figures they've calculated and the tracings they've made, the fitters work with the last-makers in the London workshop to ensure the model mirrors each foot's singular features. Meanwhile, the "clicker" selects the proper hides according to the type of shoe or boot being made, taking the weight and the lifestyle of the client into consideration—no fewer than eight pieces of upper leather are required for the simplest shoe. Then the "closer" takes over, cutting the leather to its final shape and sewing it together, incorporating all necessary linings, stiffeners and the tongue, so that the upper part of the shoe fits the last perfectly. He or she then turns the shoe over to the "maker" who completes it by attaching the sole and heel, a laborious, hand-sewn union which is crucial to the final strength of the shoe.

For first-timers the entire process takes at least six months, more like three for regulars for whom lasts have already been made. And once a client's order has been constructed by one group of craftspeople, that same team is assigned to every succeeding pair to assure continuity. Likewise, lasts are kept until John Lobb has been apprised of the demise of the client. Indeed, downstairs, beneath the showroom, some 15,000 to 20,000 lasts are catalogued in a towering wine-cellar-like storage area.

As for styling, virtually anything is possible—choose from the "stock" designs displayed in the vitrines or bring along a picture of a designer shoe that has captured your imagination. There's no difference in the pricing as, regardless of the model, each pair is made from scratch to ensure the superior fit and comfort that John Lobb clients seek. The desired skin and the complexity of the design determine the cost. If you hanker for a pair of loafers or Oxfords in crocodile, be prepared to spend upwards of £2,300. Quite an investment, but consider the amortization over the decades. They're likely to last forever, as long as you send them back at regular intervals for a tune-up. The maintenance of John Lobb shoes and boots is akin to that of airplanes—judicious repairs virtually rebuild them over the years, be they men's or women's shoes.

Yes, John Lobb *does* make shoes for women, but the vast majority of the clientele are men. Indeed, we imagine most of the ladies who commission John Lobb do so for boots, as does the Queen. Indeed, any lady or gent can feel like royalty when taking delivery of riding books. Clients make a proper evaluation of the fit of their boots astride a saddle made for Italy's last royal ruler, the unfortunate King Alfonso. Undoubtedly, the firm's founding father, once snubbed by London's practitioners of his chosen trade, would consider that John Lobb's current possession of three Royal Warrants and a king's saddle is very sweet revenge. ❧

Hilditch & Key

37, 73 Jermyn Street   071-930-5336
London SW1 6JD   071-734-4707
                                                         (FAX) 071-321-0216

Sure, you can pick up a Hilditch & Key ready-made shirt in the U.S. at certain Saks and Bloomingdale's locations, and we understand there are outlets in Australia and Austria. We *know* there's a full-fledged H & K store in Paris, but Jermyn Street is *the* source, or rather sources. In business since 1899 when Charles F. Hilditch and W. Graham Key first set up shop on Tottenham Court Road, the firm now occupies two shops on this street of shirtmakers. It's a company that remains linked to its origins with a Hilditch acting as corporate secretary—Graham, grandson of Charles. With his name on the label, Graham is especially concerned the firm lives up to its stellar reputation—London's *Financial Times* once described Hilditch & Key as Europe's leading maker of custom shirts.

Certainly, such dapper types as George Hamilton, Michael Haseltine, Christopher Reeve, Robert Mitchum, Peter O'Toole, Telly Savalas, David Dimbleby, Lord Rothschild, Marvin Heller, Senator Larry Pressler *and* Diana Rigg subscribe to the paper's assertion. Sticklers for detail, all three shops recognize the importance of the fact that all Hilditch & Key shirts are cut by hand. Shears are used for the body, but the collars are cut with a knife. After all, the collar is the most important part of any shirt; precision is paramount to ensure the manufacture of one that can be properly turned down, by hand, of course. Naturally the shirts are made in the firm's own workrooms and are sewn on flat sewing machines that have changed very little in the last century. The strong, always smooth seams are the result of a combination of twin- and single-needle stitching, flattened by hand pressing. And the buttons are all real shells, never synthetic. In fact, the buttons are so prized by aficionados that some take advantage of the H & K's practice of engraving initials on them.

If it's custom-made shirts you're after, you'll want to see Bertie Mason at number 73. Be prepared to order a minimum of six at £99.50 to £125 for Sea Island cotton. You'll be escorted to the dignified wood-panelled Wellington Room, which has the look and feel of a library with bolts of fabric subbing for books. There you'll make your choices from the substantial selection of basic and fancy fabrics, broadcloths woven in England from the world's finest cottons. All the patterned clothes are exclusive H & K designs, some new, some recycled from their "design bank," which includes cuttings of all the fabrics they've carried for nearly 100 years.

The decision making doesn't stop with the fabrics—there's the important matter of collar styles, and there are a number of them. Finally, you'll get around to the fitting, a lengthy affair involving at least eleven different measurements, copious notes, and often the taking of a photograph or two. Typical of custom-made shirt traditions, the staff will work on one sample shirt, using it first for the fitting. The total order can generally be completed in four to six weeks. If your time in town is limited, they'll rush that first shirt for a fitting within a matter of days. They'll even go so far as to work with you at your hotel or club, assuming you're staying in the West End. Just call to make arrangements—this goes for those interested in ready-to-wear as well. They'll bring the collection to you.

Ladies take note, don't be shy about taking advantage of this service. Specially made H & K blouses are a treat not to be missed. The staff will work with you on the design—choose the collar from one style, the sleeve from another for £69 to £95 for cotton, £159 to £299 for silk. Indeed, they're so accommodating to both sexes that appointments are

taken at the shops, as well, to suit tight schedules or special requirements.

Furthermore, two of the firm's most experienced representatives,
Roger Talbot and Bertie Mason, travel to the U.S. twice a year with the
latest collections and are prepared to take custom orders.

Quality and service, that's what makes Hilditch & Key so special to so
many people. There are over 10,000 current clients for the bespoke
shirts alone. The company can cite the number, because the complete
cutting pattern for each and every customer is kept on file "in perpe-
tuity."   🌰

Huntsman

H. Huntsman & Sons Ltd	071-734-7441
11 Savile Row	071-287-2937
London W1X 2PS	

It's just a coincidence that H. Huntsman's reputation has been built on
sporting clothes, suitable for riding to the hounds, and general country
wear. The shop's reputation dates to 1849 when Henry Huntsman entered the tailoring trade. His two sons joined him, and the business pros-
pered to the point where, in today's jargon, it became a takeover target
for Robert Packer, partner in another old, established clothing business.
He succeeded in 1932, and the Packer family is still in charge—though
the family long ago recognized the happy coincidence of the name and
has not tampered with it, except to state in parentheses under the logo,
"Incorporating Carpenter & Packer."

These days, 46-year Huntsman veteran, Colin P. Hammick, makes a
delightful managing director. Tall and elegantly slim, his winning smile
puts you at ease in this potentially very intimidating, very male and very
distinguished shop. Oriental rugs and library tables stacked with colourful bolts of cloth soften the effect of the soaring ceiling, highly polished
wood parquet floors and stark white walls. The stately stags' heads flanking the mantelpiece are a reminder of the firm's specialty, as are the saddles mounted on wooden "horses" in the dressing rooms.

In fact, the dressing rooms are worth a peek even if you're not here for
a fitting. Uniquely spacious, they're wood-panelled and outfitted with
very large mirrors yielding the total picture, and an inviting leather chair
or two. Then there are those precious little horses—barrel-shaped contraptions on wheels, each boasting a genuine leather (English, naturally)

saddle. They make for a perfect fit when it comes to riding clothes, be they for hunting, polo playing or just plain old recreational hacking.

Of course, any garment from Huntsman, whether or not for riding, will benefit from an extraordinarily good fit. It ought to, given the fact that measurements are taken here with uncommon care. Torso statistics are taken by one fitter, those for the legs by another. There are three people on staff dedicated to "top half" measurements and two to "bottom half." They've got assistants galore, but the apprentices are not entrusted with taking measurements until they've trained for at least five years.

Deciding what you're going to order is just as involved a process as the calculation of your measurements. There are hundreds of fabrics to choose from and an astonishing number of styles. While most bespoke tailors have a signature look, Huntsman takes great pride in a tradition of styling that aims to make what the client wants. And, when he or she has an idea for something unconventional, the staff are happy to interpret it with finesse. Furthermore, the client's nationality is taken into account—the climate is considered in the selection of fabrics, as well as the details of styling that are customary to that nation. Still, there is a special element to Huntsman's cut and craftsmanship (everything is made in the firm's own workrooms) that serves as a hallmark to cognoscenti all over the world—more than half the company's business comes from overseas.

For first-time clients, Huntsman prefers an order of a single garment, the theory being that, once the staff get that right, subsequent orders will be facilitated. Indeed, first-timers should expect four fittings—even regulars know they're in for at least two. Patience is not only a virtue but a necessity when you're dealing with Huntsman custom-made clothes. No garment is finished until you, and more importantly the staff, are absolutely satisfied with the perfection of the fit. If you can't stand the five-to six-month wait, there's a ready-to-wear range (for men only) available here, as well as at Barneys in New York and in major outlets in Japan.

But then you miss all the fun of having all those people fussing over your measurements, and the off-the-peg selection doesn't include a sporting gent's smart cavalry twill huntcoat for £1,522, or a lady's tweed shooting coat and trousers trimmed in leather for £1,891. Tweed sports jackets for country weekends start at £1,085, and cavalier cashmere versions can be fashioned for £1,722. Worsted wool suits start at £1,603 and cashmere overcoats are available for £2,660.

So who pays that kind of money and exhibits so much patience in the process? Colin, the affable managing director, told us very quietly but ever so firmly that he would have to decline to reveal names. "We are not prepared to discuss our clients from the past or of the present." The company is, however, prepared to claim the "former patronage" of such late great notables as King Alphonso of Spain, Queen Victoria, King Edward VII and King George V. That's good enough for us!   ❦

New & Lingwood Ltd

53 Jermyn Street	071-493-9621/499-5340
London SW1Y 6LX	(FAX) 071-499-3103

Still owned after all these years (1990 marked the firm's 125th anniversary) by the descendants of Miss New and Mr Lingwood, partners in business and marriage, New & Lingwood is unique on Jermyn Street in its capacity as a double threat, shirts *and* shoes of both the ready-made and bespoke species.

Should shoes be your priority, head for the little staircase at the back of the glass-enclosed shop. As you mount the blue carpeted stairs you'll be besieged with the aroma of fine leather, and then enveloped by it as you light on one of the nailheaded brown leather chairs. From your well-worn perch, you can survey the mahogany-shelved scene, brimming with traditionally styled shoes, designs that have withstood the test of time— 50 years in some cases. The ready-made numbers run £150 to £220.

If it's custom-crafted shoes you're after, ask for George Glasgow or John Carnera. They'll trace your feet and take their precise measurements, as well as act as patient guides through the innumerable choices to be made with regard to style, colour, width, weight, shape and skin. Of course, you too are going to have to exhibit some patience, as it takes about seven to eight months to make the wooden lasts and construct your order on them—six months until the first fitting. Prices start at £650 and top off at about £1,800 for a pair in crocodile. Quite an investent, but with proper care à la New & Lingwood's polishing and repair service, they could last for decades. And just about every six months either George or John visits major U.S. cities like Boston, New York, Philadelphia, Chicago, Los Angeles and San Francisco. So Americans can bring their shoes in for a tune-up or order new ones. Make sure you're on their mailing list and they'll let you know their schedule.

As for New & Lingwood's shirts, first fashioned for the scholars at Eton, the school for which the company remains the official shirtmakers, they, too, can be ordered in the U.S. Head cutter Sean O'Flynn and members of his staff join George or John on those trips. No wonder New & Lingwood figured so prominently in Tom Wolfe's chronicle of the conspicuous consumption of the go-go days of Wall Street, *Bonfire of the Vanities.* New & Lingwood's makes it easy for even the most confirmed workaholic to ante up as little as £95 a pop for cotton poplin or as much as £175 for silk crepe handmade shirts.

Still, we think it's more fun to conduct the buying business at the Piccadilly Arcade store, which may be the only one in the world where the salesmen all wear shirts with separate stiff white collars. Moreover, only by wandering about the ground level of the store can you get a true sense of the breadth of the choice of fabrics and patterns. Regardless of where you make the arrangements, Sean will make your first sample shirt himself and won't even start on the rest of your four-shirt minimum order until you're both satisfied with the sample. It'll take three to six weeks for that first shirt and a like period for the remainder of the order.

And for the ultimate in sleeping apparel, enquire about New & Lingwood's custom-made piped pyjamas for £135 to £250. A relatively new speciality here, they're the product of the years of experience of Haines & Bonner as the finest pj and nightshirt maker in the world. The august concern was incorporated into the New & Lingwood family in the 1970s and has helped make the firm what menswear writer Alan Flusser describes as "one of London's great traditional men's furnishing shops."

Thomas Pink Shirtmakers

35 Dover Street	071-493-6775
London W1X 3RA	(Telephone Orders) 071-371-0114
	(FAX) 071-225-0787

James, Peter and John Mullen, Dublin-born brothers, are certainly in the pink these days, thanks to Peter's memory. You see, he was the one who solved the problem of naming their company, which is dedicated to the classic art of shirtmaking. "Mullen Brothers" didn't sound quite tony enough to appeal to the Sloanies they hoped would frequent their shop to take advantage of Jermyn Street (the traditional home of the best of British shirtmakers) quality at lower prices. They needed a pointedly proper English name. Fortuitously, Peter recalled that a Thomas Pink had gleaned a certain amount of fame and fortune in 18th-century London due to the superior hunting coats he made. (Hence the terms "hunting pink" and "in the pink"—you were considered to be the latter, if you could afford one of his coats.)

So in 1984, the Mullen boys set up shop as Thomas Pink Shirtmakers, the right name for what has proved to be the right formula, driven by a very clever marketing gimmick. They sell classically tailored shirts (roomy but not baggy, with a traditional spread collar and French cuffs), fashioned in the Mullen family's factories out of silky two-fold cotton in at least 50 colours and patterns—all at one price, £38 for gentlemen, £35 for ladies.

They do so in elegant surroundings, resembling the tastefully decorated library of a private home in which stacks of shirts have replaced books on the shelves, and pretty, approachable young women assist customers. While the assistants are not the gimmick, they do convey a cheery warmth which is in welcome contrast to the rather stiff, though unfailingly polite, greeting at other shirtmakers. And to make their high-quality shirts even more accessible, the Mullens are expanding on several fronts. There are now three shops in London, and one each in Bath and Edinburgh, with plans afoot to cross both the Channel and the Atlantic. Should you be in dire need of a Thomas Pink chemise but are nowhere near one of their outlets, never fear, there's a mail-order catalogue *and* a shirt hotline. You can place orders 24 hours a day, seven days a week, just by picking up the telephone—add £2.50 for postage in the U.K. or £8.50 for overseas, no matter how many shirts are in the shipment. Cute and convenient, but that's not the gimmick either, though it does help explain how Thomas Pink sells more than 100,000 shirts a year.

What *is* the gimmick that has tickled the usually divergent fancies of Foreign Secretary Douglas Hurd, Billy Joel, Viscount Linley, Rachel Ward, the Duke of Bedford, Margaux Hemingway, Michael York, John Cleese and George Hamilton? Well, it, too, is in the pink—in the pink gusset sewn at the side seams where the extra-long front and back tails meet. In addition to having become such a status symbol that wags tell tales of drawers being dropped to offer proof of the wearing of a Pink shirt, the gusset does have a practical purpose. It lends extra strength to the garment and allows just a little extra roominess.

So, 200 years after the expression was first coined, to be "in the pink" (literally and figuratively) is, once again, an excessively coveted condition. But forget about being in a Pink if your taste runs to coloured or striped shirts accented with white collar and cuffs—Pink's doesn't. ❧

Tommy Nutter

19 Savile Row	071-734-0831
London W1X 2EB	(FAX) 071-734-6240

When in 1969 Thomas Albert Nutter followed in many a tailor's apprentice's footsteps by leaving his mentor to set up his own shop, savvy Savilians predicted a speedy doom for the venture. Tommy's shop was simply too different to survive. It sported a very large display window in the days when Savile Row was a series of shuttered concerns that shunned the light of day (or human eyes for that matter). Furthermore, the window merrily broadcast the fact that the shop was "Nutters." And, indeed, there was a certain outlandishness to Tommy's designs that attracted pop stars and others similarly in search of high-quality fashion with a theatrical flair. The patronage of the Beatles (three of the four wore Tommy's suits on the cover of the *Abbey Road* album), Mick and Bianca Jagger, Twiggy, Diana Rigg, Paul Simon, Diana Ross, Eric Clapton and the Duke of Bedford disproved the naysayers.

Two decades toned down some of the peaks with a few valleys, but now the dapper, moustached Tommy is back on top in a larger shop just down the street from his original digs. While many of the Row followed his lead by installing large picture windows, Tommy's current street-front wall of glass does them all one better—so do the clever, generally humorous displays. When last we stopped by, an artistic arrangement of trash cans and one of Jack Nicholson's Joker costumes from *Batman* were on exhibit (a comment on the film?). At any rate, Tommy was responsible for all those colourful suits with their flamboyant tailcoats. Jack showed up for all the fittings, which means he must have felt as if he were living at 19 Savile Row. The film's spectacular special effects tended to destroy Tommy's work. In the end, Tommy figures he made about 60 suits for the movie, his first. No wonder it went so far over budget, when you consider the fact that a conventional Tommy Nutter bespoke suit is priced at about £1,000!

We can barely conceive of what Elton John must pay for the beaded costumes that Tommy makes for him. But we got some notion when we enquired about the stunning black-and-white silk pin-striped waistcoat that reminded us of Elton—each of the fabric's stripes was overlaid with hand-beading. It alone was £350.

But Tommy's bread-and-butter customers like Rupert Murdoch and Lord Montague have less ostentatious tastes. They come here for Savile Row quality with a fashion edge, for the Tommy Nutter look which tends to be very flattering to most male shapes—wide-shouldered jackets with tailored, worked-out chests, narrow at the hips, skimming them without benefit of vents. Slacks feature deep pleats and are on the full side, but taper at the bottom and are almost always cuffed. And the look is completed with a waistcoat, often double-breasted. Come to think of it, the silhouette is equally fetching on women, but the majority of Tommy's clients are men.

Still, it's not unusual for David de Lacy Spiddal, Tommy's Mr Belvedere look-alike sales assistant who always wears a carnation, to spend a fair amount of time showing women like us the collection of ready-made waistcoats in exquisitely coloured silk and silk brocade for around £200. While we're at it, we can't resist Tommy's unique £30 ties for the men in our lives. And where else can you find suspenders embroidered with teddy bears for £25?

In case you hadn't guessed, there is a complete line of Tommy Nutter ready-to-wear here. With suits starting at £400, it is much less expensive than the custom-made line, and accounts for about 50 per cent of the shop's business. Naturally, Tommy's signature is reflected in the styles, and the fabrics, like those of the bespoke, are what he describes as "very English sorts" with subtle plaids. However, the off-the-rack suits hail from Italian factories rather than from Tommy's on-premises workrooms that turn out the custom-made goods. Available for wholesale, the line has international distribution, but this is the largest selection of Tommy's ready-to-wear anywhere in the world.

Despite this success, Tommy feels there's a trend toward the resurgence of bespoke tailoring. He notes that these days few things are original and singular to an individual. "A bespoke suit makes people feel and look good." Besides which, you can have a beautifully fitted, handmade suit for about what you might pay for a ready-to-wear Armani. All you need is the forbearance to deal with choosing the cloth, two fittings and a two-month wait. ❦

Tricker's

67 Jermyn Street	071-930-6395
London SW1Y 6NY	(FAX) 0604-249-78

While there are no longer any Trickers at the helm, the firm founded by Frederick Tricker is nonetheless a family business of long standing. Ever since Walter James Barlthrop married Joseph Tricker's daughter Clara in 1829, a Barlthrop has been in charge. Today, managing director Donald Barlthrop represents the fourth generation of a family devoted to making the Tricker's name stand for the highest quality shoes—both stock and custom-made.

The former start at £325 and are kept in an ingenious floor-to-ceiling series of wooden bins, each marked with the style number and size of the shoes contained within. You are invited to sit in one of the comfortably worn chairs while a member of the staff retrieves the appropriate pairs from their massive storage-cum-hiding place. Don't be put off by the young, hip-looking sales assistants—they're invariably friendly and they know their stuff. Despite appearances, they're eminently qualified to represent such a venerable institution, one which holds Prince Charles' Royal Warrant.

Regardless, if you've come to Tricker's for a custom-made pair of shoes, you won't be dealing with just any staff member. You'll be placed in the experienced hands of Eric Cooke who will measure your feet. While you'll be welcomed as a drop-in, it's best to call in advance for an appointment, as it can be a lengthy process to select style and leathers. Of course, you're not limited with respect to either. Tricker's will replicate any look or create one to your specifications, and if its vast inventory of leathers doesn't quite suit, the shop will secure the shade and texture you desire. Count on spending at least £450, add another £200 should you crave a pair entirely made by hand.

Either way, it'll take about three months for your first fitting, when the shoes are half finished. Three months after that you'll be the proud possessor of a bench-made pair of shoes that fit perfectly and are just as comfy as they can be. That said, we should caution that Tricker's is not necessarily for people with problem feet, but even they can get a £140 shot of comfort from a pair of heavenly Tricker's slippers, either straightforward leather or velvets dressed up with your coat of arms in gold thread. They can also chuckle over a good yarn or two from Bob Kendall who's been here as long as anyone can remember and has an amazing repertoire of shoe stories, past and present.   🍃

Turnbull & Asser Ltd

71 & 72 Jermyn Street	071-930-0502/0505
London SW1Y 6PF	(FAX) 071-930-9032

Established by Reginald Turnbull and Ernest Asser in 1885, the firm that bears their names makes some of the world's most splendid shirts. The proverbial proof of the pudding is the fact that Turnbull & Asser's Paul Cuss holds a warrant as royal shirtmaker to Prince Charles. When Cuss isn't occupied with the prince's chemise needs, he's often concerned with those of Christopher Plummer. And when he's not working with him, he's sometimes off to the U.S. to cater to customers like Steven Spielberg, John Kluge, Ron Perlman, Steve Gold and Bill Pattis. So don't be surprised if he's not around when you stop in. Don't be disappointed either—Steven Quin or Donald Amor can fit you to a Turnbull *T*.

Whoever takes your measurements, as a first-timer here you're in for quite an experience and not an inconsiderable amount of time. You see, you're up against a minimum order of six shirts, with a thousand different fabrics to choose from—from cottons to silks to viyellas, which are a wool and cotton blend. Then there's the matter of the collar shape—at least eight different styles. One's bound to complement your neck. But it can be an agonizing decision, as once you find *the* one, chances are you'll stick with it for the length of your association with Turnbull. So don't be shy about asking for a second opinion. In fact, the affable Simon Hobbs, the youngest member of the Turnbull fitting team and still in training, will probably offer his. Older, wiser and certainly more senior, retail director Eric Humbles will wait for your solicitation before proffering his opinion.

After this arduous decision-making session, it'll take about three weeks until the fitting. One sample shirt from your order is made for this specific purpose. If you've left town in the interim, the shirt will be sent to you. Chances are pretty good, you'll find it fits perfectly. If not, call or fax with the necessary modifications. . . but not too hastily. Remember, Turnbull & Asser takes the shrinkage factor into account when cutting the pattern. So wash it before making a final fitting decision. Naturally, if you go through the ritual, the practised eyes of Messrs Cuss, Quin or Amor will automatically calculate any possible reduction of fabric.

Once everyone agrees on the fit of the sample shirt, it'll take eight to ten weeks to complete the order. Classic solids tend to run £75 each, while the bold stripes favoured by Prince Charles fetch an additional £10. For white-on-white and the viyellas, count on £85 per shirt. Those made of white Swiss voile sell for £120, and plan on £140 for any in Sea Island cotton. Silk more your speed? Then you're on the fast track at £150 each.

But enough of money and back to decisions. You'll probably want to pick up some ties to go with your new shirts. Fortunately, the shop is so "men's club" comfortable, with its plush red carpeting and rich wood panelling, that you won't mind spending the additional time poring over all the gorgeous silks, with over 150 patterns, each available in twelve different colours. Nigel Butler is usually around to lend a hand (unless he's off doing tie trunk shows at various Neiman-Marcus locations in the U.S.). He'll point out the three weights of silk which determine the price—£28 to £40 per tie. Even more helpful is Nigel's flair for choosing the consummate *coordinating* pocket square. He'll never let you commit the faux pas of selecting a matching one.

Still, it takes more than a superbly tailored shirt, complementary tie and correlating pochette to proclaim your Turnbull & Asser-ship to the world. The cognoscenti know how to pick out a Turnbull & Asser client from a well-dressed pack. It's all in the buttons—bright white, made from Australian mother-of-pearl. It seems some shirtmakers cheat in the button department, using inferior material cut from the outer portions of the shell. You can tell when you turn them over, there are black flecks and other discolourations on the back. Turnbull & Asser buttons, however, are made from the very centre of the shell and are therefore just as pure as the driven snow, on both sides—and more costly. And you have plenty of opportunity to flash them with Turnbull & Asser's trademark three-button cuffs.

We guess button-flipping in the tailoring world is akin to taking a surreptitious glance at the hallmark on the cutlery in restaurants to see if it really is sterling! ❧

Woodhouse

42 South Molton Street   071-493-1524
London W1Y 1HB

In some ways, Philip Stuart reminds us of Ralph Lauren. Like Ralph, he's very attractive, he's a marketing genius, he has a flair for merchandising that testifies to an appreciation of the aspirations of his clientele, and he has a collection of menswear with his name on it. But unlike Ralph, Stuart was a retailer first, designer second, and he is something less than a household name, preferring to remain in the background. Still, like his American counterpart, Stuart has had an indelible influence on the fashion scene in his native land.

You see, Philip, who got his first taste of retailing through his family's jewelry business, was the first to sell Continental designer merchandise at accessible prices. When he opened his first Woodhouse store on Oxford Street in 1975, foreign labels could only be purchased at the high-priced boutiques on New Bond Street. Stuart searched for new names to import to England and came up with the likes of Armani, Boss and Gaultier. Then he pioneered a revolution in the way clothes were merchandised by creating more comfortable and imaginative shopping environments. His stores, now numbering eight, became benchmarks for other retailers throughout Europe, who went to London to see what Philip was doing with them in terms of stock and decor, then returned home to copy him.

What he was doing was creating the total "Woodhouse look." Fashion-wise he was making a statement with clothes for "the fashionable dresser ...he understands fashion, but doesn't have to wear over-designed clothes to say so." As for Philip's stores' interiors, they are all very sleek and sophisticated, with enough accoutrements like Oriental rugs and leather chairs to suggest the trappings that success brings. Both looks have recently culminated in the South Molton Street location, redesigned with a simple, elegant geometry that projects a cool, masculine modernism to showcase Philip's collection. It features Italian-made suits and sportswear with a decidedly British air. Philip's suits sell for an average of £250, while other designers and the Woodhouse private label go for £300 to £645.

Woodhouse has traditionally been such a successful outlet for Armani that Gerry Dixon, director of Emporio Armani UK, credits Philip with the Armani firm's ability to open the chain in Britain. So expect lots of Giorgio's ready-to-wear here, from jeans priced from £55 to £85 to suits at £250 to £650. In between, you'll find shirts at £35 to £140 and sweaters in the £200 neighbourhood.

Manager Mark Herman is usually on hand to help you wade through what may be London's best selection of ties—Armani, Woodhouse and others, ranging in price from £29 to £60. There's something for everyone, from eye-catching floral and paisley silks to club ties. The latter are, of course, the tie of choice of the would-be tycoons that frequent the shop. Woodhouse's appeal to this segment of the population is summed up by the fact that they are supplying the wardrobe for a series called *Capital Cities,* television's answer to *Wall Street.*

But lest you think Woodhouse is all business, remember that it's a favourite among pop stars, and the zany John Cleese is a regular, though he wasn't wearing anyone's clothes for his most hysterically memorable scene in *A Fish Called Wanda.*

And now that Philip Stuart has emerged from behind the Woodhouse façade to lead his own bandwagon with his namesake collection, like Ralph Lauren, he will no doubt soon be claimed by other establishments as a celebrity patron.   🍓

FOR WOMEN

Caroline Charles

56–57 Beauchamp Place	071-225-3197
London SW3 1NY	(FAX) 071-584-2521

A figure on the London fashion scene since there's been one, Caroline Charles has become a presence with the 1989 unveiling of her house, as in *H*ouse. The grand, circa 1830 double-fronted townhouse combines a retail shop on three levels, wholesale showrooms, offices, even a conservatory and a roof garden. It is a flagship fashion house in the mode of the great Parisian ones which allows Caroline to present the full breadth of her collections—her trademark, sensible interpretations of contemporary trends in very wearable day and evening clothes, along with lingerie, bed linens and men's ties.

The interior cleverly re-creates the spirit of an early 19th-century townhome, divided into distinct rooms, each one dedicated to a specific part of the collection. The street-level living room houses Caroline's day-wear and accessories and features fine period furniture, temptingly grouped in front of a splendid marble fireplace. The clothes are displayed, as they are throughout the shop, flat against the pale ivory walls, thus providing the only decor, other than the painstakingly restored mouldings and cornices. The occasional black silk mannequin, specially designed by Caroline, lends a striking contrast and the classic Grecian-style plaster busts which serve as hat racks reveal her well-documented wit. Here, you can find her large, very beautiful hand-rolled silk jacquard scarves. At £170, they prove the point that Caroline is a colourist first. They look terrific with her practical, but highly styled and very current suits for working women which sell for about £375.

On the mezzanine level, four spacious dressing rooms, each equipped with wicker armchair and full-sized mirror, are divided by a generous area with seating for weary companions. Refreshments are served to shoppers and droppers alike, and a skylight allows for the inspection of colours in natural light.

Downstairs are the bedrooms, offering evening wear, lingerie and linens. A glorious cherry-wood French sleigh-bed from the 1930s showcases the latest bed-linen designs, while the large deco mirror hanging above it reflects the delightful but tailored £155 silk dressing gowns and the flirtatious hand-finished lace teddies at £75.

Classical music enhances the elegant mood of the area for exhibiting the entrance-making gowns and cocktail suits. We adored an exquisite hand-woven brocade jacket selling for £540. Our other find was a £620 long, sequinned, ribbon-lace dress, figure-hugging and dramatic with its backless construction, not to mention one side slashed to the thigh.

Since Caroline continues to design in her studio down the street at 11 Beauchamp Place, she only pops into her headquarters to deal with the press and buyers from leading stores all over the world. As genuinely warm and exceptional in her ability to relate to her customers as she is, Caroline can't afford to spend much time in the shop. But the very capable Maureen Newton-Clare is almost always on hand to help you coordinate your Caroline Charles purchases. We find the ease with which Caroline's creations mix and match is one of their most appealing aspects. On more than one occasion, we've been outfitted for an unexpected weekend jaunt with perfectly paired jacket, skirt and trousers (about £250, £125 and £110 respectively), augmented by a chunky hand-knit £300 cotton sweater, and perhaps a pair of walking shorts for £120.

And sometimes we've come away with nothing whatsoever, except a feeling of well-being—the result of time well spent, browsing in the House that Caroline built.   🦋

Catherine Walker

The Chelsea Design Company   071-352-4626
65 Sydney Street
London FW3 6PX

As we strolled down a pretty residential street in Chelsea, en route to an appointment at Catherine Walker's boutique, we noticed a tall, willowy, coltish-looking woman in a short leopard-print skirt dashing for a taxi. Momentarily, we wondered if she could possibly be the designer whose work for Princess Diana has brought her international fame, but no... instinct told us this dark, très chic beauty was French. And someone with a name like Catherine Walker was obviously English. Well, we were right—and we were wrong. The woman we saw *was* Catherine and she *is* French. The Walker came from her English husband, whose tragic death had precipitated the birth of her business nearly 15 years ago.

True to form, Catherine had bolted just prior to our arrival. The soul of discretion with regard to her famous and not-so-famous clients, Catherine is cautious where publicity is concerned and downright skittish about interviews. She's justifiably concerned that questions about the Princess of Wales will arise. Since the subject of the divine Diana is, in Catherine's view, absolutely off limits, she prefers to avoid any potential unpleasantness by removing herself from the proximity of enquiring minds. We'd like to think we're much too well bred to have tried to solicit any information, but if truth be known, we're not. So Catherine did the right thing by leaving us in the care of shop assistant Lucy Roberts.

Slim and striking, like her clearly adored employer, Lucy's a delightful curator of Catherine's small, square, library-like boutique—clothes totally cover the walls from floor to ceiling, catalogued in tiers. There's a simple dignity, a quiet understatedness about the space which mirrors Catherine's creations. Very tailored without being uptight, there's a youthful yet formal quality about them and an unassuming charisma that never dominates the wearer's personality. *And* they are flattering to a fault for a wide range of figures. We watched a matronly middle-aged lady drop ten years and ten pounds as she was fitted for a cocktail dress for her son's wedding. Less problematic shapes like those of Shakira Caine and Lisa (as in Mrs Dustin) Hoffman are equally well served.

There are two lines of clothes, deluxe and diffusion. The latter, ready-to-wear by another name, ranges from £600 to £800 for a suit, and is much less costly than the custom-made deluxe at a minimum of £1,000. You're also looking at bagging your selections and taking them home, rather than having a six- to eight-week wait. But for suits from either line, there's a nice assortment of the bare necessities to go underneath—slim cotton T-shirts for about £65, £130 in silk, and alluring camisoles at £85.

Typically, our taste leaned toward the deluxe end of the spectrum. We coveted an aubergine velvet cocktail dress, its feminine, just-off-the-shoulder neckline accented by long slender sleeves and a bodice embellished with pearls and gold thread embroidered in a baroque motif. It was heavenly, for something in excess of £1,200. Even more magnificent was the ballgown Lucy deftly retrieved from the second tier with what we had always heretofore considered a grocers' hook. With a skirt consisting of seemingly countless layers of fine net in a predominantly green tapestry-like floral print and a bustier overlaid in a gold-thread basket weave trimmed in tassels, we've never seen anything like it anywhere. And we've seen more than our share of £5,000-plus gowns.

We had no sooner finished singing its praises, when Lucy persuaded us that we couldn't fully appreciate Catherine's considerable talent without seeing her wedding gowns. Another jolt! Not only did we not know Catherine was French, we didn't know she's the creative force behind one of London's most fashionable bridal salons. Dauntless gatherers of information that we are, we dutifully followed Lucy up the street to the intersection of Fulhum Road, where we were confronted by an odd little wedding cake of a building that doesn't look as though it could possibly be connected to anything else in the immediate vicinity. Evidently a former conservatory, it's been here as long as Lucy can remember and sets an entrancing stage for Catherine's elegant designs.

Other than the gowns lining the two long walls and the occasional plant, the principal adornment is an ornate iron-work staircase right in the middle. Otherwise more decorative than functional, the three-way mirrored space beneath is reserved for the primping, whirling and twirling of future brides. We watched a lovely young thing gaze in wonderment at her reflection in a column of heavy ivory silk crepe, its slim grandeur enhanced with a long sweeping train. The softly sensuous neckline hit just at the shoulder, and bows strung across the top of the long-sleeved bodice provided the only frill. Fit for a queen, its price fell somewhere in the £950 to £5,000 range of most of the gowns. Catherine has started doing some spectacular beading on her bridal attire, which can drive the cost into the stratosphere. In any event, we felt, under the circumstances, it was impolitic to get too specific. You see, manager Krisi McKay works by appointment, and we were intruding on a rather intimate scene.

We did, however, weasel the £1,550 figure out of Lucy for one dress, instantly recognizable to movie buffs worth their salt—the full-skirted, white Thai silk number with delicate handmade roses as the cap sleeves that Kim Bassinger wore in *Batman* when she first captured Michael Keaton's eye. Ball or wedding gown, it's a beauty. Kim should wear Catherine's designs more often—will she ever live down her disastrous appearance at the 1990 Academy Awards show?

At any rate, if you're in the market for any of Catherine Walker's wedding gowns, count on a three-to-four-month lead time. Should you wish, you can also plan on her designing a headdress to match any of the gowns. From what we've seen, you should most definitely take her up on that option. But don't look to Catherine for bridesmaid dresses unless your nearest and dearest are prepared to spring for a little something from the deluxe or diffusion line. This is simply not that sort of bridal boutique. ❧

Chanel

31 Sloane Street   071-235-6631
London SW1 9NR   (FAX) 071-408-1557

Predictably, both Chanel boutiques—there's another one on Old Bond Street—reflect the inimitable Coco's style, a combination of austerity and luxury. They're done in Coco's favourite non-colours, black and white. "It's the perfect combination. Black contains everything; so does white. Their beauty is absolute."

But not so absolute that they should not be tempered by her beloved beige carpeting. "I was the first to have rugs dyed beige," she once claimed. "It reminded me of beaten earth." Sunny gold lighting casts a flattering glow that saves the clean-cut lines, the marble staircases, the black forged iron rails and the banks of space-creating mirrors from being too stark. Designed by Christian Gallion, who's been responsible for the look of all Chanel boutiques worldwide, they are a study in sober sumptuousness.

That said, we tend to shop Sloane Street for several reasons, not the least of which is that it seems to attract a younger, classier crowd, i.e., fewer tourists. Moreover, it's bigger and, most important (in a sentimental sort of way), its street number is that of Coco Chanel's original salon at 31 Rue Cambon in Paris. Indeed, we find the Sloane Street shop irresistible on all fronts and consistently help bolster the amazing statistics that show that 99 per cent of those who turn the emerald-cut crystal doorknob and step across the threshold actually purchase goods. Browsers beware! It's tough to circumnavigate the ground floor, with its dazzling displays of the entire range of jewelry and accessories, without picking up a little something. A stunning oh-so-Chanel pair of earrings for as little as £60, perhaps? Or how about one of the signature quilted leather bags which signals your membership in an elite international sorority? You can't miss them lined up in all their glory at the front of the store—the classic envelope flap starts at £595 and an enchanting oval-shaped number with a zippered closure for £500.

Downstairs, you'll find the ready-to-wear collection, and here's where you really do need to enlist the help of a sales assistant. Once you've wriggled into that black sequinned £1,500 cocktail dress, you'll want it properly accessorized to achieve the full effect. All these girls know their stuff and think nothing of dashing around the store to pick up the perfect shoes, jewelry and purse. Indeed, most regulars have developed a personal rapport of long standing with one of the staff and wouldn't dream of shopping without her assistance.

Since we're generally on the run when we stop in, we head straight for Josianele Kabbany, the manager. No one wastes your time here, but we find Josianele particularly sensitive to tight schedules. She's able to give us a quick run-down of what's new that she thinks we'll like, from a £400 cashmere sweater to a £2,500 ballgown. Of course, that can encompass a lot of merchandise as we think that Kaiser Karl Lagerfeld's interpretations of Coco's seven sins—luxury, beauty, style, allure, elegance, taste and genuine simplicity—are nothing short of inspired. He's been at it since 1983 and has carried the mantle of Chanel to new glory. Like Coco, he seems to have a sure instinct for conquering the public's taste and, more important, for keeping its loyalty.

Certainly, he's got us and most everyone we know addicted to Chanel to some degree. Like any addiction that makes you feel as though you can conquer the world—just try on one of the suits and you'll know what we mean—it doesn't come cheap. That suit which announces your status as a *lady* to the world, costs at least £1,000. Plan on another £350 for the right blouse to go with it, and close to £200 for a pair of shoes. Talk about investment dressing! This is true blue-chip stock—these clothes exemplify Coco's edict that "Nothing goes out of style more quickly than a fashion, while elegance is for all time."   ❦

Escada Boutique

66–67 New Bond Street   071-629-0934
London W1Y 9DF   (FAX) 071-589-3020

To pass through the brass-framed glass doors is to enter a world of colour . . . and chaos. This is one store that always seems to be hectic, no matter the state of the economy or how the world's major currencies are stacking up against one another. We put it down to the jaunty exuberance of the fashions from this Munich-based house. The clothes are playfully bold and seem to bring out a sexy self-confidence in their wearers. Yet they're eminently practical—styles easily translate from day to evening with the quick change of an accessory or two and are constructed of seasonless fabrics that tend to pack well. Indeed, Escada is a master of synergetic blends—linen with silk, which has a smooth creaseless look, and cashmere with angora, which makes for a less expensive garment and produces stronger colours.

Barry Ziff, the owner of this six-year-old boutique (one of 65 Escada emporiums worldwide) maintains Americans are responsible for a lot of the frenetic activity here because prices are considerably less than those in the U.S.—by as much as a third. We've never checked out his claim, but we have noticed a number of American businessmen armed with shopping lists prepared for them by wives, girlfriends or daughters. It was pretty clear that they had their marching orders and dared not return home without the designated items.

As far as we can tell, they have very little excuse for not filling the entire order. The store is well stocked, with the collection attractively grouped by colour on brass fixtures, white walls serving as an appropriately blank canvas. It's easy to find what you're looking for, be it a smart dress in the £300 neighbourhood or a £275 blouse. And the sales ladies, no matter how harrassed by the crowds, do preserve their poise and are invariably helpful. At least those designated male shoppers don't have to suffer the indignity of the claustrophobic dressing rooms *or* stand in the often interminable lines to get in them.

While waiting, we usually take the opportunity to review the terrific assortment of accessories—belts, bags, shoes and hats—that pick up the themes of the collection. For instance, when Escada was big on hearts—heart-printed silk blouses, sequinned hearts on black satin evening jackets, and hearts embroidered on sweaters—pumps and purses decorated with cute little gold hearts were featured.

All in all, it's worth working your way through the pack to discover Escada's many enchantments...and to take advantage of Barry's self-styled bargains.   🌑

Fendi

37 Sloane Street   071-235-9966
London SW1X 9LD   (FAX) 071-581-1065

In the 1960s, it was the "fab four." For the 1990s, we've got the fab five—the fabulous five Fendi sisters, whose double *F* logo adorns an ever-growing fur, fashion, fragrance and accessory empire. It's decidedly a family business that seems destined to reincarnate the fab four during the 21st century in the guise of the Fendi sisters' daughters—Maria, Teresa, Sylvia and Federica—who are already responsible for the Fendissime collection. Designed for the younger and less affluent set, sleek-looking separates can be had for £100.

But we're getting ahead of ourselves. Before we consign Fendi's future to the next generation, we should mention that this surprisingly small and unintimidating shop (surprising if you've set foot into the Fendi's Fifth Avenue palazzo) is typical of the current generation's pioneering spirit. Opened in 1980, it was one of the first boutiques to establish a beachhead on Sloane Street. Leave it to the Fendi girls to lead a movement which has transformed a ritzy residential boulevard into one of the world's most chic shopping streets.

The ground floor is home to clothes and accessories, the Fendissime group, its more expensive "365" sister range, and the high-fashion signature collection. Meant for grown-ups, the 365 clothes are highly styled and beautifully made. Coats start at £400, blouses at £150, and dresses are in the £200-plus neighbourhood. But the pièce de résistance is the sophisticated and witty Fendi ready-to-wear. Designed for the sisters by Kaiser Karl Lagerfeld, it has a distinctive style that makes it a favourite with a cosmopolitan, international clientele. You see, just as with the Chanel line, the Kaiser does a much better job for the Fendi label than he does for his own. Prices start at about £300 and go up considerably. Suits, for our money a particular strength of the collection, start at £500.

Despite the temptations of this floor, all decked out in the Fendi signature colour combo of sand and black, it can only hold our attention for so long. Invariably, our thoughts and then our feet wander downstairs to the salon which houses Fendi's incomparable furs. There, we alight on the snug sofa to watch the video of the lastest collection, awed by the fantastic way the Fendis fashion fur. The saying that you can't tell the players without a programme takes on new meaning as we wonder at the ingenious usages, patterns and colours. We need the expert commentary of manager Patricia Silver to tell us what's what. Unless you grew up in Manhattan's fur district, you will, too. But you'll have to ask, as Patricia is one prim and proper redhead, who would never dream of intruding upon your privacy unless invited.

Once asked, she'll be more than happy to show you the stocked pieces from the collection—like a divine three-quarter length sable coat for £27,000—or to discuss a special order from the videotape. Of course, there's no such accommodation where the clothes are concerned. What you see is what you get, and it goes fast. So the trick is to stop in when the collections first arrive—August for Fall/Winter, January for Spring/Summer. Better yet, ingratiate yourself with Patricia so that she'll call you, wherever in the world you might be, the moment the clothes arrive. In fact, once she gets a sense of your individual style, she'll take it upon herself to send you polaroids of selections likely to suit you. A quick call or fax in response will assure your name is on them. 🍎

Frederick Fox Ltd

87–91 New Bond Street	071-629-5706/5
London W1Y L9A	(FAX) 071-629-3048

Despite a site right in the middle of London's traditional shopping milieu and its gracious appointments, browsers need not bother darkening the door. Australian-born Frederick Fox, milliner to the Queen (as opposed to "hatters" which is Herbert Johnson's territory), works by appointment only. He's too busy concocting hats for stores such as Saks Fifth Avenue,

Neiman-Marcus, Harrods, Fortnum & Mason and Harvey Nichols to be bothered with the merely curious. Indeed, it's his experience that if you take the time to set up an appointment, you're a serious candidate for one of his delightful creations.

And we do mean experience. Now a debonair silver-haired gentleman of a certain age, Frederick started making hats when he was only 12 years old. He took to cutting up his mother's discards and remaking them into stylish headgear for his sisters. Proud of their brothers' ingenuity, the girls started wearing Frederick's hats to church, where they were invariably complimented on the chic of their chapeaux. Word spread that the hats were the work of little Frederick, and soon he was in business — collecting the local ladies' hats one week, reshaping and retrimming them for return the following week.

At 17, he decided to head for Sydney and apprentice himself to a milliner in order to refine his self-taught techniques. Satisfied that he had no more to learn, he emigrated to England in 1958 and spent the next three years working for a series of designers. Finally, he settled at and eventually took over Langeé on Brook Street. As he solidified his position as one of London's most talented young hat-makers, he changed the name to Frederick Fox and the rest is, as they say, history. Or at least it is since 1970, when Hardy Amies recommended Frederick's work to the Queen for a state visit to Brazil and Chile. Pleased with the hats he made for that trip, she's been a fan ever since, conferring her warrant in 1974, just after he moved to his current third-floor showroom on New Bond Street.

The crystals from a graceful chandelier target spots of dancing light on the wooden trellis that serves as hat rack. You can't resist reaching here, there and everywhere for hats to suit every mood, every occasion. Since the appointment-only policy assures privacy, you can admire yourself to your heart's content with Frederick's whole-hearted indulgence. We made like one of the three musketeers in a great looking, wide-brimmed, brown fur felt number, decorated with a spray of ostrich feathers. At £165, it's perfect for an afternoon wedding or for the inauguration of the racing season. We felt more like Princess Di at a charity function in a fuschia satin pill-box, accented with a cascade of colourful handmade silk peonies.

And it was Joan Collins time when we tried on a small, black, £180 jersey cocktail hat, its crown trimmed with a fin of sequins. A coquettish veil ended just where it's supposed to, right at the tip of the nose. That's crucial, according to Frederick, so that you can wear your crowning glory without its cramping your style—you can eat, drink, and most importantly smile without any encumbrance. As a matter fact, Joan is decked out in a Frederick Fox red felt chapeau in the ads for her new perfume.

Naturally, Frederick will adjust the length of a veil on his ready-made hats to decorously tickle your nose. Or you can avoid any alterations by taking advantage of his custom designing services for a minimum of about £200. What's the maximum? Frederick laughs as he claims there is none. "A hat," he says "is a little bit like a house, isn't it? It depends on what you want. If you want the fur to be sable and the embroidery to be silk or satin, it's going to increase the price." Still, he concedes that for clients like Carol Price and Bubbles Rothermere, the average could be pegged at around £300.

When it comes to bridal veils, that figure stands as a starting point, and again there's virtually no cap on the price, or on Frederick's fruitful imagination.   🍎

Hartnell

26 Bruton Street	071-629-0992
London W1X 8DD	(FAX) 071-629-1830

For a fashion house, survival after the death of the founding designer is always a struggle. Where couture is concerned, without the support of a popular, internationally distributed ready-to-wear line like Chanel's or a perfume like Patou's Joy, it is virtually impossible. The exception that may prove the rule is Hartnell, whose Sir Norman died in 1979. There is a concentrated rally afoot led by the formidable (yet very lovable) Manny Silverman to perpetuate Sir Norman's legacy.

Fortunately, for Manny and his investors who took over the reigns of the house four years ago, Hartnell has one enduring asset, the loyalty of the Queen Mother who has worn virtually no other label since Sir Norman designed her wedding gown in 1935. But that's a double-edged sword—she is, after all, the world's most popular *grandmother*. Not necessarily a recommendation for most potential buyers of expensive, custom-made clothes. She may be perpetually adorable in her signature matching dress and coat ensembles in beautiful eye-catching (though never gaudy) colours and prints, but she also always looks ready to step in as the mother (grandmother?) of the bride at a garden wedding. Still, the Queen Mother's patronage has kept the Hartnell name in the public eye, which is crucial in the fashion game.

So Manny's challenge was to revitalize the house, to attract a younger clientele, without offending either Hartnell's most treasured client or a complement of Britain's elder society ladies who remained faithful. Many wondered if Manny was up to the task. Not us. This guy could, as they say, sell ice to the Eskimos, and he had already proved his marketing mettle by serving as saviour for Moss Bros. But the nay-sayers pointed out that the sale and rental of mid-priced men's clothing is a far cry from the rarefied world of couture, that an accessible store of racks of ready-to-wear was a long way from the hauteur of an elegant Mayfair salon. They didn't count on Manny's savvy. He understood that the hallmarks of Hartnell remained viable—Sir Norman's feminine, flattering, decorative style, as well as his passion for embroidery and glittering beadwork. All that was needed was up-to-date interpretations. And the salon itself, occupying an essentially glamorous but definitely faded 1930s building, was in desperate need of a facelift.

It took awhile for Manny to find Hartnell's version of Chanel's Karl Lagerfeld. A succession of interim "guest" designers put some much-needed vigour into the collection, capturing the imagination of the press, another important component of his campaign. Hartnell was once again gracing the pages of glossy fashion magazines with designs like the unforgettable gown "Tallulah"—all Hartnell's couture pieces are named. A drop-dead strapless evening gown in black silk gazarre, its bodice was overlaid with velvet and its full skirt was emboldened by a large romantic sweep of red net at the back. At about £3,500, it, like all the collection, was made on the premises. Once ordered, any of the couture requires four to eight weeks and, ideally, two fittings. Manny says Hartnell has been known to turn out an evening gown in six days, but that's highly unusual.

At any rate, as we go to press, it would seem Manny has found the spiritual channeler for Sir Norman—Marc Bohan, who for years had so successfully kept the Dior look alive. After a debut collection that garnered euphoric reviews from the world's fashion press, it may no longer be possible to get an appointment at a moment's notice to review the current collection.

But give it a shot. It's a treat just to step into the refurbished salon, a very grand mirrored sea of pale Hartnell green upon which a glorious crystal chandelier in the shape of a ship once again sails. The très chic, straight from central casting but refreshingly unintimidating French directress, Chislaine Lejeune, told us that until its recent restoration, the chandelier had looked like a shipwreck. Other original details, like a fire-place that had been residing at the Victoria and Albert Museum, have been retrieved and rejuvenated. It's a lavish setting, immediately recognizable as an haute couture palace to '50s and '60s movie buffs—you can almost see Fred Astaire, Glenn Ford or Rock Hudson lounging on the velvet banquette, enjoying Cyd Charisse's, Leslie Caron's, Debbie Reynolds' and/or Doris Day's delight in the passing parade of delicious fantasy fashions

Of course, with Marc at the design helm you can be sure that the clothes will spell Paris Couture (at about a third less the price, Manny is quick to point out), but will be wearable and timeless, with just the right touch of Hartnell glitz and glitter. Our guess is he has set his cap for a princess—Diana by name—and will prove serious competition to Victor Edelstein and Catherine Walker. May the best designer win! ❦

Julia's

| 12 Grafton Street | 071-629-8587/8588 |
| London W1X 3LA | (FAX) 071-629-3106 |

We've always dreamed of the day when our first names, reverently uttered, would instantly identify us. We aspire to being single-name sensations as are Cher, Liza and Liz in the entertainment world, or like Martha, America's grande dame of retail. Indeed, until recently Martha stood alone in that category. But in the irrepressible Julia, she has a challenger to her supreme status. In fact, we wonder if Julia, who runs a sophisticated operation which promotes the world's best designers to an affluent clientele, hasn't set out to be the Martha of Britain.

Of course, Julia does have a last name—it's Gale. She even has a partner in Patricia Lavender, the perfect brunette counterpoint to her own classic blond beauty who used to be her client. You see, until opening her namesake store in 1987, Julia was a vendeuse at another establishment, one frequented by Patricia. Patricia was at first fascinated then dependent upon Julia's exceptional ability to organize a flexible wardrobe, suited to a life spent traipsing around the world on behalf of Mr Lavender's antique business. Patricia knew other clients were just as enchanted with Julia's impeccable taste and uncanny empathy with their lifestyles. She reasoned that in a shop of her own, Julia could realize her phenomenal potential.

Patricia was right. In fewer than five years, Julia's (the store) has gained an enviable reputation as a "must" on any serious fashion shopper's circuit. There's a graciousness here that has a lot to do with the winning ways of the proprietors. Both have an incredible rapport with their clients, making them feel relaxed and special. Tea, coffee and even lunch are routinely served, as Julia and her three assistants assemble outfits that enhance, rather than overpower, your personal style. No slaves to designer labels, they are gifted in mixing and matching pieces.

Still, Julia and Patricia do admit a special fondness for Italy's Giorgio Grati and Germany's Rena Lange. After trying on a handsome £885 black-and-white-checked suit by Lange—a long, lean jacket over a sarong-style skirt—we could understand why. Typically, Julia produced a black skirt with a straighter silhouette for £275 to change the look altogether—the three pieces could take you all over the world.

We also liked the look of the suits by another German house, Renzo, which sell in the £730 neighbourhood. Whatever tickles your fancy, rest assured its the best of any given designer's current work. Julia reviews all the collections and edits out the styles more suited to the fashion-show runway than to real life, favouring those with a classic, timeless cachet. She looks for a chic simplicity that allows her to work her coordinating magic without producing looks that are contrived. Consequently, the names of the contributing designers to any Julia-created ensemble fade into the background, even names like Ungaro, Scherrer or Vicky Tiel. Rather, you are vaguely aware that the £165 gabardine walking shorts, the £225 silk blouse and the £460 knit jacket bear different labels, but you *know* the sum of these particular parts is a sensational look.

Furthermore, you haven't been subjected to hours in the dressing rooms, wading through countless depressingly uncomplimentary pieces—Julia and her associates know your time is precious. They assess what colours and silhouettes are most flattering to you and present their suggestions accordingly, in judicious quantities. Julia maintains, "I'd rather a woman buy two wonderful outfits from me, wear them to death and look marvelous, than if she buys millions of bits and pieces and never quite gets it right." Bravo, Julia—the store, and the person! 🦋

Pallant

19A Motcomb Street
London SW1W 8LB

071-259-6046
(FAX) 071-398-8058

There's something very appropriate about the fact that this exceptional example of Greek revival architecture, called the Pantechnicon, now houses the collection of two of Britain's most original and accomplished designers, Jean and Martin Pallant. Built in 1830 as Sotheby's arts and furniture repository, its name means "all the arts." The Pantechnicon remains home to artworks in the form of the Pallants' extravagantly luxurious, very international and superbly sophisticated designs.

This husband and wife team has been around for years; their cosmopolitan collections are sold in some of the world's most exclusive stores. And the Pallants have maintained a private clientele that's made other couturiers green with envy. But this is Jean and Martin's only shop, opened in 1988.

Here, the staggering double height of the building frames three floors of selling space, ample room to display the entire range of their work. Seemingly more like an art gallery than a clothing store, the space is linked by a spectacular staircase framed by three oversized, natural oak Doric columns, which imitate the classical façade dominated by ten columns that soar 40 feet to resemble a Greek temple. Inside, the oak columns and the refined flamboyant designs are reflected everywhere by carefully aligned mirror panels, their glimmering surfaces rivalled only by the gleaming wood floors.

It's difficult to describe the Pallant look. There's no real hallmark that consistently proclaims the label, except perhaps the quality of the clothes' construction. This is fashion for the secure, for the woman who'd rather not be identified by the designer she's wearing, who doesn't want to enter a room in an outfit screaming Valentino, Chanel or Yves St Laurent. Dyan Cannon, Lee Remick, the Marchioness of Tavistock, Lady Brocket and Greta Saachi—beautiful, self-confident and stylish ladies one and all—shop at Pallant.

Jean and Martin are masters of coordination. Monochromatic groups are complemented by smashing prints—Pallant mix-and-match designs that lend a new definition to the word *flexibility*. Select pieces can be combined to create sports clothes to business attire to evening wear. And there's always a beautifully tailored coat or jacket to go over the lot, starting at £895 and £595 respectively.

We find Pallant a particularly good source for cocktail wear. The dressy silk suits are outstanding with their flattering fitted jackets, often adorned by a flirtatious peplum. And then there are their marvellous jackets with just enough beadwork to make them sparkle. We like them with evening trousers from the £350 and up neighbourhood.

For more formal affairs, we spotted an off-the-shoulder dress, its revealing but not daring neckline trimmed in exquisite handmade silk flowers for £1,450. Ballgowns, truly grand with lavish embroidery, run the gamut from £1,800 to £4,000. Despite the lofty-ish prices, there's no pretentious arrogance about the place. Indeed, Jean, a whimsical character if ever there was one, goes out of her way to make you feel at ease. Still, there's something about her that reminds us of the haughty Balenciaga, who used to say, "I don't mind whom I dress, as long as she's the right class." 🍎

Philip Somerville Ltd

11 Blenheim, New Bond Street   071-629-4442/4443
London W1 9LE

Of course, you can purchase Philip Somerville's fantastic chapeaux in major department stores like Harrods, Fortnum & Mason, Neiman-Marcus and Saks, but given the choice, we always head straight for the source—Philip's salon on Blenheim Street. At least we have since 1986, when he expanded his wholesale business to incorporate a boutique where his fans can revel in very personal attention. Here, Philip and his staff stand ready to offer sage advice on hats to complement any outfit, any occasion. And if nothing from his three collections—ready-to-wear, "model" and couture—quite suit, Philip can be counted on to design a confection guaranteed to make you stand out in any crowd. Just ask habitual entrance makers like Queen Elizabeth, her blond daughter-in-law the delicious Diana and blonder cousin-in-law the Valkyrie-like Princess Michael. You could also speak to the Countess of Bismarck, Lady Bidwell, Kiri Te Kanawa, as well as Mick Jagger's once and current brides, Bianca and Jerry.

Even if you don't think you're in the market for a new hat, a visit to this charming little salon is a must. It's such a pleasure to venture into the forest of hat trees—hours can be happily whiled away in front of one of the many mirrors trying on one stunning headpiece after another. From the ready-made collection you'll find all the basic styles and colours in vogue for any particular season. There are lots of wide-brimmed straw and silk numbers for summer, priced from £40 to £200. Or there are velvet and felt for fall, worked into cunning shapes and sold in the £70 to £200 neighbourhood.

The new "model" collection bridges the gap—in terms of design, manufacture and price—between ready-to-wear and couture. More highly styled than the ready-made, the "model" hats are machine blocked at Philip's Luton factory and hand-finished in his London workrooms. Prices start at £120 and top off at about £200.

They're quite lovely, but for only another £50 you can wander into couture territory, which is where the real design action is. At this level, all of Philip's considerable experience, talent and imagination are brought to bear—this is the stuff the dreams of Ascot are made of. Take the knock-out halo hat we fell in love with immediately. Reminiscent of the outrageous glamour of 1940s' and 1950s' films, the leather inside headband creates a turban-like effect, while the fur felt crown and brim in two heavenly shades of grey (carbin and silver) have a dramatic sweep that delivers a fly-away look. At £525, it represents the high side of the couture price range, which is generally defined as £250 to £600.

Not bad, when you consider each of these beauties is custom-made completely by hand, blocking and all. It takes Philip's craftspeople up to three days to make one. And the skill and time involved are quite apparent in the end result—not a single stitch is visible, and the fit is flawless. These hats are truly statements in style and femininity, like the picture-perfect "Alimony" (its name, not what you need to buy it). Trimmed with sprays of egret anchored by a jewelled clasp, its deep crown and large scallop-edged brim, sweeping down at the back to frame the face, are made of a boldly patterned lace. For £340, this hat makes you look and feel like a movie star.

For that matter, any of Philip's head-turning creations lends a star-like quality to your appearance.

F. Pinet

47–48 New Bond Street   071-629-2174
London W1Y 9HA

F. Pinet is a shoe boutique that opens its doors to women who don't flinch at plunking down £700 for a handmade pair of rhinestone-encrusted evening shoes (and perhaps a matching minaudière for a mere £595). However, it closes its doors—even to *that* rarefied clientele—when Arab princesses or the wife of the Sultan of Brunei stops by for a private appointment. Make no mistake, this is a *salon*, not simply a shop.

The point is first made by the large, show-stopping windows on New Bond and Maddox streets that are more suited for museum-quality exhibition than commercial display. It is driven home by the uniformed doorman who ushers you into the salon with polite efficiency. If you're still not convinced, the plushly elegant decor should do the trick. Magnificent crystal chandeliers illuminate the sumptuous scene reflected in the ornate mirrors. Grey velvet empire sofas and antique mahogany tables dot the plush grey carpet, complemented by the grey walls. An ever-so-chic blackamoor showcases a sexy, high-heeled slipper and adds a touch of glamorous caprice, as does the gilt cupid doubling as a lampstand and the Buddhas that grace the windows.

The discreet, very professional staff are loathe to name names with regard to their clientele, but it's clear they're accustomed to dealing with sophisticated, international regulars.

Led by the wry Aubrey Mass, the staff is multilingual and exceedingly familiar with the stock, 70 per cent of it is what we consider to be ladies' evening shoes, priced from £115 to £700. But Aubrey notes that many of his clients like to flaunt them during daylight hours as well!

Besides the jewelled collection (coloured-stone mosaic styles and rhinestone-covered creations are also available), Pinet specializes in gold and silver kid, as well as satin shoes. The latter lean toward bright jewel tones, often sport decorative accents on the toe or heel and cost between £200 and £300. Here too, you can find elegant designs for daywear, like a pair of black suede pumps edged with red ruched leather for £195. But for our money, Pinet shoes for ladies are synonymous with the most special of special occasions.

For men, Pinet features an exclusive line of shoes and belts, many fashioned in exotic (though unendangered and perfectly legal) skins like stingray and shark, as well as the more familiar crocodile and alligator. Particularly popular with Arab and African clients, they range in price from £295 to £395. Presumably, Pinet's classic calf lace-ups at £115 to £155 are more attractive to the English and Anglophile Americans.

Whatever your inclination, whether or not you'd dare don a pair of rhinestoned heels or sharkskin loafers, Pinet is worth a visit, just to marvel at the art that is called shoemaking. . .*and* the one called marketing. Cognizant of the economics of the current baby boom, Pinet has ventured into new territory—the most amazing and expensive (from £50 to £300) children's shoes we've ever seen. Now, how long do you figure it takes a 5-year-old to grow out of one of those £300 numbers? 🌰

Rayne

15 Old Bond Street   071-493-9077
London W1X 3DB

Rayne's roots as a costumer were recently recalled during the firm's centenary celebration, when the company produced a pair of black satin evening shoes made dramatically theatrical, courtesy of Garrard, by diamond-encrusted bows. With matching handbag, they *were* available to anyone who might want to flaunt the work of both the shoemaker and the jeweller to the Queen for £17,000. Of course, some aspiring Imelda Marcos may have snapped them up by now. Never mind, the enthusiastic new owner, Richard Kottler, can probably be persuaded to make another pair. He appreciates the fact that the firm entered the spotlight by making similarly glamorous shoes for Marlene Dietrich, Vivien Leigh, Katherine Hepburn and Ava Gardner.

You see, Henry and Mary Rayne started out in 1889 making costumes for the stars of the day, branching into the shoe business in 1918. By 1930, Rayne had received its first Royal Warrant, and today it continues to hold those of Queen Elizabeth and her mother. Under Richard's benevolent regime, backed by a major investment from the Ensign Trust, the high standards of design and quality that brought Rayne to the attention of the royal family are being scrupulously maintained. Rayne shoes and bags are still handmade in the firm's North London factory, and the shop's craftspeople are still prepared to fashion custom-made wooden lasts for couture clients. The first pair will set you back about £600 and take two fittings, but they'll fit perfectly. And once your last is carved, you'll spend £300 for each successive pair of shoes.

Ready-made shoes, like the classic Christophe pump designed for Gertrude Lawrence in the late 1920s, start at £95. Comfortable and eternally in vogue, the Christophe comes in every conceivable colour of suede, kid or patent, with or without a pert little bow. It's typical of what Rayne has traditionally done best—very proper, well-bred shoes. But the new ownership is instilling a new vitality in the styling to broaden Rayne's appeal. We were charmed by a black satin shoe enlivened by red and white diamante detail on the heel—absolutely brilliant at £210 or so.

Something else that's brilliant at Rayne is the unique Personalized Service which enables you to order Rayne's archetypal court shoe, or pump, in *any* fabric with a variety of trims and heel heights. Normally, it takes about four weeks for delivery, but special ten-day wonders can be constructed on request. It will cost you a surcharge, though. Otherwise, you're looking at £160, which is about what you'll pay for a handbag to match.

As part of the rejuvenation plan for Rayne, the circa 1920 flagship store has been streamlined. Simplicity itself, the shoes and bags are the principal decoration, beautifully lit in their glass-shelved wooden cases. A single, large, leather sofa serves as seating, its soft contours reflected on the highly polished wooden floors. Manager Richard Collinson holds sway here. He's the one to call if you can't squeeze in a visit to Old Bond Street. Richard will do for you what he does for Elizabeth Taylor, take a selection of Rayne goodies to your hotel. It's a service fit for a queen, of both the movie and constitutional variety.　　　　　🐛

Rigby & Peller

2 Hans Road	071-589-9293
London SW3 1RX	(FAX) 071-581-8915

Except when we watched Scarlett O'Hara tighten her corset in *Gone with the Wind*, we had not given much consideration to the figure-altering undergarments until we came across Rigby & Peller, corsetieres to Queen Elizabeth. Here, we discovered what is destined to become one of our greatest treasures, a romantic-looking waist cincher with old-fashioned laces that reduces our respective waists by some five inches each. It cost £300, but who cares? We've spent more, a lot more, on fad diets and spa regimens that were much less spectacularly effective. Moreover, the waist cincher is so beautifully made, it doubles as an eye-catching belt.

And it's not the only Rigby & Peller piece that defies the "under" part of underwear. The £275 satin, strapless bras which caress and contour the torso to just below the waist play peek-a-boo under many a stylish lady's cocktail suit. Some more daring types are having them beaded or jewelled and are wearing them sans jacket with skirts or leggings, à la Madonna.

June and Harold Kenton, managing director and chairman here since 1982, applaud all such creative uses of lingerie. They've long been fascinated by its mystique and have spent the past 30 years marketing some of the world's best. Since purchasing Rigby & Peller, which had been around for more than half a century, they've been spreading the gospel to an ever younger clientele who are rediscovering the figure-flattering advantages of well-made lingerie. Indeed, Rigby & Peller does a bang-up business in custom-made items, such as merry widows for £595, bras at £150 and those clever little waist cinchers. Of course, it takes two to four weeks to make them, but only one fitting is usually required and the Kentons are very resourceful when it comes to adjusting production to fit visitors' schedules.

Should your figure not require *that* much help, ready-to-wear unmentionables are available, too. You still benefit from an expert fitter, who may inform you that you've been wearing the wrong size bra all these years. Now wouldn't that explain a thing or two? At any rate, your fitter will set you straight and show you all the latest styles from Barbara of Paris, La Perla, Van Del *and* Rigby & Peller. Prices range from about £15 to £50, and don't shy away from developing a taste for the shop's own label. It is now available throughout Britain, and you can feed your Rigby & Peller habit in the U.S. at Saks, I. Magnin, Bloomingdale's and Neiman Marcus. The Kentons' daughter Jill watches over their interests in the States. She's on regular call as a consultant to Rigby & Peller clients at Saks and Bloomies in New York. And she makes personal appearances with the line at other stores throughout the country.

As for less structured garments, there's a frivolous selection of sleep and lounge wear. True, there are some practical, simple cotton nightgowns for £85, but mostly they sell the stuff that sleepless but blissful nights are made of—namely, the silky, shimmering best of Dior, along with seductive styles by two terrific British designers, Sally Poppy and Julia Grahme.

We made one more discovery, courtesy of the Kentons and Rigby & Peller—it is possible to shop for a bathing suit without becoming suicidally depressed. Thanks to the appraising eye of their fitters and the wizardry of their seamstresses, there's no more squeezing size ten hips into a suit that is perfect for your size eight bust. Here, you can find a stylish suit that looks as if it were made for you...matter of fact, it may just have been.   ❦

Ungaro

22 Sloane Street	071-235-1357
London SW1 X9NE	(FAX) 071-235-1781

Add Ungaro to the growing list of top-drawer merchants that have forsaken the once sacrosanct territory of Bond Street in favour of Sloane Street. Actually, for a while Ungaro wavered on the fence with boutiques on both. But according to Mona Misan, the shop's clientele—the younger, more vivacious Brits and their equally self-assured international sisters—are now so used to shopping on Sloane Street that the Bond Street location became superfluous. So these days, when Jackie and Joan Collins, Cleo Laine, Koo Stark (now a photographer—talk about turn around being fair play!), Felicity Kendell and Jane Asher have a yen for Emanuel Ungaro's sexy, feminine clothes, they head straight for this spacious shop with its big bold and inviting windows.

They come for clothes bursting with colour. Ungaro is the master of sophisticated floral prints, sensuous shirring, and dramatic draping. No doubt about it, you have to have presence to wear Ungaro designs well. Money helps, too, because if you're a fan it's tough to resist the way this designer, who clearly loves women, makes you look and feel. Mona has one *very* regular client who drops £3,000 to £4,000 during every visit.

It's easy to understand how, when you consider the tempting quotient of a provocative £1,780 bronze-and-black brocade evening suit, its very fitted jacket detailed by exquisite mother-of-pearl buttons and exaggerated tails in the front. Dynamite, as was an iridescent green silk dinner suit with cheeky little ruffles at the hip for £1,590. It looks extravagantly fragile, but Mona claims otherwise. She points out that all the clothes are made of such high-quality fabrics that they're virtually indestructible. And we can attest to the fact that Ungaro's clothes pack beautifully, barely wrinkling—the difference between serious silk and its flimsy, inexpensive distant cousins.

Here, as elsewhere throughout his fashion empire, Ungaro's bold, figure-flattering dresses, starting at about £700, are very popular. They don't allow anyone to miss your entrance, particularly when accessorized by his equally theatrical jewelry, from about £150. You'll also find belts and handbags here in the £200 to £400 neighbourhood, all of which seem to have a corresponding outfit or two, since Mona not only manages the shop but also buys for it. She edits the current collection to suit her clients' tastes.

Which is not to say that they ever suffer from any lapse of judgment on her part. Ungaro led the European pack in conducting regular trunk shows in London about four years ago. Every collection in its glorious entirety is presented for a limited time for special clients. Of course, we're of the opinion that all Ungaro clients are special by definition. They almost have to be!   ❦

Valentino Boutique

160 New Bond Street	071-493-2698
London SW1	(FAX) 071-409-3012

We've always wondered where Valentino, the dean of Italian designers, came up with that singularly brilliant red that always figures prominently in his collections. Well, now we know, courtesy of Genevieve Tinto, the manager of the larger of the two London Valentino Boutiques (the other is on Sloane Street). It seems that when he was 17, studying French couture, he was invited to Barcelona where he attended a gala production of *Carmen*. "I saw flaming red—flaming all over the place, onstage and in the audience's elegant evening gowns. It was an overwhelming cascade of red, and I'll never forget it." And that dazzling display of colour became the inspiration for the red with which he is so identified, as are the many famous women who favour his clothes. They are garments meant to stand out in crowds that might include the likes of Marie Helene de Rothschild, Princess Yasman Aga Khan, Jane Fonda, Jessica Lange or Queen Sophia of Spain. Not a shrinking violet among them.

Predictably, neither is Genevieve. She's full of wit and charm. Having been with Valentino for three years, she is fully versed in the designer's enduring style. She knows his customer and knows how to dress her to accommodate her busy international lifestyle. Whether you're already a member of the Valentino vanguard or a new recruit, visit Genevieve and her New Bond Street domain where you'll find most of what represents Valentino's fashion empire—with two conspicuous exceptions at opposite ends of the economic spectrum. Here, you will find neither the cou ture nor the Oliver line. The former, priced from £3,000 to £36,000 is consigned to Rome in the care of Maria Pia (call her at 39-667-7391). The latter is Valentino's youngest and most accessible—i.e., affordable—line. It occupies a small shop at 55 South Molton Street, where you can find dresses starting at £120 and blouses at £60. Coordinating trousers and sweaters are in the £70 to £90 category.

Otherwise, the full-breadth of Valentino Garavani's prolific creativity is on view. Less expensive examples of that creativity, which fashions sensuous yet extremely modern clothes, are found in the Miss Valentino line. There's nothing lacking in the styling or the production of this collection, it's simply that less costly fabrics are used in its construction. Dresses can be had for as little as £200, suits for £250. Add a Valentino Boutique scarf, and you're bound to be a smash.

Valentino Boutique. Well, now we're talking pricy, but worth it—£600 to £850 for a dress, suits from £715 up to £1,200 for a very detailed number, and cocktail dresses that don't go for less than £1,000. If you want to ease into this collection, why not pick up one of the sensational belts for £70 or an enormous silk chiffon scarf for £150?

As Valentino Boutique veterans, we didn't bat an eye at the £3,400 pricetag on a show-stopper of an evening jacket. Flawlessly fitted, it was white with a garden of fuchsia flowers and green leaves, each one exquisitely hand-embroidered in silk, sequins and beads. A true work of art, just like the snazzy cocktail dress in black silk chiffon with a draped, sarong-like skirt. The V-necked bodice was studded with a beaded purple animal print, on which red-beaded flowers were superimposed at the shoulders. It may sound outrageous, but master colourist that he is, Valentino makes it work and worth every penny, at £4,000.

Happily, the environment that showcases all this finery is on the subdued side, with just a touch of drama here and there—black mouldings and doors stand out against the creamy yellow walls, geometrical shading distinguishes hardwood floors, marbellization brings a soaring column or two into focus, and everywhere the lighting shows off Valentino's beloved colours to their best advantage. In the store, just as in the clothes, it's the perfection of technical detail that makes all the difference. 🍃

Valerie Louthan (at Lord's)

66–70 Burlington Arcade   071-493-5808/734-1345
London W1V 9AF

Here's one for the record books—we don't usually do this. Actually, we've never done it before in our fledgling series of guides to the good life. We've never singled out a boutique within a store and treated it as a separate entity, never until we got around to considering Valerie Louthan and her phenomenal way with cashmere.

The feisty Irish redhead has been designing cashmere fashions under her own label since 1972. *Fashions* is the key word here—after years as a designer or consultant for such august names in knits as Ballantyne, Braemar, The Dawson Group and Pringle, Valerie was bored with the applications—sweaters and scarves—to which cashmere, that most luxurious yet practical of yarns, was consigned. She was convinced there was a market for cashmere clothes in simple, soft, yet fashionable shapes. She was right.

Since its debut, her label has gained an international reputation, and her chic treatments in colourful cashmere have been greatly responsible for its growing popularity as ready-to-wear—and for other designers, like Hanae Mori and Oscar de la Renta, jumping on the cashmere knit bandwagon. The boutique at Lord's, the prestigious cashmere specialists, serves as her retail flagship.

All that said, the real reason that we are focusing on this little outlet at the expense of its parent store (worthy as it may be) is that back in the mid-1970s we each bought one of Valerie's Benita capes. Heralded as the "first" cashmere cape, it's the garment that put her on the fashion map and remains one of her most popular styles. Ours have done yeoman's duty, keeping us in stylish warmth all over the world—cashmere never wrinkles, even when bundled into little, very packable balls. It travels anywhere and everywhere. And did you know that cashmere is a natural insulator—protecting you, as it does those ornery goats, from both cold *and* heat?

At any rate, we hate to tell you what we paid for our capes. Suffice it to say it was considerably less than the current £580 pricetag. But remember, we're talking about a kilo of cashmere here, and given the current supply-and-demand situation, you can count on that price escalating. You can also count on the cape being available in a dozen colours, not to mention a striking stripe or two. It's a tough call, one some avoid alto-gether by buying at least one of each—Gloria Vanderbilt happily admits to owning no fewer than 15 Benita capes.

Since our Benitas are destined for lifetime wear (cashmere is also ex-traordinarily durable, as are Valerie's designs), we were drawn to the new, very dramatic Nina cape. Trimmed with a three-and-a-half to four inch heavy ribbed ruffle, it approximates a full-length coat when properly wrapped and costs £725. Combine the Nina with another Valerie first, cashmere leggings, and you've got a smashing outfit for most seasons. The leggings sell for about £265.

Cashmere for evening? Absolutely. Take the little black dress, with the deep V-back. Sensuality personified, it has wardrobe staple written all over it for less than £500. Then there are all of Valerie's sensational combos—silk and cashmere, velvet and cashmere. One off-the-shoulder dress trimmed in velvet was a particular knockout. Cover it with a giant cashmere cape edged in a taffeta ruffle—you can't be missed for £675.

As for sweaters, of course, Valerie fashions them. But they're far from the ordinary crew-necked garden variety. Hers are playfully colourful and feature fanciful details, like zippers or bold military buttons. We're always smitten with them, as are other Valerie Louthan aficionados, like Eliza-beth Taylor and Candice Bergen. They, at least, have the wherewithal to indulge their habit to their hearts' content, while we are forced to make agonizing decisions, regretfully leaving some Louthan "must haves" behind—until the next time.   ❦

Victor Edelstein

3 Stanhope Mews West   071-244-7481
London SW7 5RB

A very talented fashion editor of a major U.S. West Coast newspaper, who in the interest of her career shall remain nameless, once told us she had interviewed just about every top designer in the business and that not one of them was very nice. She noted two exceptions to that rather dismal evaluation—Hanae Mori, the ground-breaking Japanese coutu-rier, and Victor Edelstein, who has found fame (and is working on for-tune) as one of Princess Diana's favourites.

We couldn't agree more, on both counts. And in addition to being gen-uinely warm people with a wickedly funny sense of humour, Madame (never call her Hanae) Mori and Victor share a talent for creating exceptionally beautiful clothes for clients who appreciate their timeless subtlety. They also both believe in a minimalist approach to the decor of their showrooms.

In Victor's case, a museum-quality green Beidemeyer sofa, purloined from his flat, keeps the white-walled room from being downright barren. It and a bank of mirrors are the only decorations. But anything more would be ludicrous once the collection is brought in. The glorious colours and rich fabrics bring the room to very vibrant life.

Victor's are clothes fit for a (future) queen and not an inconsiderable number of princesses—the Princess of Hanover, Princess Rupert von Lowenstein and Princess Yasmin Aga Khan among them. In the U.S., Victoria Newhouse, wife of media mogul Si; Tina Brown, one of Si's "other women" as editor of his hugely successful *Vanity Fair; Vogue* editor Anna Wintour, another member of the Newhouse family; Laura Tisch, Jean Vanderbilt, Basia Johnson and Cece Kieselstein-Cord, muse to jewelry-designer husband Barry—all are also fans. Such public ladies love the way Victor's dresses work—both standing up and sitting down. There are never any embarrassing gaps or unsightly folds, which is why you'll never see a Victor Edelstein with a cross-over front. Victor states categorically that "they never work."

He designs clothes that flatter. But once they're on, you can forget about them, secure in the knowledge that you look sensational and feel great. He doesn't believe a dress should enter a room before the lady wearing it. Rather, a Victor Edelstein ensures that *you* make an unforgettable impression, not the dress. So his custom-made—the British version of Parisian haute couture—creations are serviceable for years without wearing out their welcome.

Actually, Victor is one of the very few successful designers anywhere that relies solely on couture for his livelihood. But having dabbled in ready-to-wear and failed due to the production and delivery problems that go with the territory, Victor prefers the control he has over an on-site staff of pattern-makers, cutters and seamstresses who make one made-to-order garment at a time. And while fashion "experts" and other designers routinely sound couture's death knell for being too expensive and too impractical, Victor's business couldn't be better.

We suspect a good measure of his success is due to this most proper of gentlemen's engaging personality. He and his affable sidekick, Sara Studd, make the tedious process of measurements and fittings fun. They form warm, though strictly professional, relationships with their clients. And their knack for putting you at instant ease as you ponder spending at least £3,000 on an alluring black-lace embroidered cocktail dress is all the more astounding when you consider these are two of the tallest people you've ever encountered. Their complementary blend of elegance and earthiness make parting with copious sums of money painless.

Actually, as at Hartnell, haute couture is considerably less "haute" in price here than it is in Paris. What's more, you're not made to feel like a stranger in a strange land the first time you call for an appointment. You can usually get one with a day's notice. Count on about an hour to make your selections and have your measurements taken. The fitting—with Victor it usually only takes one to ensure comfortable perfection—comes about three weeks later. Add another three weeks or so for delivery.

In deference to his growing American clientele, Victor makes four annual treks to New York—twice to show the seasonal collections and twice to fit the garments ordered. But if spontaneity is the name of your game, you might be able to snag a Victor Edelstein at a local Bloomingdale's or Barneys. Both stores stock a few pieces from each of his collections. And if you're a U.S.-based bride, check out his dreamy wedding gowns at Manhattan's most (read *only*) elegant bridal salon, Vera Wang's on Madison Avenue in the Carlyle.   ❦

Zandra Rhodes

14a Grafton Street   071-499-6695
London W1X 3LA

Scheherazade never had it so good—she may have had a tented chambre as sumptuous as Zandra Rhodes' shop, but we're sure it wasn't filled with the fantasy creations that are the eccentric designer's stock in trade. Only Zandra of the green, blue, purple and/or orange hair would have such an outlandish boutique—its bronze Arabian Nights decor hovering dangerously close to garish—right around the corner from staid Old Bond Street. Stepping foot onto the ultra-plush peach carpeting is akin to passing through the twilight zone into a Ted Turner colourized version of a swashbuckling classic—you expect Douglas Fairbanks to leap out at you from one of the heavily curtained *and* fringed dressing rooms.

Once you've stopped cursing Ted for mucking up yet another one, you can sink into the lush, silk-pillowed circular couch that dominates the centre of the room and feast your eyes on Zandra's signature "Works of

Art" collection—masterpiece evening creations of the finest fabrics embellished with her inimitable hand-screened prints, which in turn are overlaid with exquisite jewelled beading and sequinned embroideries. Sound a bit much? They wouldn't be Zandra's if they weren't. Certainly, they're not for everyone. You need a certain hauteur to carry them off. Hence, it's the likes of Princess Anne, Evangeline Bruce, Diana Ross, Lauren Bacall, the Duchess of Kent, Jackie Onassis and her sister Lee Ross (better known as Radziwill) who act as walking, talking galleries for Zandra's flamboyant artworks. (Less active showcases display her clothes, too, such as the Victoria and Albert Museum, the Smithsonian Institution, and the Metropolitan Museum of Art.) In case you were wondering, it's no coincidence that all of these ladies are women of substance—this couture collection is priced from £2,000 to £5,000.

The first to introduce hand-cut ragged hems, the lettuce edging on jerseys, and the use of seams on the outside of a garment as detail, Zandra is universally recognized as Britain's most avant garde designer. But there's a romantic edge to her designs, a softness not generally associated with the fashion vanguard—this is, after all, the woman credited with reviving the crinoline. Consequently, she's a favourite with brides. Many choose a style from the "Works of Art" and have it made in white. Others have a vision, which they want interpreted by Zandra. No problem, after an initial consultation with Dee-Dee Edwards. Once she understands what the betrothed has in mind and has explained that it'll cost at least £4,000 to £6,000, she'll set up an appointment with Zandra herself. Once involved, she's been known to put her creative stamp on a lot more than the wedding gown. She'll whip up a headpiece for £500 to £600 and arrange for shoes to be embroidered to match the dress for £300 to £400. If encouraged, she'll even design the invitations and concoct romantically whimsical cushions for the ringbearers.

You're neither a bride nor in the market for a £2,500 silk chiffon cocktail dress? Never fear. There are two ready-to-wear collections available here, marketed under the Zandra and Zandra Rhodes II labels—after-six clothes and wearable daywear, respectively. You still get her imaginatively daring combinations of fabrics and patterns, as well as a dose of the hallmark embroidered wiggles and squiggles, but you pay a lot less for them—about £300 to £1,000. We snapped up a sinuously cut jersey dress, made bold by the artful combination of colourful striped and solid fabrics for £375.

Accessories are also important here. Glorious, 115cm square crepe-de-chine scarves sell for £120. Most are descriptively named—the Lazy Daisey, Shell and Venetian Flower Vase are three of our favourites. We secure these and many other designer scarves with one of Zandra's fantastic £135 satin flower brooches, each petal intricately hand-beaded. And we find it virtually impossible to walk out without picking up one of the fanciful hair bows, which impart just a smidgen of Zandra's artistic individuality for only £15. They are one Zandra Rhodes' creation that anyone can wear with impunity—assuming there's enough hair to warrant, not to mention anchor, them.   🍋

FURS

Birger Christensen

169 Sloane Street	071-235-5618
London W1Y 9PB	(FAX) 071-493-4263

Almost 40 years ago, Finn Birger Christensen was working in New York's fur district when he was summoned home to Copenhagen to take over the firm his grandfather had founded in 1869. Under his direction, the company branched out beyond its Danish base to make itself known throughout the world as a purveyor of high-quality, high-style furs. Birger Christensen coats are sold at major outlets in North America and Japan, as well as in the company's own boutiques in London and Paris. Moreover, the firm holds the licences of some of the world's most prominent designers, translating the distinctive styles of Donna Karen, Claude Montana, Hanae Mori, Perry Ellis and Bob Mackie into fur.

As we zero in on the 21st century, the fourth generation of Christensens, Finn Birger's son Jens, stands poised to carry on the family business. In charge of the London operation, Jens takes his father's hands-on approach to the business, often acting as the company's buyer at the great international fur auctions. Whether he's attending a sale in Copenhagen, Leningrad, London, New York or Toronto, Jens exercises his considerable expertise to select only the finest pelts—an expertise he learned from Finn Birger who defines it as 50 per cent experience, 25 per cent talent and 25 per cent sixth sense. We figure that in Jens' case at least, there's a percentage of charm in that formula as well. He's got loads of it and what better way to really get the inside track on what's what, or to sell a coat for that matter?

Tall, slender and predictably fair, with the air of the Scandinavian nobility his family has served so well for so long, Jens has a quiet charisma that has made Birger Christensen a success in London since opening in 1982. This, despite a climate of anti-fur activity in Europe, which has been particularly intense in Britain where the populace has a long heritage of being a bit of a soft touch when it comes to animals.

Jens explains Birger Christensen's ongoing prosperity in an industry that has suffered a 50 per cent decrease in sales as having a lot to do with the firm's new emphasis on shearlings and fur-lined raincoats. You see, for some reason, a lot of people don't classify shearling with fur (though we've yet to see a sheep carry on without its skin). Then, there's the school of thought that dictates if you've got it *don't* flaunt it! Fearless flaunters of fur, we prefer Jens' other justification of his business' success—high-fashion styling. According to Jens, the most interesting designs in full-fledged furs, those with lots of detail, are selling well, and Birger Christensen is noted for its fashionable renditions—"clothes with hair on," as Finn Birger says. Details like the scalloped edges on a black mink, poncho-like three-quarter coat make Birger Christensen creations so special. This particular beauty is further enhanced by the horizontal (as opposed to vertical) seaming of the pelts and sells for £6,700. We also liked a rich brown mink with an extraordinary back treatment—a centred column of vertical stripes set off by pelts angled toward the sleeves and shoulders—which carries a £7,250 pricetag. Then there was the Persian lamb jacket trimmed with ruched black satin collar and cuffs for £1,516.

Alongside such serious furs, you'll find a showcase of shearlings (£600 to £1,500), many in exciting colours, and accessories like fur-trimmed leather gloves in the £95 to £160 range and cashmere shawls decorated with mink pom-poms or tails. The wool is almost as soft as the fur, and Jens says they are very popular sellers at £350 to £1,750.

Just in case you don't see anything that suits, talk to Jens or manager John Woolf about having a little something whipped up just for you. There's a designer and fitter on the premises, ready to do your bidding. Whether your fur fantasy is produced in their workrooms or in Copenhagen, it will be executed with infinite care by expert craftspeople who hand sew the collars, cuffs, buttons, decorations and lining. Consequently, you're looking at a six- to eight-week period from start to finish—unless, of course, Jens has to go searching for special pelts to make your dream come true.   🦢

Lisbeth Buchler

14 Park Road   071-423-4033
London NW1 4SH

After all the giltz and glitter of the retail palaces of Mayfair and Knightsbridge, Lisbeth Buchler's small, unpretentious shop comes as a welcome relief. It also serves as proof that there is no law stating London's provisioners of luxury goods must be confined to Bond Street, Regent Street and Sloane Street. The Austrian-born furrier attracts a loyal clientele to her little piece of Regents Park—the Duchess of Gloucester, the Countess Di Monteluce and the late, great Ava Gardner among them.

Mild-mannered and softspoken, Lisbeth is passionate about one thing—fur. It has been a lifelong affair encouraged by her dress-designer mother, who sent her to school to learn how to make patterns for fur garments, and consumated with her marriage to first husband, furrier Philip Buchler. His business flourished on South Molton Street from 1944 until his death in 1965. By 1968, Lisbeth had a new husband, another furrier by the name of Fred Morgan; a new partner in yet another furrier, William Duke by name; and a new business.

Lisbeth and William do the designing, while Fred does the cutting and oversees the production in the workrooms behind the shop. Every piece is made entirely on the premises, benefitting from the fine handfinishing of skilled craftspeople. Lisbeth Buchler furs are so well made that many of London's skin merchants commission her to construct coats for their wives. In fact, Lisbeth ruefully claims, "Our coats last forever—I wish they didn't last quite so long."

Of course, their longevity has a lot to do with their appeal, as does their creative styling that is fashionable without being trendy. We, like many ladies around London town, are enamoured of her silk fur-lined raincoats. Made to measure, the silk shells serve as chic raincoats without their removable linings, and as superb storm coats with them. So pretty, yet so practical. We craved the nutria-lined number with mink collar and cuffs that Lisbeth was making for one of her clients for £2,500.

Another speciality here are flowing cashmere capes, hand-edged on both sides with fur. We were tempted by one in black, trimmed with luxuriant black fox at £950. But it paled in comparison to the terrific three-quarter length walking coat made of female silver-cross mink that had been dyed a devastating dark blue, highlighted by a hint of grey. Now, you should know we're not normally fans of coloured furs, but this one was smashing and well priced at £4,500. Actually, Lisbeth may have succeeded in converting us on the matter—we were also pretty taken with a £3,000 Swakara broadtail in a midnight blue, trimmed with fox.

Whether you opt for colourful or conventional fur, be sure to order a hat to match. But while you're waiting, keep your ears toasty warm with one of Lisbeth's sweet hand-knitted chapeaux boxed with mink. She's always got some in stock, and at £100 to £150 they have great gift potential. ❦

Philip Hockley

20 Conduit Street   071-493-6362
London W1R 9TD   (FAX) 071-489-1607

Hockley's has been making fabulous furs, suedes and shearlings since 1910, when Morris Hockberg inaugurated the family business in Kiev. These days, the third generation, represented by 42-year-old Michael, runs the show, but the second generation is still very much in evidence in the guise of his mama and 67-year-old papa—Philip. She oversees the front of his long narrow Mayfair shop, while he runs the factory (in between his thrice-weekly golf games) with an eagle eye for detail.

While the family's been in the business these many years, it's only been in retailing for the past four years. And we're so glad the business made the transition from strictly wholesale, because Philip Hockley is home to Zandra Rhodes' collection of furs and the top of the market Marni line, as well as its own label. Zandra's designs are executed by the Hockleys and are just as flamboyant as you might imagine, at prices ranging from £8,000 to £12,000. Even more extravagantly styled (think Fendi), the Marni collection concentrates on sable, wild mink and chinchilla. Still, some lesser furs are worked into the line, like nutria which trims a fabulous two-tiered, cape-like, cashmere coat that looked like something straight out of *Dr Zhivago*, for only £3,000. At the other end of the spectrum is the full shawl, complete with collar and deep outside pockets made from Russian sable at £36,000. Believe it or not, that's about 30 per cent less than it would be through Marni's exclusive distributors in the U.S.—Bergdorf's and Neiman's.

As for Philip Hockley's own furs, they're superb renditions of Halina Swirski's high-fashion designs. The dramatic £23,000 full-length "wild-type" (in these touchy times no one dares to admit that the little varmints are actually trapped in their natural habitat) with the 50-inch swing is one example, while the short, soft suede swing coat in chocolate or gold, trimmed with contrasting fur, for £2,500 is another. The trim in this instance is considerably more successful (not to mention appropriate) than that Philip Hockley attached to the Viscountess of Althrop's notorious wedding gown. But, hey, that's not the designer's fault. It was her idea and she is a valued client, as are Diana Ross, Barbra Streisand and Cybil Shepard. The firm would do anything in fur (or suede or sheepskin) for any of them, just as it will custom-design the fur of your fantasies.

Despite the tony clientele and prices, there's nothing intimidating about this shop. Indeed, the warm family atmosphere makes it the ideal spot for the selection of *the* first fur, be it a fox-trimmed cashmere cape for £1,200 or a 7/8ths length golden sable coat for ten times as much. Either way, you'll likely return for your second, your third, your fourth... 🐛

FOR MEN & WOMEN (& CHILDREN)

Adolfo Dominguez

57 South Molton Street   071-629-2571
London W1Y 1HH

Like many a London clothier, Adolfo Dominguez claims royal patronage, but his royals, while thanks to Queen Victoria are undoubtedly related to *the* royals, are of the Spanish variety. This makes sense, since this 43-year-old designer hails from Orense in the northwest of Spain, and 15 boutiques throughout that country claim his name. And what a name it is, which, when you hear him roll it softly and sensuously off the tongue, will immediately make you realize he has little in common with his better-known Latin namesake, though certainly Adolfo Dominguez's clothes take no back seat in the way they fit the body, be it male or female. Adolfo is of the rare breed of designers who's equally comfortable with and equally adept at dressing men and women.

His remarkably uncluttered, even stark shop stands in sharp contrast to the fluid lines of his clothes, which, of course, is the whole point. Simple functional decor with lots of light and glass is the trademark of all Adolfo's stores. In London, the street level shows off an artfully but uncontrived display of highlights of Adolfo's current collection. A sleek black stairway leads to the lower level and the majority of the stock. On both levels, opera music plays in the background and the unobtrusively attentive staff, led by the charmingly Continental Juan, await your bidding.

Adolfo's beautifully cut, up-to-date but not too trendy suits in earthy tones for both sexes are easy wearing and adaptable. For women, they tend to fall into the £400 to £500 range. Men's start at £400. But we're particularly partial to his coats, like the long, belted and boxy number we saw in a yummy wool and cashmere blend for £500. Its stunning stand-up lapels replace the need for a muffler, and the shoulderpadless, baggy sleeves leave plenty of room underneath for layering. It's available in grey, blue and green.

Adolfo's no slouch when it comes to accessories either. He covers all bases—shoes for men and women in the £100 to £200 neighbourhood, to uniquely patterned silk ties from £37, to jewelry. We're especially enamoured of the latter, which, like the clothes, is made in Spain and is very modern, yet has an ageless quality. A three-bar square-cut ring fashioned in platinum, gold and silver accented with diamonds was, as they say, to die for. In addition to precious metals and gems, the collection makes splendid use of such media as copper and frosted acrylic.

Anthea Moore Ede

26 Victoria Grove
London W8 5RW

071-584-8826
(FAX) 071-584-2717

Many a wonderful product proudly bears a "Made in America" label; however, children's clothing is not one of them. Sure, kids' clothes are made in the U.S., but they're usually very pedestrian and too trendy. Traditionally, to enter your child in the best-dressed sweepstakes means to look to European manufacturers. And there's no better source for the foremost of those than Anthea Moore Ede's charming shop.

The enchantment starts with the shop's window, which is always imaginatively decorated with clothes artistically displayed on hangers or in
boxes or playfully modelled by teddy bears. And the window treatment
literally beckons you inside; you can see through the display into the
cheery green and white high-ceilinged shop with all its tiny treasures.
Here, you'll find most everything you need to clothe a picture-perfect
child from infancy through about ten years of age, assuming that you're
aiming for a very traditional, bordering on formal, look. You know,
velvet-collared coats, dresses with lots of smocking and/or lace, short
pants with knee-socks for boys and Mary Janes and anklets for girls.

Of course, the wardrobe doesn't start out so elaborately. Anthea is of
the very sensible (not to mention practical) opinion that infants of both
sexes should live in long daygowns and nighties for the first three
months. Hers, made of a soft Swiss wool and cotton blend, are embellished with smocking or embroidery and sell for £42 to £50. For additional warmth pick up one of the adorable embroidered cardigan
sweaters or wrap your baby up in one of the satin-edged sleeping blankets made exclusively for Anthea. Both run about £25.

The real fashion fun comes during the toddler stage, when chubby
little-boy legs look particularly engaging peeking out from cotton viyella
shorts with coordinating shirts. Another Anthea Moore Ede exclusive,
they have an ingenious set of fasteners that doesn't allow gapping and sell
for £55 to £65. As for those little dears made of sugar and spice, there's a
delightful selection of dresses, each more captivating than the last. We're
told by manager Sarah Hudson that "the Frusini line is especially good
because the smocking goes beyond the yoke to embrace the shoulder."
The dresses are priced in the £135 neighbourhood.

For 8- to 10-year-olds creeping into preadolescence, there are trousers, shirts, sweaters and blazers for the boys and a line of Anthea Moore
Ede dresses for the girls. The latter fall into the £130 to £198 category—
higher, if you have something specific in mind, such as one to complement your own favourite frock. Special orders are taken with the understanding that you can wait for six weeks or so. Not to worry. The staff
take excellent measurements and are very clever at calculating how
much your little darling is likely to grow by the time the dress is finished.

Admittedly, these sound like adult-size prices. But there's real value
here. These dresses, along with every item Anthea stocks, are beautifully constructed. They are made to last, and they do, giving new glamour to hand-me-downs. Alternatively, you can look at these garments as

an investment from another perspective—resale value. There's a growing market for high-quality, previously owned children's wear, something Anthea knows a lot about. Selling used clothes and toys was how she got into the business in the first place!   🍒

Browns

18, 23–27, 38–39 South Molton Street	071-491-7833
London W1Y 1DA	(FAX) 071-408-1281

In the process of taking over South Molton, Browns has become an institution in shopping for the smartly dressed man or woman. Its appeal rests in the fact you won't have to sift through crowded racks of clothes, because the Browns staff ruthlessly edit down every designer collection to the most fabulous pieces.

Only the best selections and most perfectly coordinated collections make it to Browns. The staff know their customer doesn't follow fads but wants to be beautifully dressed and groomed. No fashion victims emerge from their doors—only perfection in style and coordination.

The guiding force behind this successful operation is the stunning Joan Burnstein. Jean Muir once described Joan as "a courageous retailer with a sense of discernment and good nose for fashion." We couldn't agree more.

With her short salt-and-pepper hair, flawless English skin, and that refined voice and ever present smile, Joan is certainly a major reason men and women of style shop at Browns.

The store was purchased from Sir William Piggot-Brown by the Bursteins in 1970. You'd never know it was the same store, as the ground-floor shop has expanded into a row of five, plus the site across the street and the Genny Boutique at number 18, with another store on Sloane Street. Browns has also expanded to include Comme des Garçons and Gianfranco Ferre, both on Brook Street.

Joan and her buying team travel twice a year to Paris, Milan, Germany, New York and Tokyo, searching for the best from established designers and innovations from new designers.

Hanging next to a Sonija Rykiel wool jersey trouser suit or a Donna Karan skirt, you're likely to see the creations of new talent like Azzedine Alaia, Romeo Gigli or Jill Sander.

In fact, many of Joan's clients call her from places like Kenya, Beverly Hills, New York and Texas to ask her what's new. She then sends them descriptions of items she knows they will love. Sometimes there are videos of the lines, and clients get those in the mail from Browns, too. It's all part of the intensive service Joan and her team provide.

Besides Joan, you'll love working with senior executive buyer Francoise Tessier, who's been with the shop for 20 years. She's always on the floor ready to help you, as are the other sales assistants. They are such a fun, interesting group of women, you can talk about the hottest plays and ballets, as well as the clothing. And if you're hungry, they will gladly fix you coffee and a sandwich from the shop's kitchen.

Browns has it's own label for men and women, and it has sensational sweaters for only £75.

One of our favourite rooms is Labels for Less, where end-of-season designer merchandise is sold for 70–80 per cent off the original prices. We saw a wonderful Jean Muir dress that was a terrific bargain.

It is clear to us that Browns' sale merchandise is better than most stores' regular merchandise. And if you need alterations, that's no problem. They will do it on the spot if you're in a hurry, or have it ready in just a few days.

In the men's department, any one of the abundance of sales assistants has the sense of style to routinely help clients like Jack Nicholson, David Putnam and Maurice and Charles Saatchi. The department has everything from socks at £10 to ties at £40 to coats and suits from £450 and up.

If you're looking for just the right shoes, handbags and jewelry to go with the latest Donna Karan, Moschino or Christian Lacroix ensemble, plan on shopping at Browns. You'll have a great time with Joan and her staff, and you won't leave empty handed. But should you be pressed for time, call Stuart Hamon on his private line 071-495-0288 and tell him about your fashion requirements. If need be, he'll pull a whole outfit (or two or three) together—from shoes to hat and everything in between—and deliver it to your hotel or home.   ❧

Bruno Magli

49 New Bond Street   071-491-8562
London W1Y 9HA

Bruno Magli's internationally renowned shoes made in Bologna first notched a London toe-hold in the late 1960s in a shop at 95 New Bond Street. They've got a much firmer foot-hold now with two spacious and elegant stores—the other is (naturally!) on Sloane Street—that reflect the classic beauty of Magli creations. We are slightly more partial to the New Bond Street location, with its pale cream walls and delicately grey marble tables topped with delicious displays of shoes. Maybe it has something to do with the inviting and uncommonly comfortable blue chairs into which we often gratefully sink after a day dedicated to shopping.

In any case, we know that at either Bruno Magli store, we can count on a marvellous selection of archetypal pumps, or court shoes, that are dependably correct and fashionable without being trendy. Colours vary with the seasons, but they're always in evidence on the shelves in the shop's well-lit alcoves. There are lots of black, brown and burgundy in the winter, and summer prompts a rainbow of bright fashion colours, as well as the traditional white, cream and navy.

While Bruno Magli does sell some pretty evening shoes and sandals, this is the place for more sensible and durable styles. One of our favourites is the popular punched-leather number with a rubber sole that is the ultimate for walking (£110). Indeed, given the excellent Italian craftsmanship that goes into every Magli shoe, long-wearing durability is a given. We're tough on shoes, putting them through rugged tours of duty on the streets of New York and London, but we depend on our Maglis to last years for the £85 to £150 we spend on them. And they do—we keep from getting bored with them by changing the charming £10 to £25 bows we buy here to dress up our pumps.

In addition to the bows, there are handbags to complement Magli shoes. Designed to match certain styles, including some of the evening slippers, they are priced from £100 to £200.

Men, while solicitously served by the courteous, even courtly, salespeople, are relegated to second-class status here by the rather limited selection which retains its undisputed classic good taste while selling for £85 to £150. Should you be disappointed by the choices for men, you might be appeased by the nice (but, again, small) assortment of reversible brown/black belts for £35, or the exclusive line of luggage. Fashioned in the softest leather imaginable, it's all very smart at £350 to £500, but we wouldn't counsel you to consign it to the not-so-tender-loving care of most airlines.

Since we don't own any, we can't say for sure, but we strongly suspect that Magli luggage, however beautiful, is not nearly so sturdy as our beloved pumps. . .that is, court shoes.

Burberry's

| 18–22 Haymarket | 071-930-3343 |
| London SW1Y 4DQ | (FAX) 071-839-6691 |

Synonymous with raincoats worldwide, Burberry's, the source of gabardine and the trenchcoat, thanks to the creativity of founder Thomas Burberry, is much, much more at this flagship store. Here, you can "Burberry" (as in active verb) just about anything—your kids in the well-stocked children's shop, your wrist with a line of watches, your stomach in the food department and even your dog with a coat in that ubiquitous trademark plaid. Many of these, as well as other Burberry products, are available only at this store that has been home to the firm since the turn of the century.

It is a spacious, comfortably old-fashioned store with high ceilings, complete with skylights, floating over wide uncluttered aisles, interrupted only by rather grand columns. The walls bear testimony to Burberry's origins as a purveyor of sporting clothes—antique cricket bats and the sepia-toned pictures of the teams that used them, oars that once swept through the waters at Henley, half models of racing yachts, golf clubs and duck decoys. The appropriately genteel staff is overseen by Graham Eunderdown, who, by appointment, makes himself graciously available to clients. Exploring the bounty that is Burberry's with him is quite an experience, as there is so much tradition and trivia connected with the place. Graham knows and tells all. For instance, did you know that the tan, red and black Burberry plaid that denotes status in certain circles was first introduced as a lining for raincoats in the 1930s? And that it wasn't until the 1960s that it was first used in scarves, umbrellas, luggage and God knows what else (it even shows up on the face of one of the Burberry watches)? How about the fact that the first transatlantic flight from America to Ireland in 1919 was accomplished by two airmen outfitted by Burberry?

With or without Graham's tutelage, Burberry's a delightful place for a leisurely browse, even for a party. If you're travelling with an entourage of 100 or so, the store can be yours for a couple of evening hours for a cocktail party, as long as you've made the proper arrangements with the estimable Graham. For smaller groups, he'll arrange for a guided tour and a spot of tea. Either way, there's plenty to look at. The lower ground floor is devoted entirely to men's rain-gear with trenchcoats starting at about

£300, while the main floor houses the rest of the men's collection—a large selection of lambswool and cashmere sweaters (many as highly styled as anything you'll find on Bond Street or Sloane Street), active sportswear, jackets, suits, silk ties for £35 and other accessories. There's also a new department dedicated to the Thomas Burberry Collection, clothes with a higher fashion quotient than the familiar classic Burberry look. The collection reflects the progressiveness of its namesake who would, no doubt, be pleased that it is attracting a younger, more diverse clientele. Burberry's is no longer the private preserve of the middle-aged aristocracy.

Which is not to suggest that the store has been forsaken by that august body. The princes William and Harry have been spotted in Burberry duds. And no wonder. Di must be just as enchanted as we are by the children's shop, also on the main floor. We were hard pressed to resist an adorably sporty tweed jacket complete with leather patches at the elbow, fit for a princeling at £75—never mind the fact that currently there are no pint-sized people in our lives. A sweet little girl's red blazer boasting black velvet collar and cuffs for £95 presented the same problem.

Upstairs is the ladies' floor, less imposingly sportive with elegant accoutrements like crystal chandeliers. In addition to the predictable sweater and skirt ensembles and sensible suits, there are some covetable items like a stylish wool jacket cut full to accommodate a bulky sweater. At £220 it's a go-everywhere-at-the-weekend necessity. You'll also find a suitably trendy Thomas Burberry Collection for women.

Of course, quality has always been Burberry's stock in trade and it doesn't stop with the merchandise. Service here is above and beyond the call of duty, particularly when it comes to the shop's visiting tailors. The 12 very qualified craftspeople detailed to this department are prepared to visit you anywhere in the U.K. to take your measurements for a bespoke suit or for alterations to ready-to-wear pieces, and to act as guides through Burberry's catalogues. At Christmas, you can wander through the various albums of goodies and, with the help of your personal consultant, purchase all your gifts and arrange for wrapping and posting without ever leaving the comfort of your home, office or hotel.

Leave it to Burberry's, in the spirit of its inventive founder, to come up with such a unique service.

Fortnum & Mason

181 Piccadilly	071-734-8040
London W1A 1ER	(FAX) 071-437-3278

Fortnum & Mason gets our vote for having the most entertaining and informative literature about its long history of any such august establishment in the city. Full of fun and the kind of hype we seldom associate with the understated British, *The Delectable History of Fortnum & Mason* declares the union of William Fortnum and Hugh Mason in 1707 as one "surpassed in its importance to the human race only by the meeting of Adam with Eve." Certainly, the comparison overstates the case, but only just when you consider the contributions Fortnum & Mason has made to the British menu—the firm's patronage of the East India Company brightened time-honoured roasted meats and boiled vegetables with spices and condiments, while popularizing the daily consumption of copious amounts of tea. Furthermore, Fortnum & Mason pioneered the production of prepared foods for sale as early as 1788—boned portions of poultry and game in aspic jelly decorated with lobsters and prawns, potted meats, Scotch eggs, mince pies and the like, all "prepared so as to require no cutting."

Thirty years later, Fortnum & Mason's tinned treasures began to make their appearance, and their hallmark hampers became de rigueur to sustaining life during such events as Queen Victoria's coronation and the Great Exhibition of 1851. Charles Dickens, a regular customer, once wrote:

> "Well to be sure, there never was such a Derby Day as this present Derby Day! Never, to be sure, were there so many carriages...so many fine ladies in so many broughams, so many Fortnum & Mason hampers, so much ice and champagne. If I were on the turf, and had a horse to enter for the Derby, I would call that horse Fortnum & Mason, convinced that with that name he would beat the field. Public opinion would bring him in somehow. Look where I will—in some connexion with the carriages...I see Fortnum & Mason. And now, Heavens! All the hampers fly wide open and the green Downs bursts into a blossom of lobster salad."

As if all that weren't enough, Fortnum & Mason can be credited with introducing the wonders of ketchup to the English palate—it was the first British company to place an order with Heinz Foods in 1866.

Okay, so everyone knows that the ground floor of Fortnum & Mason is devoted to an untold number of foodstuffs made to the store's exacting specifications, all beautifully displayed under giant crystal chandeliers and watched over by knowledgeable gentlemen in morning coats. But, have you ever considered what happens on the other levels of what, after all, is a fairly imposing building, with five selling floors in all? Did it ever occur to you that Fortnum & Mason is a full-fledged department store selling everything from fashion to candles? It didn't to us until the estimable Lilian Prescott, who's in charge of customer relations, showed us around. We'd never ventured past the unrivalled collection of teas (over two million pounds sold a year), the massive selection of biscuits, the old masters' still-life presentations of prepared foods, and the jams and preserves made from every imaginable source—try the rose petal marmalade for about £3.50 a jar.

In the company of Mrs Prescott, we discovered a whole other Fortnum & Mason world, dating from 1925 when the store was completely rebuilt. At that time, ladies' fashions, children's clothes, kitchenware and perfumes were added to the Fortnum & Mason mix. Subsequently, men's clothes were included so that today the store is an important fashion resource for professional types of all ages who appreciate its classic (and classy) approach to style and service. Customers are escorted from one area to another and introduced to experts in each department.

The men's floor on three features Fortnum & Mason's own label suits, which are made in Italy, as well as those of Chester Barrie, the Rolls-Royce of English ready-to-wear suiting. Shirts, ties, socks, shoes and braces are all available, too, in a satisfying, if not actually exciting, array of colours, patterns and styles. Think Brooks Brothers—we did as we admired a soft tweed sports jacket in an appealing green and yellow tweed with a Fortnum & Mason label for £295. But it was Armani that came to mind as we stroked an angora, tobacco-coloured overcoat by Chester Barrie—lots of 1930s chic and well priced at £995.

Still, in all, the women's collection is even better. An extraordinary array of hair accessories can be found on the second floor, along with other statement-making accents like cashmere shawls by Loro Paino in soft prints. Edged with a playful fringe, they sell in the £590 neighbourhood. But the real fashion action is on the recently renovated first floor, with its creamy salon look underscored by dreamy cloud scenes painted on the ceiling and strategically placed wall panels. An extraordinary Lalique table highlights the extensive perfume display that runs almost the entire length of the store. Theirs is one of the best perfumeries in the city. The lingerie department is equally distinguished and the millinery department is nothing to sneeze at.

As for the clothes themselves, they are mostly the products of English designers such as Jean Muir, Belville Sassoon and Max Mara. Fortnum & Mason is a major supporter of each, and is ever on the look out for new talent. We liked a black-and-white check suit by Sassoon with oversized white collar and cuffs. The long jacket fitted snugly over the slim, front-wrap skirt—ideal for business and pleasure for £475.

The lower level addresses Fortnum & Mason's roots—china, glass and silver to complement the food upstairs. The selection is vast, offering the best of English and European manufacturers. Herend's popularity here is not at all impeded by its expense, and the display is one of the largest we've ever seen. And this is where you'll find the famous hamper department. The growth of the hamper's popularity continues to be phenomenal. Some 50,000 baskets or boxes packed with delicacies are ordered at Christmas alone. Prices vary greatly, £12.50 to £2,000, depending upon the contents, but all in all they represent a good value since they are less expensive as a whole than they would be as a sum of their individual parts. While you're at it, pick up a £975 wicker picnic basket loaded with Limogesware for six and complete with cutlery, glasses, food containers and even a rug.

Here, too, you can purchase candles, which may not seem a matter of much import unless you know the 18th-century version thereof was Fortnum & Mason's first product. It was in a street stand, apparently on the current store's site, that William Fortnum and Hugh Mason first set up shop selling the used candles William received as a perquisite of his job as a footman at nearby St James's Palace. So the royal connection which continues today—Fortnum & Mason serves as the Queen's grocers and provisions merchant—was established at the very beginning. Another fascinating fact from the pages of the firm's little history book. If, hard to believe, you leave the premises with nothing else, try to coax a copy out of the staff.

There's one other important thing we learned about Fortnum & Mason, though this was from experience rather than from the store's literature. Use the marvellous grand double staircase on the west side of the building, instead of the elevators which tend to be small and slow. 🍒

Fratelli Rossetti

196 Sloane Street   071-259-6357
London SW1X 9QX

Both Rossetti outlets, on New Bond and on Sloane streets, carry the full range of the family's well-constructed shoes for men and women, but we tend to prefer the Sloane location—mostly because of the presence of Mauro Buscaglia, the very talkative manager who makes shopping here a social experience. He tells us it wasn't so long ago that the Rossettis were private-label producers of sports shoes. Hard to believe these days when Rossetti's sells fashionable shoes all over the world, manufactures over 200,000 pairs annually, keeps more than 200 people gainfully employed, and owns 17 boutiques in Europe, the Far East and North America.

The firm has come a long way since Renato and Renzo Rossetti—hence the "Fratelli"—first started making cycling shoes in the 1960s. Now a directional force in the international footwear industry, the firm remains very much a family operation. Other Italian fashion dynasties may eschew mixing business with pleasure—any discussions of work are forbidden at the Missoni lunch table and rumour has it the Fendi sisters only deal with each other in the confines of the boardroom—but for the Rossettis the two are inexorably intertwined. Renzo's wife and sons are as consumed with the business as he is (Renato died in 1986), working and playing together as a unit.

It may not be everybody's cup of tea, but it obviously works for them. The company continues to thrive as it branches out into complementary leather goods like handbags and shearling jackets. Still, the emphasis is on shoes as is evident from the extensive inventory at Sloane Street, which tends to be more fashion-oriented than the stock on Bond.

Men will find their Rossetti shoe nirvana down the stairs of this sandy beige shop, made dramatic with black accents. There, in relative privacy, since men account for only 30 per cent of the business here as opposed to 70 per cent on Bond Street, you will no doubt find a style or two that are truly *you*—practical yet versatile, classic but with a twist. We were especially impressed with the range of loafers—the sensible side-buckle version in black or brown at £160, a sportier number with tassels in black, brown, navy, beige or white for £110. In fact, tassels are sort of a Rossetti trademark. It was one of the first shoe manufacturers to use them, and seems to have a particular flair for bowed tassels, like the ones on a smashing pair of crocodile loafers at £480.

Mauro says kangaroo hide, which is extraordinarily flexible, is becoming very popular, mostly for spring and summer. And speaking of weather, it's interesting to note that Rossetti features three different weights of soles to adapt to the seasons—the summer weight is the lightest and slimmest and is only lined where absolutely necessary. The heaviest, meant to take winter's worst, can mean as much as a £50 difference in the price of the shoe. But the Rossetti sole story doesn't stop there—for the classic brogue, there is a double sole arrangement, so that the outer one can be repaired without touching the main body of the shoe. And one recent model, done with durable "pila" calf broguing, encased a delicate suede upper which sported a special rubber sole secured with Goodyear welting and then cemented for extra strength. Theoretically, the hard-wearing qualities of the rubber means the sole should never wear out...though, naturally, if it ever did Fratelli Rossetti guarantees its replacement. Available in dark brown and a stylish bottle green, a pair runs £188.

Upstairs is the ladies' domain, where the sporty versatility of the shoes reflects that of the men's. Rossetti's is beginning to get into evening shoes—and we did fall in love with a £120 pair of embroidered black satin evening shoes with a very delicate heel—but its forte is in more traditional leather and suede shoes with stacked heels. Regardless of which height heel you choose—low, medium, or high—they cost £105 in suede and leather. And, again, loafers are special here. We liked the side-buckle style in lizard with a crepe sole for £230. The only problem was that it was difficult to see how it looked in the very decorative, but rather impractical, pyramid-shaped mirror that dominates the centre of the room. In heels, you get the right perspective, but in flats—forget it! Indeed, since we couldn't really assess their foot-flattering potential, we had to pass on a beautiful two-tone evening slipper, its deep purple toe elaborately embroidered in black for £85.

It was a pity. Mauro assured us the style was a winner, and we trust him implicitly. Still, there are some things we just have to see for ourselves.

Gallery of London

1 Duke of York Street	071-930-5974/925-2082
London SW1Y 6JP	(FAX) 071-930-9216

For years we've been just wild about Tender Buttons in New York, awed by its astonishing selection. We've always wondered where the store found all those ornamental buttons. Now we've discovered one of its heretofore secret resources, the London Badge and Button Company which seven years ago opened this retail outlet (Gallery of London). It is, bar none, *the* best source for blazer buttons—plain or fancy, enamelled or not, brass or silver, shiny or matte finish. And the best news is that they're all beautifully catalogued to accommodate the firm's far-reaching mail-order business.

Most styles are £2.75 to £4.50 each for either large or small buttons. They're sold individually so you can assemble a set according to what you need. However, you can drive up the cost considerably by getting involved with the engraving of initials or crests (allow two or three weeks) or by commissioning a set in gold.

With so much to choose from, you can be forgiven for becoming a bit befuddled. Fortunately, the softspoken Michael Coleman is on hand to help plot a course through this sea of buttons. If you're of a mind to salute your favourite sport via your blazer, Michael will guide you to the buttons emblazoned with symbols of every imaginable outdoor activity. Take it one step further, with matching cufflinks (or button covers), tiepin and keyring. All of the stock is made in the company's own Birmingham factory, which Michael tells us is where most British jewelry is manufactured.

Not quite coordinated enough for you? How about a corresponding handmade patch, embroidered with gold and silver threads? Alternatively, should you care to be true to your school, you can wear buttons with its insignia. Chances are London Badge and Button already makes the blazer crests sold in your alma mater's bookstore, be it British or American. And it's doubtful there's a regiment anywhere in Her Majesty's Service that isn't represented here. Prices tend to range from £15 to £17 for the standard size, around £12 for what Michael describes as the miniatures. But, again, you can up the ante with special orders.

Since the company supplies royal families of the Continental strain, we imagine that there have been some pretty interesting demands made upon its creativity. Naturally, Michael wouldn't 'fess up to their exact nature, but his rueful smile said it all.   🍒

Georgina von Etzdorf

149 Sloane Street   071-823-5638
London SW1X 9BZ

Walking into this tiny, glass-encased shop is to be enveloped in a sensuous sea of sumptuous fabrics, fashioned into luxuriously indulgent clothes and accessories. They're the creation of the store's namesake, but the result of a team effort. Georgina's design sense, augmented by Martin Simcock's production knowledge and Jonathan Docherty's technical skills, has built a business which, in a decade, has grown into an extraordinarily successful silk printing and design company with worldwide distribution. It produces intricately designed, completely hand-printed textile products destined to become collector's items.

While you can find Georgina's colourful, innovative prints in outlets such as Harrods and Liberty, the complete collection is on view only here and at the firm's boutique in Picketts in the Burlington Arcade. Opened in 1988, the soft curves and neutral colours of the Sloane Street location make it the flagship—it's the perfect showcase for Georgina's long, silk, jacquard scarves which virtually fly out of the store at £45 to £185 each. At the higher end of the price range, they're lined with insulating cashmere, and all are hand-fringed.

It's the colours that really stun you here. So unusual, so vibrant, yet they have a chameleon quality. At first glance the gorgeous wool challis scarf wouldn't seem to go with anything in your closet, but upon closer inspection, it turns out to be the perfect complement to the very suit you're wearing. No wonder Gayle Hunnicutt, John Hurt, Glenda Jackson and Mel Brooks enjoy stopping by to see what's new, what they might be inspired to add to their Georgina von Etzdorf collections. Mick Jagger and David Bowie buy the £35 ties, and we get a kick out of the boldly patterned braces, which we buy for our most self-assured menfolk at £49.50 a pop.

But for extravagant luxury, it's tough to beat the dressing gowns suitable for both sexes. Available in caressable panne velvet, cotton velvet or wool challis, all enhanced by Georgina's fabulous prints and lined with silk, they're the ultimate in lounging comfort and sell for £525. From £325 to £525, you can get an unlined silk, jacquard kimono-style robe.

For more formal at-home activities, made-to-measure smoking jackets are offered at £600. Jack Nicholson explored the seductive properties of one of these sumptuous numbers in *The Witches of Eastwick*. Ask manager Alison Baigrie about the relative merits of a plain velvet version trimmed with printed silk collar and cuffs versus a patterned velvet with unadorned silk.

Either way, they're beautifully made, the work of the skilled craftspeople Georgina and her partners employ at their Salisbury headquarters. Once a 17th-century barn, it is now a fully equipped studio and manufacturing facility dedicated to textile design and development. It's a long way from the garage of Georgina's parents' home where she first started printing fabric. As such, it's also testimony to the team's recognition of a void in the British textile industry—namely, a desperate lack of design and colour—and Georgina's team's ability to fill it.

Gilbey's Waistcoat Gallery

2 New Burlington Place   071-734-4877
London W1X 1FB   (FAX) 071-434-2533

Gallery is the operative word here. The minimalist, whitewashed, skylit decor facilitates the aesthetic display of a dizzying array of waistcoats (also called vests) as artworks—always an adaptation of Salvador Dalí, Gustof Klemt and Monet. Tom Gilbey, a consistently employed if unsung designer of men's and women's wear for the last 20 or so years, has finally found his calling in his inspired interpretations of this most adaptable of garments. Both decorative and functional, the waistcoat has a distinguished history dating from 1580. By the 1660s, it had become a revolutionary British fashion statement as part of Charles II's radical three-piece suit. According to chroniclers of the period, the king meant the vest to challenge the fashion dominance of the French court. Louis XIV countered his sartorial sally by dressing all his servants and lackeys in waistcoats in an effort to downgrade the garment's chic. The ploy didn't work, and before long the French king had succumbed to the vest's charms as an unrestricted jacket and as an effective tool for the display of dandyism.

It wasn't until the latter part of the 19th century, when colour virtually disappeared from male wardrobes, that waistcoats were consigned to traditional woollen cloths rather than luxuriously flamboyant satins, velvets, brocades and cashmeres. Thanks to Tom, the garment is regaining its status as a fashion statement reflecting the wearer's personality, be he—or she—butcher, baker, candlestick maker, banker or beachcomber. Tom designs for one and all in innovative fabric combinations that enable his vests to be styled for innumerable occasions. In fact, largely due to his influence, one could make the argument that the waistcoat became to the '80s and '90s what the T-shirt was to the '60s, with no end of the trend in sight—just ask Mick Jagger, Paul McCartney and Eric Clapton, who often don Tom's creations on and off stage.

Off the rack, or more accurately in this case, off the "peg," waistcoats range from £75 to £350. We were especially taken with a black velvet beauty accented by an elaborately hand-embroidered shawl collar for £250. For a more sportive look, there's the traditionally cut doeskin-fronted number at £175. If you want something truly unique, talk to Tom about his bespoke service—he has a staggering number of fabrics to work with and a boundless imagination. You just have to stand still for the fitting and pay the bill, £195 to £400 or more if you and he get carried away. But if you're from overseas, you won't have to stand still very long—he can do it in 24 hours. And if you have a particular visual theme in mind, Tom will execute it on a hand-painted or appliqued waistcoat, just as he did for Rupert Murdoch—the media mogul now wears Tom's rendition of Bart Simpson.   ❦

Giorgio Armani

178 Sloane Street	071-235-6232
London SW1 9QL	(FAX) 071-823-1342

The opening of Giorgio Armani's London base on Sloane Street in 1989 was yet another indication of that street's growing prestige, and of Bond Street's decline. A decade ago, Mr Armani would surely have elected to situate this highly stylized shop with its attentive doorman on Bond Street or thereabouts. But times have changed, and his store serves as one more magic magnet drawing fashionable shoppers to Sloane Street—Tina Turner, Linda Carter, Shakira and Michael Caine, Jonathan Ross and Stefanie Powers among them.

They pass through the welcoming foyer in its soothing tones of grey in search of the uncomplicated sophistication of Armani's clothes, separates, mostly, displayed as complete ensembles. There's plenty here to choose from for both men and women, in the signature black label and the lower priced "diffusion" line with the white Mani label. But manager

Joanna Binder works with Armani devotees to develop special orders from photographs of the seasonal collections months before they appear in the store. She's equally accommodating when it comes to special services, like bringing a selection of clothes to your hotel room or home. Just give her a call, tell her what you're looking for and schedule an appointment. And if you've come across an Armani piece at another store and are desperately seeking coordinates, give her a description and she'll make her selections accordingly.

Still, we think it's more fun to visit the store. It's divided up into such manageable sections with mirrors everywhere. We just love to run our hands over the richly textured fabrics that are Armani's hallmark. We had to be dragged away from the unconstructed-looking suits that make such excellent use of men's wear shapes at about £895. And, oh, that classic cashmere jacket at £1,100! His fluidly sensuous eveningwear occupies the rear of the store and is in the £1,000 to £4,000 neighbourhood.

In the Mani section, you'll find more fitted and less costly garments that tend to be more flattering to the smaller woman. Here, a silk blouse runs about £195, as does a pair of trousers (more like £350 with the black label in the waistband).

Upstairs is devoted to the Armani man. He gets a bit less space than his female counterpart, but the display of clothes is equally slick— museum-like tableaus that nonetheless invite you to touch and even to disassemble in order to try on a coveted piece. Suits run about £800— £550 for those of the Mani label. Good-looking, but their easy, unstructured cut isn't for everyone. Not so the sportily chic leather jackets at about £1,250—they should be a staple for any gentleman's wardrobe, as should the singularly handsome silk ties for £55.

After a stroll through the store, it's easy to understand why over 2,000,000 people acquire a piece of Armani every year. After our last visit, make that plus two! 🥀

Harrods Ltd

Knightsbridge   071-730-1234
London SW1 X7XL   (FAX) 071-581-0470

There's no doubt that you will become one of the 50,000 people who visit Harrods each day. You cannot leave London without wandering the 22 acres of trendy and traditional merchandise, seeing for yourself why

Harrods' motto is "Omnia, Omnibus, Ubique," or all things, for all people, everywhere.

Certainly, few stores have the history and heritage of Harrods, which began in 1849 as Henry Charles Harrod's tea and grocery shop. By 1864, the business was earning £1,000 per week under the management of Harrod's energetic son, Charles Digby Harrod, who added perfume, medicine, stationery, flowers, fruits, vegetables and cooked meats departments to the store. By 1880, Harrods employed more than 150 people.

During the next 100 or so years, Harrods would experience phenomenal growth and prosperity, despite some very challenging events: a devastating fire caused the entire store to be rebuilt in 1884, and then in 1959, Harrods was taken over by Hugh Fraser. In 1974 and 1983, there were bomb explosions in and around the store. But, throughout its turbulent history, Harrods has reigned supreme for merchandise and service, due to the skill and dedication of its owners and managers who were determined that Harrods would survive, thrive and prosper.

And prosper it has, from a £20 per week grocery store to a £1,000,000 per day organization.

M. Al Fayed bought the store in 1985, and he is the epitome of the hands-on chairman. You may spot him walking throughout the store, as he likes to keep an eye on things, checking on quality and service.

It is totally impossible to see the store in one visit, but perhaps we can give you a brief idea of what is where, so you can do some research before you go.

The Food Halls on the ground floor are probably the most famous section of Harrods. There are 18 departments, including liquor (which stocks 163 different brands of whiskey), cheese (which offers 500 varieties), the bakery (which sells 130 kinds of bread) and the confectionary (selling 100 tons of chocolates each year). You might like to take home a vacuum-packed Scottish salmon, which can go right with you on the plane or can be shipped.

Also on the ground floor are the fine jewelry room, the leather room, stationery, cosmetics and perfumes, and the men's fashion departments. Since Harrods is known for service, on the ground floor you can have your broken lighter repaired, look for lost property, check your parcels, leave valuables in the safe, or ask the liveried doormen, the "Green Men," to hail a taxi.

On the first floor is fur storage, although Harrods no longer boasts a fur department, alterations, baby and children's clothing, and a children's hair salon, where your child will receive a "first cut diploma," if it's his or her first hairstyling.

You'll also find what we love most about Harrods: the Executive Service Suite. Just call Brian Ames or Julia Eccles direct at 071-581-4874 with your shopping list, and they'll collect all the merchandise into one enormous room for your arrival. They'll even serve you breakfast or lunch. Should you overindulge in the bounty that is Harrods, have them send up the Givenchy skin-care and beauty line in the company of a makeup artist. The combo will have you looking glamorous in time for cocktails and dinner.

Imagine stopping into Harrods, seeing everything you need all in one place, and having it all shipped home for you. This is the perfect service for any busy executive.

The second floor has books (you can pick up another copy of this one!), china, linens, glass engraving, cookshop, kitchen designing, radio and television sets and pets.

If you need an eiderdown quilt, there are wonderful ones in fine linens, but be prepared to spend £2,350 for this ultimate luxury.

The third floor features furniture, pianos, posters and prints, dry cleaning, corporate interiors and picture framing.

The fourth floor is our favourite because of the Toy Kingdom: four huge rooms filled with toys for every age, from rattles for tots, to computer games for adults.

There's also Harrods Bank, a customer service department, gift wrap and certificates, travel booking, tourist information, coach tours, theatre tickets, photo processing, optical testing, Way In Hairdressers, and a credit department. Be sure to arrange for a Harrods charge card, so you will get all the store's wonderful catalogues, especially the marvellous Christmas one—sorry, U.K. mailing only of the catalogue.

In 1989, Harrods opened its new Fine Jewelry Room, featuring treasures designed by N. Bloom, Cartier, David Morris, Theo Fennell, Garrard, Lalaounis and Mikimoto. You will surely find something perfect for that Vicky Tiel evening gown in this department.

If we're going too fast for you, perhaps you'd enjoy some refreshment, which is easily found at one of the store's 11 bars and restaurants on the ground, first and fourth floors. You can have a full meal, a light snack, a cup of tea or a cocktail. Just ask any of the ultra-polite and gracious sales-people to direct you.

You certainly can count on Harrods for expert help, even in the most unusual circumstances. One lady we know lost all her luggage on an air-line, just four hours before she was leaving on a cruise. She called Harrods in a panic and, within a few hours, they had assembled a week of cruisewear for her, which was delivered to her ship just as it pulled away from port. Now that's service!

We hope you won't be shopping at Harrods under such duress. We do advise you, however, to arrive at 9:00 A.M. (9:30 on Tuesdays) when your feet are fresh, so you can spend a leisurely day discovering the store that truly is all things, for all people, everywhere.   🍎

Henrys

201 Regent Street   071-437-6579
London W1R 7WA

Founded in 1926 by Jonathan Falkner, Henrys remains a family business steeped in the traditions of superior design, excellent craftsmanship and fine service. His grandson, also named Jonathan Falkner, is now in charge of this leather goods business and is committed to the firm's hall-marks, despite an aggressive expansion program—shops in Glasgow and Birmingham, as well as in other London locations on Brompton Road and Golders Green and a recently opened flagship store on New Bond Street. While the latter occupies the site of the former stately home of Lord Nelson, we like the Regent Street store best. Once the Italian State Tourist Office, the elegant building with its marble walls and floors, and its tall graceful windows evokes the days when travelling was a luxu-rious affair.

It still is, if you avail yourself of Henrys' sophisticated luggage made exclusively for the firm in Italy. (The store also carries other labels like Longchamp, Hartman and Lark, but since you can get these anywhere, why bother with them here?) Henrys' look in luggage is self-consciously old-fashioned, solid and extravagant. It announces not only that you have arrived, but also that you knew what you were doing on the way there. There's a varied range of fabrications—from basic, boxy, hand-stitched cowhide in black or tobacco, at £400 for a vanity case, to £700 for a 32-inch wardrobe, to glamorous crocodile, starting at about £2,600 for a Gladstone bag, the ultimate overnighter/weekender.

We were drawn to the handsome, rigid cases in glazed green canvas, trimmed in rich brown leather. They stand out in airline or ship terminal luggage piles and cost from £500 to £700. But the real knock-out here is a ladies' crocodile travelling case, sized just right to slide under any airplane seat, though at close to £4,500, it deserves first class. Truly the pièce de résistance, it splits into two halves. The top portion is a vanity complete with a mirrored lid and storage compartments for cosmetics and jewelry—the latter constructed so that your baubles are concealed and secured in place. The bottom half has enough room for some seductive underwear, a negligee and a change of clothes and shoes. It'll take you anywhere in the world in undeniable style. And to protect it from the rigours of travel, it comes with a tough, fitted cover at no extra charge, as do all Henrys' pieces.

The store also has a lovely selection of handbags in leather and lizard in seasonal colours from £75 to £160, and distinguished-looking briefcases averaging £300. There's also a line of leather-trimmed handbags and accessories in quilted paisley-patterned canvas. Described as Henrys' "country pursuits," the prints feature Regency hunters riding to the hounds. Prices start at about £70 for a lady's wallet and go up to £135 for a hunting shoulder bag.

You'll even find an assortment of evening bags, but we remain committed to what Henrys does best—equipping you to travel with élan. 🦃

Herbert Johnson Ltd

30 New Bond Street	071-408-1174
London W1Y 9HD	(FAX) 071-734-8119

You may not be aware just how familiar you are with hats from Herbert Johnson. But think about it. When was the last time you saw Her Majesty Queen Elizabeth II sans chapeau? Okay, for formal occasions she might don a crown, but for daywear she often relies on Herbert Johnson, which has been in the hatting business since 1889. Like mother, like son—the firm holds Prince Charles' warrant as well, although he seems to prefer the windblown look. Perhaps as that dear little bald spot of his grows, the prince will follow some of his illustrious ancestors' steps in originating fashion trends. (Actually, he's already had some influence with regard to the double-breasted suit.) Maybe one day, following Charles' example, hats will once again become de rigueur for a well-dressed man.

In fact, when real men did wear hats, many were outfitted in Herbert Johnson's Grovesnor model—a rabbit fur, felt number which now sells for £75 and was once favoured by Humphrey Bogart, Spencer Tracy and Bing Crosby. Latter-day machos may prefer the Safari, which survived snake pits, jumps from airplanes, and runaway horses atop Harrison Ford's head throughout the trilogy launched by *Raiders of the Lost Ark*. Then there's the prosaic tweed hat with the turned-down brim that suffered through all of Peter Sellers' misadventures in the *Pink Panther* series. It remains a bestseller at £49.50.

Should you have something a little dressier in mind, think Fred Astaire or Rex Harrison and go for one of the splendid black silk top hats at £450. For winter wonderland warmth, there's quite a selection in fur, including some Daniel Boone trapper looks in wolf, for up to £400. And to capture a little of the dashing presence of Charles Lindbergh, check out the £89 leather flying helmets.

If you're wondering where the ladies fit in among all this male finery so pleasingly exhibited in graceful, glass-fronted armoires, head downstairs. There you'll find the captivating styles that have made habitués of Joan Collins, Jane Seymour, Joanne Lumley and Mrs Dustin Hoffman (he eats, she shops). We were enthralled by a flirtatious, red silk cocktail hat in the guise of a perfectly petalled rose for £165. Another entrance-maker was a black velvet hat, approximately the size and shape of a frisbee, crowned with a pert little silk cone encircled with rhinestones at £195.

As you may have guessed, Herbert Johnson is the source for many of the winsome designs that show up at Ascot every spring. Although a custom-made hat generally only takes two to three weeks to construct, Royal Enclosure-bound ladies start coming in as early as January to order the crowning glory of their Ascot duds. They consult with head designer, Sylvia Fletcher, who likes to see what they plan on wearing, at least from the waist up. Of course, she'll work from a fabric swatch and your description of its ultimate form, if that's the best you can do. In any case, it will cost *at least* £150 not to mention the £35 for the beautiful burgundy hat box which all Herbert Johnson creations deserve, be they ready-to-wear or custom-made.

If you opt for the latter, you can depend on a perfect fit. Naturally, sizing or blocking changes may be required with the off-the-hat-rack specimens, and they are done on the house. Likewise, perfectly acceptable bags for your purchases are offered free of charge, but they don't have the cachet, or the practicality, of those distinctive boxes—we've been known to stop by just for a box or two. They make such stylish storage bins!

❧

Hermès

179 Sloane Street	071-823-1014
London SW1X 9QG	(FAX) 071-259-6662

Hermès is yet another testimony to French style in London. Founded by Thierry Hermès in Paris in 1837, the company originally supplied beautiful harnesses to the carriagemakers of the Champs Elysées. In 1879 Thierry's son Emile-Charles transferred the business to 24 Faubourg St. Honoré, where it has remained ever since. Besides making harnesses, Hermès began to produce saddlery. Before long, it became established as the best in France, and could count several crowned heads among its loyal customers, including the Imperial Court of Russia. With the advent of the motorcar and the impending demise of the horse-drawn carriage, Hermès was quick to realise the need for diversification, and it began to produce wallets, travelling cases, handbags and luggage, using the same techniques and craftsmanship the firm had applied so successfully to harness-making. Indeed, Hermès saddle-stitched finishing technique became and remains all the rage. Leather goods were soon followed by clothing, clocks and watches, diaries, costume jewelry, travel accessories, goldsmith's objects, gloves, ashtrays and, of course, silk scarves and ties.

Hermès arrived in London in 1964, with an enchanting little shop in Jermyn Street, which is sadly no longer with us. A Bond Street shop was opened in the early 1970s and the Royal Exchange shop, so beloved of City gents, followed in 1979. In 1988, the most ambitious shop was opened on Sloane Street in the heart of the Knightsbridge shopping village, testimony to the success of Hermès with its English patrons. The shop is beautifully designed by French interior architect, Rena Dumas, with cherry wood panelling and gleaming brass and glass. Presided over by the delightful Genevieve Payne, the shop is a haven of self-indulgence.

With its saddle-room background and equestrian motifs, Hermès is a natural favourite with the horsey set. Over the past ten years, however, its influence has become far-reaching, and the company's peculiar brand of easy elegance permeates fashion at all levels. Thierry Hermès may be long gone, but the standards of craftsmanship which were his trademark are still very much in evidence.

The Sloane Street shop is notable for its reflection of the latest development of Hermès in ready-to-wear, with considerable space devoted to both men's and women's collections. The entire lower ground floor is devoted to ladies' ready-to-wear. From classic jodphurs and impeccably cut suits, to reversible silk scarves, windbreakers and natty shorts in jewel colours, Hermès has emerged as a name to remember in the fashion stakes. Hardly surprising as the fashion director is none other than Claude Brouet, the doyenne of Parisian fashion as the former fashion editor of French *Elle* and *Marie Claire*. (Shoes, too, are winners.)

Menswear, too, is the epitome of that well-mannered wit which is synonymous with Hermès—i.e., ties, ties, and more ties. But this is also the place to find impossibly soft cashmeres, silk-lined sports jackets and wild, silk bomber jackets. Beautiful "made-to-last-a-lifetime" shoes and finest Sea Island cotton socks should be replaced at night by the deliciously traditional velvet slippers. Best of all is the heavy, heavy silk dressing gown in midnight blue (£725).

Leather goods are displayed in every nook and cranny from the sublime (the infinitely desirable and always classic crocodile Kelly bag at £5,250) to the deliciously ridiculous (a leather chewing gum holder for £65). There is currently a nine-month waiting list for the Kelly bag, which takes up to 20 hours' work. Our hearts were won by the stunningly simple "Constance" bag with the lines of a classic sports car and the classic *H* motif (£1,500). Equine roots are very much in evidence with stunningly crafted saddlery, bridles, bandages and blankets. We were sorely tempted by a riding crop (in an outrageous shade of yellow!).

If you are feeling really extravagant, there is a selection of delectable cushions covered in the ubiquitous Hermès scarves. One entire corner of the shop is given over to such "simply must-haves" for the home. Vividly coloured tableclothes, mats, oven-gloves, all strikingly and definitely "Hermès"—lots of horsey hardware designs. There are also acres of deep and richly patterned towels, that would seem sufficient to wrap an entire family (we were told there are seven kilos of dye in each!), and lovely featherlight pareos.

Watches, jewelry and costume jewelry—well, we just had to have the wonderfully heavy chaine d'ancre bracelet in silver (£380) and a pair of the sellier leather and gold earrings (£55) which are young and fun and available in myriad colours.

Oh, and then there are the "oh-so-soigné" gloves, and the hats and the belts and the diaries and the secateurs and the ashtrays and the scent in all its glorious incarnations. . . .

Converts to Hermès include the divine Yasmin Le Bon, charmer Nigel Havers, and transatlantic refugees, Sigourney Weaver and Bruce Willis. There is little that is cheap, but whatever you end up with in this bastion of bon chic bon genre, it will be undeniably exclusive and enduringly fashionable.

James Smith & Sons Ltd

53 New Oxford Street   071-836-4731
London WC1A 1BL

Founded in 1830, James Smith & Sons specializes in two accoutrements inexorably associated with the English gentleman—umbrellas and walking sticks. Indeed, we have a theory that the British were successful at ruling much of world because most of the colonials simply cowered in the face of these strange contraptions. These days, while the continuing demand for umbrellas is obvious, the fact that Smith's still considers walking sticks an important part of its business bears explanation. After all, the walking stick has long ceased to be an essential part of the well-dressed gentleman's attire, but the market remains surprisingly strong—primarily among collectors and Americans who consider them a very British souvenir indeed.

Today James Smith & Sons operates out of the unique Victorian shop front it has occupied since the original Mr Smith's son, also named James, moved the business there in 1857. Just two blocks from the British Museum, the corner building was once a dairy and was transformed by James Smith, the younger, to house not only his business, but his family as well. He, his wife and nine children lived above the shop until the prolific Mr Smith seemingly got bored with his various business interests (six others, including a barber shop and a hatters) in London and moved the family to Tasmania, in the remotest wilds of southern Australia, to engage in farming. His grandson R. H. Mesger, one of Smith's current directors, was born there and entered this particular family business about 1930.

It is a business that despite the modern use of plastic and nylon has changed very little—the basic structure of the umbrellas remains the same and the sticks are made of the same woods and made by much the same methods as they were when Smith's was founded. To pass under the British and American flags painted on glass (apparently James Smith has long valued its American clientele) and through the oak and glass doors is to travel through time to a more gentle era. You enter a forest of umbrellas, walking sticks and canes in every conceivable colour and wood, a scene surveyed by three majestic maces. Representative of the thriving business Smith's once did in ceremonial umbrellas and maces for African tribal chiefs, they are topped by proud silver animals—an elephant on the tallest and a rhinoceros on the other two, presumably symbolizing the strength of the chiefs for whom they were made.

You, too, can feel like a chief with a more modest but still impressive stick made of an exotic wood like ebony, rosewood or malacca and also sporting cunningly carved handles—dogs, foxes, birds or horses in ivory, horn, tortoiseshell, silver or even wood. Most can be fitted with bands for engraving and all can be cut to your height. Prices range from £10 to £650.

As for the umbrellas, they, too, are available in a number of treatments, from basic black for conservative males to tartans for the more adventuresome distaff. And, Smith's will gladly accommodate you with regard to school, club or corporate colours, just don't ask for silk—umbrellas require so much fabric that no matter how much you may normally abhor nylon, swallow your pride and go with it in this instance as the practical alternative. Custom orders take about three weeks and cost at least £50.

Off-the-rack brollies range from £40 to £250 for men and £15 to £200 for women. Unisex golf umbrellas start at £50. Don't be put off by those prices at the upper end of the scale. Assuming you don't lose it, a Smith's umbrella could last a lifetime. They're that well made and James Smith & Sons will happily effect any repairs that may ever become necessary. In fact, umbrella repairs represent a substantial portion of their business. They generally sell about 1,500 umbrellas a month (depending upon the weather) and fix 500—accepting faulty ones and then dispatching them, fixed good-as-new, by mail if need be. It's all part of the service. Remember Smith's hundred-year-plus love affair with their discreetly unnamed American customers.

True to the etiquette of a bygone era, the gentlemen at Smith's politely decline to drop any specific high-profile names. Rather, they diplomatically declare their pride in their international band of devotees, and then allow a tiny, titillating tidbit—James Smith & Sons supplied *The Avengers'* Patrick MacNee with his enviable umbrella wardrobe.

Katharine Hamnet Shop

20 Sloane Street   071-839-1002
London SW1

If you consider yourself sexy and like to dress that way, then this store is your mecca.

The clothes are meant to make men look studly, and women irresistibly seductive. At least that's what Katharine's PR person told us, and judging by the clothes, we do agree.

We saw the shortest, most flirtatious skirts, and black lycra/cotton/wool "cat" suits with spaghetti straps and sculptured bras. These are not for the office, ladies, but we know you'll find the right time and place to wear them. Just do your sit-ups and leg lifts before you try one on.

Everything tends to be tight and sexy, à la Madonna, even the tailored jackets, such as the long riding habit in khaki wool with a black velvet collar. At £228, this sultry number would be pretty hot over stretch leggings, and you don't need a horse either.

For men, there are some great leather and suede jackets in the £1,500 neighbourhood and an unusual blouson-cut style in black wool for £400.

This store is definitely not for the faint of heart. You've got to be in great shape physically and mentally to wear these clothes, which the hip clientele is. These people are definitely used to attracting attention.

The young and fashion-forward staff will help you put together just the right ensemble for that night on the town. Once you get used to the store, you'll realize that the clothes are actually more wearable and flexible than you first thought. Just relax and open up, maybe you'll find a seductive new you lurking under that tailored suit.

The store itself, designed by Nigel Coates, is certainly a fashion statement, on sophisticated Sloane Street. At first glance, the front window looks like a multiscreen, multimedia presentation, with video monitors piled high. Then you realize that they are fishtanks serving as a backdrop for shelves! Very clever. The leather couch is in the shape of big, bright red lips. Sculptural fixtures topped with glass globes accent the walls, and the fitting rooms form a semicircle at the back, with heavy, oversized curtains draped to the floor. It really is quite a dramatic setting for selecting a trendy look.

Who would have thought a woman graduating from Cheltenham Ladies College would grow up to be such a provocative and savvy clothing designer? But that's just what Katharine Hamnet did.

She freelanced in New York, Paris, Rome and London before launching her first store back in 1979. In 1982, she received a "Designer of the Year" award from the International Institute for Cotton. You may remember her "Choose Life" T-shirts of 1983, emblazoned with messages like "Education Not Missiles" and "Preserve the Rain Forests." Clearly a designer in touch with the world, before the world was in touch with itself.

After she won "Designer of the Year" from the British Fashion Industry in 1984, she designed for "Fashion Aid" and "Clean up or Die" in the late 1980s. She moved her production to Italy in 1989, and today you can find her fabulous designs at shops in Australia, Germany, Japan, the U.S. and Spain, just to name a few.

So, if you're already avant garde, or want to be, stroll into Katharine Hamnet's store and unveil your most daring enticing self.   🌱

Loewe

25 Old Bond Street	071-493-3914
London W1X 3AA	(FAX) 071-408-1370

Loewe and leather, leather and Loewe—virtually interchangeable words in certain circles, ours included. Ever since a German emigrant by the name of Enrique Loewe founded the company in his adopted Spain in 1846, Loewe has been making leather goods and garments with "passion and precision." Indeed, 145 years after the first Loewe boutique opened in Madrid, Enrique's great-grandson is in charge of the firm's ever-expanding fortunes. Under his skilful management, Loewe has broadened its horizons well beyond Spain to Hong Kong, Japan, Australia, France, the U.S. and Britain, while maintaining standards that require the purchase of the finest skin and the workmanship of true artisans.

Loewe hit London in the late '60s, and the city embraced the company's winning way with leather. There really is something distinctively soft about Loewe leather—there is a sensuality about it, tempered by meticulous detail. Many of the techniques used to tan and work the leather are identical to those first employed by Enrique in the middle of the 19th century. Loewe maintains that its artisans feel an affinity with the leather, that their work is "as much an 'affair' as it is a 'labour'; as much a subtle art as it is a craft." And it shows.

It also smells—upon entering the monochrome, tan shop with its pear wood and brass vitrines as counterpoint to a rather imposing staircase, you have to take a moment or two to recover from the dizzying effects of the enticing aroma of fine skins. Once you've steadied yourself, take advantage of general manager Edwina Ellis's exceptional knowledge and aesthetic sense. Pretty, pert and with a complexion for which we would glady die, she offers terrific guidance when it comes to assembling a leather wardrobe. She understands how Loewe leather caresses the body with its extraordinary, not to mention long-lasting, flexibility and knows what styles will best suit you—just as she knows what the Duchess of York and Lady Rothermere should wear.

Like those two good-time girls, we find the skirts, jackets and trousers irresistible. They feel and look like liquid on our bodies—liquid gold, that is, at prices that start at £320 for a skirt and can go up to £1,600 for a jacket made of nappa, the Rolls-Royce of leathers, worked to a buttery softness from calves' or lambs' skin. For men, the heavenly suede and leather jackets styled to withstand fashion's test of time run from £950 to £1,250.

At the other end of the scale, we were smitten with a precious little nappa changepurse. Round and sealed with a jazzy zipper, it's available in a broad range of colours, from bright to basic, and costs only £13. It makes a great souvenir gift for the folks back home. For more serious money, there are wallets, made of grainy, durable astragalina and derby leathers, designed to encase specific currencies. The billfold meant for pounds sterling and credit cards runs £120, its American counterpart £150. And there are a couple versions for yen, from £98 to £129.

Naturally, handbags are an important part of Loewe's business and, just as naturally, they incorporate the company's distinctive insignia— four fluid *L*s joined so that they could almost (but not quite) be mistaken for just a pretty pattern worked into the leather. You see, if they were too circumspect, it would take all the fun out of proclaiming to the world that you had spent £400 on a pocketbook! In all fairness, many sell for considerably less. Even a small nappa bag can be had for about £110.

Still, we think clothes are what Loewe does best. Where else could you find a fitted, navy blue, pinstriped suede jacket coupled with a slim white leather skirt? Where else, indeed.

Marks & Spencer

458 Oxford Street   071-935-7954
Marble Arch   (FAX) 071-486-5379
London W1N OAP

Enter this amazing 100,000 square-foot store with four gigantic floors overflowing with absolutely everything, and you'll understand why Marks & Spencer's Marble Arch store is featured in the *Guinness Book of World Records* as "the store with the fastest moving stock in the world."

On a typical day, you'll see customers carrying home 200 men's suits, 3,000 pairs of socks, and 600 pairs of ladies' shoes. And that's just from the Marble Arch store. If you can't find it here, it doesn't exist.

It's hard to believe this empire grew from a simple peddler named Michael Marks, who first sold his wares at Leeds-Kirkgate market in 1884. Mr Marks was a great public relations man and had a natural flair for attracting customers: he marked all his items with a note that read, "Don't ask the price. . . it's a penny." Of course, he became the most popular merchant at the market and soon had a thriving business.

In 1894, Marks teamed up with Tom Spencer, and by 1900 the team had penny bazaars in 23 market halls, and "branch establishments" in 11 other places. Fifteen years later, they had grown to 145, and by 1988, Marks & Spencer—M&S—had become an international corporation with an incredible 292 U.K. stores, 11 in Europe, 275 in Canada and the U.S., one in Japan, 33 in Hong Kong and one in Hungary. Who could ever have dreamed two young merchants would create such a successful empire?

One reason for its continuing success is that the company has stayed in the family for quite a number of years. The chairman from 1972 to 1984 was Michael Mark's grandson, Lord Marcus Sieff. Although Lord Sieff is now retired, he's still honorary president of M&S, and takes note of everything that goes on. Lord Rayner, the recently retired chairman, had started as a trainee manager when he was 26, as had his successor, Richard Greenbury. Today, he's still expanding the M&S empire. So you can see this is a business that has stayed in the family a very long time and is still run today by people who manage it with familial care.

Marks & Spencer has about 2.2 million charge customers, and somewhere around 100,000 people shop there every day. You will find the diversity of goods incredible: from designer bras to delicate bone china, from pillows to peppermills. A bar of chocolate is 22p, a man's suit from

£99 to £225, and a furniture suite is £1,000. No matter how much is in your budget, there's something at M&S you can buy. Of course, browsing is perfectly acceptable, but we think you'll be tempted by at least one item.

We found lots of great bargains: silk shirts for women at £35, men's shirts from £10 to £27.50, and sensational leather bomber jackets from £125 to £250.

The lingerie department has an enormous selection of classic silk robes at £90, nightshirts at £20, slips in every length from mini to midi and underwear (called knickers, by the way) from £2.50 to £8.99.

The kid's department for 1 to 14 year olds has darling sneakers that zip on the side, and cute snowsuits for £20.

Don't miss the home decorating department, with the fantastic selection of bedding, sheets, duvets and wallpapers. Everything is coordinated so you could design an entire room here.

The feather and down quilts run from £25 to £27. (Overseas visitors should remember to take the length and width measurements of their beds, because English sizes differ from those in the U.S., Japan, and other countries.)

One special aspect of M&S is that the store has its very own label, called St Michael. Throughout the store you'll see it on a number of beautiful, reasonably priced items. In fact, 90 per cent of everything in the store is British made. The management truly believes in supporting the local economy, and feels the British dedication to quality is what pleases customers most.

One department we promise will please you is the downstairs supermarket of delights, which sells smoked salmon, lobster, fresh crab, pork pies, vegetarian goodies and even spicy Indian cuisine. If you're dieting, you'll be happy to know that M&S hasn't forgotten you, because there are luscious low-calorie foods as well. No one has to leave hungry.

One last reminder: remember to bring cash with you because M&S does not take credit cards (except for its own, which only U.K. citizens can get). There's a bank on the second floor, though, where you can exchange your travellers' cheques for cash or get cash from an American Express card, if you've brought your personal identification number.

In any case, with all the wonderful bargains at Marks & Spencer, you'll surely find the perfect something at the right price. Or at the very least, you'll have a delightful time looking.

N. Peal

37, 54 & 71 Burlington Arcade   071-493-2990
London W1V 9AE   (FAX) 071-734-1345

Much of the fashion passion for cashmere can be traced to Nat Peal's wartime service for his native Britain. You see, the wool knit hats, gloves and scarves he sent home to his wife from his Shetland Islands post proved to be best sellers in the family's Burlington Arcade shop—a notable discovery, given the fact that it had opened in 1939 as a shop specializing in silk goods. Slowly the focus of the business changed, and by 1946, N. Peal was so established as a purveyor of fine woollens that Ballantyne cashmere adopted the firm as an outlet—the Scottish connection was solidified and the cashmere connection made.

Nat broadened his market, and that for cashmere, by being one of the first Brits to travel regularly to the U.S. to stage very successful trunk shows. But the shot heard 'round the world was N. Peal's gift of a cashmere jacket to Jackie Kennedy during the early days of "Camelot." A photograph of the charismatic First Lady modelling the jacket was widely published, and N. Peal found itself firmly positioned on the international fashion map. Today, the firm enjoys a worldwide reputation for fashionably styled, superior Scottish cashmere.

And, in fact, N. Peal has been in the fashion vanguard by expanding cashmere's application from casual V-neck sweaters and sensible cardigans to sultry, spaghetti-strapped dinner dresses, delicate camisoles and body-hugging minis. The person responsible for the recent styling innovations at N. Peal is Gillian Hunter, who has a flair for shape and colour—for both sexes. We could live in her wide-legged, turtleneck jumpsuit, available in up to 30 colours, for about £650. Cashmere leggings topped with a long, cable-knit sweater is another terrific informal look for £475 to £700, depending upon the intricacy and weight of the cable stitching. For decadent summer relaxation, check out the single-ply sweatshirt at £210.

Gentlemen can assume a similar comfort level in a dreamy, reversible, argyle sweatshirt for £645. But given the fact that it's a snug eight-ply weight, it's more suitable for autumnal leisure hours. And if we were Rosalynn Carter, we'd update hubby Jimmy's look with a très chic double-breasted cardigan, sporting a jaunty shawl collar at £575.

As appealing as both the merchandise and the glass-fronted stores are, shopping here does require a modicum of patience. Square footage is not a Burlington Arcade strong suit—the tiny shop is almost always crowded. To avoid the hordes, you can seek N. Peal's "caress of cashmere" in its boutiques at Harvey Nichols and Liberty, but you'll suffer in the selection department. Here, men, women and children can, quite literally, be outfitted head to toe in cashmere—what a happy thought!

Even happier is the notion of combining two of our favourite luxury items—cashmere and fur—to create the ultimate oversized cape, trimmed with sable tails. At £1,200, it's the closest we're likely to get to ownership of a sable coat in the foreseeable future.   🍎

Polo/Ralph Lauren

143 New Bond Street	071-491-4967
London W1Y 9FD	(FAX) 071-409-2603

If ever an American designer and a foreign country were made for each other, it's Ralph Lauren and Britain. This good old boy from the Bronx has for years been peddling the contrived, yet casual look of the English aristocracy when esconced on their sprawling estates. He's done so with such great success that their American counterparts, and those who strive to be, have adopted it as a veritable uniform. So it follows that Ralph experimented with creating a selling environment, mimicking the lifestyle he perpetuates here, in London, before pulling out all the stops in the Madison Avenue mansion that now is his flagship store.

Originally opened as a franchise in 1981 by the Burstein family, the proprietors of Browns who know a thing or two about retailing and merchandising themselves, the store was bought by Ralph in 1983. He took the long, narrow, former chemist's shop, which once dispensed Lord Nelson's prescriptions, and refitted it to create a cultivated, homely atmosphere. The delightful scent of potpourri greets his "guests," while handsome area rugs soften their tread on the lustrous hardwood floors. Muted, easy-listening music (as opposed to Muzak) permeates the air and two cosy sitting rooms at the rear of the store, each with a fireplace, extend cordial hospitality—flames crackle in the grates during the winter and almost any holiday justifies the serving of festive refreshments. And everywhere—always—arrangements of fresh flowers brighten the decor. As anticipated, you feel as if you're being regally entertained by the

Laurens themselves and find yourself wondering when Ricki is going to announce dinner.

Despite all appearances, however, this most definitely is a commercial establishment, chock full of very buyable merchandise. Cases at the front of the store contain antique jewelry and silver frames, most of them late Victorian, and all of them instant heirlooms. You'll also find handsome pocket flasks dating from the early years of this century, mixed in with Ralph's small leather goods, circa 1991.

But the real draw is the clothes that define the Ralph Lauren lifestyle—an array of country chic garments, from sweaters, ties, suits and vests for men along with slacks, skirts, blazers and blouses for women. The selection is more than adequate but by no means vast. And what with the demand of the Japanese, French and even Americans who flock here, nothing seems to stay in stock very long, not even (maybe *especially* even) the gorgeous £400 hand-knit sweaters or the £300 crocodile belts.

Even the British, who ostensibly originated the look, update it with Ralph Lauren fashions. Margaret Levin, whose hubby owns the Capital Hotel, is so fond of Ralph's interpretations of aristocratic casual that she not only dresses in his creations, but she also decorated the rooms of the family's charming hostelry with his fabrics and linens. Ironic isn't it? One of the first of London's English country home hotels owes its quiet elegance to a poor kid from very urban New York City, who made good— *very* good.   ❦

Skindeep

49 & 53 South Molton Street	071-499-3550
London W1U 18E	071-493-4920

In Greece, Dimitri Pappas' family is famous for shoes, made of leather. In London *he's* famous for leather of all kinds—leather jackets, leather suits, leather skirts, leather belts and leather cowboy boots. Indeed, Dimitri is the proud possessor of the largest selection of cowboy boots in town.

Made in Spain by Tony Mora, they are, according to Dimitri, the "Rolls-Royce of boots," though at £100 to £220 a pair their modest price doesn't reflect their status. While the boots are available in a wide variety of leathers, from cowhide to lizard, there are just two tried-and-true styles—the classic Cuban heel with pointed toe and the more subdued flat heel with rounded toe. Either way, they're blissfully comfortable, once on the foot. It's getting them on that can be a bit of a problem, but at SD, the larger of the two shops, Dimitri's charming assistant, Jacqueline, is generally around to lend a hand. She's an expert at the fine art of booting and is a patient teacher to the novice. Jacqueline puts your foot in a plastic bag and guides it down the shoot while you grip the loops on either side of the boot and shove. As you might expect, getting a new boot off can be just as difficult as getting it on. Once again, it's Jacqueline to the rescue as she pulls while you sit on the stairs and clutch the railing.

If all this seems like too much trouble, and you have no interest in playing at Clint Eastwood or the Lone Ranger, there's still plenty of reason to stop by Dimitri's shops. For one thing, there's that divine, seductive scent of fine leather everywhere—it's worth a visit just for a whiff. Indeed, Skindeep, decorated in warm tones of russet and brown from floor to ceiling, highlighted by bright spots on the most dramatic jackets and boots seems like a cosy leather tent.

SD (son of Skindeep) is larger, more subdued and arguably more elegant than its predecessor, all done up in white and grey. One wall boasts two tiers of artistically arranged jackets, basically designed for men but quite capable of being worn by women. Towards the rear of the shop is an area definitely devoted to the ladies, with suits and skirts made of the most supple of leathers and suedes, from £245 to £345, depending on your preference for a full or straight skirt.

Both SD and Skindeep specialize in sheepskin jackets. While the skins comes from Italy, the garments are manufactured in England. Designed by a young team, the look is definitely masculine, but there tends to be enough detail on the jackets to make them appealing to women. Sheepskin collars are processed to stand in for leopard or mink and are detachable, as are the cuffs. The collars and pockets of other jackets are trimmed in calf and accented by leather buttons. Prices of the sheepskin numbers start at about £150 and go to £700, while more traditional (and basic) suede jackets stay in the £100 to £300 range.

Dimitri's shops also feature something called the New Buck Jacket. The "New Buck" refers to a recently refined technique of leather processing which involves removing the top layer of skin and then oiling and waxing the newly exposed stratum. The result is an all-weather leather impervious even to London's rainy days—a New Buck Jacket, once drenched, can simply be hung up to dry, rather than rushed to the dry cleaner for some tender loving care to restore its colour and shape. Durable, handsomely cut in a square silhouette with two deep pockets and benefitting from the insulating powers of a quilted lining, the New Buck Jacket is a must for the outdoorsman, from £150 to £350.

For women who are more interested in making an entrance than in being a knock-out outdoors, there are graceful, three-quarter length suede coats with a cape effect in the back for £295, full-length suedes for £425 and leather coats from £400. On the accessories front, there are belts, gloves and hats for both men and women starting at £30.

At Skindeep and SD, with their soft, sumptuous, yummy-smelling goods, it's very clear that Dimitri Pappas' knowledge of and experience with leather is more than. . . skindeep!   ❦

Swaine Adeney Brigg & Son Ltd

| 185/186 Piccadilly | 071-734-4277 |
| London W1V OHA | (FAX) 071-494-1976 |

Like many English firms, Swaine Adeney Brigg goes to great pains to trace its lineage as far back as possible, taking what might be considered the occasional liberty. In this instance, they peg the date of the firm's founding at "sometime before 1750," when James Ross started making whips. Apparently he was pretty good at it, as he held the Royal Appointment of Whip Maker to King George III and "probably" to King George II before him. In any case, you notice there's no Ross in the company's name these days—seems he was "succeeded" by a Swaine, James by name, in 1790. James managed to hold on to the Royal Warrant, as have all his successors to this very day. Indeed, in addition to being Queen Elizabeth's whip and glove makers (the two going hand in hand), the shop supplies umbrellas to her mother and leather goods to her bonnie Prince Charlie.

But we digress in tracing the shop's long history. At some point the Adeneys entered the picture, consolidating their position in 1802 when one married a Swaine. The last chairman, Robert Swaine Adeney, was a member of the seventh generation, but sold the business to Reg Connell.

So where does the "Brigg" come from? Well, Thos. Brigg & Son was famous in its own right for its superior handmade, wooden shaft umbrella, first introduced in 1836. The company was acquired by Swaine Adeney during World War II, creating a double identity. To this day, the firm tends to refer to itself and to most of its products as Swaine Adeney or Swaine & Adeney, yet it is internationally famous for the Brigg umbrella, which is the only one in the world still made entirely by hand. Indeed, a not inconsiderable number of people insist on calling the store "Brigg's." You see, a Brigg umbrella is virtually a required accessory for anyone serious about demonstrating their discerning taste. Although, we don't recommend the £7,500 gold-handled number mounted with diamonds and rubies for that purpose! But you might get away with the £2,400 solid ivory crook (read *handle*) and malacca stem (shaft) beauty, adorned by a nine-carat gold collar.

If you're an habitual loser of umbrellas, don't choke on these prices. The classic Brigg, complete with malacca handle, gold-plated collar on which initials and date can be engraved, and "best English black silk" covering is £365. And it's an investment you can expect will last a lifetime. Witness the elderly gentleman who recently strolled into the ground-floor umbrella department, intent upon having his Brigg repaired because the silk was slightly frayed. Actually, he stalked in as he was upset by the necessity of the repair and was not at all placated when the salesman politely pointed out that the date on the collar read 1923. The gentleman still felt that, despite 65 years of loyal service, this should not have happened. Since he allowed as how the umbrella had accompanied him during the "troubles with India," on his honeymoon, and in countless other significant events during his life, we imagine his angst was more related to being separated from his precious brolly than by anything else!

At any rate, Swaine & Adeney was happy to restore it. The Essex factory is as devoted to repairs as it is to new production, regularly dispatching fixed Briggs to their owners all over the world. So, what is really behind the mystique about these umbrellas? It has a lot to do with their height and the size of their handles. At Swaine & Adeney you are essentially fitted for an umbrella—the appropriate size is selected to match your frame. The result is that its height and feel are just right for adding a little confident swagger to your walk.

Determining the correct size is the easy part. After that comes the dilemma of which umbrella is really *you*. To begin with, you have to decide whether to go with the classic or traditional construction. The latter is produced by tapering a solid walking stick, producing an umbrella which is particularly strong. When folded, the tips of this style lie above the handle. The classic incorporates a separate handle and stick, and its tips nestle below the bottom of the handle, creating a slim, elegant appearance. Either way, there is an amazing assortment to choose from, involving handles made of every conceivable material, including silver, lizard and ostrich, devised for every imaginable purpose—for travelling there's one with a detachable tip and top, allowing it to fold into a more manageable size at £110; for drinking, there's one with a flask; for defense, there's one with a sword; and for betting, there's one outfitted with a gold-plated racing pencil. Should you have yet another need for an umbrella, the shop will custom design one for you. It takes three to six weeks, and the costs vary, as you might expect.

For those who expect nothing more from an umbrella than for it to protect them from getting wet, there's the standard £75 model, produced in bulk with a nylon cover. ❦

Trussardi

51 South Molton Street   071-629-5611
London W1Y 1HS

Arguably South Molton's most elegant shop, this two-storey melody of marble, glass and brass fittings harmoniously blended with caramel coloured walls houses all that is Trussardi, from clothes to perfumes. As such, it is the flagship of Italian designer boutiques in London—Nicola Trussardi was the first to establish a British beachhead. But then he's been the first to do a lot of things. In the days before *glasnost,* he was the first Western fashion designer to be invited to stage a show in Moscow, and his was the first Italian house to export.

Even his entry into the world of fashion was something in the way of a first. Having expanded a leather goods company to include clothes, he was denied a bid to participate in the seasonal Milan shows, the best organized of European fashion exhibitions, stalked by John Fairchild's *Chic Savages.* He promptly hired La Scala and produced his first show without the sanction of the Italian version of Paris' Chambre Syndicate for a stellar audience from the worlds of politics, finance, business and arts. The response was rousingly enthusiastic, launching a fashion empire which now spans the globe with Trussardi boutiques in 15 countries.

In London, one of Nicola's fellow Milanese is in charge, Fabiana Baiardi. She's rightfully proud of his innovative but never overstated designs and the high level of personal service her little shop affords its clients. Indeed, Fabiana encourages out-of-town regulars to call ahead when they're planning a trip to London so that she can put together a sampling of things Trussardi that she thinks they might like.

For the younger set, she might select from Trussardi's gesture to the trend of modifying the classic tuxedo for both sexes. For men, there's a handsome, short-cropped evening jacket accompanied by trousers with a built-on cummerbund for £650. More traditional looks sell for £580 to £600. For women, we vote for adopting his long, tailored, black wool crepe jacket with oversized pleated satin collar over a short straight skirt for *the* evening uniform.

More sporting looks include figure-flattering pleated slacks for men and women in richly coloured wools for £150, cotton shirts and silk blouses to top them, sumptuously textured and printed sweaters to complement the lot (£200 to £250), and softly constructed coats to layer over the whole ensemble. Time-honoured camel-hair coats range from £400 to £600, and chic shearlings start at £1,200. Indeed, Signor Trussardi seems to have a particular facility for leather (not surprising, considering his roots)—we were mad about a sensuously cut suede suit at £660. And leather goods remain a part of his repertoire. There's a complete line of luggage in black or tan, including a £290 tennis bag and a £400 golf bag that any caddy would be proud to carry. We also liked the distinctive collection of purses in tan with contrasting trim—bright colours for spring and summer, dark for autumn and winter and priced at £150 to £250.

The range of Trussardi accessories includes address books and the omnipresent Filofax. Finally, there are the luminously printed silk scarves starting at £80, as well as a group of body lotions and scents for men and women that should not be overlooked. In the unlikely event that nothing strikes your fancy, ask Fabiana about the briarwood handled Parmesan cheese knife. Usually tucked away, almost hidden, in a display cabinet, it's a practical, yet frivolous gem for £80.

Trussardi truly is a unified little world that reflects a precise and very refined taste.

FOR SPORTS

Captain O.M. Watts

49 Albemarle Street	(24 hours) 071-493-4633/8845
London W1X 4BJ 3FE	(FAX) 071-495-0755

Yes, indeed, there really was a Captain Watts who first opened a ship's chandler's on Maddox Street in 1927. In fact, he was a mariner of some note who plied the seas during the last great days of sail. Later, his instruction of emergency off-shore navigation courses to essentially on-shore sailors was crucial to the dramatic evacuation of Dunkirk. There is much about this paradise for seafaring browsers that the old salt would recognize today—the store that bears his name is fully prepared to outfit any yacht—power or sail—from stem to stern, from brass portholes to automatic pilots. It is a genuine, fully equipped chandler's right smack in the middle of Mayfair, just steps from the Ritz and Brown's, that draws serious yachtsmen from all over the world.

It also attracts plenty of what yacht brokers like to call "lookie-loos"—people who have nautical aspirations, but not the money to realize them. Here, at least, they can fulfil their dreams to some degree, if only with the purchase of books from London's largest sailing library, or a £3.95 brass keyring fashioned as an anchor. Indeed, the main floor resembles nothing so much as a giant blond-wood footlocker, loaded with gear—watertight jackets and trousers, bulky knit sweaters, rubber boots and leather topsiders. There are always plenty of people routing through it, plenty who know what they're looking for and plenty who don't. Proud members of the former group, we were impressed with the Musto foul-weather gear which is worn by the Whitbread racing crew. What hasn't been provided for on the £199 bright red Ocean jacket in the way of safety has no business being there.

Not into the finer points of thermal clothes or buoyancy liners? Well, you can certainly appreciate the nautical antiques department with its fascinating assembly of sextants, barographs, bells, lamps and tele-scopes, which harken back to a time when form more beautifully fol-lowed function than it does today. This is an essential port of call for gift hunters and collectors, both of whom should know that Captain Watts' undertakes commissions to locate and obtain specific items. Talk to

Gillian Gould about what it is that you've been looking for to no avail—odds are she'll find it.

Which is pretty much the case for contemporary equipment as well. Down the stairs at the front of the shop is the chandlery floor. There you can happily indulge in the yachtsmen's practice that William F. Buckley describes as standing in a cold shower and tearing up thousand-dollar bills—actually, he said hundreds, but we're allowing for inflation. At any rate, what Captain Watt's doesn't sell neither you nor your boat needs—the oversized glossy catalogue is 103 pages long, and each page profiles as many as 50-plus items. Staggering isn't the word for it.

But Captain O.M. Watts isn't just about products; service plays a proud role here, too. That 24-hour number is put to good and frequent use by clients from all over the world. Not too long ago a customer of long standing called from Singapore for £50 worth of badly needed parts. Watts delivered them to him within 48 hours. Furthermore, the firm offers insurance, boat maintenance and valet plans, navigation courses, and chart updating on a weekly basis, if necessary. In other words, you can buy a boat, any boat, and then consign it and yourself to Captain Watts' caring, knowledgeable hands to be made ready for conquering the seven seas.

No wonder that people who grew up with a yachting heritage—people like the King of Norway and Prince Michael—as well as those that did not, like Michael Caine, rely on Captain Watts. Whoever you are, or aren't, you can be sure of the great equalizer that is the sea washing ashore here. Courteous, respectful service is the norm. No one brooks special treatment, not even Princess Alexandra. When she recently wrote a cheque for a purchase, the clerk politely gave it back to her, asking for an address!

W. & H. Gidden

15D Clifford Street	071-734-2788
New Bond Street	(FAX) 071-494-2388
London W1X 1RF	

The intoxicating aroma of top-grade leather lures you off New Bond Street, up an ancient lane and across a well-trod threshold into horse heaven. Take a good look around. You're likely to spot Paul McCartney, his ex-Beatle buddy Ringo Starr, Rod Steiger, or the Queen of Spain ordering a new saddle or tack for their trusty steeds. They rely on the expert advice of Michael Gidden, the great-great-grandson of the firm's founder, and you should too, no matter the calibre of your star status. In Michael's benevolent eyes, all horse fanciers are created equal.

Of course, some are more equal than others. And the purchase of a Stuben saddle, priced from about £610 to £850, may be the dividing line. Gidden, founded in 1794, is the British distributor of these famous saddles and, as the result of the fine seat of their own brand, is the proud saddlemaker for the Queen.

As you might expect of such a venerable company, standards are high in terms of quality and service. All Gidden's saddlemakers are required to serve long apprenticeships, and the manufacturing process is done the old-fashioned way—one craftsman lovingly works with a saddle from start to finish in the firm's London facility. Equal care and attention are paid to repairs. If your harness needs some work, this is the place to take it. It's also the place to visit for the best selection of bits; headstalls, including copper snaffles; plastic and rubber pelhams, and all thicknesses of reins in the city. Head for the saddlery proper on the lower level of the shop, which looks deceptively small from the outside.

It turns out that there are three floors, connected by a perilously narrow staircase. Indeed, although Gidden started out strictly as a saddlery, these days they carry just about everything associated with riding, "except the feed," jokes Michael. Upstairs, there's a complete line of clothes for men and women, including classic habits, like the master hunt reds, and terrific looking sports separates that make you look like the proud owner of an expensive mount, even if you've never put boot to stirrup.

We loved a beautifully tailored ladies' country tweed jacket in subtle shades of brown and just a touch of blue for £160. And, of course, there are plenty of those oh-so-necessary riding helmets, as well as a range of saucy reinforced top hats.

Equine accessories are equally well represented. What horse wouldn't be eternally grateful for a soft lambswool saddlepad, sized and styled to match each of the saddles offered?

The ground floor is the source of that aroma that so effectively attracts people here in the first place. It's chock full of all sorts of wonderful-smelling leather goods and gifts. We were very taken with the handsome, very solid-looking saddle-leather briefcases with the eye-catching brass buckles. Think of the impression you'll make plopping one of those babies down on a conference table!

Besides all the functional and tweedy clothing we've already told you about, not surprisingly Gidden is a first-rate source for fantastic riding boots. They range in price from £190 for basic ready-to-wear designs to £700 for custom-made. All are beautifully constructed, and many of the styles are quite fashionable. You don't have to be a horse lover to adore these boots. Just wear them with a sporty tweed jacket and a suede skirt to effect that classic Ralph Lauren look. Perfect for a country weekend.

Whether you're a true equestrian or just a leather connoisseur, a visit to Gidden's is not to be missed. It may even inspire you to take those riding lessons you've been putting off.

Holland & Holland Limited

33 Bruton Street	071-499-4411
London W1X 8JS	(FAX) 071-499-4544

Generally speaking, hobbies are gobblers of vast sums of money, but occasionally an enthusiast turns his avocation into a money-making enterprise. Such is the case of one Harris J. Holland, a successful tobacconist and noted shooter of his day, who in 1835 opened a shop dedicated to the highest state of the gunmaker's art. Today, the firm he established 156 years ago is internationally known as the world's finest maker of double-barreled rifles for big game and is one of only two major manufacturers of firearms left in London (see James Purdey & Sons Ltd).

Left is the operative word here. At one time there were any number—mostly concentrated in Mayfair and Soho—indicative of the fact that, by the turn of the century, London had become the gunmaking capital of the world. It was an industry born of the 1780s when the growing popularity of sport shooting throughout the country launched the emergence of the British as the world's premier crafters of guns. The advent of the practice of animal husbandry substantially increased the game population by the mid 1800s just as the ranks of the middle class were growing. And the Industrial Revolution gave them more leisure time to indulge in shooting. The law of supply and demand kicked in and the English game gun appeared. Light and well balanced, it was meant to be carried in the field all day, yet it was unfailingly reliable, called upon to fire hundreds of rounds a day.

Shooting was so much in vogue that competitions were held every Monday (when there was no racing to bet on) in Hyde and Battersea Parks. In fact, legend has it that London's legions of pigeons are the descendents of the proverbial ones that got away. At any rate, the competitions were testing grounds for the city's great gunmakers, most of whom operated along the lines of a cottage industry. Only Holland & Holland and Purdey had their own factories, which gave them considerable advantage in terms of design and technical innovations.

Still, the basic firing mechanism has changed little in the last 200 years. According to Holland & Holland's ruggedly blond sales manager, James Booth, there have been "certain refinements over the years, but basically the design is a thoroughbred"—a description that is equally appropriate to the shop he oversees. Stately stag and other game heads dot the pine-panelled walls, surveying a clubby scene reminscent of a gun library. New guns, including a spectacular presentation model embellished with elaborate ornamentation in precious metals for £200,000, are displayed on one wall, while their older brethren are lined up for repair along the opposite.

Indeed, vintage guns are treated with special care and affection here. We watched one member of the staff reverently unpack a 50- or 60-year-old rifle which had suffered badly from too many years of storage in a dank cellar. As he laid it out on a leather-topped table, he muttered about what a shame it was to allow such a fine piece to get into such condition. Then he looked up and told us not to worry, "we can fix it." Of course, it wasn't our gun, but he just assumed we would have the same concern about its sorry state as he did. Indeed, it is a pity that it should have been treated so cavalierly, when you consider a new Holland & Holland gun requires about 700 to 900 hours to make and costs from £5,000 to £37,000.

Of course, we're talking about the haute couture of guns here. Each is made to "fit" its purchaser. Measurements are taken at the firm's shooting grounds on Ducks Hill Road, Northwood, using an adjustable gun. The hand-finished stocks are made of the finest French walnut—the English variety grows too slowly and is therefore too dense and too heavy. And the ornamental engraving is exquisitely hand-carved to the customer's specifications. Indeed, James tells us that in recent years there has been a renaissance in that particular facet of gunmaking. Much more ornate artwork has come into play since World War II.

If you can't wait a year or so for a gun, there's usually a good range of second-hand models for sale in the £8,000 to £10,000 neighbourhood. And if that's more money than you had in mind or if you're in the market for a starter gun, Holland & Holland does sell "other people's" (read *cheaper*) guns. Whatever you purchase, they're prepared to teach you to use it properly and safely at the shooting grounds, where lessons for every type of shooter are available—from novice to experienced competitor. And they'll make sure you look the part—the Holland & Holland shop next door to the gun store carries a complete line of sporting togs and accessories.   ❦

James Purdey & Sons Ltd

57–58 South Audley Street	071-499-1801/5292
London W1Y 6ED	(FAX) 071-355-3257

For six generations, more than 175 years, James Purdey & Sons have been supplying exceptional, hand-crafted guns to the world's sportier sportspeople—those who can afford to ante up at least £23,000. Actually, you don't have to fork it over all at once. You see, the painstaking nature of the work involved in the manufacture of Purdey guns means that it takes at least two years to produce each one. So there is what might be described as an easy-payment plan—one-third deposit when the order is placed, another third when the action (the firing mechanism) is forged, and the final third paid before delivery.

True works of art, Purdey guns are built in the company's own factory where craftspeople are trained under a traditional apprenticeship scheme. There are six distinct categories of production—barrel making, actioning, ejectoring, stocking, engraving and finishing—each of which requires at least five years of training to master. To connoisseurs each is worthy of rapturous praise, but even pikers like us can appreciate the beauty of the finished product, particularly the rich glow of the French walnut stock and the intricacy of the engraving on the metal casing that encloses the working parts.

The stock is cut to ensure absolute wood-to-metal fit, a hallmark of Purdey quality and essential to the inherent strength of the gun. Then it is shaped to meet the client's measurements. Measurements? Yes, indeed. These are bespoke guns and require the recording of precise physical dimensions, like "centre back to point of shoulder" and "bend of elbow to trigger finger." There are 10 measurements in all, which explains why it's necessary to visit the red-brick monument to Victorian excess that quarters Purdey's offices and showrooms. You can't just call up and say, "I'll take two."

Furthermore, there are other decisions to be dealt with, decisions best made in the red splendour of the Long Room. Its walls filled with Purdey family portraits and shields, along with an interesting collection of shooting photographs and records, the chamber is both boardroom and showroom. You sit at the massive centre table in one of the ornately carved high-backed chairs and chat with managing director Lawrence Salter about your needs, gun-wise. Purdey guns are designed according to clients' shooting preferences—i.e., pheasant, grouse, quail, duck, upland game, etc. Each may require different barrel lengths or triggers. Moreover, *where* you shoot is important. English game guns are chambered for $2^{1/2}''$ cartridges, while American and Continental standard cartridges are $2^{3/4}''$.

Having dealt with all that, there's still the issue of engraving. A pattern known as "fine rose and scroll" has long been a trademark of Purdey guns and is included in the basic price. However, the firm has a tradition of producing extra finish guns upon which the engraving is done entirely to the customer's specifications, often incorporating game scenes or gold inlay lettering. Naturally, the price depends upon the extent of the work and can be estimated once you've settled upon the design.

Having gone to all the trouble and expense of owning such a fine machine, you should probably take it one step farther and be completely outfitted for the sporting life by Purdey. On Mount Street, right next door to the gun shop, is the James Purdey and Sons Accessories Shop, where you can find quality clothing along with such necessities as shooting seats, gun covers, clay pigeons and cartridge cases. Talk about one-stop shopping! One visit to Purdey and, two years plus a probable minimum of £25,000 later, you will be all set to make a real impression at one of the prestigious annual shoots on assorted Scottish estates. Of course, you'll need two years to wangle an invitation.

FOR THE HOME

Asprey

165/169 New Bond Street	071-493-6767
London W1 OAR	(FAX) 071-491-0384

One of the most beguiling stores in the city, inside and out, this resplendent emporium is truly an Aladdin's cave of treasures. Anticipation ripples through our bodies whenever the uniformed doorman ushers us through the concave paned-glass doors. We're ready to be enchanted and our first sight of the old-fashioned columned interior that fairly sparkles with crystal, silver and objets d'art never disappoints. Nor does the exceptional and often unique quality of the merchandise ever fail to yield gift-giving inspiration.

Furthermore, the staff, benevolently overseen by chairman John Asprey and his cousin Edward, are unwavering in their polite helpfulness. Newcomers and old reliable regulars are treated with equal respect. No one is ever allowed to feel like an intruder in these hallowed halls, an impression all too often given in other such tony stores. This is a family owned and run operation dating from 1781, and it shows. John and Edward are always here and usually available to any enquiring client. In fact, the ever-charming Edward claims, "I'm just a shopkeeper."

But, oh, what a shop—full of exquisite jewelry, rare antiques, gorgeous leather goods, sensational silver, captivating crystal, fine china and truly one-of-a-kind objects like the beautiful rock crystal horse highlighted by 18-carat gold and diamonds which sells for £185,000. Such precious pieces are, for the most part, housed in the Gold Room, the oak-panelled chambre which doubles as John's office. Executed in the firm's own workrooms on the upper floors of the building, they are true flights of fancy, never duplicated and often winding up as gifts for heads of state. We're sure that's the destiny of the set of three delicate rose quartz scent bottles mounted on 18-carat gold for £32,500. Naturally, Asprey is prepared to design and construct an object that tickles your particular fancy. A replica of your yacht in silver, perhaps? The design is free, but to render it into reality, plan on spending at least £12,000.

Lest you think Asprey is out of your league, consider its incredible range of goodies. A silver bookmark will set you back less than £100, while a leather-bound contemporary volume from Diedre Hart's book department to go with it can be had for as little as £250. Of course, if you happen upon a first edition Dickens, the price will be closer to £25,000.

For less literate antiques, head for the gracefully balustraded mezzanine. There, Paul Clarke is the resident expert on the admirable collection of predominantly 18th-century English furniture. If it's silver you're after, talk to Alistaire Dickenson, unless you want the newly minted kind. In that case, you need to speak with Stephen Eaves in the extensive silver department on the main floor. And just because it's new, that doesn't mean it isn't capricious or expensive. Take, for example, the rather amazing sterling caviar server shaped like a sturgeon which retails for £5,000.

Predictably, the jewelry selection is comprehensive and bewitching. Asprey's agents travel the world over tracking the best pieces from showrooms and estates. If you have something in mind but don't see it, trust Peter Barry to find it for you. And don't overlook the small leather-goods department, which is worthy of a visit if only to get an intoxicating whiff of the rare skins. We were sorely tempted by the crocodile wallets, crafted on the premises—£500 for a man's wallet, £800 for a lady's French purse.

No wonder Asprey is the proud possessor of three Royal Warrants. It gets our "Shopoholics' Award" for being one of London's most gracious and fascinating stores.   🐛

The Conran Shop

Michelin House	071-589-7401
81 Fulham Road	(FAX) 071-823-7015
London SW3 6RD	

We've already addressed the architectural treasure that is Michelin House in our discussion of its resident restaurant, Bibendum. But we would be remiss in our duty if we did not additionally point out one unusual physical feature of the shop that occupies its ground floor and cellar—you can see right through it. Windows line the front and the back of the main level, yielding an additional light and airy feeling to the already sprawling store. And the somewhat heady atmosphere is further enhanced by a world-class sound system playing tapes that prompted us to give the Conran Shop our "Best Music" award.

Last time we went a-browsing, the liquid velvet voice of Johnny Mathis went with us as we cruised what is best described as a department store minus the clothes, except for children's which it does carry. There are no fewer than 33 named departments, from baskets to tea and candles to upholstery; and you can be sure that Sir Terence Conran has his hand in every single one of them. This is, after all, his flagship store and is worlds apart from Conran's in the U.S. or Habitat in Britain. To express it in fashion terms, the Conran Shop is couture, while Sir Terence's other stores are ready-to-wear.

Actually, the fashion analogy is very appropriate as the clientele is a decidedly trendy lot, design aware but not necessarily wealthy. Still, the Conran Shop is particularly popular with pop stars and has acquired a reputation as being *the* place to re-do your home once you've made money. And rumour has it, many a would-be success shops the store simply to give the appearance of having made it. The Burnham sofa, a classic Conran piece that can fill up virtually any room with its massive rounded back and arms, is especially sought after. At £1,500 it makes a statement and is so large you practically live in it—no need for much else in the way of furniture.

More self-assured types, like us, are enchanted with the strikingly unusual archangel trolley, a dreamy deco bar cart with a beautiful arcing sweep to its chrome frame and staggered shelves—a knockout piece for £195. We were also smitten with the Pliable Man's Chair (bit of an oxymoron, there). Made of birch plywood, it is exceedingly comfortable, despite what appear to be very hard edges, and very practical. The arm rests double as side tables.

Indeed, when it comes to contemporary styles, the Conran Shop is tough to beat, with its novel chair rack—a wall of chairs, each showcased in a theatrically lit bin. The stylish sales assistants, all in black looking like the staff of Ian Schrager's chic Royalton and Paramount hotels in New York, encourage you to take out the chairs and "try them on." A very creative merchandising technique, it is typical of the store's approach—nothing about it resembles a typical furniture showroom. There are no matched sets or overtly coordinated displays anywhere on the floor.

Down the large, divided staircase at the entrance, you'll find smaller goods and a familiar Conran touch, shopping carts. At the bottom of the stairs, you're confronted with what must be one of the world's largest collections of baskets and vases, from £12 to £170. A plump tortoiseshell glass vessel caught our eyes and wallets at £99. And, just beyond, we were very tempted by the fluid lines of a group of sculptured, cast aluminium candlesticks by Matthew Hilton, for £87 to £150 a pair.

There's a lot more aluminium in the kitchen department which boasts every pot, pan and utensil known to man. And if you'd rather eat than cook, you'll find food here, too, including an ever expanding range of Conran-labelled condiments. In an increasingly health-conscious country, Conran's is becoming very well known for its olive oil.

Fortunately, with so much to look at, the staff take a very relaxed attitude. You're left to browse at your leisure. And it can take hours to pour through the travel books and agonize over which of the huge assortment of collectible boxes would make the perfect housewarming gift. But there's a method to Conran's madness. The staff know that if you wander long enough, you're bound to find something you can't live without, whether it's a 90-pence soapdish or a £2,500 handmade oak table. So be forewarned. Don't kid yourself about just looking—if you go to the Conran Shop, you'll do some buying as well.

Eximous

10 West Halkin Street	071-627-2888
London SW1R 8JL	(FAX) 071-498-0552

We have it on good authority that the Royals like to personalize gifts with appropriate crests, coats of arms and, at a pinch, plain old initials. Maybe it reminds them of their elevated station in life—after all, they have more impressive crests and coats, and usually *more* initials than most anybody else! In any case, Eximous is the place for them, and for you, if you choose to follow their lead. Eximous will stamp or engrave any conceivable object, which pretty much states the range of merchandise it stocks. Describing itself as a "manufacturer of monogrammed accessories," the firm claims it was founded in 1978 with the notion of providing the "answers to all gift-giving occasions...." We wouldn't care to quibble with either assertion, and we've often followed the lead of Prince Charles, who, it is claimed, calls in his orders by the score.

Since Eximous holds His Highness' Royal Warrant, we presume he's never been disappointed, and we know that *we* never have been. The selection is extraordinary and often unique as the majority of the products sold are designed and manufactured exclusively for Eximous. One such item is the white porcelain and quilt cachepots which can be personalized with a hand-painted coat of arms. For those, of course, who can claim their own crest or insignia, it's the perfect gift at £225. Allow at least eight weeks for delivery and rest assured that the folks at Eximous will not question the validity of whatever design you send. Yes, they do know what's legitimate and what's not, but they have a discreet sense of humour about that sort of thing.

For less pretentious types, we find a dozen navy blue pencils with the giftee's name inscribed in gold block letters an always appreciated offering at £8.50. And we haven't known a bride and groom yet who have been anything less than thrilled to have their wedding invitation preserved under glass in the center of a lovely (and practical) gilt-edged wooden tray for £120. There's also a large selection of leather goods (wallets to jewel boxes), picture frames made from virtually every possible material (silk moiré to silver), and some trinkets for the kids (monogrammed christening mugs to playful cotton-knit sweaters).

The choice of givable goodies is seemingly endless. At Eximous you can browse with the assurance that inspiration will surely come. And while you're waiting for that lightning bolt to strike, pointing to the exemplary present for that special someone, it's a very nice place to stroll through—spacious, but cosy, with its rich mahogany decor. Still, however, attractive, one of the shop's best features is that you don't have to go there to take advantage of its stylish goods and excellent services. Eximous has a booming, worldwide mail (and telephone) order business, thanks to its beautiful catalogue. It's an invaluable resource, one we always consult when a gift-giving occasion looms. You should, too. 🐛

General Trading Company

144 Sloane Street   071-730-0411
London SW1X 9BL   (FAX) 071-823-4624

In 1920, the General Trading Company was founded by Dealtry and Alfred Part to provide unusual and superbly made goods for its discerning clientele, in a comfortable atmosphere.

Today it's no different. The familiar Sloane Street mansions contain one of the finest collections of traditional household furnishings and gifts for every occasion. We always leave ourselves at least an hour, there's so much to see.

On the first floor, you'll find a unique collection of 18th- and 19th-century furniture, porcelain, prints, silver and accessories. We loved the brass door stops at £55 and £65, and yearned for the library ladder covered with antiqued hide, at £700.

Next to Antiques, in Decorative Living, there's an irresistible collection of fabrics, rugs, modern upholstery, lamps, painted furniture, cushions and Venetian glass. We fell in love with a 19th-century chest of drawers that was decorated with hand-painted flowers and fruit, for £1,850.

We're sure you'll find the perfect tableware, as the china department has famous names like Coalport, Worcester and Spode, as well as newer designs from Hinchcliffe and Barber, and Emma Bridgewater.

The kitchen department has a fabulous collection of stylish equipment and utensils, like a beautiful butcher-block trolley at £288 and terra-cotta pots for slow cooking at £12.50.

Don't miss the Eastern Bazaar, front right-hand corner on the ground level. It has a truly exotic collection of silk quilts, dhurries, kelims, antiques, porcelain, carved wood and wall hangings from Indonesia, China and the Philippines.

One of the utter delights of shopping at the General Trading Company is stopping for a meal or snack at the cellar café, Justin de Blank's. Try the vegetable tartlets and sinfully rich pot au chocolat during lunch or dinner in the pretty, walled patio garden. Of course, there's plum pudding, as well.

If you're shopping for a unique wedding gift or something wonderful for your own home, the General Trading Company will be a fruitful and relaxing experience.   ❦

Halcyon Days

14 Brook Street   071-629-8811
London W1Y 1AA   (FAX) 071-409-0280

An authority on 18th-century English painted enamels and the founder, in 1950, of Halcyon Days, a shop devoted to antique objets de vitrine, Susan Benjamin has spent her life collecting and reviving very special, traditional English crafts of the highest order. In 1970, she formed an association with a Staffordshire-based company to produce finely detailed enamelled boxes and bibelots in the spirit of the past—a spirit that was all but forgotten since the 1830s until championed by Susan. Then, just recently, she launched a new rivival—a collection inspired by the charming 18th-century miniature porcelains produced by a Chelsea factory between 1750 and 1784, among the rarest and most sought-after of 18th-century English ceramics.

Dubbed, respectively, Halcyon Days Enamels and Halcyon Days Porcelain they are available at fine shops worldwide, but there is no better selection than at *the* source at Susan's original Brook Street shop and her annex at 4 Royal Exchange. The artfully decorated display window under the elegant white awning beckons you inside to a world of enchanting, mostly useless, but undeniably beautiful and oh-so-dear (literally and figuratively) decorative "things." The walls are lined with cabinets loaded with enamels—boxes in every imaginable shape, frames, clocks (porcelain miniatures, too), seals and scent bottles fitted with gold and vermeil mounts, some even studded with precious stones.

For us, it's fun to know that the trinkets we consider here may have been pawed over by Prince Philip, the Queen Mother and Prince Charles (Halcyon Days enjoys the Royal Warrant of all three). Of course, we can't speak for them, but we were enchanted by one of the dainty teal green and 24-carat gold enamelled limited edition music boxes (only 750 made) for £1,450.

Should you be seduced by these little treasures but haven't the foggiest idea how to exhibit them properly, never fear. Susan's scholarship (her books, *English Enamel Boxes* and *Enamels* are considered invaluable reference materials) is matched only by her salesmanship. Halcyon Days sells delightful collectors' cabinets, including a rich-looking £695 burr-walnut table-top vitrine and a £375 rosewood, Regency-inspired, gilt-edged book tray, suitable for wall-mounting or for a table top. Fill either with diminutive Halcyon Days delights, which start for as little as £30 and go as high as £3,900. Before long, you'll look like a world-class collector of the real thing.

In fact, Susan's reproductions are as enthusiastically pursued as their prototypes, and well they should be because they are made by the same, painstaking processes. A team of artists in her Brook Street studio is constantly at work on ideas for the company's collections and for special commemorative pieces—one of the most successful components of Susan's business.

If you remain unconvinced about the worthiness of Halcyon Days' productions, but are a lover of exquisite displayables, Susan's shops are still worth a visit. Collectively, they house the largest and most comprehensive selection of antique English enamels anywhere in the world outside a museum. ❧

The Irish Linen Company

35–36 Burlington Arcade   071-493-8949
London W1V 9AD   (FAX) 071-499-5485

Linen, that most durable and comfortable of fabrics, has been in use all over the world for some 10,000 years. It can be traced to the stone and bronze ages when it was used to make fishing nets and lines, as well as ropes for hunting. It was even used as a sturdy building material. Today, linen is associated with considerably more luxurious purposes, and, since 1875, the Irish Linen Company has been a purveyor of linen at its elegant best—from sumptuous table settings in rich damask to cool and covetable sheets, to delicately embroidered handkerchiefs.

Still a family-owned and operated business, it sells, as its name suggests, only Irish linen, considered to be the best in the world. The superb quality of the merchandise has, over the years, attracted a host of personalities who appreciate the air of gratifying exclusivity imparted by linen. Winston Churchill, Charlie Chaplin, members of the Kennedy clan, the Queen of the Netherlands, Douglas Fairbanks, Jr., and Paul McCartney—all have stroked the inviting products in this discreetly refined shop, with its bird's-eye maple panelling, its display alcoves lined in luscious green velvet and its creative lighting. The latter shows off the superior workmanship involved—exquisite appliques, detailed embroidery employing the unique skills of Madeira, and ethereal French lace adorn many items.

We were smitten with a lovely, hand-embroidered, eight place-setting luncheon set, costing £450. Less elaborate, but still sporting the handiwork of Madeira, was a set for four at £85—an incredible bargain when you consider that you can spend £69.50 for a handkerchief here. That handkerchief, though, is probably the most beautiful one you've ever seen, lavishly embroidered all in white and ideal as an accessory for the sentimental bride. For everyday use, there is an assortment for as little as £5.95, each edged in drawn threadwork. But we feel the £37.50 alençon lace-bordered number does better justice to Chanel bags, especially if they're faux Chanel—the expensive hankie lends credence to the illusion.

As for sheets, nothing compares to linen. It virtually ensures a restful night's sleep. A simple king-size pair goes for about £395 for two flat sheets (ever try to iron a fitted sheet?). And make no mistake, linen does require ironing. What it does not need, however, under any circumstances, is bleach, which can do irreparable damage. Generally speaking, it doesn't require starch either, as there is a natural crispness to linen. At any rate, you're talking another £71 for a pair of pillow cases, £59 for a set of shams.

For something a little more ornate, there are sheets trimmed with faggoting at £465 for a king-size pair. They, like their unembellished brethren, can be sent to the laundry. Just make sure they are ironed by hand—with care. To add a little colourful lustre to your bed, there's a large assortment of pillows in a rainbow of colours in linen or organdy for about £30 for the 12″ by 16″ size. Decorated with some of that extraordinary Madeiran embroidery, they can go for as much as £150.

In the gift category, we found the set of six cocktail napkins from £22.50 a winner. Beautiful and practical, with a little tender loving care, they'll last a lifetime, according to manager Marianne Master. She told us linen is resistant to tearing, doesn't wear out from washing (it's the only fabric known to be stronger wet than dry), and is totally mothproof. What more can you ask from such a fine indulgence? 🦗

Jo Robinson Ltd

| 8 Yeoman's Row | 071-589-3354 |
| London SW3 2AH | (FAX) 071-584-3958 |

In an age when American decorators have become "interior designers," shamelessly courting celebrity-dom and inflicting their instantly identifiable look on every client that has more money than taste, their British counterparts are often a breath of refreshingly creative air—none more so than the delightful Jo Robinson, of the genuinely warm smile and twinkling eyes. She doesn't rankle at the term *decorator.* Jo's spent her entire professional life becoming one of the best, under the tutelage of her cousin Jean Munro, internationally known for her knowledge of Georgian architecture and her collection of "Munro" chintz. Having worked her way up through the ranks of Munro Ltd to become its director, Jo has now struck off on her own with a decorating business ensconced in this charming shop.

Just a short walk from Harrods, it occupies an old mews coach house decked out in an elegant, faded green on the outside and a blaze of colour and pattern on the inside. Jo tailors her decorating to her clients' individual requests and lifestyles. Her versatility is reflected in the merchandise of her shop. Set against the rich Russian red walls is an extremely attractive selection of vintage and new lamps, 19th-century decorative china, antique furniture, mirrors, chandeliers and objets d'art.

We were intrigued by the large collection of late 18th- to mid 19th-century works featuring botanical, architectural and natural history themes. Including their hand-painted ornamental frames, they can generally be had for £120 to £350 each, and can be purchased individually or in sets.

The atmosphere here is informal and friendly. You're encouraged to browse to your heart's content, which can keep you happily occupied for quite some time—there's a lot to look at here. Questions are knowledgeably fielded by the affable staff of four, headed by Jo. When she's out travelling with clients or scouring the Wiltshire and Norfolk countryside for new additions to the shop's inventory, Guy Wilkins is in charge, ready to assist in any way he can to guide you through the nuances of the decorative arts. Actually, Guy saved us from ourselves, from our impulsively passionate desire to own a lovely £2,000 Victorian marble-topped conservatory. After hearing descriptions of our respective domiciles, he convinced us that the table might be better suited to the Duchess of Devonshire (one of the firm's clients) than to either of us.

Instead, we opted for a couple of pillows from the shop's assortment of antique needlework and hand-painted numbers, for £75 to £250 each. That's what's so special about Jo's shop—there's always an alternative, in fact, several choices when you're in the market for objects, from a £14, 19th-century ashtray to a £4,000 oriental rug.   ❦

Keith Skeel

94–9 Islington High Street	071-226-7012/359-9894
London N1 8EG	(FAX) 071-226-0935

Keith Skeel's handsome, late 18th-century house, filled to the brim with an astonishing profusion of eccentricity, is a familiar haunt to the many dealers and collectors who regularly prowl nearby Camden Passage in search of unique antiques. Indeed, because of his philosophy of purchasing only pieces that are unusual, striking and an excellent representative of their genre, Keith's "Aladdin's cave" of treasures is such a reliable resource that many skip the hustle and bustle of the Passage altogether. Instead, they content themselves with Keith's nine beguilingly arranged showrooms in the main shop and the mind-boggling warehouse just around the corner. There's plenty of bounty to occupy their attention—one illustrious decorator and his equally distinguished client spent three whole days perusing Keith's stock.

However, not even they could give a completely accurate description of it, since Keith's stock is far from static. He says he buys, quite literally, every single day. All that remains unchanged is his reputation for stocking the largest single collection of unusual and eccentric antiques in the country.

As you sink into one of the pair of £9,500 button-backed leather wing chairs to survey the almost bewildering scene of amazing objects, you might spy Calvin Klein, Ralph Lauren or any number of wealthy Eurocrats. Just like you, they're having trouble concentrating on any one item. There are just *so* many screaming for your attention—like the remarkable, 18th-century, French ormolou mirror, its ornate filigree soaring to the ceiling, as well it should for £10,000. Then there's the eye-catching pine-cone sculptures that make up a veritable forest of "fir" trees. Though not antique, they meet Keith's criteria of being arrestingly uncommon and of exceptional quality. Made in the Philippines, they range in size from three to five feet and are bestsellers at £120 to £300.

More antique and just about as popular are Keith's collection of 19th-century decorative bronze animals—there seems to be a particular passion for pugs these days at about £1,000 each. Smug-looking cats can cost as much as £2,200. Being more people-oriented, we were struck by the turbaned bronze bust, his exquisite features cast in Austria, circa 1840. At £3,900, he was a bargain, compared to his rather surrealistic Austrian brethren—100-year-old life-sized figures of black minstrels, of which Keith had a number when last we visited. Extremely rare and very valuable, they're the kind of thing you'll want to chat with Keith or his assistant Neil McKay about to determine price. But, don't try the old bargainer's ploy of pooh-poohing their quality in order to get a deal. Keith appreciates and works with people who share his excitement about the pieces in his possession. In fact, his taste in customers can be just as quirky, just as persnickety as his taste in curios. Still, he's incredibly tolerant of indecisive browsing, allowing free rein for you to wander up and down, round and round, for as long as you please—which, at Keith Skeel's, can be a very, very long time indeed.

Maggs Bros., Ltd

50 Berkeley Square   071-493-7160
London W1X 6EL   (FAX) 071-499-2007

While the ritual has never been documented, it is certainly plausible that, on occasion, bibliophiles all over the planet position themselves to face the general direction of the west side of Berkeley Square and pay homage to their mecca—Maggs Bros., since 1853 one of the world's leading dealers in rare books and manuscripts. Occupying virtually every storable inch, including the former stables, of an imposing townhouse that once belonged to statesman George Canning, the Maggs family's collection currently numbers some 2,000,000 books. And as far as we can tell, John Maggs, great-grandson of founder Uriah, is intimately acquainted with each and every one of them. Certainly, he has no trouble quickly retrieving anything you ask for, from the stacks in the stables or from the beautiful, antique wooden cases that line the walls of the house—whether your interest is in a £20 "starter book" or a £1,000,000 collector's collectible.

This is a man truly enthralled by his work. People who share his passion for books, particularly tomes on travel which are his speciality, spend hours with Mr Maggs (he's so dignified, we dare not call him John). You see Mr Maggs is quite a talker and a fascinating one at that. As he recounts their history, he makes books come alive, and his vision of a collector's mission truly is compelling. Then there are the anecdotes, like his story about the late Queen Mary, who presented a bit of a problem for the patriotic Maggses. It seems she was an avid collector; consequently, the firm was one of her regular haunts. Naturally, when the Queen expressed an interest in a particular book, the only correct response was to offer it to her as a gift. It got to the point that, when informed of her imminent arrival, the staff were instructed to hide anything of great value!

While Mr Maggs is usually on the premises and a visit with him is definitely "worth the price of admission," remember he has a staff of 20, each a specialist in a particular field. If your interest is in military books, you should see Nicola Hemingway, who pleasantly stuns starchy old warhorses with her vivaciousness. As for anything by or about T.E. Lawrence, Mr Maggs' son Edward is the resident expert.

Typical of venerable British family firms, the emphasis here is on personal service. Maggs doggedly pursues requests for specific books, no matter how long it takes. Our pal David Andelman once told Mr Maggs he had been unable to find a copy of the two-volume *Journey to Arabia* by William Gifford Paulgrave, the first Englishman to explore that part of the world, preceding the more famous Lawrence by a century. Mr Maggs said he'd engage in a search and would notify our friend of the results. Two years later, David received a letter telling him the set had been secured and Maggs would be happy to send it along "on approval." Granted, the object of our friend's desire fell into the category of Mr Maggs' personal preoccupation—he is particularly keen on such chronic travellers as Captain Cook, George Vancouver and those intrepid Victorian ladies who broke all stereotypes by making the most astonishing journeys—but that didn't matter. Whatever our friend had asked for, Mr Maggs or his agents would have found it, eventually.

Not surprisingly, Maggs enjoys a huge mail-order business, with clients in almost every country in the world. They look forward to the company's extraordinary catalogues, organized around specific subjects and published several times a year. Over the years, there have been more than 1,100, some of which have become collector's items in their own right, like the lavishly illustrated *Provincial Bookbinding in Great Britain*, produced in 1981.

Obviously, Maggs Bros. exists to cater to those bent on amassing a serious book collection, defined by Mr Maggs as boasting at least one volume worth around £1,000. Still, if you have anything more than a passing interest, you shouldn't miss Maggs. We even did what one would have thought was the impossible—we fell in love with a book about birds, full of pretty pictures. Upon asking the price, we were astounded to learn it was only £1. Mr Maggs was astonished too! ❧

Monogrammed Linen Shop

168 Walton Street	071-589-4033
London SW3 2LJ	(FAX) 071-823-7745

Being French (her name notwithstanding) and therefore accustomed to the wonders of Leron and Porthault, Anne Singer was struck by London's dearth of shops dedicated to linens. It was one of her first impressions of the city when she moved here with her husband and children. As her family settled in, Anne found she had time on her hands and began to think more and more about what she considered a great void in London's vast inventory of shops.

Eight years ago, she turned thought into action and opened this treasure trove of linens from France, the Philippines, Portugal and China, while throwing in, for good measure, some household accessories and children's clothes (infant to five years). Anne and her shop have made such a name for themselves that the powers that be at Thomas Goode, *the* authority on up-market accessories for the home, installed a Monogrammed Linen boutique in its store on South Audley. There Anne stocks an admirable array of table linens, but the real story in this category is her novel concept of creating tablecloths, placemats and napkins to match china patterns at prices ranging from £150 to £3,000. The notion has become so popular that Anne's orders keep an entire French embroidery factory busy all year. The factory routinely produces embroidered linens to complement particularly popular patterns like those of Herend and Limoges. But literally any design can be copied. . .or invented.

One client from Greece wanted aquatic-looking placements and napkins for her yacht. Anne and her factory devised a set, sporting colourful and exotic fish—each different, each exquisitely worked by hand.

But if your interest lies in bedding, towels or children's clothes, head for the original Walton Street location. It has such a whimsical air, its walls and ceilings covered with mattress ticking of the palest blue-grey. Hand-embroidered sheets are stacked high on the shelves, next to luxurious towels in a delightful rainbow of colours—blues, pinks, and greys. Baby pillows form an inviting pile on a cunning little cot in front of racks of neatly arranged children's clothes, while teddy bears beckon from an alcove. Anne's office occupies the rear of the shop, and behind it all, sits the sewing machine used for monogramming.

Though tucked neatly away, the machine is seldom idle, due to the shop's renown as a supplier of especially fine towels. The rich white terry, bound in a contrasting colour, are especially popular—washcloths at £7.50, hand towels £24.95 and bath sheets for £79. If you have a special binding in mind, just tell Anne. Special orders take about two months and the price depends on the cost of the binding. Unbound towels tend to sell for a little more than half their fancier brethren. Regardless, monogramming costs £5.50 for one initial, £7.50 for three, per item.

As for sheets, there is a large assortment in both cotton and linen—embroidered sheets, floral sheets and sheets with pulled threads. Prices range from £100 for a plain cotton single-size set to £650 for a lovely linen king-size set.   🍒

Nina Campbell Limited

| 9 Walton Street | 071-225-1011 |
| London SW3 2JD | (FAX) 071-225-0644 |

To many Americans, Nina Campbell burst upon the scene when the Duchess of York, forced by patriotic censure, dumped the American decorating icon Sister Parrish in favour of her. In actual fact, Nina's been around and making design waves since 1970, when she set up business in a small, 18th-century house in Belgravia. Her shop, along with Geoffrey Bennison's neighbouring antique shop, is credited with establishing Pimlico Road as *the* place for connoisseurs of the unusual to shop. One can only wonder if Nina's subsequent move to Walton Street will set a similar course for this neighbourhood.

Here, in another former residence, she maintains all the outlets of her considerable energy under one roof—a retail and wholesale operation as well as the offices for her design firm. These days, she's helped with the latter by the tall, angular self-described "Colefax & Fowler renegade," Henry Greenfield. It's not surprising that their tastes should coincide, as Nina, too, served an apprenticeship with John Fowler. Both she and Henry inherited from him a passion for the rigorous aesthetic of the 18th century, skilfully combined with the painted furniture, sumptuous trimmings and floral chintzes of a later age.

Still, while Henry may be managing director, it's Nina's cachet that draws the crowds to the shop and has clients, both corporate and residential, lining up for her decorating services. Recent commissions, in addition to the Duke and Duchess of York's mansion, include a house for Rod Stewart, Paris' Hotel Bentley and Christie's new premises in London. All benefit from Nina's extraordinary use of colour, commanding sense of proportion and flair for mixing patterns and textures, styles and epochs. Despite a leaning toward deep, dusty hues, her colour palette is decidedly contemporary, lending a fresh look to antiques, as well as to modern furnishings. And her daring combinations assure her interiors never look "done," while always reeking with comfort. Her moniker as the master of country house chic has become world famous, but what truly distinguishes Nina's work is perfect placement of an unusual, perhaps bizarre or even ugly object that has the panache to set off a whole room.

Predictably, such objects set her shop apart from other more run-of-the-mill decorator showcases, a peculiarly British phenomenon. An elaborately beaded £1,200 chair and a £900 Dutch coal bucket used as a planter are two cases in point. More conventional, but still capable of imparting drama to a room, is the large assortment of tapestry and needlework pillows, ranging in price from £50 to £120.

The front room resembles an overcrowded parlour, a studied hodgepodge of singularly striking furniture and eye-catching accessories. Towards the rear, the shop takes on a more commercial look. The back room houses Nina's line of soft goods, many featuring her trademark hearts—from £9 fabric-covered coat hangers to a £55 set of tea-for-two china. Nina claims she even wears heart-shaped glasses. But we've never seen her dark dancing eyes framed by them, as she invariably tells us she's just sat on her last pair whenever we run into her!

Downstairs you'll find Nina's fabrics and wallpapers. Sold wholesale as well as through the shop, the lines have been tremendously successful, due to their stunning simplicity and sophisticated coordination of colours. Henry makes the interesting point that nothing frustrates designers more than being compelled to use the papers and fabrics already on the market, which never quite seem to suit their purposes. So it makes good practical sense for them to devise their own, besides which, he laughs, "there's nothing greater for the ego, either, than putting your name on both. It's really your only stab at eternity." Nina's shot at it goes for £15 to £30 a metre for the fabrics, £15.95 a metre for the wallpapers. In both instances, we're attracted to her creative twist to traditional Regency stripe patterns.

Clearly, you don't have to be bankrolled by a queen to purchase a touch of the irreproachable (except, in our view, where the restaurant of The Capital is concerned) taste of Nina Campbell, the decorator of the decade.

Paperchase

213 Tottenham Court Road   071-580-8496
London W1P 9AF

There are few reminders here of Paperchase's mid '60s roots as a source of supplies for trendy art students, except the basic product profile which remains a happy alternative to that of more conventional purveyors. The store has a well-deserved reputation as a supplier of amusing, captivating, exclusive and thoroughly unconventional paper products. It also now has 22 branches, proving the point that there is indeed a passion for paper—from a 45p card to a spectacular black mesh wrapping paper that sparkles and glitters at £10 a metre.

The Tottenham Court Road store is the largest of the lot and serves as headquarters for the chain. It's always bustling, as there's certainly something for everyone. An utterly enchanting browser's paradise, the selection is enormous and so entertaining. Don't plan on a quick trip here to grab a card and run. It's next to impossible not to be caught up in the colourful displays of distinctive merchandise, especially during the fall when the second floor becomes a Christmas wonderland, beautiful to look at and a delight to shop in. Anything meant to embellish the holiday can be found here, from little 15p candles to entrancing handmade decorations for as much as £30. Beautiful gift boxes in every shape and size are available for homemade goodies or that abomination of a gift from last year you intend to pass on to a deserving someone this season. There's even a gift-wrapping service. Place all your Christmas purchases in the staff's ingenious hands. Select your favourite boxes, papers and ribbons, then leave the tedious wrapping to them.

You can take care of other special occasions in the store's incredible card department. If you can't find one here that tickles your fancy, you're hopeless. There are thousands to choose from, including exquisite handmade pieces for £3. All are cleverly displayed in cellophane, so there's none of that dog-eared look that is the bane of many a card in less resourceful stores. We've had many a giggle looking for just the right card to express a particular sentiment, and we've always found it.

Just as we've always found the perfect stationery to serve as the invitation for a theme party. Indeed, themes are a bit of a speciality at Paperchase. Once the store selects a new theme, it appears on stationery, wrapping paper, tissue, ribbons, cards and even desk accessories, including disposable fountain pens for £1.40. If your signature style doesn't seem to be in stock, ask managing director Timothy Melgund and he'll find it for you from the store's extensive resources all over the world, or he'll have it designed.

Still, function is just as important as form at Paperchase. All those practical little items like paper clips, tape and note pads are available, too. And in its bid to save the world's forests, the store does a lot with recycled papers.

But for pure impractical whimsy, nothing beats the selection of doll-house papers for 40p a sheet—chintz wallpaper, bathroom tile paper, wood floor paper—all in precious, precise detail. Actually, there is one item here that beats even those on the fun scale, and that's the python-skin printed tissue-weight paper at £1 per sheet. Now wouldn't that dress up the goodie bags for your next charity affair—of course, it could be your last!

Royal Doulton

167 Piccadilly   071-493-9121
London W1V 9DE

Unless it's Wedgwood you're after, you can fulfil just about any English china or crystal dreams by exploring this cavernous showroom. With its brilliantly polished light-wood floors and sleek glass cabinets framed by lustrous redwood, there's a Scandinavian look to this sparkling empo-rium. The domain of the estimable Miss N O'Donnell (with an empha-sis on the *Miss*—we had to use all our considerably persuasive powers to elicit the first initial), the shop features the largest selection of stock pat-terns from Minton, Royal Crown Derby, Paragon, Royal Doulton and Royal Albert in London.

So why, if it carries all that, is the store called simply Royal Doulton? Well, it seems that the company founded by John Doulton in 1812 (now officially called Royal Doulton Tableware Limited) has, over the years, judiciously incorporated other firms to become England's leading manu-facturer of bone china and handmade, full-lead crystal. Does that mean that Minton and Royal Crown Derby are now indistinguishable? Not by a long shot. The artistry, traditions, facilities and techniques of each of Royal Doulton's acquisitions have been scrupulously maintained.

Therefore, Royal Derby's elaborate red, gold and black Imari pattern looks just as richly detailed as it did when first introduced—although at

£215 for a five-piece placesetting, it costs a lot more these days. Ditto, Minton's lyrical, floral-pattern Haddon Hall, which made its debut in 1949. It's still made just as it was all those years ago, but it is pricier. Count on spending £52.50 a placesetting, even here at what can certainly be described as *the* source. The shop routinely ships to all parts of the world. And the service is so good that you can order a whole set of Royal Doulton crystal liqueur glasses in the delicately cut Windsor pattern (approximately £22.50 each) and rest assured that they'll arrive on the appointed doorstep intact.

In addition to the tableware, there's a terrific collection of decorative items, such as the beautiful, gold-banded ginger jars from Royal Crown Derby for £425. Brightly coloured paperweights in 31 different designs make perfect gifts from £39, as do authentic collectors' objets d'art at closer to £300. And speaking of collecting, the three-year-old shop serves as the home of the Royal Doulton International Collectors' Club.

Start your own collection of the world-famous Royal Doulton figurines, many of which sell for £65 to £95. If you want to ease into the habit painlessly, pick up one of the exquisite miniature porcelain bouquets of flowers for less than £8. Equally intriguing, and collectible, are Royal Crown Derby's dear little animal figures—£35 for an engagingly cheeky chipmunk, £75 for a sensational dragon.

Should you be feeling especially extravagant, talk to Miss O'Donnell about arranging for a set of Royal Doulton dishes embellished with your monogram or family crest. It's easily done, albeit costly. Naturally, the degree of expense depends upon the complexity of the design. Again, should you wish to slide into the custom-made arena without spending a sum which approximates the gross national product of a small Caribbean island, investigate having the Minton studio execute a commemorative piece for a special occasion. Its artists will paint a portrait of a loved one—human or not. Alternatively, they can immortalize your home or some other significant edifice. Miss O'Donnell can make it happen, if you have a lead time of four to six months and about £450 for an 11 1/4" or £225 for a 9" plate.

But the best news is that whether you drop in just to cruise the exhibit, to pick up a humble gift or to fill up the china cabinet of your new country retreat, you'll benefit from the same graciously deferential treatment by the congenial staff. Royal Doulton truly puts England's best foot forward in terms of product and service. 🐀

Smythson of Bond Street

44 New Bond Street	071-629-8558
London W1Y 0DE	(FAX) 071-495-6111

Status symbols come and go—yesterday's de rigueur accessory is now ostentatious. Indeed, to describe something as chic almost guarantees that one day it will also deserve the appellation of "passé." Of course, there are exceptions and Smythson's signature personal diaries are notable ones. Long considered "social passports," their cachet is acknowledged, quite literally, all over the world—they've gone to the North and South Poles with the Transglobe Expedition and accompanied Sir Edmund Hilary on his epic Mount Everest climb.

The brainchild of Smythson's founder, Frank Smythson, the diaries set a style and standard that have been widely imitated since they first made their debut toward the end of the last century. There are now over 100 different types for pocket and desk use—from the classic Featherweight, $5^{1}/2'' \times 3^{1}/2''$ in blue lizard with gilt corners and closure for £65, to specialized diaries like the blue leather book for ski notes at £10.75. Then there's the split pigskin, £50 Hunting Journal with headed columns for recording the details of all outings, and the desk-top buffalo calf album for recording one's association with the "sport of kings"—the $11'' \times 8^{3}/4''$ Polo Book for £150. Any can be monogrammed to the tune of £2 per initial.

Since Frank Smythson first opened for business in 1887 as "Stationer, Engraver, Die Sinker, Printer, and Publisher," the shop has also specialized in superior writing papers for distinguished people or for those with aspirations. As stationers to Her Majesty the Queen, you can be sure that Smythson's engraves some of the world's most coveted invitations. Its papers have also been a perennial favourite of the international diplomatic corps. Treaties have been signed (and broken) on Smythson's papers, marriage proposals made, and takeover attempts have been tendered on them. The uses are myriad—so are the choices. When making your selection, it's best to enlist the help of a veteran like Peter Lippiatt, who's been here for over 20 years.

There are 10 distinct kinds of paper; each is specially milled and subtly displays Smythson's exclusive watermark. The papers come in a beguiling range of hues, including the hallmark Bond Street Blue, introduced by the firm's founding father in the late 1880s. They can be plain or hand-bordered in a variety of colours. Prices start at about £16.50 for 100 sheets, with matching envelopes available from £25— more if you want them tissue-lined. But that's just the beginning. There are 20 different hand-engraved monogram styles—£84 to £148 to cast the dye for your initials and £75 for the address. Or you can have a dye custom-designed to emblazon your family crest or to commemorate the family manse, for about £600 or so. Don't forget the choices, and costs, associated with the actual printing. Most colours, including black, go for about £45 per 250 pages, more like £90 for white. Gold or silver runs £158. Making a personal stationery statement with Smythson style doesn't come cheap (or easy), but it does make your footing on the social ladder a little firmer.

Beyond diaries and papers, there's plenty to capture the browser's attention in this large, invitingly laid-out store. From the beginning, Smythson offered innovative gifts. An early catalogue features an electric bedside clock capable of projecting the dial onto the ceiling at night. Less novel but equally clever is the pound case in sterling silver, which holds six £1 coins (paper pound notes are no longer minted) and sells for £31.50. We were also intrigued with the dark green, buffalo calf table planner. Decoratively trimmed in gold, it boasts slots for 10 place cards which you can arrange and rearrange with impunity until you settle on the perfect social dynamic. Once you get it right, the planner is handsome enough to warrant displaying, so that your guests can easily find out where they'll be sitting and with whom. We've known of world-class hostesses like Anne Bass who possibly rely on computers for this sort of thing, but for £94 we prefer this hands-on approach.

It's so much more personal and, somehow, makes us feel good, reassuring us about our good taste . . . which, in a way, is what Smythson is all about.

Thomas Goode

19 South Audley Street	071-499-2823
London W1Y 6BN	(FAX) 071-629-4230

As a rule, we find table-top shops on the cold side—endless displays of china, glass and silver glistening under harsh lighting which, despite the plentitude of merchandise make the stores look somewhat barren. Not so Thomas Goode—Goode's to the cognoscenti. There's a lavish opulence about this store that envelops you with glamorous luxury. It starts with the palatial exterior, a massive, rather flamboyant red-brick Victorian structure, loaded with nooks, crannies, peaked roofs and chimneys. Stately columns frame a bank of display windows that stretch the length of the building. They're all masterful still-lifes of some of the world's finest decorative home accessories, except for the two that provide sanctuary for a couple of London landmarks—seven-foot high, richly ornamented ceramic elephants made by Minton for the Great Exhibition in Paris in 1889. They've stood guard on South Audley Street ever since Thomas Goode's son William bought them, along with the rest of the Minton exhibit, for his family's china and glass shop. Centred between the two colourful behemoths is an unusual mechanical door which automatically opens, triggered by the weight of a person standing on the platform. A very rare example of Victorian design, it is believed to be the only model in the world still in use.

Inside, the splendid skylit setting that William Goode created in 1845 is just as effective at showcasing contemporary treasures as it is at displaying the finest china, porcelain and glass of the 19th century. Thirteen showrooms lined with rococo cabinets and laden with sumptuous displays of merchandise laid out in their intended environment encourage endless browsing. And so do the experienced staff, led by Helen Robinson. They're alert and helpful, but not overly solicitous.

We suspect their friendly attitude has a lot to do with Helen's relatively recent stewardship. Prior to the arrival of the former executive editor of British *Vogue*, Goode's had a reputation for being a bit on the stuffy, intimidating side. After all, the store has been supplying the royal family with china and glass since 1863, currently holding a hat trick of warrants from the Queen, her mother, and her eldest son. Furthermore, Thomas Goode is the sort of place you can spend £2,500 on a five-piece place-setting of its Flora Danica, your expensive taste recorded for posterity in the archives that track every single purchase ever made here. But Helen understands that, like a magazine, a successful store must be accessible to a broad range of people. So these days, you can spend as little as £5 here and still be treated like royalty.

Weak for Waterford, from chandeliers to goblets? Beside yourself about Baccarat? Speculating about Spode? Longing for Lalique? Hot for Herend? Or wondering about Wedgwood? This is the place for you. And if the awesome assortment of merchandise seems overwhelming, ask for our favourite salesman, John Fleet. He's been here for over 16 years— what he doesn't know about Goode's goods isn't worth learning. And he'll help you with any of the store's special services, such as monogramming glassware or creating china with your family's crest or company's logo.

Among the stocked merchandise, take special note of the Minton. Ever since William Goode bought those elephants, there's been a unique association between their manufacturer and the store where they now stand watch. Minton makes patterns exclusively for Goode's—our favourite is the Imperial Gold pattern with its rich colours at £102 for a five-piece placesetting.

As for silver to go with it, investigate creations by Comyns, a firm that's been in the silversmithing business for some 300 years. Comyns, too, makes special pieces just for Thomas Goode. And the store is very accommodating when it comes to designing silver to your specifications.

In case you hadn't guessed, London's, indeed the world's, most fashionable brides register at Goode's and have been doing so since it opened. Consequently, many take the opportunity to glimpse at history by consulting the archives to see what their ancestors chose when setting up their households. Shopping at Goode's is a time-honoured tradition in all the best families. Why not make it one in yours?

The White House

| 51–52 Bond Street | 071-629-3521 |
| London W1Y 0BY | (FAX) 071-629-8269 |

Once upon a time, an arcade and art gallery separated the *two* White House stores on Bond Street, at Numbers 51 and 52, which specialized in the finest quality linens. In 1929, work commenced to combine the two premises with the happy result that, today, walking into the former arcade space—now the entrance of the White House—is one of London's shopping treats. Natural light streams through the glass ceiling, dancing on the crystals of a spectacular chandelier. There is an unparalleled sumptuousness here, from the creamy peach decorations to the cool green carpets to the tableaux of lavish bedrooms and dining rooms.

Since the unification all those years ago, the store has expanded its brief to include lingerie, hosiery, men's accessories and women's and children's fashions. Still, it is best known, and indeed beloved, for its exquisite linens, including the D. Porthault line from France, exclusive to the White House in the whole of Britain. Lesley Butcher, the linen buyer, showed us a fabulous king-size set of sheets and pillow cases in cotton voile with eyelet embroidery for £1,825. We were also enthralled by the immense, beautifully detailed tablecloth and its 12 napkins. But our fondness for red wine stopped us from shelling over the £2,730 necessary to make it our very own. We reluctantly left it to those among the store's large Arab clientele who presumably do not drink.

More, shall we say "accessible," are the lovely percale six-piece sheet sets that start at £330 for queen-size, or the crisp organdy placemat, fit for a boudoir breakfast tray, for £56. There's plenty to choose from in both the outlandish and modest categories as the entire ground floor and one mezzanine level are devoted to linens. Be sure to check out the elegant damask tablecloths, cashmere blankets and Irish linen sheets.

And don't miss the lingerie, which is a very special and natural extension of the White House's speciality. Since 1920, workrooms upstairs have been turning out a collection of sensuously silk unmentionables trimmed in antique lace, much of which is bought at auction. Each piece is designed around the lace and fashioned by a team of seamstresses, many of whom have been here for some 40 years. A slip can take four days to make and can occupy the tony £335 neighbourhood. By the same token, the store carries less costly, but certainly not mundane, versions for more like £75. A pink silk jacquard crepe de chine negligee, like the one we fell in love with, might take eight days of labour and sells for no less than £990.

The other department we find enchanting here is the one dedicated to children. Once called the Fairy Corner where the world's most fashionable babies and children were dressed under a glass dome etched with the moon and stars, it remains the preserve of pampered tots. Remember all those pictures you've seen of tiny royals in velvet-collared coats? You'll find the real thing here for £325—plus £90 for the corresponding hat. Little girls' dresses with sweetly traditional details like smocking range from £60 for a daytime number to £450 for a silk party frock. For boys, there are blazers, trousers, shirts, sweaters and even Little Lord Fauntleroy-like velvet breeches for formal occasions—the silk shirt to go with them sells for £150. The entire collection travels to the U.S. twice a year with the paragons of patience who are the sales staff. Under the leadership of children's wear buyer Josey Kentish who has been here 20 years, they even make house calls to take measurements.

As for catering to those too young to have whims, the White House does that, too. There's lots here for the infant in your life, from a cotton crawler at £55 to a satin romper at £165. And if making a statement about a baby's future is your intent, how about a £1,900 creamy silk and antique lace christening gown? Those workrooms upstairs can even incorporate your heirloom lace into one, or rejuvenate a gown that has occupied the bottom of a trunk for far too long.

Finally, we should mention the men's and women's clothing departments, which are perfectly nice and have their followers. But fashion is not really the White House's forte—with the possible exception of swimwear. London boasts many better emporiums for clothes and accessories, but few can hold a candle to the White House when it comes to linens and lingerie.

CHAPTER SIX

Jewelry

Baubles, bangles and beyond

*L*ondon may be home to the crown jewels, but not all of them are locked up in the fabled tower. There's a reason some of the big-time international dealers in staggering stones—Harry Winston and Van Cleef & Arpels, to name some names—who are major players in other repositories of the world capitals, haven't set up shop here. The competition's too stiff. Homegrown jewelers like Garrard have been around for centuries creating baubles to tickle the royal fancy. And even many of the "newcomers" to the trade, like Kutchinsky, have been around for well over a century or more and are in the habit of producing *important* pieces.

Tiffany touched off a trend when it opened its first European outpost here. But it was rough going for a while for this colonial upstart. It took the patronage of a newly crowned king to put Cartier on the map at the turn of the century. Still, there's always room for new talent if it's truly distinctive. And, in fact, several natives have recently carved out niches for themselves with inimitable styles that are developing global followings.

If you thought it might create a little stir to show up at your next dinner party in the diamond tiara Queen Elizabeth wore to her coronation celebration, you don't have to go to the lengths of robbing the Tower of London. You see, the city is a treasure trove of fabulous fakes—contemporary and vintage—often costly enough to make you wonder about the proverb, "all that glitters isn't gold." At these prices it should be, and often is. London's artisans are quite accustomed to fashioning specially commissioned jewelry, even to reproducing a favourite faux as a priceless gem, or vice versa. Either way, these sparklers are capable of blowing any budget, no matter how much money you have to spend before tea.

Annabel Jones

52 Beauchamp Place	071-589-3215
London SW3 1NY	(FAX) 071-589-0546

There's a seductive, boudoir-like quality to this treasure chest of a shop, owned by its namesake Annabel Jones, aka Annabel Astor. This aristocratic blond beauty is married to William Astor, grandson of Nancy Astor, the Virginia-born belle who became the first woman to take a seat in Parliament. No doubt the feisty Nancy would be proud of her grandson's choice of bride—certainly, she would appreciate Annabel's enterprise.

Passionate about jewelry since childhood, Annabel made her hobby of collecting antique pieces into her vocation by opening her first boutique in the Brompton Arcade in 1967. She moved to Beauchamp Place in 1969 and has deservedly acquired a reputation for collecting some of the world's most exciting vintage and antique jewelry. If you share her infatuation with precious finery, you'll be hard-pressed to pass by her cream encased window with its distinctive ruby-red display pieces dripping with exceptional jewels. It will stop you dead in your tracks, somewhat like Fred Leighton on Madison Avenue in New York. The difference is one of attitude. At Fred's you are all too often made to feel like an unwelcome trespasser, while at Annabel's you are welcomed with genuine warmth and interest.

You're encouraged to take the load off your feet by settling on one of the sumptuously patterned sofas or chairs, where you'll be offered tea or coffee. From your perch, you can take in the exceptionally pretty scene. Brilliantly lit glass cases shimmer against the pale yellow walls. They are loaded with jewelry—both antique and contemporary—and silver, another speciality here. Racing-green, velvet-draped tables take the place of the black velvet trays of most jewelry stores, and act as desks when not strewn with the pieces that intrigue you most. One important piece that captivated us was a necklace of graduated and faceted emerald beads, separated by 18-carat gold and calibre-cut ruby roundels, and punctuated by a pair of oval Ceylon sapphire, diamond and ruby motifs. Breathtaking, and well it should be for £62,500. Or perhaps something a little more romantically subtle is more to your taste. Fork over £21,750 for a four-strand necklace of cultured pearls accented by a baroque Victorian diamond creation which may once have been a brooch.

You see, redesigning and updating antique jewelry to make it more wearable is another of the firm's fortes. Furthermore, Annabel and her team of designers do it with such excellent taste that the integrity of the pieces remains intact. Peter Hubble, the resident expert on antique jewelry and silver, would just die if it was done any other way. He's the one to contact about selling your family jewels or having them appraised for insurance purposes. Ditto on any old silver you have lying about. And you should speak to Peter about any silver repairs or engraving you might want to have done.

As for pearl and bead restringing, yet another strength of Annabel's outstanding range of services, ask for Albina Evans.

If you think all this service sounds nice, but the prices sound high, think again. Annabel's original signature pieces start as low as £40 for a 9-carat gold charm. We were charmed by the mini 9-carat pendant in the shape of a bee, which is her hallmark. At the other end of the scale are the strikingly unusual 18-carat gold and black onyx earclips, highlighted by gold and diamond stars, which can be worn with or without matching pear-shaped drops. Yours for £4,490. All her designs are executed in very limited quantities, so should you succumb to their special appeal, you'll be joining a select club of collectors.

Speaking of collecting, don't forget to check out the silver, some of it on the serious side, such as the pair of Victorian silver letter scales with weights, which sells for £4,450. Then there are the examples of whimsy. Take the circa 1920, silver-plated travelling cocktail shaker, which contains four beakers, three glass bottles, a lemon squeezer *and* still has room left over for an ice compartment. It must have come in handy during Prohibition and is equally useful today at £1,350. And for the man who exercises, there's another silver plated shaker, fashioned by Asprey in the shape of a dumb-bell, for £750.

No wonder Annabel Jones' superbly produced catalogues are eagerly anticipated by devotees all over the world. Hers is one mailing list you'll want to be on.

Anne Bloom

10A New Bond Street   071-491-1213
London W1Y 9PF   (FAX) 071-409-0777

Just short of three-quarters of a century *young*, Anne Bloom remains very much a hands-on proprietor of the jewelry business she moved here from Grosvenor Street in 1980. In fact, she's pretty much a one-man band in this tiny gem of a shop, which is dominated by a dazzling display of sterling frames, many dating from the late 1800s. Ranging in price from just over £100 to closer to £3,000, they represent the best of English silversmithing traditions in every conceivable size and shape.

Once you've torn your eyes away from the frames, you'll probably be mesmerized by Anne's small but very special collection of exceptional jewelry. She specializes in authentic Edwardian pieces, starting at £1,000 and climbing to £3,000. Each has been carefully chosen by Anne, reflecting her exquisitely refined taste, tempered with a sense of humour. We spotted a glorious stickpin that would lend distinction to even the most prosaic lapel—a Chinaman carved in glass with an amusing, rounded diamond tummy. French, circa 1915, it sells for about £2,500. Another French vintage stunner was a Cartier cufflink set from 1950— sapphires set on 18-carat gold fans for £3,900.

Of course, English firms are represented as well, like Bracher & Sydenham of Reading who were responsible for a gold bangle made unusual by a detachable diamond target that doubles as a brooch or pendant. Still in its original box and complete with the brooch clasp and pendant holder, it can be your conversation piece for £12,200. But as amiably chatty as Anne is, she wouldn't tell us the price of the diamond and platinum collar with its intricate pattern of baguettes and brilliants. It was dripping with authentic 1930s glamour, but Anne will only talk about money to really serious potential buyers.

We guess she'd decided the extraordinary set of eight tortoiseshell place-card holders, made by Asprey in 1910 and inlaid with delicate silver animals and birds, was more our style. At £1,900, she was right.

Boucheron

180 New Bond Street	071-493-0983
London W1Y 9PT	(FAX) 071-493-3153

The allure of Boucheron jewelry, carefully shepherded by four generations of the venerable French family, dates from 1858 when Frederic Boucheron opened his first shop in Palais Royal in Paris. In an era when the wonders of "world exhibitions" were legend, Frederic's jewelry attracted notoriety with 1st-prize awards at the Philadelphia Exhibition in 1875 and the Paris fête in 1889. By 1893, fame had generated the need for expansion, and Frederic moved his shop to the Place Vendôme, becoming the first jeweler to stake out territory there for those that would follow.

The beneficiary of global attention, Frederic set his sights on the world and opened branches in London and Moscow—the latter going the way of so many other vestiges of the finer things in life with the onslaught of the Revolution. His son and successor, Louis, expanded on the global theme, as did his sons Fred and Gerard. So today Boucheron claims clients in virtually every country in the world—the Saudi Arabian royal family, the Begum Aga Khan, Elizabeth Taylor, members of the British aristocracy, Sophia Loren and Elsa Martinelli.

In London, many of them seek the services of managing director Norman Lane. He's seen a lot of spectacular gems come and go, yet he's not the tiniest bit jaded. Quite the contrary, in fact. Whether he's showing a delicately modest bracelet for just under £1,000 or a magnificent collar of white and canary diamonds set in geometric patterns in 18-carat yellow gold with matching earclips for closer to £500,000, he's got a sparkle in his eyes and an infectious enthusiasm. Indeed, when it comes to the subject of Boucheron's legendary craftsmanship, design and original creativity, he's downright reverent.

After he introduced us to "Les Pluriels," we were ready to worship at the same temple. This collection of cufflinks, rings, necklaces, watches, earrings and bracelets is an extraordinary combination of beauty, intelligence and flexibility. In each category, an 18-carat gold base piece is constructed to accommodate nine different inserts that transform the look of the piece. This is jewelry that defines yet defies traditions. Take the cufflinks. Give the £350 classic base to a deserving someone, and then commemorate a special anniversary annually with a rainbow of semiprecious stones that slide into place for £150 to £490. By the same token, there's not a woman worth her salt who wouldn't appreciate the exquisite design (not to mention the tradition) of an impressive link collar that converts from business to pleasure with its set of bejewelled implants.

For more solid investments, take a gander at the result of the current scion of the Boucheron clan's passion—jewelry and objets d'art incorporating the fascinating, half visible, half invisible proportion of rock crystal. The tall, debonair Alain Boucheron was the first to couple crystal with precious gems, while maintaining the family's custom of pure lines, simple curves and a density of carats that walks the fine line between plenitude and overkill. We were enchanted by the purity and transparency of a gold-rimmed, six-sided crystal box, its top decorated with a crest of diamonds, jade and coral. At £25,000 it may be the ultimate in coffee table boxes!

And speaking of ultimate, no profile of Boucheron would be complete without a mention of its ever so understated watches for the truly discriminating. Nothing about these unmistakably elegant timepieces screams status, as in *Rolex*. Their strikingly fluted gold cases come in three shapes—rectangular, round and square—and are interchangeable with all available bracelets and straps, allowing a total of 77 possible combinations. Prices start at £2,200 for ladies' styles and £2,450 for gents' watches. It's a small price to pay for admission to the select international club that recognizes their classy signature.   🍒

Butler and Wilson

189 Fulham Road	071-352-3045
London SW3 6JN	(FAX) 071-376-5424

Despite the records set by the auctions of the *real* jewelry collections of the likes of the Duchess of Windsor, there has, in the last decade, emerged a taste for and a massive cult devoted to the delightful fantasy of their costume cousins. In fact, costume jewelry has been transformed from a rather déclassé substitute for the real thing to high-fashion status. And if anyone could be fingered for playing the central role in this metamorphosis, it'd be Nicky Butler and Simon Wilson. Harrods' Fall 1989 retrospective exhibition of their work (the first ever such event held in the store's hallowed Jewelry Room) both commemorated their 21 years in business and confirmed the impact that Butler and Wilson have had on the British attitude toward costume jewelry.

Butler and Wilson started out selling the work of other designers, decorative jewelry chosen for its style, wit and fashion, primarily with art nouveau and art deco origins. The lavish displays in their tiny stand in Antiquarius on Kings Road caught the attention of Britain's fashion press. And soon they were inundated with customers demanding the items they had seen in various fashion spreads. Of course, given the lead time between a photographer's shoot and publication, the featured pieces had often been sold by the time the magazine or newspaper article came out. So, Nicky and Simon decided to start making their own designs.

They began by basing their styles on the 1930s, but as their confidence grew, Nicky and Simon began to combine old and new elements to create some of the most fantastic, unabashedly fake and quite quickly, talked-about jewelry around. They opened their first shop on Fulham Road in 1972. The South Molton location opened in 1984. While both stores have a stylish, minimalist non-decor, with black walls and bright spots aimed at the simple blond-wood and glass display cases, the legacy of Nicky and Simon's early market-stall days is still clear. The shops are crammed with a dazzling array of designs, as many as 6,000 pieces—from the Butler and Wilson hallmark heart-dangling-from-a-bow earrings, fashioned in glass for £18.50 to the classic "pearl" choker with "diamond" clasp at £98, to Nicky and Simon's glamorous diamante lizard for £198.

The dizzying selection, the generous range of prices (from £10 to £200) and the almost constant, attentive presence of Nicky or Simon have made both Butler and Wilson shops frequent haunts of Jerry Hall, Faye Dunaway, Lauren Hutton and, most impressively, the Princess of Wales and the Duchess of York. The first three ladies are presumably pretty well-off, but we *know* Di and Fergie have access to very serious jewels, yet still get a kick out of Nicky and Simon's splendid creations.

Even if a trip to London is not in your immediate plans, you can still enjoy the pleasure of wearing Butler and Wilson jewelry—their designs are now available in stores throughout Britain and the U.S. Nicky and Simon have even opened their own Butler and Wilson outposts in Glasgow and Los Angeles. Since some of their bestsellers are rhinestone incarnations of popular Walt Disney characters like Mickey and Minnie Mouse, Donald Duck and Goofy, we wonder if a shop in Orlando, Florida, looms in their future, too. Now there's an opportunity, Michael Eisner!

❦

Cartier

175–6 New Bond Street	071-493-6962
London W1Y 0QA	(FAX) 071-355-3011

There may be 145 Cartier stores around the world, but none has such romantic origins as the London beachhead. Opened on Burlington Street in 1902, the branch was the direct result of the intimate friendship and inter-marrying of the Cartier family with English couturier Charles-Frederic Worth's family. The mutually beneficial bond between the two designing families—Cartier's jewels and Worth's clothes—was ever so complementary, particularly on royals like Britain's Princess Alexandra, a Worth fashion fanatic. Through Worth, the Cartiers became friendly with the princess' husband, the future Edward VII. He announced their association to the world in 1902 when he placed an order for 27 tiaras for his coronation. With the patronage of the new king so eloquently (and profitably) expressed, the future success of Cartier in Britain was assured. And, indeed, to this day, the London store is second only to the Paris operation in sales per square metre.

One reason for the shop's ongoing popularity is the fact that many of the staff have been here for years and years, 45 years in the case of designer Dennis Gardner who worked with the store's founder, Jacques Louis Cartier's younger brother. Dennis' interpretations of traditional Cartier design themes are superb. So if you have an unmounted stone or two lying around or you want to reset that inherited brooch, make an appointment with him or his jewelry manager Terry Davidson. For as little as £1,000, the firm's in-house workrooms will whip up a little custom-made something for you.

As for the stock merchandise, it's predictably special, fit for clients like Elton John, George Michael, Paul McCartney and the Queen Mother whose Royal Warrant the shop holds. Jan Havlik usually works with special customers as he's the man in charge of the truly fine jewelry. With the exception of Her Majesty, who has the privilege of making selections in the privacy of her own home, Jan escorts them into the precious little "high jewelry" room, with its fireplace and majestic 19th-century panelling. There, the high-rollers review inestimable trinkets, such as the exquisite diamond symphony necklace we coveted—all 62.83 carats and

£102,000 of it. Then there's the famous Cartier cats so beloved by the
Duchess of Windsor. Double diamond-studded panther heads adorned a
truly fabulous bangle bracelet in 18-carat gold for £110,350.

You might even see a cat that actually belonged to Wallis, since Cartier
makes a habit of repurchasing its pieces. The firm keeps track of them,
with records of every single creation ever designed and sold in any of its
stores. So if an antique ring just cries out to be yours, its pedigree may
tell you who else was seduced by it.

Speaking of rings, if you're in the market for one of sentimental significance, take a look at Cartier's unparalleled collection of engagement
rings—from diamond solitaires to the sapphire and diamond combinations so popular in Britain. Prices range from the relatively affordable to
the outlandish, depending upon the flamboyance factor of you or your
intended. For less meaningful expenditures, investigate the new range of
Egyptian-inspired jewelry that starts at about £1,600.

And if you are in need of a gift of a more modest nature, showroom
manager Tessa Ley will show you the assortment of accessories that
have made Cartier quality so accessible to the masses. We were drawn to
a burgundy leather credit-card case for only £65. Unfortunately, it was
too slender to hold all the plastic we'd need to purchase that sensational
panther bracelet!   ❦

Cobra and Bellamy

149 Sloane Street	071-730-2823
London SW1 X9BZ	(FAX) 071-730-5286

Draped from floor to ceiling in dashing black and white pin-striped fabric, this little deco jewel box is just as striking as its two owners. Tania
Hunter is the engaging blond British woman. Veronica Manussis' dark
good looks, zest for life, and artistic spirit are of Greek origin. Together,
they travel the world in search of spectacular pieces representative of the
best of 20th-century costume jewelry—works by Chanel, Nina Ricci and
Trifari. When they're not out treasure hunting, Tania can usually be
found on the premises, while Veronica busies herself with designing a
line of jewelry for this store as well as for the Cobra & Bellamy outposts
at Liberty and the Joseph's store on Sloane Street.

Veronica's work is very large and very graphic with sleek, simple lines,
usually executed in sterling silver, although most pieces can be done in
gold by special request. It has a timeless quality about it, which is com-

forting when you're contemplating spending £840 (sans tax) for an enamelled silver necklace. Equally stunning was a tubular necklace, lent subtle detail by the clever use of various widths for £126. Add £50 for the earrings, plus the tax for both.

When we're looking for something glitzier than Veronica's glamorous designs, we turn our attention to the couture costume pieces that make up the bulk of the inventory in the black lacquered cases. Much of it dates from the '20s, '40s and '50s, like the crystal bead Chanel necklace made extraordinary by flower-shaped "garnets" for £680. Like everything else here, it's in mint condition. And, as with all the Chanel pieces, it has been authenticated by Madame Gripoix, who ought to know. Her family has been making all Chanel's jewelry for three generations.

This is where Jerry Hall and Lady Conran find some of their favourite earrings, like the circa 1940 Chanel earrings, sporting three full mobi pearls set in a field of green cut glass and rhinestones at £300. And we had to drag ourselves away from a £620 Nina Ricci star-shaped stunner, a brooch fashioned in pearls, rhinestones and large cabachon "emeralds."

There is a reward for resisting temptation here. After all, you have to come back to take just one more look, and it's always a treat. Tania and her sales assistants make every effort to pamper you. They encourage you to linger as long as you can, with genuinely warm hospitality, dashing to the café next door for coffee or a snack to make up for that lunch you skipped. Of course, a little nourishment helps you digest £1,400 plus tax for an earring and brooch set. Remember, this is costume. But it does make a sparkling (and very real-looking) statement with "rubies, diamonds, and emeralds" clustered in invisible settings to resemble carnations. For the real thing, check out Bertagnolli & Blum's work in sterling silver and 24-carat gold inspired by the Vienna succession movement— gemstones sparkle in earrings and rings, £780 and £650, respectively.

The girls have been here for 12 years, well before the Bond Street to Sloane Street exodus, proving they have just as good an eye for real estate as they do for jewelry. And just in case you were wondering why the shop is named Cobra and Bellamy, instead of Hunter and Manussis (or, to be symmetrical Manussis and Hunter), there's a predictably good reason. It seems that Tania Hunter's maiden name is Bellamy; however, Veronica thought Manussis was a bit of a nuisance on a logo. But her influence is there nonetheless—Cobra refers to a group of '50s painters and sculptors whose work Veronica admires. They hailed from Copenhagen, Oslo, Brussels, Rotterdam and Amsterdam—get it? ❦

Elizabeth Gage

20 Albemarle Street   071-499-2879
London W1X 3HA   (FAX) 071-495-4550

We first ran across Elizabeth Gage in a suite at the Carlyle, where the
ebullient blond was showing her distinctive jewelry to a very appreciative
audience—many of whom were already avid collectors, the result of her
annual treks to New York with the best and brightest of her collection.
Indeed, an argument could be made that Elizabeth is better known in
the U.S. than in her homeland. Articles in glossy publications like *W*
have positioned her as *the* reigning British jewelry designer, citing her
flair for creating exceptionally striking pieces. But often when we have
mentioned her name to even our most sophisticated London friends, we
are met with blank stares.

When that happens we make a date to take them to Elizabeth's Albemarle Street salon, where, invariably, they become instant devotees.
Their enchantment begins with the salon itself, which once bore the
Cartier name. Most jewelry showrooms are purposely understated to the
point of dull, generally done in elegant hues of blue, grey or beige. Not
so Elizabeth's lair. There's a festive, sophisticated, Laura Ashley look to
it, thanks to the rose and green (her favourite colour combination) paisley print wall covering. A curving banquette in green is made all the
more conversational, not to mention comfortable, with fluffy, ruffled pillows. Metal jardinières painted to look like baskets overflow with colourful silk flowers, and a gloriously fake dogwood tree, rooted in a corner,
hovers overhead. All in all, the salon, like Elizabeth's jewelry, is an oddly
intoxicating blend of kitsch, classic and contemporary.

It is conspicuous, substantial-looking jewelry which immediately identifies itself as hers and is most definitely not for the faint (or dainty) of
heart. Elizabeth states, "Jewels for the modern woman are jewels to be
worn day into night, bold, sumptuous, with an elegance to take her anywhere." One signature style that we've seen adopted by classy ladies all
over the world is the wide templar rings featuring intriguing textures in
gold and studded with stones. They start at about £1,100 and are representative of much of Elizabeth's work in that they echo Greek, Roman
and medieval themes. Furthermore, in these, as in so many Elizabeth
Gage pieces, the gold is richly worked, using ancient techniques such as
granulation and beading—the setting is as important as the stones to the

total effect. It's the stunning, architectural combinations of gold and colourful stones that truly differentiate Elizabeth's work.

She is one designer who is not afraid to revel in brilliant colour. She uses stones the way an artist uses a palette, often concocting seemingly discordant mosaics, which always work almost in spite of themselves. She's not afraid of mixing the precious with the semiprecious, with studied abandon, either. We were mesmerized by a brooch and earring set of blue tourmaline, mobe pearls, rosy-red rubellite, white hot diamonds, and South Sea pearls, set in 18-carat gold. Dramatic is not the word for it. We imagine the price is equally extravagant, but Zoe Simpson, the self-assured executive director, is loathe to quote specific numbers for publication. Fair enough. Suffice it to say, that at Elizabeth Gage, you're looking at a broad range—from about £1,000 to upwards of £75,000. They're "not so extravagant that people have to lock them up in the bank," says Elizabeth; "they are jewels to be worn and enjoyed". . .and to stop traffic—the show-stopping collar of briollet-cut aquamarines and tourmalines surrounded by diamonds, accented with a detachable 31-carat aquamarine pendant, for instance. Then there's the massive triangular-shaped watermelon tourmaline, encased in grainy gold, dripping with frosted onyx. Generally speaking, neither one of us is much for broaches, but pieces like this seem destined to change our minds.

Maybe we'll even have Elizabeth make a couple for us using the stones from the ugly, inherited pieces that clutter up our safe-deposit boxes. She delights in creating special jewelry for clients and has a knack for knowing what would suit them best. And she's a miracle-worker when it comes to redesigning dated jewelry, turning it into one of her timeless works of art—like her Charlemagne ring, a huge purple amethyst set in a crown of green enamel, punctuated by small round cabochon amethysts. Or one of her Agincourt range, flexible rings in the manner of old-fashioned metal watchbands of finely sculpted gold, set with resourceful combinations of stones. Their intricacy of detail teases and surprises the eye, providing the enjoyment which is endemic to Elizabeth's jewelry. Her work very much reflects her attitude that jewelry should be first and foremost an investment in pleasure.

Garrard

112 Regent Street   071-734-7020
London W1A 2JJ   (FAX) 071-439-9197

Designated the official keeper of the crown jewels since 1843, Garrard's recently found itself in the middle of the quintessential good-news/bad-news scenario. The good news is that as of January 1990 the eminent firm holds Prince Charles' Royal Warrant; the bad news is that every piece of letterhead, every card, every bag, every catalogue, every any-thing sporting Garrard's logo had to be reprinted to incorporate the Prince of Wales' three-feathered coat of arms. Our guess is that the shop was happy to do it. Not only is the appointment prestigious, it hearkens to the company's origins when George Wickes set up shop as a gold-smith on Ponton Street in 1735. One of his earliest and best customers was the then Prince of Wales, Frederick.

That prince was especially fond of the ornate rococo style so popular at the time, and Mr Wickes was a master of it. Indeed, it would seem the prince was a little too fond of Mr Wickes' exquisite renditions in silver— not only was Frederick one of his first clients, but the prince's excesses represented one of the young firm's first bad debts. Despite that unfortu-nate incident, the royal connection, once established, has never been broken. The company has consistently fashioned state and personal jew-elry for the royal family for over 250 years. Garrard adapted the Imperial State Crown for Queen Elizabeth's coronation and, more recently, sup-plied the engagement rings for both the Princess of Wales and the Duch-ess of York.

So much for the pedigree of the clientele. But what about the family tree of a firm started by a man named Wickes and now called Garrard? The name change stems from the 1790 employment of one Robert Gar-rard, who gained control of the company during the early years of the 19th century. It remained in his family's hands until 1952 when it was amalgamated with another venerable jeweller and moved to the present, palace-like Regent Street site.

Don't worry about having to flash your coat of arms to gain admission, though. The discreet, well-informed staff are just as solicitous of com-moners as they are of their titled patrons. Furthermore, you don't neces-sarily have to worry about the number of figures in your bank account or the limits on your credit cards. Perhaps taking a cue from Tiffany, with whom Garrard would appear to share a passion for blue, the firm has expanded its inventory horizons to include an abundance of gift items, including calculators, decanters, ice buckets, briarwood veneer and leather briefcases, Herend elephants. They range in price from only £10 to virtually limitless amounts. But unlike Tiffany/New York's (as opposed to London's) frenetic atmosphere, all is calm and decorum here. The spacious showrooms, recently refurbished, benefit from aisles and are dominated by a majestic double staircase of Sicilian marble.

Fit for a king, it looks as if it belongs in one of the enchanting precious metal, mineral and gemstone castles which are a Garrard tradition. Gold and silver towers and turrets are surrounded by lapis lazuli moats and adorned with glimmering stones. Only two or three are made annually by the gifted William Tolliday, so there's always a waiting list. Suffice it to say that if you have to ask the price, you can't afford one.

We did talk about money in the extensive antique jewelry department, which specializes in 19th-century pieces. We just had to know about the stunning emerald and diamond bracelet which had belonged to the Duchess of Windsor. A token of the Duke's affection, it is inscribed with their initials and the date of its presentation. And it could have been ours for a mere £1,000,000.

Less budget-stretching are the custom-designed signet rings that can be had for as little as £325. Still, it's likely you'll spend considerably more for one fashioned in 18-carat gold that sports an elaborate coat of arms or symbol of your profession or whatever you have in mind. Garrard's in-house designers can create or re-create just about any motif, and they are ready, willing and able to work with you to realize the jewelry of your dreams, be it a simple ring or an entrance-making necklace. We don't know whose idea it was, but we were taken with the striking diamond necklace composed of alternating emerald and round-cut stones and sporting a solitary (albeit enormous) pear-shaped sapphire—price upon application (British for request), but undoubtedly a fortune in any language.

More modest, but still an excellent example of Garrard's fine design and workmanship, is a group of jewelry made of yellow-gold oval links, set with pave diamonds, each distinguished by a single gem seemingly floating in the centre. You could look and feel like a queen with the matching necklace and bracelet, £35,000 and £18,000, respectively.

And speaking of workmanship, don't miss the shop's collection of trophies upstairs. Garrard's has traditionally made them for many of the world's most prestigious sporting events. The firm was responsible for the fabled America's cup, and a number of similarly impressive pieces are on display, including the 96-ounce, 18-carat gold cup commissioned by George V for Ascot in 1923. You can't win it, but you can buy it. (You can *claim* you won it in a polo match—one you played in with Prince Charles.)   ❦

Graff

55 Brompton Road	071-584-8571
London SW3 1DP	(FAX) 071-581-3415

Our guess is that if Laurence Graff had his way, when Marilyn Monroe crooned "Diamonds Are a Girl's Best Friend" in *Gentlemen Prefer Blondes,* she would ask him to talk to her rather than Harry Winston. Ever since he "went public" in 1974 by relinquishing his family's wholesale gem business in favour of a retail operation, Laurence has been dogging Harry's dear departed heels to become "King of Diamonds." Indeed, he seems to beg the comparison between the two firms—Laurence takes a P.T. Barnum approach to the business, constantly criss-crossing the globe in his relentless pursuit of the most important stones and exhibiting them with the appropriate hyperbole. Challenging but, we think, not attaining Winston's tagline of being the "ultimate jeweller," the purveyor of "rare jewels of the world," Laurence unabasedly declares his "the most fabulous collection of jewels in the world."

Certainly, it's one of the most dazzling. Once through the vault-like entrance of the salon, you are assaulted by the brilliant radiance of (literally) tens of thousands of carats of masterfully lit jewels. It's like strolling into the Smithsonian's Hall of Gems and, indeed, there is a museum-like look to the display—a solid stream of eye-level glass cases lines the perimetre of the room. They almost seem to float in mid-air, as the supporting walls, as well as the floor and ceiling, fade into the background. There is nothing to compete with the contents of the cases for the attention of the eye—at Graff the jewelry *is* the decor.

And what a resplendent decor it is, featuring such astonishing sights as what Laurence considers to be the most fabulous stone that has so far passed through his hands. Unnamed when we were introduced to it, this extraordinary pear-shaped diamond is aptly described by Graff's spokesperson, Gwendoline Farrow, as "a drop of frozen light." Some drop—it's a whopping 85.91 carats, the fourth largest flawless, pear-shaped diamond in the world. Naturally, the gracious Gwendoline, a beautiful jewel in her own right with her luxuriant red hair and creamy skin, declined to discuss price. Suffice it to say, we're talking millions, and Graff will have no trouble selling it—but not before Laurence produced a replica for his Hall of Famous Diamonds, a memorable exhibit of some of the major stones that have been in the firm's possession at one time or another.

One we found especially intriguing is Le Grand Coeur D'Afrique, at 70.03 carats the world's largest flawless, heart-shaped diamond. It is truly a Graff creation, the product of Laurence's imagination fired by the discovery of an exceptional 278-carat rough diamond in 1982. After months of delicate negotiations, he purchased it and turned it over to his two best diamond cutters. It took them a year of painstaking work to cut three stones from the rough—two "satellites," a 14.25-carat marquis and a 25.22-carat, heart-shaped diamond were fashioned before the pièce de résistance emerged. The magnificent gem was eventually coupled with its smaller heart-shaped satellite (Le Petit Coeur d'Afrique) and set into a spectacular necklace.

But not all Graff jewelry is quite that serious. Prices start at about £3,000 and some of the pieces are downright amusing, like the precious (literally and figuratively) cuddling koala bears, available as pendants, earrings and brooches in pink, yellow or white diamonds. Think £5,000 and up. The adorable bears are indicative of Laurence's new-found interest in coloured diamonds. His craftsmen have been working with them a lot lately, turning out pieces like a very unusual ring featuring pink, blue and yellow stones cut—respectively—in square, pear and oval shapes. The centre, pear-shaped, blue diamond sported 7.5 carats, with the total weight of the ring being close to 14. The ring (as opposed to the bears) ranks among the store's significant jewelry. Gwendoline once again avoided the question of cost. To our way of thinking, whatever it is, it is definitely worth it, as the ring is truly unique.

More traditional was an immense, unbelievably green, emerald-cut emerald ring, surrounded by diamonds. But it was made unmistakably Graff by the baguette cut of the diamonds, each secured by 18-carat yellow-gold prongs that highlighted the design. We still covet it.

No doubt it will have been sold when next we visit—Laurence has more trouble finding worthy stones than he does well-heeled customers from all over the planet. And Laurence tries to make sure they keep coming back by developing personal relationships with many of them, encouraging them to call him or his son François before hitting town. If they can't get through, it's only because he and François are off in search of splendid stones that will give additional lustre to the growing legend of Graff.   ❦

Ken Lane

66 South Molton Street   071-499-3700
London W1Y 1HH

Our New York pal, Kenneth Jay Lane, established his first international beachhead in London in the 1960s. It was on Beauchamp Place and is still going strong, as is the tiny shop in the Burlington Arcade. But when we're in the market for Ken's fabulous fakes, we head for the latest of his retail gems in South Molton Street. Leave it to our dear Kenny to dive into the sophisticated up-market frenzy on this street, so recently anointed as one of the world's most fashionable. Kenny's never far from the action, which has a lot to do with his incredible success.

You see, he's always had the good sense to attach himself to very grand ladies with world-class taste, ladies who adore him for his sophisticated charm and incisive wit. Kenny's their escort of choice when their husbands are unavailable (and even when they are). Consequently, he's constantly exposed to the most amazing jewels, which he happily and expertly copies. Kenny views it as a compliment to the jewelry, asserting "you are nobody, if I haven't knocked you off." And, fortunately, his influential mentors subscribe to his theory. They're amused when he conspiratorially tells them they'll see his version of their baubles for a small percentage of the amount they paid.

In fact, they're not only fans, they're customers. Jackie Onassis, Nancy Reagan and Nan Kempner routinely opt for Kenny's costume jewelry in lieu of the real thing. Then there's the matter of Barbara Bush's omnipresent pearl choker—it, too, can be yours.

In London, the clientele includes Kate Aidie, Liza Minnelli and Princess Di. Even Prince Philip has dropped by, and Jack Nicholson seems to find Kenny's jewelry the perfect (not to mention economical) gift for his ladylove(s) of the moment. We suspect that they, like us, choose the Molton Street shop because of the mind-boggling collection of earrings which is even larger than that of the New York store, and the presence of manager Pam Lewis. She's a whiz at sorting through the vast selection and coming up with just the right pin, bracelet or earrings to go with that new suit. Just describe (or show) it to her and let her fingers do the walking.

She may steer you toward Kenny's most popular copies, those of Cartier and Bulgari pieces. The traditional Cartier animal brooches favoured by the Duchess of Windsor (naturally a dear friend of Kenny's) are a speciality—£10 to £130. Very nice and dead ringers for the real thing, we still prefer the more contemporary look of the chunky gold "Bulgari" chains, set with cabochon stones for £195. We also liked a multi-strand, jet bead necklace sporting a statement-making centre hook clasp set in diamante highlighted by black enamel at £135—matching diamante and enamel earrings in a knot configuration go for £108.

In this instance, we can't pinpoint the source of inspiration—it could be a Ken Lane original, of which there are many, all cleverly inventive. So much so that some of his clients have been known to have his work copied by fine jewellers using precious metals and gems!

We're glad Kenny has finally taken our cue and replaced the faux flowers at the front of this otherwise sleekly mirrored jewel box of a store—they weren't nearly as good fakes as his.   ❦

Kiki McDonough

73 Elizabeth Street	071-730-0248/3756
London SW1 W9J	(FAX) 071-730-2708

We first heard about Kiki McDonough and her eye-catching but understated jewelry from one of her biggest fans. We'd like to say it was the Duchess of York, who is one, but alas we're not on such intimate terms with that vivacious royal. But we are chummy with Justin de Blank, whose first-rate food shop is right across the street from Kiki's precious little boutique. He told us we couldn't leave the Eaton Square area without visiting her. We were amenable, thrilled to juxtapose the pursuit of our two greatest passions—food and jewelry.

It turns out Kiki is a newcomer to London's large and diverse jewelry scene, but in only five years, she's carved out a respectable niche to call her very own. She designs modern pieces at reasonable prices, from £200 to about £2,000—a price range that on Bond Street wouldn't buy you much of interest.

Here, there's plenty to warrant your perusal, brought to you by a dynamic redhead who's never had any formal training in jewelry design. It would seem she didn't need it. She knew what she liked and what she wanted—elegant jewelry that works as well with jeans as it does with cocktail dresses—she just couldn't find it. So she started making it. Of course, the fact that she came from a family of jewellers didn't hurt. Kiki knew the ropes and the resources. What she didn't know was how to sketch, and she still doesn't. But she's a great communicator, who inspires craftsmen to translate her ideas into functional works of art, into jewelry for the 1990s.

The shop itself reflects the progressive, clean lines of Kiki's work. . . and its romantic warmth. Neutral tones in the fabric-padded walls, the carpet and the display cases set off the rich colours of her favourite stones—amethyst, onyx, hematite and lapis lazuli. Stunning marbleized, obelisk-shaped vitrines dominate the room and mirror the fanciful touch in the very wearable jewelry.

It's the flexibility of Kiki's pieces that her customers find so appealing. Many of her necklaces come with detachable decorative clips that can instantly transform a simply elegant strand of beads into an authoritative piece of jewelry. For instance, a lovely 9mm baroque cultured pearl necklace stands on its own but becomes a knockout with the addition of a large, heart-shaped mobe pearl, set in an intricately twisted 18-carat gold rope mount—string of pearls and clip are £1,900. We were also intrigued with the blue-black radiance of a hematite bead necklace. The gold loops separating the beads at the front are distinguished enough details, until you add the glamorous barrel-shaped hematite and 18-carat gold clip. The set sells for £650.

On the earring front, the heart-shaped onyx pair with diamond-punctuated, 18-carat gold bows are stylishly whimsical at £495. And once you put on the sizable mobe pearls encased in an elaborate scroll setting for £1,200, you'd be tempted to never take them off. You wouldn't have to, either. They outdo even Chanel, with their go-anywhere, anytime flair. And the pear-shaped faceted rock crystal drops, topped by gold-embellished sapphires are show-stoppers at £495.

Kiki doesn't ignore gentlemen's needs for good-looking practical pieces either. She has a nice selection of cufflinks and moneyclips done in 9-carat gold and semiprecious stones for £275 to £395.

If you're in the market for handsome, serviceable "fine" (as opposed to costume) jewelry at accessible prices, head straight for Kiki's. Don't even stop by Justin de Blank's. Save that particular treat for afterwards, as a reward for your good taste.   🍐

Kutchinsky

73 Brompton Road	071-584-9311
London SW3 1DB	(FAX) 071-589-4385

We admit we didn't know much about Kutchinsky when we first entered the jewelry firm's soft and creamy showroom. We had been referred by one of our London sources. But things got off to a rocky start when it was clear there was a mix-up about our appointment with Paul Kutchinsky—he was out of town and hadn't told anyone we were expected. But typical of a company and family whose middle name must be gracious, we were nonetheless greeted like long lost friends (or clients) by the dashing David O'Connor, who, like most of the staff, is on the fair side of 45 and has spent the bulk of his professional life here. He ushered us through the calm sanctuary of the front room, its dreamy atmosphere dotted with little Regency desks, as only the subtlest reminder that this is a place of business, to a private alcove toward the rear.

There, he started to tell the Kutchinsky tale, only to be usurped in his labour of obvious love by an even better representative—Paul's brother, Roger Kutchinsky. Together, Paul and Roger maintain a jewelry legacy that dates to the reign of Queen Victoria in London, but traces its origins to the Continent where the family served as jewellers to King Ludwig of Bavaria. Given Ludwig's extravagances, it's not surprising that Kutchinsky continues to produce extraordinary objets d'art as commissioned and stock pieces. A remarkable natural rock crystal fruit compote trimmed with 18-carat gold, its columned pedestal encasing a 4,350 carat citrine, took our breath away. So did the price at £96,750.

Just as we were recovering, Roger, who resembles a jolly Peter Lorre, presented us with what he described as "the ultimate in Dinky toys"—a miniature Ferrari made of rock crystal with ruby seats, an 18-carat gold roof, diamond tail-board and onyx wheels. Keys dangled from the ignition and the gold steering wheel worked. Roger's eyes danced as he told us he wouldn't want any of his customers to come to harm, so he had insisted on the gold seatbelts and emerald-cut diamond rear-view and side-view mirrors. It took 18 months to manufacture and was created for stock, quite an investment in time and materials for a toy selling for £160,000. You could buy a garage full of the real thing for that!

The jewelry is equally spectacular. Take the emerald and diamond collar, handmade in the firm's own workshops, as is all Kutchinsky jewelry.

Its staggering centre square-cut, 38-carat Colombian emerald was high-lighted by another 50 carats of pavé diamonds. Roger reminded us that the £556,000 pricetag would be somewhat slashed by the tax refund if it was sold for export. Comforting thought, one we also applied to a £385,000 necklace with its 62.56 carats of diamonds arranged in a deli-cate floral pattern. And what a thrill it would be to offer a pair of Kutchinsky's diamond cufflinks as a token of affection to an equestrian type. Gold horseshoes enshrine the most imaginatively cut diamonds we've ever seen. They're in the shape of a horse's head, making the links gloriously unique, as well they should be for £10,000.

While we're on the subject of diamonds, we should mention the shop carries the U.K.'s largest selection of diamond watches. It has every brand you've ever heard of and one you probably haven't—Kutchinsky's own, available in an amazing range of styles fashioned in a vast assort-ment of materials. There's no real signature, except that they may look small to an American eye. Roger explained that his watches are made primarily for Europeans who tend to have smaller wrists than those of us from the colonies, and who therefore tend to go for more modestly scaled timepieces. Whether it's Kutchinsky or otherwise, watches start as low as £750 here and can go as high as £300,000.

Probably higher, as Roger made it clear that the firm will go to virtually any length to produce phenomenal watches, jewelry and objects. As far as we're concerned, he proved it without a shadow of a doubt when, for Easter of 1990, he and Paul unveiled a giant egg with a sparkling pink di-amond shell, concealing a wealth of movable delights, including a fantas-tic gallery of tiny portraits. King Ludwig would have loved it.

Tiffany & Co.

25 Old Bond Street
London W1X 3AA

071-409-2790
(FAX) 071-491-3110

Could this *really* be Tiffany? Where are the unwashed masses? Where are the harried sales staff? Where is the interminable wait for a lift? But, yes, the cunning eggshell blue boxes with their white ribbons are in evi-dence, and that is an Elsa Peretti open heart, sterling silver pendant in the glass-topped, almost black-matte finish mahogany case. If it's Peretti, it must be Tiffany, as she is one of the stars of the firm's stable of exclu-sive designers. Indeed, nothing but the quality of the merchandise and service of this small, quiet store even vaguely resembles its New York parent. An overstuffed, linen tapestry-covered sofa and armchair separated by a magazine-strewn coffee table dominate the centre of the room. Need we say more?

Opened in 1986 as the first international outpost of this most identifiably American of jewelry concerns, the shop is a genuine charmer, not the least bit intimidating, with its picture window framing (of all things) a comfy window seat. Still, despite its inviting atmosphere, we're told it got off to a slow start in terms of sales. Perhaps as the American upstart—the New York store was founded in 1837, young by English jewelry standards—Tiffany had to prove its mettle and metal before being adopted by British buyers. And speaking of metal, only that hallmarked as 18-carat gold or sterling silver is sold here—no 14 carat and no plate.

Prices for what manager, Christopher MacDonald, described as the store's collection of "fancy goods" start at about £40. Properly discreet, however, he indicated the sky can be the limit, particularly when you get into custom-designed items, a Tiffany specialty in olde London towne. We understand one client was intent upon a very special gift for his clearly beloved spouse, a gift that would be an appropriate token of their whole family's appreciation of her years of devoted service. He consulted each of the couple's three daughters about their favourite colours, and then brought Christopher into the loop. The result was a spectacular bracelet made of precious stones, corresponding to each of the girls' colour choices, fashioned into four fanciful flowers. The back of each was further adorned by a facsimile of their signatures—one of hubby's too, ergo, the fourth flower.

Now that she truly has everything, maybe next time he'll bestow upon his wife a considerably less costly bauble that caught our eyes—a beautiful powder brush with an ornate silver and gold handle for £235. And for the man who has *almost* everything, may we suggest the sterling silver stays for £40?

As for our wish list, put us down for the triangular-shaped Paloma Picasso rubellite earrings, their edges softened by bevelled gold frames— real statement-makers for £17,280, only the ozone layer in Tiffany's price atmosphere!

Van Peterson

117A–119 Walton Street	071-589-2155
London SW3 2HP	(FAX) 071-584-8165

A real-life Connecticut Yankee (almost) in King Arthur's Court, Van Peterson is actually from Washington, D.C., where he studied to join that city's legion of lawyers. Still, like his fictional predecessor, he's been shaking things up in merry old England since he emigrated a decade ago. Indeed, Van is almost single-handedly responsible for broadening Englishmen's horizons when it comes to cufflinks. He noticed that choices of these necessary little furnishings were decidedly limited in his adopted country and rather prosaic at that—oval, round or square. So he designed his own collection featuring airplanes, ships, turtles, racing cars and, for the theatre buff, a set of Comedy and Tragedy masks. In sterling, Van Peterson links cost £100; in gold they're £300.

Either way, they're one of the highlights of the store he opened eight years ago, after refining his jewelry-dealing skills at a stall in Camden Lock. He operates it with his charming (and British) wife Lynn— apparently Van has found more than a new career since setting foot on English soil. His large selection of vintage sterling and costume jewelry is proudly displayed in a brightly lit, caramel-coloured environment, designed to make the most of all that sparkles here. It's an eclectic lot, though Van's fondness for the best of the 1920s' and 1930s' offerings is evident in the original pieces like the men's Rolex watches or the eye-catching diamond and platinum studs (£2,000 for the set), and in the assortment of reproductions. Of special note in the latter category is a group of exquisite, flamboyantly deco picture frames. Crafted in sterling silver and accented by paste "gems" with a touch of colourful enamel here and there, they spell glamour. We were particularly taken with the cunning little travel frames, the glass protected by very decorative pairs of doors. A Van Peterson exclusive, the frames range in price from £275 to £350.

Van and Lynn's collection of women's jewelry is streamlined and elegant in sterling, opulent and colourful in 18-carat gold plate and stones, and traditional in paste diamond and emeralds. They discovered a designer in Barcelona named Michael John, who's a master with silver. His bracelet, resembling a Henry Moore sculpture, is a stunning conversation piece at £400. Less attention-grabbing, but equally beautiful, is his featherlight rope bracelet for £300. Other silver focal points include a necklace, bracelet, brooch and earrings for Flipper fanatics. Fortunately, these lovely dolphin pieces are priced individually—£500, £350, £210 and £150, respectively. En masse, they're a bit overpowering.

The current crop of 18-carat, gold-plated creations looks as if it once graced Cleopatra's jewel box—lavishly studded with pearls and coloured stones, opulent, but priced to be extremely affordable. Prices start at about £50 and go up to £200. However, most items are tagged at around £100.

If your taste runs to the more traditional costume look in paste, head for the case to the left of the door. It's full of Trifari—jewelry made shortly after World War II by a group of veterans of such great European houses as Cartier and Boucheron who had been brought together in New York by a couple of American entrepreneurs. Charged with making high-quality costume pieces that approximated the fine jewelry they used to make, the enterprising craftsmen succeeded admirably. Van and Lynn's collection of Trifari is one of the best around, with prices that begin in the £100 neighbourhood and escalate considerably from there.

Still, jewelry isn't the only story at Van Peterson. The shop has started selling original photographs by the likes of Norman Parkinson, Cecil Beaton, Horst and Hoyningen Huene. More precious, or at least more costly, than most of the jewelry—Norman Parkinson's renowned "The Art of Travel" is £900 and the average price for a Huene is £730—the photographs are, nonetheless, an appropriately glamorous complement. And, of course, they're not exactly what most Brits (or anyone for that matter) would expect to find in a jewelry store, which is just the way Van likes it.

CHAPTER SEVEN

Beauty and Health

Now, if they could just bottle that picture-perfect English complexion

P erhaps it's all that rain—the ideal natural moisturizer—or Sherlock Holmes' famous fog or the fresh air at all those country houses. Whatever it is, British women, not to mention their male counterparts, have beautiful skin. So in all respects, it's not surprising that beauty products have put London on the map, in a certain sense, preserving all that glowing skin and making the most of their other endowments! The best advertisement for beauty products, after all, married into the royal family—over the last 10 years or so Princess Di has glowed from magazine covers around the world.

So it shouldn't be too surprising that a long tradition developed of chemists and barbers concocting potions meant to enhance the human countenance. Indeed, neither sex has ever been shy about indulging in them. Remember, the term *dandy* was coined in London, and for good reason. The gentlemen were the ones who popularized perfumes by indulging in the scents created for them by their barbers. And a strong case can be made that the first establishment in the world to cater to female beauty needs was in London.

In any event, there's no doubt that since the 1960s, since the advent of Vidal Sassoon, Jean Shrimpton's luxurious locks, Twiggy's crop-top, and the Beatles' bangs, London has had an international influence on hair care. What the city's hairmeisters do best is develop a look uniquely suited to you in terms of colour and cut—just as they've done for the divine Diana, not to mention her spirited sister-in-law.

From emporiums devoted to the closely guarded secrets of century-old formulations, to high-tech salons, to ancient enclaves of masculine pampering, there is a place to appeal to everyone's taste—and deep pockets.

SUPPLIES

Czech & Speake

39C Jermyn Street	071-439-0216
London SW1Y 6DN	(FAX) 081-981-7232

For years, Frank Sawkins felt that bathrooms, no matter how contemporary, lacked what he considered one essential element—elegance. He was drawn to a time of fewer modern conveniences but considerably more grace, that of the Edwardian era. The more he thought about it, the more he was convinced there was an unfulfilled niche in the market for bathroom equipment that was both functional and elegant. So, Frank set out to fill that void by designing an Edwardian range of "sanitaryware" and fittings, a happy combination of the engineering feats of today and the beauty of a bygone age.

Frank and his Edwardian line found a niche all right. When was the last time you opened a glossy decorating magazine that *didn't* feature a brass-footed tub and pedestal washbasin? They may not be Frank's, but he deserves some credit for the trend.

He also deserves a kudo or two for taking his vision of Edwardian elegance one step further by creating sophisticated toiletries. With the help of designer/perfumer Shirley Brody, he concocted a strikingly packaged aromatic line—soaps, bath oils, shampoos, colognes, talcum powders and potpourris. Now partners, Frank and Shirley have developed six distinct fragrances which curry favour with a broad range of customers who share their view that bathrooms should be seats of indulgent relaxation—

people like Susan Hampshire, members of the Rothschild family, Billy Joel, David Frost and Victoria Tennant. Presumably, they all appreciate purity—a quality that Frank and Shirley have gone to great pains to incorporate. Everything is made with natural essences—no synthetics—and old-fashioned touches abound. The soaps are handmade and triple milled, each wrapped in the Edwardian manner in glycerine paper. It seems those dawn-of-the-century types knew what they were doing—the glycerine paper keeps the fragrance from dissipating almost indefinitely.

Should redoing your bathroom be more than you can cope with, you can certainly dress it up with Czech & Speake products. There's a lovely group of accessories, including our favourite, the £69 free-standing brass toothbrush holder—it's also handy, not to mention chic, for makeup brushes. And it's easy to take care of as the price—excluding tax—includes a coating that prevents tarnish. Equally handsome, a porcelain soap dish floating in a brass, wall-mounted fitting sells for £65, coated and minus tax. For a mere £12.50, you can change the entire ambience of your bathroom with one of the shop's scented burning oil rings. Fill the ring with the fragrance of your choice and sit it on a light bulb to release its alluring scent.

Actually, any of the toiletry products lend a touch of class to the environment—like the line for men which Frank and Shirley named after the address of their first shop at 88 Jermyn Street. An intoxicating blend of some 100 essential oils yielding an enticingly masculine aroma, the No. 88 cologne comes in a distinctive satin-finish black bottle—£34 for 100ml. So does the No. 88 aftershave, and Frank and Shirley have been clever enough to devise a jell formulation especially for travelling. No worries about broken bottles in your luggage. The regular aftershave sells for £27 for 100ml, and it costs £17.50 for 50g of the jell.

While it pleases us to dispense No. 88 products to worthy males, it pleases us more to soak in a bath laced with Czech & Speake's rose bath oil. The scent is divine, a charming blend of English roses, jasmine and geranium bourbon, and the oil doesn't leave any telltale blobs. It just leaves your skin smelling sensational and feeling invitingly soft, at £25.50 for 100ml, £37 for 200ml. Add some rose soap for £6, along with the rose candle at approximately £20, and you've gone a long way toward transforming your bathroom into the elegant sanctuary Frank and Shirley feel it should be.

The shop is set up to show off all the Czech & Speake products in their natural settings, demonstrating their best uses (within reason, of course). Towels drape on brass and enamel racks, bathrobes hang on hooks, soaps and shampoos nestle in brass and nickel bathracks. The oversized porcelain bathtub lounging on its claw-like brass feet (£1,798) in front of the fireplace may be a little far-fetched, but it is representative of Frank and Shirley's idea of a truly contemporary bathroom. 🍇

D.R. Harris & Co. Ltd

29 St James's Street	071-930-8753
London SW1A 1HB	(FAX) 071-925-2691

The little bar once populated by the city's swells who would come to nurse their hard-won hangovers from a night of carousing in St James's "clubland" no longer exists, but the tradition remains. D.R. Harris, established in 1790 just down the street at No. 11 and still operated by the Harris family, continues to produce its patented Pick-Me-Up, known to the cognoscenti as the Original. Herbal-based with a touch of ammonia for a little zing and priced at £1 per glass, it has been reviving and stimulating jaded senses since the 1860s. And according to Pat Assirati, one of the sympathetic staff members, it really works. She ought to know—not because she depends on its powers on a regular basis, but because she's seen countless regulars down a glass. You see, this handsome, 40-something lady started working here when she was 18, left to raise her family, and she has returned to the Victorian grace of this chemists, which serves as a sanctuary to a number of old-time characters who find D.R. Harris a haven from the rigours of modern society.

Pat told us the origins of the Original stem from the fact that during the last century no chemists could exist in the area without offering some sort of a "morning after" remedy. Today, D.R. Harris is the sole remaining dispenser of such a tonic—£13.35 for 500ml, £4.25 for 100ml, just in case you want to keep some at home. Alternatively, for what Pat describes as more contemporary tastes, try the big tablets of vitamin C which do the trick and are good for you or take advantage of both the new and the old remedies with a combination pack for £5.

The establishment's location fostered other time-honoured products as well, namely a line of luxury shaving toiletries, so necessary for a gentleman to regain his composure after a night on the town. Both the soap and the cream lather easily with a rich masculine-scented foam—£4.55

for the soap in a convenient 50g plastic-cased stick, £4.75 for the cream in a 75g tube. For traditionalists, the soap is available in hand-turned wooden bowls for £8.95 to £11.25.

In fact, Harris' (or Harris's as some of the labels are marked) tenders a complete range of bath preparations, soaps, toilet waters, razors and brushes, and is also a working pharmacy. We've found the almond oil soap to be a godsend when travelling as it lathers fast and furiously in either hard or soft water. A box of three hand-sized soaps is £8.45 or £12.35 for the bath-sized soaps. And we find the very famous £12.95 Old English Lavender Water with its hint of musk, almost as restorative as the Original.

Actually, we're inclined to agree with Pat's parade of old-timers who find just being here an invigorating breath of fresh air. The shop's authentic period interior is instantly recognizable as a bit of Victoriana, perfectly preserved and uncluttered by modern point-of-sale displays. If D.R. Harris has never been used as a location for the filming of a Dickensian tale, it should have been. Apparently, our brothers under the rising sun agree—a Japanese consortium was so enchanted by the shop that it built an exact replica outside Tokyo. Of course, given the Japanese routine of nightly "business meetings" made into male-bonding sessions by copious amounts of alcohol, the shop is tapping into a huge new market for the Original—not to mention vast potential for its Crystal Eye Drops that put the sparkle back into tired or reddened eyes. Not medicated, purely a cosmetic solution, the drops are quite miraculous and, at £4.75, already have an international following, particularly among Hollywood types who consider them a necessity for facing the camera for close-ups.

James Bodenham & Company

88 Jermyn Street   071-930-5340
London SW1Y 6JH

Back in the 1860s, Mary Anne Floris, the heiress to the fragrance fortune, married one James Bodenham, thus changing the name of the family that to this day runs the charming Floris shop next door, at 89 Jermyn Street. Being just as proud of its Bodenham heritage as it is of the Floris name, the family decided to immortalize the former with a range of skincare and bath products, housed in its own shop which was named after Mary's husband.

More rustic, more English country than its internationally famous sister store Floris, James Bodenham & Company is run by the same managing director. John Bodenham is Mary and James' great-grandson, and his own son Edward is, at 16, already representing the ninth generation of an unbroken chain to be involved in the family business. Here, one treads on rough-hewn hardwood floors rather than plush carpet, and sturdy provincial-looking furniture rather than highly polished, glass-fronted cabinets serve as display vehicles. Whereas Floris merchandise is flower based, much of James Bodenham's is redolent of fruits—orange, grapefruit, apple and lime among them. We've become addicted to the apricot range, particularly the £3.50 bath oil.

And while Floris only touches on products for the home, James Bodenham stocks them en masse. Knee-high baskets overflow with aromatic potpourris. A small bag sells for as little as £2.50, and you can extend its fragrant properties with a similarly scented room spray, starting at £4.50.

The back room is an ever-changing, seasonally geared gift wonderland. This is serious browsing territory that can always be counted on for gift-giving inspiration, whether from the enormous selection of children's books or the intriguing assortment of gourmet foodstuffs. The bagged herbal teas from £2.95 a box are winners, as are the creatively flavoured jams, honeys and vinegars with prices from £2.95 on up.

Having enjoyed the bucolic charms of James Bodenham, don't miss the refined sophistication of Floris next door. The talented and dedicated Bodenham family wears two distinct hats, with equal aplomb.

🐛

Floris

89 Jermyn Street	071-930-2885
London SW1Y 6JH	(FAX) 071-930-1402

In 1730, when Juan Famenias Floris set sail for England from his native Spain, he did so with the intent of finding fame and fortune as barber to the gents of London's fashionable St James's. He succeeded admirably, operating out of the Jermyn Street shop, which still belongs to his direct descendants. But he didn't hit the jackpot until he started fooling around with oils and essences in the back room, trying to approximate some of the captivating fragrances of his homeland. At that time perfumes were a novelty, and each scent was concocted for the exclusive use of a specific client, its formula carefully recorded so that it could be re-created.

Scents being what they are, they proved to be Juan's and their own best advertisement. They wafted their way into society through the swank clubs of the area, they were carried on the perfumed handkerchiefs of the card-playing dandies, they entered stylish salons on the ruffled cuffs of gentlemen intent upon seduction. Soon it seemed as if all of sophisticated London was clamouring for Juan's flower-based fragrances, so happily named Floris. He was able to forsake barbering in favour of devoting his shop to a luxurious setting for the sale of all manner of perfumed products.

Seven generations later, it remains just that, a gracious, somewhat old-fashioned, family-run emporium, dedicated to superior quality and service. Gleaming Spanish mahogany showcases, acquired from the Great Exhibition of 1851, display the full range of Floris merchandise—perfumes, colognes, bath preparations, talcum powders, gentlemen's toiletries, soaps and fragrances for the home. Quaint touches like the presentation of change on a velvet pad may be responsible for Floris' slightly stuffy reputation. But any such impression is quickly dispelled by a discussion of the clientele with manager Andrew Puckering—Mick Jagger, Tatum O'Neal, Robert Wagner—or R.J. as we know him—and Princess Di are all devotees.

We can make an educated guess about what attracts Mick and R.J. It's either the No. 89 or Elite range, the only two Floris bouquets for men. Prices start at £3.95 for a deodorant stick and stop at £29 for 200ml of cologne. Shunners of facial hair, the rocker and the charmer may also stop in for the handmade, badger shaving brushes—£17.25 for "pure" badger, £32 for "best."

Otherwise, they probably pick up a little something for Jerry and Jill. There are 16 Floris fragrances for women, with names like Wild Hyacinth and Rose Geranium. Perfumes can be had for as little as £7.25 for a spray refill and as much as £36.50 for 30ml in a classic, square-stoppered glass bottle, while toilet water ranges in price from £11.25 for 50ml to £29 for 200ml. The heavenly scented dusting powders in their distinctive Floris blue and gold boxes are another popular item at £11.50.

While you're pondering the practicality of a £35 polished wooden bowl filled with a fragrant soap, wander into the back room where Juan first started experimenting over 250 years ago. Long the sanctum of

Floris directors, it also serves as a museum. Glass-fronted cabinets exhibit the paraphernalia of the scent-making business—testers, sample
bottles, packaging designs and ancient formulas. And pay special attention to the ornate hair ornaments that were once a Floris speciality. Indeed, the firm's first Royal Warrant was attained as combmaker to King
George IV. The company still boasts a nice selection of decorative
combs, but these days, in deference to ecological concerns, they're made
of very fine faux ivory and tortoiseshell. Furthermore, they're hand cut,
so we think they're a relative bargain at £7.40 to £14.75.

Having been soothed and pampered by the refined sophistication of
Floris, take a walk on a slightly wilder side—right next door at James
Bodenham. A different look, different products, but the same quality,
service, and family. Look it up!   ❧

Molton Brown

58 South Molton Street	(Ladies' appts.) 071-629-1872
London W1Y 1HH	(Office) 071-491-2478
	(FAX) 071-491-0350

Back in 1971, Caroline Burnstein (of the Brown's Burnsteins) and Harvey
Collis founded Molton Brown as a hairdressing salon with environmental
concerns that may have been a bit ahead of their time. Today they're
right on target, and the products, made of natural ingredients, have
drawn a deserved international reputation for excellence. Indeed, the
Molton Brown line of cosmetics and hair and skin care products, which
is handled by Caroline, has become so successful that it has far out-
stripped the salon side of the business.

It all began with Harvey's then novel approach to hairdressing as a
more natural-looking alternative to the stylized set and sprayed do of the
day. Caroline found that the conventional products on the market were
too harsh, too perfumed and too coloured to yield the effect Harvey was
striving to achieve. Together they developed a hair-care line based on
herbal infusions, and the rest, they say, is history. Handmade and
fragrance-free cosmetics followed in 1978, and Molton Brown skin-care
products, made with natural sugars and amino acids (as opposed to animal extracts), was launched in 1980.

The Molton Street shop sells it all in a setting that mirrors the firm's
image of natural simplicity—white walls, bleached-wood display cabinets
and highly polished parquet floors. Hair-care products for men and

women range from the familiar chamomile shampoo at £4.95 for 10 ounces to the exotic Nettle Deep Shine. Made from stinging nettles, it's a unique dressing that gives hair a shiny, just-washed look when applied between shampoos and sells for £4.85.

The extensive line of merchandise for the bath is a soaker's delight. We love the aromatic bath milks that emulsify to turn water into a soothing moisturizing solution. Our favourite is called Deep Relaxing and contains chamomile, marjoram and clary essential oils, which seem to have very relaxing and rejuvenating properties. Every Deep-Relaxing-laced bath leaves you calm and refreshed, and it is only £8.50 for 1.5 fluid ounces. For a change of bathing pace, we like the sea moss bath sachet salts at £1 for 7/8 ounce. Rich in trace minerals, the salts, when dissolved in water, yield a fresh, invigorating effect on the skin. Pure vegetable soaps, handmade in Molton Brown's own labs in formulations such as milk and oatmeal, mint, eucalyptus, rosewater and marigold, complete the bath picture and sell for £1.95 each.

Advocating the soft, natural look, Molton Brown cosmetics have a matte finish, but they are, nonetheless, vibrantly rich in terms of coverage and colour. The knowledgeable staff are on hand to instruct you on the makeup's proper application. They will outfit you with the appropriate complement of their wonderful pony hair or sable brushes which sell for £2.50 to £14.00, and they'll suggest a regimen of gentle Molton Brown skin-care products best suited to your skin.

Mount a flight of grey stairs to the first floor hairdressing salon where you can get everything from a manicure to a complimentary scalp massage. Here, also, you can have your hair cut, coloured with natural vegetable dyes or permed on the Molton permers without fear of damage. The hairdressers can give a fantastic cut, and they equally specialize in work on long hair. They will shampoo and style for £22 to £28, depending on the seniority of the stylist.

Up another flight to the third floor, you're enveloped by the feeling of entering a sanctuary that pervades the men's salon. The delightful Kayvan, along with Mia and Clare, presides over all the activity here. They run a tight, smooth-running ship and offer one of the best cuts in town from £23. A wash and what they call a "finger dry" goes for £12.50. Just what it sounds like, with well-trained fingers acting as aerators, the finger dry is a Molton Brown speciality for both men and women—it limits the damage done to hair by blow drying.

Whether it's the finger dry or the vast array of products, Molton Brown attracts a glamorous clientele—Cher, Christie Brinkley, Brooke Shields and Roger Moore among them. A number of royals are also regular shoppers for the handmade colour cosmetics and the beautiful assortment of bows and bands. 🌿

Penhaligon's

41 Wellington Street   071-836-2150
London WC2E 7BR

If Americans find something vaguely familiar about the bottles encasing Penhaligon's fragrances, something about the graceful lines and the fetching crystal ball-stoppers, it's because Victoria's Secret—the U.S.-based chain of lingerie stores—knocked off Penhaligon's for their line of scents. But if there was ever any question about bad blood between the seven-store chainlet, founded by a barber from Penzance in 1870, and the contemporary retail giant, it has now become a moot point. Les Wexner, founder of the Limited, now owns both, having recently acquired Penhaligon's from the Laura Ashley Group.

A legendary worker of merchandising magic, no doubt Les has big plans for Penhaligon's, but we hope he doesn't mess with this particular store. It's our favourite, despite the fact that the Burlington Arcade and Brook Street locations tend to be a bit more convenient. Occupying a former greengrocer's space in a 17th-century building, it could, in a city of charming emporiums, win the "quaintest" award. A colourful array of oriental rugs is scattered over the ancient, almost black wood floors. Each wide, rough-hewn plank displays its centuries proudly—looking every bit its age, in an au courant sort of way. If they weren't still fulfilling their function as flooring on their original site, they'd be in someone's *Architectural Digest*-worthy country home.

During the winter, a fire flickers in the homelike, rather than grand, fireplace which is flanked by well-broken-in leather chairs. Old-fashioned cases complement the Victorian packaging of the products, original right down to the flirtatious little bows on the bottlenecks which are still tied by hand—each and every one. It's all so very picturesque. Even Disney couldn't do any better than this!

Nonetheless, the Covent Garden shop would be unfamiliar to William Henry Penhaligon, who established himself across town in fashionable St James's. There, like Floris before him, he acted as barber to the court and first developed his fragrances for his male clients, especially those who frequented the famous Hammam Turkish Baths right next door. Dating from 1872, the Hammam Bouquet, a blend of rose and jasmine with an undercurrent of sandalwood, remains a popular seller at £58 for 200ml of the toilet water or £32 for 100ml of the aftershave. Like each of the traditional scents, specifically for men and for women, it infuses a full range of toilet necessities—bath oil, soap and shampoo.

Not surprisingly, the Blenheim Bouquet, named after his birthplace, was Winston Churchill's favourite. Described as a discreet Edwardian citrus fragrance enhanced with a lingering note of pine, which endures "like all good relationships," it could be yours as well at £8 to £75 for the eau de toilet, depending upon the size. And we can only wonder whether or not the princes Philip and Charles are attracted to the stately Lords—whatever their preference, they've both honoured Penhaligon's as manufacturers of their toilet requisites.

As for more delicate sensibilities, the ladies seem to be most satisfied with Elizabethan Rose and Bluebell. One mysterious, the other beguiling, we love the aroma they bestow upon our tresses—£8 for a bottle of shampoo. But it may be that the new Racquets version could be better for our hair. The first fragrance to be introduced in decades, it was created for sporting men and women. The hair-care products are specially formulated for daily washes, and there's a moisturizer designed to protect the face from the elements. Generally speaking, all the Racquets products—from cologne to body lotion—with their invigorating lemony smell are less expensive than the rest of the Penhaligon line, as they are all packaged in plastic.

Of course, the departure from tradition is welcome when it comes to travelling, but if you hanker for some home-bound Racquets merchandise, you might want to explore Penhaligon's impressive collection of antique and modern silver containers. Traditionalists, we're drawn to the former—like a bottle overlaid by an ornate silver casing by William Combs circa 1876 for £1,595, or the £395 turn-of-the-century garlanded globe glass jar with silver top. But we do admit to having a soft spot for their contemporary renditions, which are plain, elegant and handmade for Penhaligon's. The little round scent jar, its glass body distinguished by fluting and an oversized silver lid, is a charmer at £140.

No doubt about it, Mr Wexner has yet another winner on his hands. But how's he going to improve upon perfection?   ❦

UNISEX SERVICES

Daniel Galvin

Hair Color Consultants Ltd	071-486-9661/8601
42–44 George Street	(FAX) 071-487-2597
London W1H 5RE	

We first ran into Daniel Galvin, who is to colouring what Harry Winston is to jewels, at La Coupe in New York, where he visits regularly to care for some of that city's prettiest heads of hair. When he's not on Madison Avenue, he's overseeing this very busy salon where he recently celebrated 30 years in hairdressing. It's a career he was born to—his grandfather and father had been hair-care professionals. Early on, he realized his interest lay more in colouring than in styling, so at age 18 he applied to London's top ten salons and accepted a position with the only one that replied, Olofson of Knightsbridge. There, his extraordinary skill became legendary, and within a year he was approached by every establishment that had failed even to acknowledge his earlier applications.

Turning the other cheek, he signed on with Leonard to head what was then the largest tinting department in Europe and spent the next 15 years perfecting the techniques that would keep him much in demand by the world's top fashion magazines. In 1978, he left Leonard to open his own enterprise, which today employs 14 colourists, 14 stylists, 16 assistants, three manicurists and a hair doctor—or trichologist—by the name of Lynn Barker, not to mention the four receptionists required to man the telephones and keep all the appointments straight.

Naturally, dealing with Daniel's schedule is their biggest headache. He's so much in demand, and he's got the New York operation to deal with, as well as film company assignments that can take him just about anywhere. Still, his greatest challenge occurred in his own back yard, when Albert Finney was simultaneously shooting *Murder on the Orient Express* and appearing nightly on stage in the West End. The movie role required that he have jet black hair, while the play featured a character with basic brown hair, approximating Finney's own. Daniel developed a black gel that gave the proper effect for a day's filming, but that could easily be washed out in the evening. At any rate, to get Daniel's personal attention, you're going to have to book way in advance and be prepared to cough up a minimum of £50 for a tint or vegetable dye. A full head of highlights will set you back £150, but you can pay less for the services of any of the other very capable stylists in Daniel's stable. True, they're not Daniel, but they're close. He doesn't let anyone loose, no matter how experienced, unless they've been thoroughly trained by Galvin. Actually, two of his best colourists have been apprenticed to him for their whole lives—his daughter Louise and his son Daniel, Jr. Then there's Lousie Vyse and Sharron Chantal, along with Stacy Green, no relation to Daniel except in their extraordinary talent. But his second in command for colouring is Jo Hansford.

As with colouring, there's plenty of talent on the styling front to take care of you. A cut and blow dry for ladies runs £25 to £45; for gentlemen, it's £16 to £30. But if you decide to wash at home and trek to George Street with a wet head for a stylish finish, we're talking about £14 to £25. For cutting and styling, book with Celine Tapp or Karin Brown, who's been known to attend to Princess Di's golden locks.

Now, we all know how traumatic changes in hair colour and style can be; after all, there is absolutely nothing else that can affect the way you present yourself to the world (except, perhaps, for a 100-pound weight loss). At least at Daniel Galvin, you can get a sense of what you're in for in advance. You can either check out the colour and coif of Al Pacino, Stefanie Powers, Ringo Starr and wife Barbara Bach, Jane Seymour and Anthony Andrews, or you can pick up Daniel and brother Joshua's book *Hair Matters* that sums up and showcases their hair-care philosophy. As Daniel says, "Hair is the only accessory you wear 24 hours a day." We're thrilled that hair matters so much to them, because it matters so much to us . . . and to you.   ❦

John Frieda

4 Aldford Street	071-491-0840
London W1X 5PU	(FAX) 071-494-1649

Born clutching silver scissors, the son and grandson of successful hairdressers, John Frieda entered the family business as a teen—first as a helping hand at his father's salon on weekends, then as a full-fledged apprentice at the legendary Leonard. At the time, the late 1960s, Leonard was the leading salon in the city, and during his nine years there, John learned every aspect of the business, becoming heavily involved in the creative side. By the time he opened his own hairdressing emporium at the tender age of 25, he already had an impressive list of magazine credits notched on his blow dryer.

That first establishment went the way of so many that are spawned by partnerships, and since 1979 John has been flying solo—at a pretty high altitude. He now owns three thriving salons in London, staffed by over 85 employees and has opened one in New York. His John Frieda Hair Care System is a national bestseller at Boots, the U.K. chemists chain. And in 1989, John walked away with the ultimate accolade from the industry he has served so well, the title of British Hairdresser of the Year. Add to this, devastating dark, good looks and a client list that boasts some of the world's most beautiful (or at least most famous) heads— Jerry Hall, Mick Jagger, Raquel Welch, Michael York, Helena Bonham-Carter, Michael and Shakira Caine, Catherine Oxenberg, Jane Seymour, Linda and Paul McCartney—and we could really begin to dislike this guy. But we don't really know for sure, since we've never met him. He cancelled his appointment with us moments after we arrived at the Aldford Street shop. Did we not pass muster?

Okay, so we know he's rude and/or not available to ordinary mortals. But we also know he's a formidable force on the international hair-care scene. His John Frieda Precision Styling System, devised for the trade in book and video form, has had tremendous impact at a time when hair is moving away from the "wash-and-wear" era to a period in which dressing and styling are increasingly important. And John's personally trained staff are the world's best purveyors of his revolutionary techniques, providing expert hair care with a relaxed affability in attractive surroundings.

The Aldford Street salon is the newest and most stylish of John's real estate, convenient to such Mayfair mainstays as the Connaught. Formerly a fur shop, it took John a year and, by the look of it, a fair bit of change to renovate the premises—grey marble floors are softened by cream walls, punctuated by mirrors and sleek black wall sconces. High ceilings, arches and skylights bestow a luminous, airy atmosphere. No wonder so many clients have standing appointments two or three times a week. This is a pleasant place to spend an hour or so, while everyone works at making you look and feel your very best.

A cut and blow dry will cost £24 to £44, depending upon the stylist. Since he's the designated artistic director of this salon, you can't go wrong with Kevin at the high end of the fee range. We know people who swear by Melanie and her £40 attentions. Manicures start at £8.50; pedicures are £15.

As for colouring, the dashing resident expert, Steven Little, tells us it runs £20 to £90, hinging on the extent of the work. The good news is that whatever you're having done, you'll have it done downstairs, out of sight. No one, except your hairdresser, who knows for sure anyway, will see you all gooped up. With such consideration for his clients, John must not be totally heartless, and we do have it on pretty good authority that these days when Lulu sings "To Sir with Love," she's saluting him, not Sidney Poitier. You see, the redheaded spitfire is Mrs John Frieda.   🦋

Michaeljohn

25 Albemarle Street	071-629-6969/499-7529
London W1X 3HA	(FAX) 071-495-0152

Few partnerships last as long or are as successful as that of Michael Rasser and John Isaacs. They've been in business in Mayfair since 1968, catering to the coiffures of royals and commoners alike, women *and* men. Of course, it may help that 13 years ago they expanded to Beverly Hills, and John spends much of his time there. So they're not in each other's hair all the time. Furthermore, there is a third party here in the guise of Frank Warner, who's been the driving force behind the successful development and promotion of the Michaeljohn Hair Care products.

We think the secret to the shop's success is that Michaeljohn clients are not subjected to the latest trend in styling or colouring. . . unless they want to be. Michael, John, Frank and their staffs treat their clients as individuals, creating looks that suit their looks, personalities and lifestyles. It's an art that can only be practised by stylists that have undergone the extensive training Michaeljohn insists upon. For the London salon that means technical study at the London College of Fashion, underwritten by the firm, coupled with three years' apprenticeship on the salon floor, followed by two years as a junior stylist before making fullfledged senior stylist.

So don't be disappointed nor skip the Michaeljohn experience altogether if you can't get an appointment with Michael himself. It's practically impossible, unless you're Princess Anne and even she has been stricken to find out he's off on a photo shoot when her royal locks were in need of touching up. The point is, any of the salon's senior stylists will take excellent care of you. Take Denis, for instance. He's French and is especially good at creating softly full, beautifully feminine coifs. Then there are Clive and Charlie who have a special knack for those really strong, angular cuts. For long hair or formal dos, depend on Gerald or Martin. All of them, as accredited seniors, described on the tariff card as the "creative design team," charge £39.50 for cut, shampoo and finish— that's for the ladies. Gents are charged £32, and most aren't too interested in Denis' services. Michael and Frank, by the by, as "creative directors" charge £52 to cut and style women's hair, £29.50 for men's.

For younger, hipper street looks, check out the talents of some of the juniors or "creative stylists" who charge £34.50 and £25. And the entire staff are available from Monday thru Saturday, from 8:30 A.M. to 5:00 P.M., except on Thursdays when the salon is open until 8:00 P.M. Should their schedule not fit yours, special arrangements can always be made for staff members to visit your hotel or home. Prices upon request.

If privacy is your concern, you can seek that of the "royal enclosure" where Princess Anne and cousin Princess Alexandra hang out. Personally, we prefer the friendly buzz of the ladies' salon on the ground floor. Classical music muffles the chatter, while bunches of fresh flowers warm the white-and-black-tiled floors and rusticated walls.

One side of the salon is devoted to the needs of men, except for the space allocated to the royals and to colouring, a department which is overseen by Richard Burns when he's not off doing film work or consulting for the BBC. His clients have included Julie Andrews and Marcello Mastroianni, so you can understand why his rates are "on quotation." His team's fees range from £20 for a semi-permanent rinse to £75 for a full head of highlights.

Manicures and pedicures, £11.50 and £19.50, almost complete the picture of services available at Michaeljohn. We should mention that children's hair, male and female, is tended to here, and the salon is the source of the best bargain lunches in town, courtesy of the adorable Sylvestro. He specializes in creative salads and sandwiches that have become so popular that regular clients have been known to take time out from their Bond Street shopping just around the corner to pop in for a light lunch—75p for a cup of coffee to £3 for a delicious, filling salad.

And, we guess, no discussion of Michaeljohn would be comprehensive without the ritual recitation of a portion of the shop's most impressive and very international client list. And the following doesn't even take into account the firmament that haunts the Beverly Hills salon. So here goes—Candice Bergen, Barbara Taylor Bradford, Richard Chamberlain, Michael Crawford, Faye Dunaway, Blake Edwards, Fiona Fullerton, Lee Remick, George Segal and Kathleen Tynan. Any questions?

Nicholas Theodor

45 New Cavendish Street   071-486-0411/0412
London W1M 7RL

The formal, turn-of-the-century façade belies the contemporary symphony of black-and-white interior, which enshrines a salon dedicated to the personalized pampering of its clientele. There's another applicable *p* word of primary importance here, and that's *privacy*. There's no factory atmosphere at Nicholas Theodor. Indeed, downstairs there is a beauty department which takes only one person at a time for a full regimen of facial, massage, manicure, pedicure and waxing—the ultimate in privacy, supervised by the super Suzanne Daily. Her £13 pedicures bestow new life on your tired old feet as she massages them with truly magic fingers, while her soothing facials (from £22) will put you right to sleep. Who needs Canyon Ranch in Arizona for stress reduction? A couple of hours in Suzanne's care will surely do the trick!

Upstairs is Nicholas' preserve, where he, three other stylists and three apprentices endeavour to make hair look the very best it can, based upon a world-class cut. Nicholas, whose own receding hairline is more than compensated for by an abundant moustache, says that's key—without a good cut, hair never falls right no matter how much it's blown, crimped or curled. If you want him to prove his point with your hair, you'll need to book at least a week in advance. The same holds true to take advantage of his expert styling. Regardless, you can count on his approach to your hair being creative without being gimmicky. In fact, this Cyprus native firmly believes that "the best way to look is looking natural."

Appointments with Nicholas start at £30, but you can benefit from his technique by putting yourself in the well-trained hands of any of his stylists, from £28 for a cut and blow dry or set. Shampoo and sets can be had for as little as £15. Whatever the differences in price, you'll get the same very solicitous personal service from everyone on the staff, no matter who you are. . .or who you're not. Nicholas is no prima donna. He insists that no one on his staff is, and hopes that none of his clients are. And most take the cue. If your idea of fun is lording your singular status over other mere mortals by having the proprietor of an establishment fawn all over you at the expense of others, seek beautification elsewhere.

Easy going, well-spoken, and unimpeachably mannered, Nicholas treats everyone equally.

Not surprisingly "names" don't impress him, so he doesn't bother to drop them to us or anybody. But we can assure you that the devotees of this salon are an extremely attractive lot who lead very busy lives. They depend on that Nicholas Theodor cut to see their hair through long days and, often, longer evenings. They also rely on getting a reviving dose of the three *p*s here—personalized pampering in private. ❧

The Ragdale Clinic at Michaeljohn

25 Albemarle Street	071-409-2956
London W1X 3FA	(FAX) 071-495-2461

Snide colonials that we are, we listened indulgently while some of our London friends waxed poetic about the inch- and cellulite-reducing properties of a painless treatment offered by the Michaeljohn Ragdale Clinic. Then we dismissed their ramblings, assuming they were but another manifestation of the world renowned, charming eccentricity of the British. What we couldn't ignore, however, was the actual existence of the clinic as an oasis of revitalizing pampering peace right smack dab in the middle of bustling Mayfair. Once owned by the same folks who brought you the prestigious health hydro (read *spa*) Ragdale Hall, the clinic opened in 1989 as a smaller, city-bound version of its country-based parent.

Here you can escape for an hour or two or three or even a day, to relax and re-energize, courtesy of a full complement of regimens from £12 manicures to £28 super firming facials to £36 aromatherapy—a one-and-a-half hour glimpse of heaven via a head-to-toe massage with therapeutic oils.

A unisex operation, you *could* run into George Hamilton, Lulu, the Duchess of York, Rod Stewart or George Michael, but it's unlikely. The Michaeljohn Ragdale Clinic is committed to privacy and discretion. Witness the tiny lounge where you just might get a chance to quaff a cup of coffee or a glass of mineral water before being delivered into the hands of the highly skilled therapists. There's no interminable waiting for appointments here—schedules are taken seriously and are adhered to. Manager Sarah Reed sees to it, just as she makes sure that each of the therapists has spent at least two years training in the fine art of administering beauty treatments—no graduates of bogus beauty schools will ruin your day with a botched leg waxing or unfortunate eyelash dye.

For a real treat, commit yourself to the staff's care for a morning or afternoon. Three hours and £65 get you a manicure, pedicure, facial, sun tan and massage. We also highly recommend the rejuvenating "Sisley facial," particularly one by the delightful Helen. It starts with a relaxing back massage and gets better, minute by minute, for the entire one-and-a-half hours it takes. Truly the Rolls-Royce of facials, it preserves, protects and repairs your skin—be you male or female—for £35, thanks to the liberal use of an exclusive line of French botanically based products called (you guessed it) Sisley.

As for that miracle treatment we scoffed at . . . it's called Ionithermie, and we must admit we were so impressed with the Ragdale Clinic that we finally succumbed to the hype and gave it a go. And were we glad we did! The results were indeed visible—a reduction in the girth of our respective waists, hips and thighs and a notable smoothing of our little ripples of cellulite. If you watch your diet, drink lots of water, but very little coffee, tea or alcohol, and go heavy on fruits and veggies, the effects even last for three weeks or so. And we're told that if you elect the clinic's advised course of five sessions for £150, the improvements to your figure may even be permanent. But we can't attest to that, as we've only had the pleasure of our one go-around at £36.

What exactly is Ionithermie? Developed in France and not yet approved for use in the U.S., it involves a potpourri of fat-busting and fluid-draining creams, topped with clay and then zapped with two types of stimulating electric currents. Admittedly, the experience is somewhat unnerving, but ultimately it's amazingly soothing. You feel and look terrific afterwards. God bless the idiosyncratic British and their penchant for embracing the most unlikely sounding procedures.   ❦

Richard Dalton

Claridge's	071-409-1517
Brook Street	(FAX) 071-499-2210
London W1A 2JQ	

Even though this intimate, glamorous, high-tech salon is open on Saturday, a strong case can be made for making appointments for Monday to Friday only. You see, if Richard Dalton is in town (a big *if* given his wanderlust), he only works on weekdays. It just seems silly to pick a day when you know there's no chance he'll be around. Richard is, after all, one of the world's most renowned hairdressers, due to his former eight-year collaboration with the Princess of Wales, which kept her so picture perfect. Despite the notoriety, however, Richard remains unabashedly himself—a gentleman, in every sense of the word.

In deference to his clients, some of whom obviously have considerable clout, Richard plans his travel schedule three months in advance. So if you plan ahead, you'll be sure to get an appointment and be assured that he'll keep it. Generally a week's notice will do for a cut that costs £35 to £40, or a £25 blow dry. Inveterate traveller that he is, Richard will go to your hotel or home for an additional £25—it's only £15 if you're staying at Claridge's, since he only has to trot upstairs. Richard has also been known to venture farther afield on behalf of a client. It's not unusual for his services to be requested in the U.S. or on the Continent.

If Richard's not around, don't be too disappointed. True, you won't be worked on by the same pair of hands that cared for Di's do, but you will reap the benefit of Richard's expertise from any of his four stylists. He trained them all, and by osmosis you'll even get a little dose of Richard's mentor, the legendary Alexandre de Paris. His influence is evident in the salon's special way with long hair, chignons, hairpieces and headpieces. With a client list that reads like *DeBretts Peerage*, it's a good thing Richard and his crew are handy with tiaras.

When Richard's on the road, we're torn between Luigi, Anthony and Tara. But when it comes to a manicure, there's no contest. Yvonne gives the best in town—£12 for a regular manicure, £15 for the French version. In any case, you can take advantage of the salon's location and order a spot of tea or a glass of champagne, delivered by a liveried footman. No matter who's tending to your tresses, you can sit back, sip and relax in one of London's most stylish salons. The pale, blond-wood walls lend elegance to the spaces in which your every beauty whim is indulged, even during extended hours—Richard Dalton is open on Thursdays until 8:00 P.M., Saturdays until 6:00 P.M. Gentlemen usually make their appointments late in the day; they find the atmosphere so relaxing after the daily grind.

GENTLEMEN'S SERVICES

Geo. F. Trumper

9 Curzon Street	071-499-1850
London W1Y 7FL	(FAX) 071-281-9337

They say "living well is the best revenge"—Ivan Bersch lived so well that he was able to buy the very establishment that dashed his youthful dreams by denying his application for a position as barber. At the time, he vowed he would return to Geo. F. Trumper as its owner. He did just that, purchasing the circa 1875 firm from the founder's daughter. He did so "about 30 years ago," according to *his* daughter and current proprietor, Miss Paulette.

While owners may come and go, much of the institution that is Geo. F. Trumper remains pretty much the same. Touted as the world's most celebrated gentlemen's hairdresser and perfumer, it stands as a refreshing refuge of gentility in an often harsh modern world. It's not just the old-fashioned polished mahogany booths, leather upholstery and marble counters, nor the sporting prints and faded pictures of royal patrons adorning the walls that mirror another era. It's the sense of decorum, of courtesy that pervades. There are standards here that are preserved at all costs—standards of service, of products and of the clientele.

Granted, even at Trumper's some concessions to the realities of modern life have been made, according to 44-year veteran, Mr Leonard. But he claims it was only a few years ago that a gentleman who arrived wearing shorts for a haircut was asked to leave and return more properly dressed. Mr Leonard regrets that those days are over, but we suspect most real gentlemen would never dream of showing up at Trumper's in such disrespectful attire—certainly not regulars like Di's dad, Lord Spencer, and Fergie's father, Major Ferguson. And we doubt the American contingent, including Douglas Fairbanks, Jr., Tony Curtis and Tom Selleck, does either.

Whatever the gentlemanly quotient of the clients, the staff is downright courtly and clearly devoted to the firm. In addition to the esteemed Mr Leonard whose advancing years now prohibit him from working full time, there's the charming Mr Charles, who commutes 150 miles a day. Sure, there are other establishments closer to home desperate for his skills, but how many of them have been known to make house calls to

Buckingham Palace? How many can boast the world's largest collection of shaving brushes, let alone a large assortment of Geo. F. Trumper preparations—bottled lotions and balms, boxed soaps, potted shaving creams, each sporting its own heady perfume redolent of other times with names like Wellington and Marlborough? Where else are the arts of beard and moustache trimming so well preserved? And who else still offers a shave and hot towel for £10.50, or at any price?

The preparations have a history dating to the mid-19th century when George Trumper first opened his shop as Court Hairdressers—his Victorian patrons would recognize it today as all subsequent expansions have been done with the express purpose of preserving the original look. From the beginning, he manufactured perfumes, toilet waters, pommades and other products in the vaults beneath the shop. The tradition continues. All Geo. F. Trumper products are still made by hand, often by the original methods and special skills that have been handed down. Indeed, until recently they were still made in the cellar, and many were developed by Mr Trumper himself, like the Extract of Lime Cologne and Aftershave (£11.50 and £10), and remain popular today. A new product only appears every three years or so after being thoroughly tested for the quality and consistency that are the Trumper's hallmark.

The hairdressings are particularly noteworthy, responsible for many a well-groomed head all over the world. Packed in handsome, crown-topped bottles, they're available, as is the complete Geo. F. Trumper range, by mail-order. We know several gentlemen who swear by San Remo, described as "a light preparation with just a touch of oil and delicate perfume, which cleanses the hair and improves growth"—£10.50 for the 205cc bottle, £4.75 for the 100cc plastic travel pack. We understand the shampoos and conditioners are also worthy of a pledge of allegiance. Some, like the Thyme and A-D, are extremely effective against dandruff, while others, like the Melissa and Chamomile, are extra mild for heads that are washed daily. All of these herbal-based shampoos come in 200cc and 500cc plastic bottles, £5 and £8, respectively.

Which to choose? Take advantage of the talents of Mr Leonard, Mr Charles or any of the barbers for a £16.50 shampoo and cut or a £10 head massage and shampoo. Once they've worked with your hair, they'll tell you which Trumper products will keep it looking its shiny best.

Of course, the selection of shaving soaps cannot be ignored, especially Trumper's Potted Shaving Cream. Generations have counted on its excellent lather and glycerine base which leaves the skin ever so soft.

Available in six different aromas, it comes in a replica of a 19th-century ceramic bowl for £19.75. And, in another concession to modern times, it's also packaged in plastic tubes. However, the blow is softened by the fact that those tubes come in Edwardian-style cartons. Standards, don't you know!   ❦

Truefitt & Hill

| 23 Old Bond Street | 071-493-8496 |
| London W1X 3DA | (FAX) 071-499-5325 |

This is the only hairdresser (for gentlemen or otherwise) on Bond Street and it is arguably the oldest, continually operating establishment of its kind in Britain, maybe the world. Truefitt & Hill has been clipping and snipping on or near these very premises since 1805, when Francis Truefitt set up shop as "Court Hair Cutter." Indeed, the firm's court connections remain intact—Prince Michael and the Duke of Kent entrust their locks only to Truefitt & Hill, as does Prince Phillip, for whom house calls are made. Mr Willison, who's been here for 41 years, makes the regular trip to Buckingham Palace to keep Phillip's head looking regal.

Frankly, we think Phillip gets the raw end of the deal. Truefitt & Hill is such a warm, welcoming sanctuary—much more comfortable than that drafty old palace. Here, the gents that consider the shop somewhat of a club, nestle into the soothingly worn leather chairs in the front while they wait for their appointment with one of the 10 barbers or two manicurists. Most take a stab at reading the newspapers left on the solid-looking drum table, while others simply relish the quiet luxury of the heavily carpeted, fragrantly scented shop. In either case, they're not left to linger long—appointments, which should be made a day in advance, are sacrosanct.

Don't expect to be coddled with offerings of tea or coffee, or lulled to sleep with music (or Muzak). This is essentially an old-fashioned barber shop, nothing chi-chi about it, despite the glass cases full of shaving and hair brushes, along with all the other toiletries required by men. These are all steadfastly traditional products, like the Car hairdressing cream first produced in 1900 when a couple of patrons persuaded the owner that such a treatment for men was needed to keep their hair shiny and in place. Having come up with the notion at their RAC, the cream was named after the source of its inspiration (Car equals RAC spelled backwards) and today sells for £8.60.

Even ancient barbering traditions are adhered to here—no electric clippers or razors. The expert £17.50 shampoo and cuts are done entirely by hand, as is a £9 beard trim. If a manicure is what you have in mind, count on spending £8, and if you want to give your face a refreshing treat, have a massage for £10.50. We know gentlemen who opt for the works just to lengthen their stay in the tranquilizing, relaxed atmosphere. Afternoons can happily be whiled away here, but never on Saturday since Truefitt's closes for the weekend at 12:30 P.M. From Monday to Friday, the shop's open from 9:00 until 5:30. Should you require its services before normal business hours, call Mr Dennis who will make the accommodation for you.

CHAPTER EIGHT

Miscellaneous Services

In a city where "service" is an active verb

*L*ondon's not yet the 24-hour go-go town that New York is. Round-the-clock is more likely to mean two left turns past Big Ben and Westminster Abbey. Korean grocers who never sleep haven't bloomed yet in Bloomsbury. Most sidewalks do get rolled up by midnight. But the city's increasingly international and sophisticated citizenry—not to mention visitors who still haven't quite made it through their £1,000 by tea-time—are pushing to pick up the pace.

Whether you want to save time or waste it creatively, whether you exercise your angst or your argyles, whether you're fastidious or frivolous, a new breed of London's perennial entrepreneurs are on the cutting edge of ways to tempt you into parting with what's left of the £1,000 before tea, that no other Brit has managed to get from you.

Anne Walker

32B Leverstock House   071-584-0198
Sutton Estate
Elystan Street
London SW3 3QZ

If you've been steadfastly resisting the onslaught of the 20th century, let
alone the 21st, and have succeeded in stubbornly remaining computer il
literate, you may need to call upon Anne Walker's 30 years of experience.
That's how long she's been typing novels, scripts, proposals, reports and
correspondence for a diverse clientele. A former legal secretary and
more recently a grandmother, she combines professional perfection with
soothing concern.

Serendipity figured prominently in Anne's career. When she left her
law firm employer to raise her family, she agreed to continue doing some
typing for the firm at home. Seeking more regular and gainful part-time
employment, she answered an author's ad in a newsagent's window for a
charlady. The author was Gavin Maxwell, and it turned out that what he
really needed was a typist to pound out *Ring of Bright Water.* Anne used
to show up at his otterless Chelsea residence and take dictation. She did
the typing then, as she does now, at her own residence.

Since her book debut, she's worked for other notable authors like
James Thackery and James Mitchell, but her fees remain modest. At
£5.75 an hour, which averages about 2,000 words for typing from text,
Anne charges considerably less than most agencies we've come across—
and we can attest to her accuracy. If you draft your work on tape, she'll
work with that, too, for £5.75, but she says that the figure translates into
more like 1,500 words an hour. For scripts, she charges £2.75 per 1,000
words.   ❧

A Place Like Home

63 Sisters Avenue   071-228-4668
London SW11 5SW   (Toll-free from the U.S.) 800-526-0215
                                                  (FAX) 071-738-1626

During her 25 years in the real-estate business, specializing in reloca-
tion, Silvia Lawson-Johnston had discovered what she describes as "an
incredible need" for short-term housing other than in hotels. It's a need
generated in some instances by economics, in others by personal prefer-

ence. So in 1989, Silvia went into the business of finding rentable "places like home" for visitors wishing to stay in town for a week or more.

With an inventory of properties, ranging from 1960-ish one-bedroom flats to a magnificent, fully staffed six-bedroom, six-bath mansion, she has pioneered an alternative passport to London living. Virtually all the properties are within walking distance of Harrods—i.e., in some of the poshest residential territory in the city. Yet prices are surprisingly modest, especially when contrasted with the daily hotel tabs outlined in this book. Most are in the £350 to £1,500 a week neighbourhood including gas and electricity. The only additional charge is for the telephone, which all of them have, along with televisions and maid service.

Furthermore, the comforts of your new home are shown to you by one of Silvia's representatives. No wandering about aimlessly mistaking the hall closet for the bathroom and vice versa. You're also presented with an information kit about local attractions, such as grocery stores and dry cleaners, as well as a complimentary food starter kit. Silvia says that basically it's breakfast—coffee, tea, milk, sugar, croissants—since so many international flights arrive at ungodly early hours. This way you can get settled in without worrying about dashing out to pick up basics.

Silvia will even make transportation to your new digs easy by arranging to retrieve you from Heathrow or Gatwick at £40 and £50, respectively, for standard cars (more like £60 to £70 for limo service). You might as well splurge, as you'll save on food. One dinner at home and you've paid for your transportation from the airport.

Generally speaking, Silvia can locate accommodations to suit your budget and space requirements—two-bedroom, two-bath flats for two people or two couples are the most sought after—but not if you want that six-bedroom beauty. Even at £4,000 a week, it's seldom vacant. When last we spoke with Silvia, she told us in a conspiratorial whisper that it was occupied by "a very well-known person." No amount of pleading could induce her to reveal her client's identity, which brings up another reason for not lodging in a hotel—privacy, complete and utter privacy.

Counter Spy Shop

62 South Audley Street	071-629-0223
London W1Y 5FB	(FAX) 071-629-9538

On a street otherwise populated by august purveyors of upscale goods like Thomas Goode and James Purdey & Sons, this glass-enclosed storefront stands out. A cursory glance yields the impression it's a rather pedestrian electronics shop with a window full of telephones, computer monitors and other gadgets. Upon closer inspection, it becomes clear that this is no ordinary electronics outlet—an outlet for the high-tech wizardry of James Bond's faithful Q is closer to the mark. The telephones are equipped with anti-bugging devices, the monitors are part of a surveillance system and the pocket-size computer has a built-in modem with an automatic scrambling device.

Inside, the deception continues. The non-decor enhances the appearance of a nondescript, probably discount emporium in which you can purchase anything from clocks to clothes. . . except these clocks conceal cameras, the clothes are bulletproof and pricetags are virtually nonexistent. Indeed, the issue of cost here is as sensitive as the equipment. We could only persuade manager and fellow Yank, Joe Brocia, to reveal one price for publication, that of a handsome leather briefcase wired with an electronic shock system. Should anyone walk away with it, the simple push of a button on a beeper-like device will get their attention with a painful pang—one guaranteed to make the thief drop the case. Its yours for about £1,000.

Actually, we were a little shocked when we asked to see the manager— Joe suddenly emerged through the back wall of bookcases which had seemed to define the length of the shop. Wrong. For the few moments the "door" was open, we spied a large, secret back room that looked like NASA Mission Control. From there, CCS Communication Control, the Counter Spy Shop's U.S.-based parent company, operates the service end of the business. With over four decades of experience in assisting individuals, corporations and law enforcement agencies with their security needs, these are the folks to call if you have any reason to believe you have an espionage problem. They'll conduct a complete sweep of your hotel, car, home or office to determine whether or not it's "clean." Their analysis will ferret out any surveillance equipment. After disposing of it,

CCS will then install devices that will ensure the invasion of your privacy will not be repeated.

Furthermore, CCS can help protect you from any harmful intrusion on your person. In addition to the bulletproof clothes, including Burberry raincoats, they offer armour-plated cars—BMWs and Mercedes are stocked. And, according to Joe, 12 to 15 a year are sold from this location alone (there are five others in the U.S. and one in Paris). CCS or standard issue, Joe can arrange for a car to act as a video monitor by installing a camera in the antenna.

But the electronic trinket that most intrigued us was a hand-held voice stress analyzer—i.e., a lie detecter. Kept next to a telephone, in a desk drawer or in a purse or pocket, it offers virtually instant verification of fact or fiction. We were dying to know the answer to the "how-much" question, but we suspect Joe used one on us when he asked if we could be counted on to refrain from publishing the price. No doubt it's costly, and perhaps we should all hope it stays that way. Should its technology go the way of VCRs and laptop computers, making truth detection a household reality, just think what havoc it could wreak on all our lives!

❦

London Unlimited

3 Dunraven Street   071-499-3382
London W1Y 3FG

Obviously, we think we know London pretty well, but occasionally even we are stumped about how or where to obtain a particular item—a pal's hunt for 17th-century church pews comes to mind. When that happens, when we don't have a ready answer, we call our secret resource—Bernice Cooper, the Canadian born dynamo who owns and operates London Unlimited, a personal shopping service.

Having lived in the heart of London for decades, many of those years spent renovating houses, projects which required resourcing all sorts of unusual bits and pieces to restore them to their original grandeur, Bernice Cooper is a one-woman Rolodex of contacts—contacts for everything from china to couture clothes. If your plan is to shop London, call Bernice. She'll take you on a half-day spree for £50 which takes you to places "much more interesting than Harrods" where she will pass on her trade discounts to you. Alternatively, if there's a certain something you simply must have—a vintage Astin Martin Volante perhaps or a perfect 18th-century ancestral portrait—the charge is £150 a day. If you're looking for things decorative, she suggests bringing along swatches and colour chips to make sure the hues are appropriately complementary.

But you don't have to be in London to take advantage of Bernice's expertise. She will undertake a specialized search for you on her own for a negotiated fee up front, "just to make sure there is genuine interest."

Treasure hunts for the rare and precious aside, Bernice has come in most useful to us when our luggage has gone missing. One call to her and she rounds up enough fashionable clothes, accessories, underwear and toiletries to keep you going for a couple of days. No more hiding out in your hotel, waiting for your bags to appear or missing appointments because in your traveling clothes you were under (or over) dressed. In short, carry Bernice's number with you at all times! ❦

Moss Bros.

88/90 Regent Street	071-494-0666
London W1R 5PA	(FAX) 071-350-0112

So you've played the game and played it well. You've been rewarded with a last-minute invitation to the Royal Enclosure at Ascot. Good for you . . . or is it? Do you have the foggiest idea what to wear, how to adhere to dress regulations so strict that you'll be censured by the attending stewards if you're improperly outfitted? Mercifully, it doesn't really matter whether you do or don't, because Moss Bros. does. For generations the firm has been recognized as *the* expert in matters of formal attire. Naturally, it sells a full range but, more important for your purposes, it rents clothes as well.

In fact, according to President Monty Moss, great-grandson of founder Moses Moss (honest!), the rental of formal clothes "brings more customers through our doors than any other of our services." And he does mean doors (as in plural)—there are outlets all over the country, many trading under the name Suit Co.

Fortunately, Moss' inventory is so vast that most any request can be handled on short notice. (The real swells, however, start reserving their Ascot morning suits in January.) Moss Bros. carries three versions that will pass muster—the Elite, the Ascot and the Classic, each about £37 for the first 24 hours, half for each subsequent day. Still, the affable Monty tells us there are certain accoutrements that are de rigueur—the top hat, for instance. You must have it and wear it. A bare pate in the

Royal Enclosure will earn you a disapproving tap on the shoulder from a steward. Then there are the gloves, which must be grey and are always carried, never worn. Both come as part of a £14.95 accessories package, which also includes the appropriate shirt, tie and handkerchief. By renting at Moss Bros., you can be sure you will not commit any sartorial faux pas.

You'll probably also be saved the embarrassment of doing or saying something stupid, as Monty and his staff will tell you exactly what to expect and how to act. It's a matter of professional pride—they don't want their clothes associated with any boorish behaviour. You see, everyone knows Moss is *the* source. Monty's broad smile gets downright titanic when he talks about the client who went to Buckingham Palace in a morning suit to receive an honour from the Queen. "How very nice you look," she said. "Did it come from Moss Brothers?"

No racing or knightships in store for you? Moss is still the solution to that unanticipated black-tie affair. The store can even help you out should an important meeting present itself just when all your suits are being cleaned—tuxedos run in the £22 to £32 a day neighbourhood, and the Harvard, a very dignified, double-breasted business suit is available for £27.95. And what about that Highland ball that sounds like so much fun? You guessed it, Moss can outfit you in proper Scottish evening wear, kilt to sporran for about £45. Though we must warn you, these people are sticklers for etiquette, which dictates that only subjects of the U.K. or those of verifiable Scottish heritage may wear Highland dress. If you don't qualify on either count, you may find them steering you toward a conventional tux.

Naturally, Moss is equally adept at handling your anticipated needs. Telephone or fax ahead with your measurements. The staff will select the proper garments, make any necessary alterations and have them waiting for you upon your arrival—either at the store or, if you prefer, at your hotel. You can even make arrangements for weekly rates in certain instances . . . all of which means you may be able to travel lighter than you ever imagined.

After generations as Britain's premier supplier of rental formal wear, you can just imagine the stories Moss Bros. can tell. And Monty's just the brother—there are three genuine siblings involved in the business— to tell them. "It's strange," he says, "the things we find in the pockets of the clothes returned from hire: marriage certificates, rings, a glass eye on one occasion, and money frequently. Everything is meticulously returned to its owner; but not the pound of butter we found inside a top hat soon after the war—obviously 'lifted' at the reception during rationing." If only Moss Brothers' clothes could talk. Come to think of it, maybe they do!   🌱

Newgate Communications PLC

21/22 Chelsea Garden Market	071-352-8040
Chelsea Harbour	(FAX) 071-352-3430
London SW10 0XE	

He may have been a son of mother Britain, but Stephen Morris had a lot of Yankee ingenuity. So much in fact, that at the tender age of 26, he founded and managed a publicly held company that employed close to 300 people. This after having already racked up capitalistic successes as a futures trader and as a stockbroker. It was during his broker days, when he worked in New York, that he became enamoured of the instrument of his future fortune—the cellular telephone.

He loved the idea of never being out of touch, and discovered that in his business his constant availability gave him a competitive edge. Stephen reasoned he wasn't the only one who could benefit from this wonder of modern technology. The idea of Newgate Communications was born and became a reality in November 1988. Stephen armed a couple of fellows with a list of Britain's top CEOs and instructed them to start telephoning, to call these top business guns and tell them about Newgate's ability to supply their companies with cellular telephones on a rental basis.

It didn't take long for the idea to catch on and Stephen's business to take off. When President Bush came to town, the American Embassy ordered ten, while the Russian Embassy asked for five. Even the metropolitan police department has become a regular client, as has B.A.T., and Newgate is proving to be a godsend to high-tech Americans who are invariably disappointed that the telephone they brought from home won't work here . . . or anywhere else. So don't bother packing yours. Just call or fax Newgate and reserve one of the 300 to 400 telephones always on hand. You can secure a number at the time of your reservation, which you can distribute to those you consider worthy before you leave. Your telephone will be waiting for you at your hotel. Or if you're susceptible to dialing withdrawal, Newgate will hand-deliver the telephone to you at the airport.

When you consider the surcharges most hotels tack onto telephone bills, renting from Newgate is very practical—£9.95 per day, plus tax. Incoming calls are free, and outgoing ones are charged at 33p "per unit" (approximately one minute). Weekly hires can be had for £59.95. A month will cost you £175. And if you're in town to do a deal, weigh the privacy factor—there's no possibility of hotel operators or porters delivering messages that might tip the scale, whether inadvertently or not.

The telephones work anywhere in London—except in the underground (but you knew that). They work anywhere in the U.K., for that matter. And they keep you even more connected than you might think. Each has a preprogrammed number that links you to a Newgate secretary to whom you can dictate a letter or fax. Copies of the finished product are dispatched to your hotel, office or home. Call director Christopher Norman to get plugged in—he's been in charge since it became clear that Stephen's abilities were more creative than managerial.

The Newgate story doesn't stop with telephones. You can rent a fax machine, as well, for £15 a day. If you're a fax fanatic and staying in a hotel, this is definitely the way to go. Most hostelries charge £3 to £5 per page, both for sending *and* receiving. It really hurts to pay that kind of money (as we have had to do) for a communication you neither solicited nor wanted.

And if you want to be even more plugged in, Newgate can supply you with a computer—£30 for a laptop, more for larger models. All are IBM compatible.

Need we spell it out for you? Newgate can set you up with a temporary and largely portable office during your stay. For more permanent business ventures, this firm, which sensibly proclaims that the "wide choice of product and systems should lead to better business solutions, not confusion," can automate an office suite or an entire building. Service-oriented, Newgate will service any product from any manufacturer at the right time and at the right price. What more could you ask?   ❦

One Night Stand

44 Pimlico Road	071-730-8708
London SW1 8LX	(FAX) 071-730-2064

Back in the early 1980s, Joanna Doniger had a good idea, one that she has successfully exported to New York and one that has been widely copied. She reasoned that renting was a viable option in an age when economics and common sense deny the impulse to go out and purchase a new frock for every dressy occasion. After all, men have been doing it for decades. And no one sniffs at a rented tux. Of course, who can tell, unless the fit is dreadful?

Cognizant of that one potential drawback when she opened for business, Joanna inaugurated a policy of making alterations where they count. Today, in two airy rooms she presents a dazzling selection of cocktail dresses and evening gowns, complete with accessories. Items are routinely adjusted, as are those telling sleeve lengths. Don't count on more, but her stock is so large and varied that you're bound to find something suitable in something that approaches your size. Actually, more than suitable when you consider you'll be dishing out as little as £60. However, you *can* spend as much as £120—still, you're talking about a third of a comparable dress retail. And you can keep your rental for up to four days. Joanna figures you need some time to get ready for the big do—time to get the right colour lipstick and nail polish, find the perfect shoes, locate the correct stockings and work out the hairstyle issue.

It's always a good idea to make an appointment ahead of time with manager Jane Heron or with Daisy Cook. Tell them what you think the occasion calls for, and they'll pull the appropriate pieces from their collections of Terence Nodler, Anna Leise Sharp, Diana Callas, and Frank Ushee lovelies. Joanna stays away from Britain's couturiers as the cost of their clothes would drive her prices out of the ballpark of the 24- to 40-year-old young professionals who make up the bulk of her clientele. You see, she purchases everything for One Night Stand brand-spanking new. No seconds, samples or previously owned pieces cross her threshold.

Not that we necessarily have anything against used clothing. Indeed, February and August are our two favourite months to visit London—that's when Joanna sells off her stock in preparation for the new season!

❦

Sidi Tickets

30-A Jubilee Hall	071-240-8808
London WC2H 9BD	(FAX) 071-836-9910

Picture Eliza Doolittle's affable cockney daddy singing "Get Me to the Church on Time" in the movie version of *My Fair Lady*, and you've got a handle on Sidi Hoyes, who makes any number of the city's hall porters look good. He's the guy they go to when all other resources for tickets—

any tickets, from *Phantom of the Opera*, to Wimbledon, to the next royal wedding—have dried up. They know they can depend upon him to fulfil just about any request, short of a ticket to heaven. That is the *one* instance that Sidi, in an atypically modest fashion, admits he can't help.

Otherwise, due to his diligent pursuit of tickets anytime, any place, constantly culling what he calls his secret sources, Sidi always delivers, literally. Alternatively, you can pick up your tickets from any one of three locations, though we tend to frequent the Covent Garden stall, which is where Sidi first set up shop. Prior to that he had operated out of a restaurant in Drury Lane, where customers called him on the public telephone, while the diametre of his table defined his office. Despite the rudimentary facilities, Sidi developed a word-of-mouth reputation for reliability, and his business thrived. Indeed, he claims that, when *Cats* made its much ballyhooed debut, through the purchase of tickets Sidi had more money invested in the show than Andrew Lloyd Webber.

Be that as it may, Sidi's now certifiably successful enough to employ a staff of ten and to offer tickets for literally any event in the world. So call or fax ahead to make arrangements to attend whatever you want, wherever you want. Sidi's a delightful character, and we highly recommend you make his acquaintance, but he's often off securing blocks of tickets. In his absence, direct your enquiries to his most capable, though more sombre, manager, Colin Martin.   ❦

Take-A-Guide Ltd

11 Uxbridge Street	081-960-0459
London W8	(FAX) 081-964-0990

"Dreams can come true, they can happen to you, when..." you call Fred Pearson's exceptional service, affectionately known as TAG (get it? *Take-A-G*uide!). Fred's in the business of making fantasy trips into reality. Tall, elegant and urbane, he's about the most enthusiastic, most optimistic man we've ever met. For this guide par excellence, nothing is impossible—the word *no* has been banished from his otherwise comprehensive vocabulary (Oxford graduate, don't you know?).

The idea of TAG's service is simple—its execution is most often not. Essentially, TAG offers personal touring throughout West Europe via private car in the company of a mature, intelligent and highly entertaining guide. While there are brochures filled with tempting, set-price itineraries, like a day in the country for about £315 in a Grenada, or £457 in a

Mercedes limousine, TAG really hits its stride in the customizing depart-ment. Fred and his staff thrive on special requests and have successfully dealt with more than their share of those bordering on the bizarre.

Take, for instance, the case of the woman who was convinced she had once been a poetic pal of Will Shakespeare's in Elizabethan England. She wanted to right an ancient wrong by laying a wreath at the tomb of her "uncle," who had been a favourite of Elizabeth I and is buried in the church at Warwick Castle. The present Earl of Warwick is not in the habit of allowing strangers to muck about with his family's sacred tombs, but for Fred. . . .

And if you have more modest sightseeing aspirations, you can always count on Fred to come up with something unusual to augment the old standbys like Westminster Abbey or the Changing of the Guard at Buck-ingham Palace. He turned us on to a nightly ritual we had never heard nor read about—the 9:30 closing of the Tower of London, dubbed the Ceremony of the Keys. Historically fascinating and visually moving, it's free and, even more unusual, uncrowded.

Naturally, prices are tagged (sic) to the itinerary you work out with Fred or any of his very knowledgeable people. And you don't have to wait until you get to London to start the process, or incur huge long-distance telephone bills. There's a U.S. toll-free number—800-825-4946—which puts you in touch with TAG's International Booking Service. All TAG telephone numbers are manned 24 hours a day.

Having perfected TAG's service to the point of winning major interna-tional travel awards, Fred ventured into new territory in 1989 with tours by helicopter. The concept remains the same, tailor-made trips in the company of an informative guide, but the experience is even more unforgettable—faster, too. It adds a new spin on the old "If it's Tuesday, this must be Belgium" syndrome of fast-paced sightseeing. Indeed, we got a chuckle out of the brochure's seemingly straight-faced assertion that this is the ultimate sightseeing experience for "those who like their history and culture condensed" and who want to see "England in hours rather than in days." Via TAG "Helicop*tour*" you can "do" London in an hour for £835. A tour of romantic castles and gardens takes a little longer—a whole day to be precise—and costs about £2,380 for a maxi-mum of three, including transportation to Wycombe Airport, as well as lunch with wine at one of the legendary English country house hotels.

Since we like our history in long, relaxed doses, we prefer sticking to the road with TAG. But that's what it's all about—it's a matter of preferences. Whatever you want to do, however you want to do it, Fred Pearson and TAG will make your travel dreams come true.   ❦

Acknowledgements

To Passport Books' Bill Pattis for being exactly what you are—a man of honour and integrity.

To Mark Pattis for his continued support and enthusiasm for all my books.

To Michael Ross, my extraordinary editor, for his invaluable advice, recommendations, patience and encouragement.

To Sharon Spence, who showed and shared her editorial expertise on this book.

To Sandy Mendelson of Hillsinger Mendelson, who helped make *New York on $1000 Day (Before Lunch)* come to life on film and in print.

To Ilene Kadish for all of her time and talent in research, fact-checking and help always above and beyond the call of duty.

To Ruth Renoit for her continuous help and support.

To my friends and colleagues on both sides of the Atlantic whose kindness and professional cooperation made the research such fun.

Many, many thanks,
F.W.K.

To Ferne for exceptional patience and understanding which was— evidence to the contrary—always noted and appreciated.

To Mama Margery Clark and perpetual pal Hollister Lindley for their invaluable help in the research department.

To Ed Callaghan for his compassionate ear and boundless faith.

To David Andelman, who was instrumental to the first book and who remains indispensable to me.

Always,
S.M.C.

Index

ABOUT THE AUTHORS

Ferne Kadish

Born in Chicago and raised in Beverly Hills, Ferne Kadish is now bicoastal, dividing her time between New York and California. She attended Boston University and the University of Southern California and has served on the faculty of the New School of Social Research in New York City. An avid world traveller, Ferne is much in demand as a speaker to women's groups throughout the U.S. and has written on the subject of travel for numerous magazines. Her successful writing career also includes a novel, *The Golden Circle,* of which she is co-author. Drawn from her various experiences and expertise in travel, fashion, marketing, and design—as well as her intimate knowledge of the lifestyles of the rich and famous—*New York on a $1,000 a Day (Before Lunch)* and *London on a £1,000 a Day (Before Tea)* are the first two titles in Ferne's new travel series.   ❦

Shelley Clark

Raised in both Rehoboth Beach, Delaware and Chevy Chase, Maryland, writer/publicist Shelley Clark has had an eclectic career. After graduating with honors in history from Kenyon College, Shelley gained hands-on experience in a variety of fields, including tape editing, sales, marketing, and public relations. Following a stint with the first Reagan inaugural, Shelley joined a D.C. consulting firm, where she was responsible for organizing conferences and special events for the National Institutes of Health. Her skills as a writer and publicist caught the attention of Hanae Mori, for whom she became director of communications based in New York City. Shelley's lifetime fascination with hotels has been transformed from an avocation to a vocation, culminating in her current position as director of public relations of Holiday Inn Worldwide's international flagship property, the Holiday Inn Crowne Plaza—Manhattan. When not meeting the press or organizing parties, Shelley enjoys cooking, sailing, theatre and travelling.   ❦